Semiotic

| 128 | Internationale Forschungen zur
Allgemeinen und
Vergleichenden Literaturwissenschaft |

In Verbindung mit

Norbert Bachleitner (Universität Wien), Dietrich Briesemeister (Friedrich Schiller-Universität Jena), Francis Claudon (Université Paris XII), Joachim Knape (Universität Tübingen), Klaus Ley (Johannes Gutenberg-Universität Mainz), John A. McCarthy (Vanderbilt University), Alfred Noe (Universität Wien), Manfred Pfister (Freie Universität Berlin), Sven H. Rossel (Universität Wien)

herausgegeben von

Alberto Martino
(Universität Wien)

Redaktion: Ernst Grabovszki

Anschrift der Redaktion:
Institut für Vergleichende Literaturwissenschaft, Berggasse 11/5, A-1090 Wien

Semiotic Encounters
Text, Image and Trans-Nation

Edited by
Sarah Säckel, Walter Göbel and Noha Hamdy

Amsterdam - New York, NY 2009

Cover Image:
Elena Bautz

Cover design:
Pier Post

Le papier sur lequel le présent ouvrage est imprimé remplit les prescriptions de "ISO 9706:1994, Information et documentation - Papier pour documents - Prescriptions pour la permanence".

The paper on which this book is printed meets the requirements of " ISO 9706:1994, Information and documentation - Paper for documents - Requirements for permanence".

Die Reihe „Internationale Forschungen zur Allgemeinen und Vergleichenden Literaturwissenschaft" wird ab dem Jahr 2005 gemeinsam von Editions Rodopi, Amsterdam – New York und dem Weidler Buchverlag, Berlin herausgegeben. Die Veröffentlichungen in deutscher Sprache erscheinen im Weidler Buchverlag, alle anderen bei Editions Rodopi.

From 2005 onward, the series „Internationale Forschungen zur Allgemeinen und Vergleichenden Literaturwissenschaft" will appear as a joint publication by Editions Rodopi, Amsterdam – New York and Weidler Buchverlag, Berlin. The German editions will be published by Weidler Buchverlag, all other publications by Editions Rodopi.

ISBN: 978-90-420-2714-5
E-Book ISBN: 978-90-420-2715-2
© Editions Rodopi B.V., Amsterdam - New York, NY 2009
Printed in The Netherlands

Table of Contents

Introduction   7

Theorising Textual and Visual Encounters

Mary Orr
Intertextuality: Old Debates in New Contexts   15

Harish Trivedi
Anglophone Transnation, Postcolonial Translation:
The Book and the Film as Namesakes   31

Renate Brosch
Migrating Images and Communal Experience   51

Textual Encounters

Caroline Lusin
Encountering Darkness:
Intertextuality and Polyphony in J.M. Coetzee's *Dusklands* (1974)
and Matthew Kneale's *English Passengers* (2000)   69

Georgiana Banita
Affect, Kitsch and Transnational Literature:
Azar Nafisi's "Portable Worlds"   87

Walter Göbel
Washington Irving's "Rip van Winkle", A Postcolonial Reading or:
In Search of a Usable Past   103

Irina Bauder-Begerow
Echoing Dickens: Three Rewritings of *Great Expectations*   119

Sarah Säckel
What's in a Wodehouse? (Non-) Subversive Shakespearean
Intertextualities in P.G. Wodehouse's *Jeeves and Wooster* Novels   137

Ida M. Samperi
"No Text Just Comes out Ex Nihilo, It Always Comes out of Other
Texts": Christine Brooke-Rose's *Thru*   155

Visual Encounters

Nicola Glaubitz
Transcribing Images – Reassembling Cultures:
   Kazuo Ishiguro's Japan   175

Joachim Frenk and Christian Krug
Handovers of Empire:
Transatlantic Transmissions in Popular Culture   191

Sonja Fielitz
Fish and Chips with Marshmallows?
Possibilities and Limitations of Trans-Cultural Intermediality   209

Susanne Gruss
Shakespeare in Bollywood? Vishal Bhardwaj's *Omkara*   223

Amira Nowaira
Text and Pretext:
Reading Cultural and Ideological Paradigms in the Hollywood and
Egyptian Movie Adaptations of Tolstoy's *Anna Karenina*   239

Noha Hamdy
Revisiting Transmediality: 9/11 Between Spectacle and Narrative   247

Wolfram R. Keller
"Long Live the New Flesh"?
David Cronenberg's *Videodrome* and the Limits of Ovidian
Metamorphosis   263

Introduction

This is a collection of essays which originated in an international symposium on intertextuality but was substantially expanded. The essays aim at opening up scholarly debates on the contemporary challenges of intertextuality in its various intersections with postcolonial and visual culture studies. Having become a catchphrase for modern art and literature, the term has seeped into the aesthetic imaginary of the twentieth and twenty-first centuries. But is intertextuality mainly a modern/postmodern phenomenon or merely a neologism for phenomena which have previously existed in different, albeit less critically discoursed and consciously articulated guises? Another challenge is to delimit the discursive contexts of intertextuality. In terms of disciplinarity, is intertextuality confined to the bounds of contemporary literary theory or is it sensitive to conceptual imports from other disciplines and so likely to engulf other discourses such as those of the natural sciences and the visual arts? These are theoretical concerns and debates which *Semiotic Encounters* is interested in highlighting and bringing to the forefront.

The first section begins with metatheoretical reflections on the interdisciplinarity of the subject and by engaging the readers in mapping its future trajectories and configurations in an age of digital technology. In this light, Mary Orr, in a programmatic initial statement, maps out the scope of intertextual theory and raises the vital question of whether intertextuality has been surpassed by the hypertext. She explores the dynamic potential of the concept of intertextuality and the new dimensions it has gained since the 70s in the sphere of oral, visual and electronic media and even in the bridging of the 'two cultures'. Furthermore, Mary Orr observes a tendency towards the accelerated decentring of traditional demands of authorship by digital technology and towards the erasure of traditonal national and cultural boundaries and of 'author-itarian' power structures. Harish Trivedi takes up two of Mary Orr's main issues: the inter/transcultural dimension and the intermedial one. Much more so than Orr, he is sceptical of the indiscriminate use of metaphors of cultural translation (Bhabha, Lahiri) which more often than not lead to entire misprisions, and he exemplifies this in a comparative analysis of Jhumpa Lahiri's novel *The Namesake* and its film version. Trivedi praises the film for its convincing representation of bilingualism, e.g. by means of 'hybrid scripting' or by synaesthetic audio-visual effects, which tend to compensate for a lack of cultural subtlety in the novel. The concept of 'cultural translation' appears for Trivedi much more in need of circumspection and inverted commas than for Mary Orr. Renate Brosch finally seems to share Mary Orr's intercultural optimism to some extent. She focuses on visual culture and migrating images, specifically on the importance of global icons for collectivities and their 'visual imaginary' or 'storehouses of images'. In their global transmission images can often cross intermedial boundaries as well and become 'global icons', but they can also call in question individual and collective identities. Paradoxically, the succumbing to the power of the visual and the iconoclastic questioning of the validity of images can go hand in hand and thus grant some latitude for audience agency.

The three main areas of semiotic encounters presented in this volume are thus explicitly plotted out in the theoretical section: (a) the dimension of the intertextual in the traditional sense (as specified e.g. by Genette), (b) the widening of the concept towards visual and digital culture and (c) the frictions between the intertextual and the transnational. The first two aspects govern the structure of our volume, while questions of the transnational and/or postcolonial form a recurrent subtext.

Following the trajectory from textuality to intermediality, the second section begins with Caroline Lusin's analysis of polyphony in Coetzee's *Dusklands* and Kneale's *English Passengers* and their postcolonial/postmodern rewritings of Joseph Conrad's master narrative *Heart of Darkness*. Lusin explores the ways in which Coetzee and Kneale take the uses of parody into account, the projection of 'otherness' or 'alterity' and epistemological issues. Her observations dovetail with Harish Trivedi's as far as questions of subversion, but also of mistranslation and opacity in intercultural exchanges are concerned. Quite a diffferent, more affirmative reading of the relationship between centre and margin is offered by Georgiana Banita, who interprets Nafisi's *Lolita in Tehran* as a novel which confirms neo-orientalist fantasies of the 'West'. Banita focuses on the well-known photograph on the cover of the paperback edition and its ideological bias, defining the novel finally as 'kitsch', though in a very specific sense of the term. A reinterpretation of Washington Irving's "Rip van Winkle"-story from a postcolonial perspective follows, which focuses on paratexts and on contradictory and partly subversive mythological intertexts as well as on Irving's own belated rewriting by adding the postscript with its Native American focus. Walter Göbel's interpretation of this famous short story opens up vistas on the historicity of intertextual ambiguities and of postcolonial rewritings, while also presenting an in-depth analysis of what Renate Brosch has called 'collective frameworks of knowledge' and how they can determine the formation of the textual/visual imaginary. Irina Bauder-Begerow's reading of two Australian rewritings of Charles Dickens' *Great Expectations* broadens the theme of postcolonial revisionary encounters. The monological Western viewpoint is in both novels undermined by a multiperspective structure. In Peter Carey's novel the Australian convict Magwitch plays a key role, even moving to the centre of sympathy, while in Lloyd Jones' *Mister Pip* the female protagonist from 'down under' gradually comes to question Dickens' classic as the narrative against which she plots her own female Bildungsroman.

The final two contributions to this section are case studies on forms of intertextuality within the monolingual English culture. Sarah Säckel's object of study are P.G. Wodehouse's *Jeeves and Wooster* novels, whose concept of Englishness is constructed through a dialogue with mainly English literature, e.g. Shakespearean drama, while Ida Samperi analyses the use of a bricolage of theoretical jargons in Chistine Brooke-Rose's novel *Thru*, resulting in a playfully intertextual, interdisciplinary and mainly parodic form of discourse which signifies upon the proliferating critical debates of the sixties and deconstructs their boundaries.

The second part of the volume engages in debates on intertextuality as a cross-medial phenomenon. Migrating images are traced on their voyage across medial and national borders and are studied within the theoretical framework of inter- and transmediality and what Renate Brosch has called their links with frameworks of knowledge. Nicola Glaubitz unites questions from both sections by focusing on the novel *Artist of the Floating World* and its presentation of the transcription and the translation of cultures, while on the other hand investigating to what extent Ishiguro's writing is indebted to Japanese cinema as well as to mass media images of other cultures for the constitution of the hero's identity. In this and the following essays the global redistribution of images and its implications for contemporary theories of intermediality becomes a crucial factor when 'reviewing' the medium of film, as it crosses cultural, ideological and national borders and negotiates cultural identities on a global scale.

Joachim Frenk and Christian Krug follow suit with an investigation of the translation of the visual imaginary and of imperial gestures in a number of novels and films. Their main focus is on Bond films whose iconic focus moves from Britain to the US and in the figure of the ubiquitous Bond even becomes transnationally dislocated – which can be interpreted as part of a loss of specific Britishness by a figure on its way to becoming a global icon. At the centre of their investigation is the visual encoding of the *translatio imperii*-theme which is presented and deferred at the same time, as it must come into conflict with the transnational imaginary. The negotiation of cultural identities on a global scale is also a theme of Sonja Fielitz's essay. Like

Frenk/Krug, Fielitz observes a tendency to Americanise the British cultural heritage, in this case the Shakespeare film industry, and like Frenk/Krug she sees a form of 'handover of Empire', or simply of American neo-imperialism, at work. Cultural misprisions must multiply in due course within such unbalanced semiotic encounters.

The Hollywood industry is also at the centre of Amira Nowaira's comparative analysis of film versions of *Anna Karenina*. She examines the cultural and visual transcoding of literary texts into film language, her case study being the Hollywood and Egyptian movie adaptations of Tolstoy's novel. Questions as to how producers from other cultural and national contexts deal with the challenges of American media imperialism or how national and cultural identities are devalued and influenced by Hollywood are again raised. Susanne Gruss, on the other hand, interprets an example of Bollywood Shakespeare. She shows how the visual imaginary of both cultures is fused in the course of translations of genre conventions and contexts, leading to a hybrid visual product for both Indian and world markets, an observation which strikes a common note with Harish Trivedi's observations on bilingualism in *The Namesake* and Frenk/Krug's conclusions on the internationalisation of the Bond-figure.

Noha Hamdy analyses intermediality within the US visual imaginary: she examines the various narrative and visual templates of a recurring theme of 9/11 iconography, the representations and ideological renderings of the shocking image of *Falling Man*, which was however religiously and mythologically recodified in the process of intermedial translation in order to transform the chaotic into various forms of heroic iconography. Her contribution focuses on the complex interactions between remediations and ideology. Wolfram Keller finally targets the translation of Ovidian poetics into David Cronenberg's aesthetics of metamorphosis, adding a structuralist and historical dimension to the exploration of the visual imaginary. At the same time, he points out how the implicit parodying of traditional Virgilian imperialist discourse can become problematic when it assimilates elements of a somewhat intimidating and dystopian future, as is the case in David Cronenberg's film *Videodrome*. As in many of the former contributions, questions of remediation are at the centre of attention in the effects of a pervasive Ovidian aesthetics upon 'local' Canadian cinematography. A core concern of the entire volume is to be located here: the question how local remediations reflect the emergence of global iconic discourses and how containment and subversion interact in various forms of intertextuality and intermediality – most obviously in the tensions between the strict codifications of the international film industries (Hollywood/Bollywood) and their appropriations of national pretexts, which are explored in the final section. As Renate Brosch pointed out, the seductive emotional power of globalised images and their iconoclastic (local) potential have to be mediated in any process of remediation.

Marbach, June 2009 *The editors*

Theorising Textual and Visual Encounters

Mary Orr

Intertextuality: Old Debates in New Contexts

In the face of its rivals – 'interdisciplinarity', 'intermediality', 'interdiscursivity' – and of the explosion of virtual, visual, and postcolonial forms of cultural expression, 'intertextuality' holds a more tenuous critical position today than it enjoyed in the 1970s and 1980s. Is the word merely a shorthand for 'connection', the specificities of which are redundant since the nature of the texts being connected assures them? Is the nodal term 'text' in 'intertextuality' a major reason for its shift from centre to margin in critical debate and terminology, and hence for its replacement by the vocabularies of virtual media? Or does 'intertextuality' remain useful for unpacking ever more complex twenty-first-century 'semiotic encounters' in their translation of texts and images? This essay seeks to address these questions by also exploring an additional dynamic ('window') to the four which structured my *Intertextuality: Debates and Contexts* (2003).

It was an enormous pleasure for me to accept the email invitation to give the opening plenary at the conference which preceded this volume. Organised by Sarah Säckel and Noha Hamdy, postgraduates learning the academic trade and following in the interdisciplinary footsteps of Walter Göbel, Head of the American Studies Department at the University of Stuttgart, the occasion had particular personal significance. First, I revelled in the opportunity to return to Germany, the language, literature and culture of which has had to be displaced, but not erased, by my research and teaching in French studies. Second, the altogether German yet Anglistik/English Studies contexts of this invitation encouraged me to reflect further upon the inspirations of *Intertextualität: Formen, Funktionen, anglistische Fallstudien* by Ulrich Broich and Manfred Pfister, which had shaped and clarified my own work as a doctoral student in 1985 on the 'intertextual dimension' in the works of Claude Simon. From the semiotic learning curve for the doctoral thesis eventually emerged my *Intertextuality: Debates and Contexts* of 2003. In its study of the forms, functions, and appeal to a more multilingual as opposed to monolingual English understanding of 'intertextuality', my book owes much to Broich and Pfister's subtitle. I note again here that their study has still not been translated for monolingual English speakers to appreciate the English 'Fallstudien'. In being invited to address semiotic as opposed to linguistic encounters in the opening plenary, however, three elements stood out as central: the formal, the functional, and the personal. They are also central to the plenary genre itself. In its very format and forum, this plenary offered me an unprecedented space in which to rethink the subject of intertextuality, its debates and contexts, since I could incorporate oral, print, visual, and electronic texts in semiotic encounter. Furthermore, because few of the transnational English Studies audience of fellow speakers were known to me except in print, the nature of our semiotic encounter(s) could be gauged as an immediate and mediated set of exchanges.[1] Finally, the conference organisers had given me a cue I had never envisaged literally for myself, the final words of my own *Intertextuality*, 'speak again!' These words are a direct quotation from the opening act and scene of Shakespeare's *King Lear*, Lear's dissatisfaction with his daughter Cordelia in her refusal to express love for him in the false terms of her sisters. Picking up her answer ('Nothing.'), Lear's invitation to her to speak again is in apposition to "Nothing will come of nothing".[2] In this plenary, mine was to find us an intertextual talking point of semiotic encounters of text, image and trans-nation, in order to address the relevance and future of 'intertextuality' as critical term.

The plenary, especially an opening one, is synonymous with and epitomises a context of 'high' cultural and intertextual status. The generic remits of this transnationally recognised form of communication function as a codified space of paradox and tension, namely that thanks to the *gravitas-auctoritas* of their speaker, ideas can be expressed anywhere on a scale from the most polemical to the most reactionary. The speaker's freedom is boundless, yet bound by audience expectation and permitted questioning after the plenary's conclusions. Like an inaugural speech or lecture, the plenary therefore sets out a stall, but according to respected rules and discourses governing setting and occasion, whether academic, political, religious. Form and function are then almost ideally allied and codified by this genre. For these reasons, I decided to test it as the almost optimum locus of 'intertextuality' (and 'intermediality') by directly challenging some of its parameters. Such a move exemplifies the dynamic of any revisionism: innovation must combine with artful imitation in self-reflexive (dis)play. The success of the experiment will depend upon, and be determined by, the critical audience testing acceptability or unacceptability against expectations set by the pre-given norm. To guarantee some moderate success for my experiments on the plenary within one, into which I wanted to factor interdiscursive reflections, intertextual reference, intermedial practices and modes of communication, I opted for cultural reference points designed to appeal to an academic audience gathered to discuss semiotic encounters. Visual impact being key as well as a compact form of illustration, interpretation, and suggestion, I completed my set of media by presenting my plenary with an accompanying power point presentation including use of a hypertext link. My words were now set to images of words and images. The floor was mine to 'speak again'.

---

[1] It was also an opportunity to question 'high' (finished/published) and 'low' (unfinished, collaborative, work in progress) as qualitative classifications of cultural forms.
[2] King Lear 1.1.89

Old Debates in New Contexts

The prologue, like the above introductory remarks or the introduction to a critical essay, shapes the whole of what follows, encapsulating and describing in concise shape and form the questions at stake. One of the main pressure points on the concept of Kristevan 'intertextuality' as a 'mosaic of texts' is the word 'text' as its core idea or generator. While 'text' remains a highly malleable container for new cultural work – in filmic and electronic media, in postcolonial and non-European contexts, tongues and settings – it still prioritises more well-worked, constructed, and finished products over those that are deemed less so. For a text to be a text even in its broadest definition or recent text messaging sense, human production is recorded in such a manner that another may 'read', respond, and engage with it. Assumed behind this minimum definition lies the machinery of 'publication', whether presses or personal blogs. Preservation therefore goes hand in hand with maximising communication and dissemination. Current urgency to digitise earlier textual productions and recordings (for example newspapers, tapes) before their very fabrics disintegrate marks this double spirit, to ensure that generations to come can know of print text worlds freely, and as exhaustively as possible.[3] But in such laudable agendas lies the gulf between the internet and intertext rich and the internet and intertext poor. One of the open conclusions of my book was to signal the necessity of increasing intertextual wealth for not just some privileged communities, but for those cultural producers largely excluded from (print) text, and hence hypertext.[4] Such problems regarding the ethics of managing whose pieces were included in the 'mosaic of texts' informed the overriding question posed by my book, 'whither intertextuality?' The 'inter-' prefix of the term in theory suggests an unbounded, inclusive community of equals, whereas in practice some texts, media, languages, and generic forms are clearly given much higher status and priority than others. The recent displacements of 'intertextuality' by rival terms such as 'intermediality' or 'interconnectivity' do not resolve the ethical issues, issuing as they do from the same prefix. The relegation of 'intertextuality' in critical theoretical importance thus results from the historical contexts of the core and prefix terms that combined to form it in the first place. A powerful neologism with huge scope to denominate in many European languages, 'intertextuality' ('intertextualité', 'Intertextualität') remains a term with no verb form (unlike

---

[3] Open access versus copyright protection debates in the face of the digital revolution are a further test of the idealisms of creators of information superhighways. Information overload is a further reality check upon the limitlessness of transnational intertextual potential.

[4] It lies outside the discussion of this essay, but privilege is not only on the side of 'high' cultural production. Popular ('low') culture and its media also openly embrace digital forms of communication.

for example 'imitation'). It is then inevitable that rival terms such as 'intermediality' have challenged it as better suited to describe twenty-first-century semiotic forms and encounters, just as 'intertextuality' had likewise displaced earlier (but very similar) concepts such as influence, imitation and quotation. In *Intertextuality: Debates and Contexts*, I envisaged this process as four electronic windows, with the most recent, 'intertextuality', now hidden by its others as it had itself occluded them ('influence', 'imitation', 'quotation'), although all four share the same (trans)cultural screen. The book's conclusions about these four terms in process used the analogy of classical drama. By heralding its end as a fourth act – normally a point of waiting – its expected dénouement in a fifth act was to come. In these analogies with contemporary electronic windows and enduring drama, my concern was to illuminate patterns of cultural recycling which were not bounded by historical, geographical, linguistic, generic or material hierarchies of knowledge. In challenging linguistic and other blind spots in Anglo-American critical theory, I also wanted to restore to intertextual work by others an enormous vocabulary and terminology that had been sidelined by the catchall word 'intertext'. I surmised that any replacement term for 'intertextuality' was inherent within its own and its predecessors' structural dynamics.

One way therefore to rethink the question, 'whither intertextuality?', is to rewind to the contexts and debates in which Kristeva coined the term as also the potential space for discovering successors. 'Interdiscursivity' was one such rival covered in my book. With wider currency, 'intermediality' as recent rival has retrospectively sharpened the ambiguities of 'text' in 'intertextuality' as filmic, print, radio etc., by capitalising on the explosion of new technologies since the 1970s. However, as argued above, any coinage with an 'inter-' prefix stands to be replaceable. Rewinding to the place before 'intertextuality' *inter alia* then begs the more interesting question. What had 'intertextuality' occluded *collectively* with 'influence', 'imitation' and 'quotation'? Context certainly informs the debate as it did my study of it. The conceptual design for my book was thought at the end of the last century, and hence has open conclusions and space made for a fifth act or window. In a new millennium, I now see the problem of this incompletion in the grounding of other beginnings. By its double opening prior to its introduction, my book in fact already posed important questions about the form and function of prologues and opening remarks as points of departure, whether as rupture or new variation. The idea of departure(s) might go far in circumscribing the missing fifth 'window' that is the subject of this essay.

New Debates in Old Contexts

Openings and introductions remain common and fundamental to any kind of cultural encounter or engagement, whether interpersonal, intertextual or intermedial. But how much do we know about what happens culturally and linguistically when we are introduced to someone or something new for the first time? What constitutes or contributes to a 'good' or 'bad' semiotic encounter, let alone an optimum one?[5] To move my new audience towards the place of these questions, in a play (plenary) in search of a fifth act, we viewed an ordered list of synonyms for 'openings': '1. aperture, break, chasm, chink, cleft, crack, fissure, gap, hole, perforation, rupture, space, split, vent; 2. beginning, birth, dawn, inauguration, inception, launch, onset, start; 3. chance, occasion, opportunity, place, vacancy; 4. (antonyms): closing, closure, end; 5. *décor, frame, mise en scène*'. To underscore such encounters with difference and similarity, this thesaurus exercise was repeated with the word 'beginning(s)': 'birth, commencement, establishment, fountainhead, inauguration, inception, initiation, introduction, onset, opening, origin, outset, preface, prelude, prime, rise, root, rudiments, seed, source, start, starting point; (antonyms) end, finish; *epigraph, foreword, homepage, hyperlink, incipit, overture, palimpsest, paratext, preliminaries, prolegomena, prologue, titles*.' The more 'textual' terms came last in italics, but other patterns and orders were of course also embedded in these lists. Transnational and translingual critics of 'openings' were cited.[6] Lulled into a frame of the familiar plenary format, my audience was now ready to be shocked, from passive into active participation in the forms and functions of the genre. In the promise of all the above-listed words, the introduction of such activity would either produce the most negative response (Cordelia's 'nothing'), or positive engagement that might collectively reveal the illusive fifth term. I therefore proposed a collaborative task eminently suited to rethinking first things in the cultural imagination as mosaic of texts – oral, textual and hypertextual. Each delegate was asked to envisage an example of a medium of semiotic encounter with the following transnational parameters: it was to have (1) no 'text' (i.e. words), but many sub-texts; (2) conventions of form; (3) silence and gaps that were nevertheless audible and/or visible; (4) allusions that were cross-cultural, multilingual; (5) reinterpretability from surface readings as much as from references relying on more extensive or specialist knowledge

---

[5] Classics of reader response theories remain Wolfgang Iser, *The Act of Reading: a Theory of Aesthetic Response*, London: Routledge and Kegan Paul, 1978, and Michel Riffaterre, *Semiotics of Poetry*, Bloomington: Indiana University Press, 1978.

[6] See for example Edward Said, *Beginnings: Intention and Method*, New York: Basic Books, 1975, and Gérard Genette, *Seuils*, Paris: Seuil, 1987.

and (6) a mode of 'telling' (significance) pertaining to retelling. Delegates were then invited to discuss their example with those beside them. Their discussion and my silence would end when I reassumed my proper plenary speaker position by giving my own answer to the same task. To capture this unique initial dialogue between speakers/readers in semiotic encounter was to try to circumscribe that moment which spawns new relationships, passing acquaintance or rebuff. In all three reactions lies the germ of plot, the potential for new cultural production and articulation.

Possibly because of shock, my audience rose to the challenge. My own response, the medium of the visual arts, echoed theirs in a variety of genres. My particular example was the artistic visualisation of the famous myth of Narcissus and Echo (as told in Ovid's *Metamorphosis*) in two forms, chosen not least because of the different cultural contexts and aesthetic priorities of their painters. Again I invited 'intertextual' reactions and responses to each version in turn (shown through power point) to maximise our perspectives on 'texts' that were also mixed media, as well as being illustrations of our conference theme, *Semiotic Encounters: Text, Image and Trans-Nation*. The first was John William Waterhouse's picture/reinterpretation of the story, painted in 1903 and now housed in the Walker Art Gallery Collection, Liverpool. This 'naturalistic' take on the text was then compared and contrasted with Salvador Dali's more famous *Narcissus's Metamorphosis* of 1937 (in the Tate Britain, London) as a 'culturalistic' take on the text. Ida Samperi spoke eloquently for collective response to these two works, by highlighting how they encounter the place of representing realities that are contingent (the world of the upper half of the paintings and the world of the lower part, the reflections in the water), but that in the encounter, they also defer approach to, or designation of, 'reality' as fixable in form.[7] In the impasses of making sense, the desire for meaningfulness none the less exists. Amira Nowaira beautifully captured the paradox of postmodern sensibility to there being no ultimate 'sense' and 'meaning' as however the space of postmodern meaning by drawing our attention to both, couched in a very specific question. What was the significance, she wondered, of the straw hat she saw immediately in the centre of Waterhouse's painting (and which others had to have pointed out to them because they did not 'see' it)? Interesting speculations in the discussion at the end of the plenary demonstrated that we were all as much

---

[7] In both paintings, the effects of (non)symmetry work on vertical and horizontal planes. In identifying this inbetween (the surface 'world' and it reflections in the water as submerged world) as Derrida's arche-writing, Ida Samperi encapsulated understanding of the non-origin of sense which lies between differing realities and 'intertextual' responses to them. The reality of things does not exist, because 'reality' is altered by our reflection of it.

meaning addicts as we were deft practitioners of postmodern intertextual and intermedial theories allegedly defying the existence of meaning.[8]

It was at this point that I revealed my experiment to bend the formal yet unspoken rules for the conduct and content of plenary lectures. While we had been overtly engaged in an exercise in thinking about highly codified cultural (re)productions and their media, and examples *par excellence* of 'intertextuality' and 'intermediality', in fact the oral genres of my frame demonstrated that these are often the most stylised and ritualised, because they pertain to speaking events for a general public rather than to an audience of private readers. Television news broadcasting, courts of law, classical drama share similarly ritualised codes and practices, functions and forms. Clearly, the illusive fifth term in the beyond or before 'intertextuality', influence, imitation and quotation would need to encompass oral and 'textual' semiotic encounters and 'non-word' media such as painting and its reproductions electronically. We had also been engaging overtly with the many unspoken messages of these two visual arts texts as illustrative of highly complex semiotic encounter and its impasses or failures. Many 'intertextual' lessons could indeed be drawn from the Narcissus and Echo configuration, given that the end of the story is clearly introduced before it begins in the foregrounds of both paintings, symbolised in the narcissus flower. From the Waterhouse version, Narcissus' blindness (monologism and monolingual discourse?) and deafness (solipsism?) results from intractable, pre-set ways of approaching the world when one's others (Echo) are ignored. Narcissus' many interreflections may scintillate or fascinate in Dali's painting. They do not illuminate in any of their wall of mirrors where Echo might exist let alone sound the surface depths of the male imaginary. Has Dali captured in the intertextual allusions, for example to Rodin's *Thinker* and to Greek/Latin philosophical traditions and models, narratives of superior male identity and discourse holding *ad ovo* their own creative birth? And for a digital age, what is the meta-narrative of the (male) fingers holding the egg from which the narcissus flower breaks forth fully formed, instead of a chick?[9] Is hypertext merely a belated, variant, form of human creativity in the arts of recording for posterity? What of its earliest forms as the more revelatory of the 'intertextual' or 'intermedial' dynamics of cultural production?

---

[8] My own answer to the question is that the hat clearly belongs to Narcissus, and were he wearing it, he would more readily recognise himself as the reflection in the pool.

[9] Visual media manipulation is surely one of the advances available to current virtual media, returning in consequence some very old questions about the truthfulness or error of any form of representation.

Prior to Greek and Roman cultural forms, and Latin illuminated manuscripts as their legacy, the rich amalgam and dialogue of text and image in several 'hands' had already been developed to a very high degree of formal stylisation and experiment, in ancient Mandarin for example. Were the ends and hence the beginnings of Mandarin and later Latin illuminated manuscripts truth, beauty or utility? Or were these cultural productions as much a celebration of national cultural prowess, the highest excellence in draftsman-ship, creativity, knowledge and imagination in their encyclopaedic semiotic encounters? Did supreme mastery of the medium define the ideological, pedagogical, and cultural power of a counter elite between the highest and lowest economically and politically in society, and in response to complex international and internal social upheaval that included the disempowerment of rival others? Were these ways to build imagined or real communities of cultural capital for some, but not for others? Or were these superlative compositions of text and image vying with other transcultural ways of picturing the world that 'intertextuality' and 'intermediality' also largely forget?

Some of the most important achievements of human endeavour are among the most ancient ways of regarding and recording experience in media other than word and/or image. The ancient Chinese invented the calendar. Astronomy and astrology were one and the same in ancient Babylon and Egypt, to elucidate the movements of the gods and the natural world pictured in zodiacs. Major epistemic breaks in human cultural development map onto discovery of new natural and mathematical laws, or encryption and encoding devices such as the printing press. The development of the computer is then but another calculating-figuration machine as useful and marvellous as the abacus. Numbers, their patterns and power to shape new discovery in the form of differential equations for example, are a further semiotic, figurative system and language that 'intertextuality' and 'intermediality' allegedly encompass, but also distinguish themselves from. Is this the zone in which to rediscover missing terms, the place of new figurations of space and time in the contexts of the 1960s as the era of the Cold War, the space race, the internet and major developments of our virtual economy and communications networks? Prior to Kristeva's *Semeiotikè* and the launch of 'intertextuality' in the critical marketplace, structuralism focused very specifically on mathematical equations as 'proofs' for textual relations. Numbers have always been deemed more undeniably factual and objective than letters, a language of correction of previous error and calculation from informed hypothesis of new discoveries beyond that which is visible, even with the most powerful of telescopes or microscopes. One nineteenth-century example makes the case, the discovery attributed to Johann Galle in 1845 of Neptune in our solar system. However, it was also largely thanks to calculations made by John Couch

Adams (1819-1892) for the probable existence of a planet which was affecting the orbit of Uranus. George Airy, the English Astronomer Royal, failed to investigate these claims passed on to him by Adams' professor, John Challis, who was charged by Airy later in the year to mount a search. On the other side of the Channel, Urbain-Jean-Joseph Le Verrier (1811-1892) published his prediction about a similar planetary body. The Paris Observatory being as deaf to these ideas as Greenwich to Adams', he approached Johann Galle at the Berlin Observatory. Le Verrier had come to his conclusions thanks to working on laws of gravitational pull and the tilt of known planets as calculated earlier by Pierre-Simon Laplace (1749-1827). In diverse 'hands', this truly transnational discovery and encounter with numbers rewrote the facts of our solar system. Although it avoided the religious outrage that the earlier discovery of planetary motion had caused (such as the reality that the sun did not revolve around the earth), scientific authorities failed equally to acknowledge the new truth.

Thus the textual imagination that richly acknowledges and encompasses the scientific imaginary is, in a nutshell, the cultural domain where attention needs to be turned for rediscovery of the term preceding and succeeding 'intertextuality', which, because it is a neologism, can be dated very specifically to the late 1960s. Structuralist fascinations with numbers and formulae are then belated manifestations of among the oldest recorded human activities. Ancient Chinese traditions (of painting on silk, bamboo and other media) speak of the non-division of macro- and microcosm, nature and culture, science and art, content, medium, and form. The world and its representations were similarly of a piece in ancient Babylonian and Egyptian cultures and monument making. Medieval manuscript traditions enacted and recorded the shift that would lead to the oppositions of religion and magic/science, of numbers and letters in the Western psyche and its institutions. Classifications of disciplines in European University curricula from the nineteenth century onwards, for example, increasingly dichotomised sciences and social sciences (as more important) than the non-factual humanities (because these are allegedly closer to religion, myths and creative texts). Hypertext, by contrast, has been hugely corrective of such ideological divisions and uncrossable frontiers through its interdisciplinary agendas for the revivification of biblical, mediaeval and Renaissance subjects as well as encyclopaedic and scientific dimensions of pre- and postmodern knowledge and cultural production. If Kristevan 'intertextuality' already attempted to bridge such discipline divides with the concept of a 'mosaic' of texts from any subject domain or medium operating contiguously, the world as tissue of (authorless) texts became increasingly unsatisfactory as model of inclusion. The case of English studies (*aka* Broich and Pfister) is again richly illustrative of intertextuality's hypothetical range, yet sociopolitical shortcomings.[10] Like many humanities disciplines, English Studies in universities in the 1970s (particularly elite Ivy League institutions), awoke to the need for an institutional survival strategy to widen its contexts and spheres of interest, yet hold to core linguistic and cultural agendas. Intertextuality was thus displaced and then replaced post 1970 with interdisciplinarity on the one hand as the more able to promote comparative literary, cultural, gender, and postcolonial studies if semiotic encounter was to have a constructive (rather than destructive or deconstructive) cultural force. On the other hand, intertextuality was further sidelined in its forms and functions by the digital, hypermedia, revolution. 'Intermediality' has in consequence, and since the late 1990s, become the new 'intertextuality', to show the latter's belatedness as form of cultural remediation.[11] But 'intermediality' as theory and concept, creative and theoretical exploration of virtual and multimedia relations, remains a mode of fixing forms of expression. This returns us to the definition of text with which we began, as place where human production is recorded in such a manner that another may read, respond, and engage with it. 'Intermediality' certainly increases the transnational possibilities of such encounters and engagements, making communication at once more simultaneous and durable across time and space. However its multipliers remain almost greater ethical dividers between the 'intermedial' rich and the 'intermedial' poor. The question, 'whither intertextuality'? is now equally 'whither intermediality?' since both terms point to their others while seeking to usurp these absent voices by circumscribing them. Or put this back into the terms of the two paintings of the story of Narcissus *and* Echo above. They nicely configure present absence in both 'intertextuality' and 'intermediality'. Two particular dimensions deserve very serious attention. The first is formal: cultural construction in every sphere occurs by means of oppositional classifications and representations. The huge vibrancy of gender, postcolonial, and translation studies in the twentieth century emerged from greater understanding of the need to rearticulate the cultural politics of binary oppositions and hierarchies of power. The second is functional: cultural dissemination and hence revivification in every sphere is severely limited by monolingual or 'mono-medial' production in the hands of authorities. While poignantly portrayed in the

---

[10] By 'English Studies' I encompass its many constituents, such as Anglistik or World English.
[11] The contexts and debates of 'intermediality' studies replay many of the confusions and possibilities that critics discovered with 'intertextuality' in the 1960s and 1970s. For a useful article exploring many of the key proponents and theories of intermediality, see Irina O. Rajewsky, "Intermediality, Intertextuality and Remediation: A Literary Perspective on Intermediality." *Intermédialités: Histoire et Théorie des Arts, des Lettres et des Techniques* 6 (2005): 43-64.

eradication of the audible (Echo) in the worlds of the (in)visible in Dali's painting, digital hypermedia also risk at their peril other echoes. There are too many lessons in the Narcissus story to allow one sense, discourse, genre, language, discipline or medium of production (however multimedia it might be) to predominate to the detriment and hence erasure of others.

New Debates in New Contexts

In this avowedly digital age, where copyright is increasing problematic through cut-and-paste borrowing, sampling, and purloining, the work that was essential to pre-print production – of diverse hands, collaborative and often anonymous projects, translations and adaptations – is visible and accessible once more. Increased understanding of the complexities of cultural production as informed and arbitrary encounters and networks of creators and other creations has also brought the demystification (and demythologisation) of major nineteenth-century paradigms for authority and authorship, namely genius and invention, epitomised in a discovery or work by the (lone) scientist or artist. If 'intertextuality' as 'mosaic of texts' paved the way to questioning influence, imitation, and quotation as ever being singular, or the particular property of one individual, language, creed or group, hypermedia in turn challenge intertextuality's tacit preoccupations with nameless official (high) over popular (low) cultural forms.[12] Through website names or homepages, electronic inter-networking productions name collaborations much more visibly, including rival, parallel, transnational, contributors to the scenes of dominant cultural expression and innovation. Interestingly, my example above from nineteenth-century scientific advancement already made the point that singular discoveries, works, or paradigm shifts rarely originate from one author or genius. Electronic hypermedia remind us the more forcibly not of the current sense of "invention" ("to find out in the way of original contrivance; to devise first", OED), but its earlier meanings from the Latin *invenire*, "to come upon", "discover" and "to fabricate, design, 'make up', devise" (OED). These are illustrated in the fascinating world in word and image of early science writing, from the earliest recording in almanacs and zodiacs, myths and travelogues, to tall tales and early compendia of the marvellous creations of the known world. Critics in the humanities formed in textual, cultural, and transnational studies are then ideally placed to engage with modern science and scientific discourse, especially with their claims to encode 'reality', because scientific work (especially the collaborative) is

---

[12] It lies outside this essay, but Bakhtin's rich legacies behind Kristevan 'intertextuality' – heteroglossia, the carnivalesque – similarly prioritise and return to high cultural forms, especially those that are polyphonic and dialogic.

allegedly more verifiable than the work of the (artistic) imagination. Both 'intertextuality' and 'intermediality', then, have much new work still to do to recover and unpack the significance of the 'diverse hands' contributing to a famous discovery by some single, usually European male, scientist. It is only by active remembering of things past in often uncatalogued archive collections that lost work in science by women or non-European men will be seen as remarkable in its own right, not least because this science was conducted outside official institutions or scientific establishments. In my plenary, I briefly presented one fascinating examplar, the science writing and its illustration by the English-born Sarah Bowdich (1791-1856). A woman scientist, explorer, and discoverer of new fish species among others in the Gambia, when no woman in science is recorded in the official history of the discipline for the nineteenth century before Marie Curie, Sarah may also be counted among the earliest anthropologists and ethnographers (male) of the period.[13] In terms of text, image and trans-nation, 'intermediality' also needs to encompass scientific and anthropological plates, photographs, and text within its remits, particularly materials pertaining to the study of non-Western cultures. Only by so doing may it become increasingly aware of its Narcissus models of cultural reflection on the one hand. On the other hand, and given the increasingly visual priorities of hypertext culture, 'intermediality' needs to guard against neglecting and excluding voices and their media outside itself (the hypertext 'poor'). Translating multifarious Echo back into electronic visual-cultural agendas will be the art of any forthcoming technologies and their scrutiny, to ensure that cultural meta-discourses (science, technology) are never taken as neutral, let alone objective or universal.

Yet any reinstatement of Echo (the discursive, aural, multilingual) needs at the same time to transfigure the Echo-Narcissus binary investments that have produced, articulated, and institutionalised Western cultural heritages and their others. So while 'intertextuality' and 'intermediality' have work to do in terms of promoting greater intercultural inclusiveness and synergies to realise their prefix, neither can be a last word on the forms, functions, and modes of cultural revivification. This is in part because of the 'inter-' prefix discussed above (which also pertains to 'interdiscursivity' as alternative model within the same family of terms). To replace this prefix with another,

---

[13] See http://www.ansp.org/museum/digital_collections/fish/bowdich.php (last accessed 1 November 2008) for the only readily available image of one of Sarah's exquisite drawings of fish. The short synopsis given here about Sarah is however erroneous in various details ('facts'). For much more reliable information, see Donald de Beaver, "Writing Natural History for Survival – 1820-1856: the Case of Sarah Bowdich, later Sarah Lee," *Archives of Natural History* 26.1 (1999): 19-31. For work on the extraordinary qualities of Sarah's science and its writing as a woman, see Mary Orr, "Pursuing Proper Protocol: Sarah Bowdich's Purview of the Sciences of Exploration" *Victorian Studies* (2007): 277-285.

such as 'trans-' as in 'trans-nation', permits only relative room to manoeuvre in the same dominant cultural spaces. Is more radical cultural understanding of the place of Echo a way to rethink the impasses of Narcissus' distorting mirrors? Has the illusive element and our fifth 'window' to do with roots, introductions, departures and the unfinished as precisely the inexhaustible melting pot for culture's representations in imitation of the cornucopia of nature?

In his megalomania and madness, Lear was adamant that speaking held the key, not silence. Cordelia was, however, aware that clichéd language for powerful sentiment provided no useful communication for the ears of her interlocutor either. Speaking *again* is the potential bridge between, the 'Emperor's new clothes' of stating realities that are so hidden because they are so obvious. Texts and media likewise depend for their sense of potency not so much on blanks and silences, but on speech genres and speech acts that have evaded them and hence make a difference as to how to apprehend the world. In that we have never had so much daily access to multimedia cultural environments, to the many popular, high, scientific, economic, legal, fictional, national discourses, views, and voices, the potential to stumble upon the elusive term preceding and hence succeeding 'intertextuality' (and 'intermediality') has never been greater. Yet in this clamour, how does one distinguish heartfelt expression from cliché, or tell again so that one's voice is heard and recorded, despite the penalties for painful truth in the ears of dictators? Numbers, laws, and the proofs of science have rarely been used as a political instrument, although the announcement of profoundly reverberating scientific discoveries has brought challenge to prior 'authorities' (and their pronouncements of these new ideas as anathema or heresy). Humanities' sensitivities to reading the unspoken in the spoken and the unseen in the visible (in times of censorship, the genres of satire and allegory, the pointed message of a cartoon with or without a caption), therefore offer many ways to reappraise the presumptions of discourses of 'expert' knowledge (including their deconstructions). It is then not sufficient to find alternative metaphors to reclassify such statements and positions, although reconfiguring or remapping well-trodden territories may add new players, details, topoi or perspectives to the picture.[14] Rather, it is in the non-formulaic one-liner, the

---

[14] See Franco Moretti, *Graphs, Maps, Trees: Abstract Models for a Literary History*, London and New York: Verso, 2005. These models remain two-dimensional and work of a single expert. More interesting are metaphors of filigree work involving a variety of skills or workers (with which I concluded my *Intertextuality*), or of geological remappings which include physical and collaborative efforts. The first geological map was published by William Smith in 1815. Mapping the strata of any place in a given country or on several parts of the globe returns a very different picture of the connections between places than is otherwise apparent on the cultural surface, yet this cultural surface is also shaped by the strata (real and meta-

quip, the artless ready-response which may go unrecorded, that we need to look. There is a word for such a scene of potential meaningfulness, the form of which punctuates the early parts of this essay, the anecdote. Literally that which is not published, this transnationally familiar form of cultural expression may function as the telling remark, the witty turning of another's coat, the satirical point that evades the censor because dressed in a personalised short narrative that, apparently, has no wider political significance. Or the anecdote is illustrative of more highly wrought expression to come.[15] Without laws or theories as to its length or breadth, it pertains to the sciences as well as humanities contexts and is defiantly omnivorous in its materials.[16] In an age of alleged electronic sophistication, forms such as the anecdote with their pejorative, marginal connotations and denotations (as of the speech of women, or those of non-white ethnic or lower class status) represent the enduring elusive power of knowing how and when to speak again. Amira Nowaira's question about the significance of the hat in Waterhouse's painting of Narcissus and Echo came to be the anecdote that enabled a fuller story to be told, and a point to be made.[17] The personal can indeed speak again in the most politic of terms through the anecdotal as seemingly minor aside in cultural history. In consequence, the teller of an anecdote outside the written text or digital medium may then paradoxically be the richer culturally, if verbal profligacy, immediacy, independent creativity, and potential untraceability are expedient to the regeneration of the cultural imagination as multiform not uniform. Such potential gains for the greater cultural fabric in the making are also liberating for the myriad voices, texts, and artefacts that have so far defied print collection or digitisation. The losses are thus on the side of those charged with the surveillance of the machinery of culture, its forms and functions. The internet and intertext rich may in fact be the poorer after all since their materials are, by default, iterative, and according to patterns and systems of knowledge.

---

phorical) beneath it or the fossils to be found there. Discovery and understanding of the importance of such rock as the metamorphoses of microfossils constituted a reappraisal of the orders of creation in mid nineteenth-century Europe that led, by diverse hands, to the human genome.

[15] Although translatable into many European languages, 'intertextuality' (as also 'intermediality') has no verb form. It is worth noting that 'anecdote' similarly has no verb form.

[16] There are surprisingly few comprehensive studies of the anecdote (as opposed to the fragment, or paratext) apart from Marie-Pascale Huglo's *Métamorphoses de l'insignifiant. Essai sur l'Anecdote dans la Modernité*, Montreal: Balzac and Le Griot Editeur, 1997. The scientific pertinence of anecdote is perhaps well-illustrated in the short-lived French journal launched in 1854 entitled *L'Anecdote: Revue Scientifique et Littéraire Suivie de Faits Divers et de Pièces Récréatives et Instructives.*

[17] Barthes defined such 'hotspots' in photographs as the 'punctum'.

In response to the invitation to speak again, my plenary set out to question the current status of 'intertextuality', its debates and contexts, by challenging the remits of the plenary itself as among the most intertextual and formal of speech genres, yet also the least explored. By adding to verbal illustration through power point slides of text, image, and transnational subjects, I was able to extend, visibly and aurally, the 'intermedial' import of the plenary genre. But most of all, I was interested in the experiment of breaking the mould of the plenary form by actively eliciting the comment of my audience within, and not just at the end, of its performance. If this was my only solution to the knotty problem of finding distance from my own positions, I was not interested in self-reflexive play with the plenary's forms or functions (in this case academic) so much as with its possibilities for concentrated, collaborative, cultural work. In my search for a fifth act lying behind quotation, imitation, influence and intertextuality, I felt sure in the preparation of my materials that because I was myself as yet blind to their 'point', my audience would see it. I was therefore completely open to changing the end of my prepared talk had a new term or debate emerged.[18] Possibly the shock of involvement, or interest in my illustrations from Sarah Bowdich's work as challenge to the gender and transnational politics of intertextual and intermedial criticism, meant that I did not depart from my script:

> But a further term [for 'intertextuality'] has surely been presenting itself throughout our engagement in semiotic encountering this afternoon? In thanking you again for being my interlocutors in these opening thoughts, many dialogues and interlocutions have richly been brought into interplay. If the 'inter'- allows of no outside of its locutions, collocation in its translocations might better encompass such contexts. It is only through the collocations of debate (its disposition, arrangement with, or relation to others) in diverse tongues and hands that new collocution can take place. Where better might I then look for the ideal space for exploring collocution than to finish my plenary, so that we can enjoy the colloquy of this colloquium?

If this conclusion opened up the formal plenary genre to gather in its related but more informal speech genre, the concluding term, 'collocution', did not resound in later panels. By contrast, informal discussions between panel sessions allowed me to hear without hearing the 'point' I had made without seeing it. It has only been in the process of including the normally unpublished edges to any plenary in essay form here that the unfinished stories and 'points' have taken shape into the elusive term which 'collocation' had not quite put its finger upon, 'anecdote'. Where better can 'anecdote' then be

---

[18] None did, although questions at the end focused more on 'intermediality' than on 'intertextuality'.

positioned than as coda to the words of a plenary talk in more wrought form, since anecdotes already promise speaking again?

Works Cited

Beaver, Donald de. "Writing Natural History for Survival – 1820-1856: the Case of Sarah Bowdich, later Sarah Lee." *Archives of Natural History* 26.1 (1999): 19-31.
"Bowdich's British Fishes (1828-1838)." *The Academy of Natural Sciences* 1 Nov. 2008
<http://www.ansp.org/museum/digital_collections/fish/bowdich.php>.
Broich, Ulrich and Manfred Pfister, eds. *Intertextualität: Formen, Funktionen, anglistische Fallstudien.* Tübingen: Max Niemeyer Verlag, 1985.
Dalí, Salvador. *Metamorphosis of Narcissus.* 1937. Tate, London. *Tate Online.* 21 Nov. 2008
<http://www.tate.org.uk/servlet/ViewWork?workid=2987>.
Genette, Gérard. *Seuils.* Paris: Seuil, 1987.
Huglo, Marie-Pascale. *Métamorphoses de l'insignifiant. Essai sur l'Anecdote dans la Modernité.* Montreal: Balzac, 1997.
Iser, Wolfgang. *The Act of Reading: a Theory of Aesthetic Response.* London: Routledge, 1978.
Kristeva, Julia. *Semeiotikè.* Paris: Points, 1969.
Moretti, Franco. *Graphs, Maps, Trees: Abstract Models for a Literary History.* London: Verso, 2005.
Orr, Mary. *Intertextuality: Debates and Contexts.* Cambridge: Polity Press, 2003.
—. "Pursuing Proper Protocol: Sarah Bowdich's Purview of the Sciences of Exploration." *Victorian Studies* (2007): 277-85.
Riffaterre, Michel. *Semiotics of Poetry.* Bloomington: Indiana UP, 1978.
Said, Edward. *Beginnings: Intention and Method.* New York: Basic Books, 1975.
Waterhouse, John William. *Echo and Narcissus.* 1903. Walker Art Gallery, Liverpool. National Museums Liverpool. 21 Nov. 2008
<http://www.liverpoolmuseums.org.uk/walker/collections/20c/waterhouse.aspx>.

Harish Trivedi

Anglophone Transnation, Postcolonial Translation: The Book and the Film as Namesakes

The Anglophone Transnation comprises migrants from the postcolonies struggling to survive in the metropolis and swiftly losing their own language and culture as they try to assimilate. Described as 'cultural translation' in postcolonial theory, notably by Homi Bhabha, this vexed process is further complicated for those migrants who are even residually bilingual. Their double enunciation is represented through varying semiotic strategies in the different mediums of novels and films, as for example in the case of Jhumpa Lahiri's *The Namesake* (2003) made into a film by Mira Nair (2007). Such negotiations with diasporic bilingualism serve at the same time to reveal a new dimension of the expressive capability of films compared with that of novels, which may help us re-think some aspects of the entrenched aesthetic debate on books vs. films.

Semiotic Encounters and Postcolonial Bilingualism

The Anglophone transnation is a recent and thoroughly postcolonial development. In what is basically a glaring example of colonial discrimination, a substantial proportion of the population of the world is regarded not as 'English-speaking' but rather as 'Anglophone' – in the sense of not having been born to the language and speaking it as their mother-tongue (as in the title of Winston Churchill's celebratory 4-volume work *A History of the English-Speaking Peoples*) but rather as having been obliged by colonial rule to learn and use it; such language-use is often seen as a deviant variety of the 'standard' version of the language such as spoken by the white citizens of Britain and subsequently and arguably also the United States. Thus, while colonial subjects began speaking in English on their home ground (as notably in the West Indies and in parts of Africa) often due to the suppression and even extermination of their native languages, the Anglophone 'transnation' was born when they began to migrate out of their own countries after the conclusion of the Second World War, to what some of them were culturally conditioned to regard as the Mother Country or as Home, and that is when the fact that they were 'Anglophone' was underlined, in contrast with the native population who were of course properly 'English-speaking'.

In the 1950s, while still under British rule, a large number of West Indians migrated to England to take up lowly jobs that no native Englishmen were available or willing to fill and they were shortly after joined by (East) Indians too, who had gained independence in 1947. In the 1960s, a higher class of migration began from India, by trained professionals such as engineers and doctors, not only to the U.K. but also to the U.S.A. which still continues though now somewhat restricted and abated, and it is basically these migrants who have gone on to form the Anglophone transnation. It is their success not only in their professions but in the areas particulalrly of creative writing and indeed of postcolonial theory (which was in effect founded by three such migrants, Edward Said, Gayatri Chakravorty Spivak and Homi Bhabha) that has given this tiny segment of world population a disproportionately high visibility and academic value.

All such Anglophone migrants have of course a first language, their mother-tongue, which could not be left behind in one abrupt move as the Motherland was. This native language persists under the hegemony of pragmatic Anglophony and continues to permeate the more intimate aspects of a migrant's existence which English cannot reach. It coexists with English and contests with its professional and social as well as domestic and personal spaces which constitute a migrant's life and sensibility. It fights a constantly losing battle, especially in the case of second-generation migrants, but it also mounts rearguard resistance as in the case of many of the so-called 'heritage kids' wishing to reclaim, as they grow up, the language of their forbears and consciously seeking to reconnect with the lost Motherland through indirect access to it via books and even more films in the language of the Motherland. This is perhaps especially acutely the case with migrants from India, for several obvious reasons. Not only is India one of the biggest producers of books in the world, in its own languages as well as in English, but it is also the biggest producer of films in the world, nearly all of which are in one or the other of its own languages, with only a handful of films being produced in English.

Nor is India by any plausible definition an Anglophone country, unlike several other former colonies. Though English continues in a colonial hangover to be one of the two official languages of the state together with Hindi, there are only a handful of mother-tongue speakers of it in the country and the proportion of competent second-language speakers of English is estimated to be no higher than 5%. In a huge colonial paradox, Shakespeare for example was taught in India in the original English even to those seeking to learn basic English as a second language, as if Shakespeare's was the kind of English they were best off learning (Trivedi 2006, 195f.). The ground-reality of India being an intractably non-Anglophone country is obscured in Western (and especially English-speaking and Anglophone) perception mainly by three factors: that even 5% of the Indian population amounts to over 50 million people, i.e., nearly the whole population of Great Britain; that the Indians who circulate overseas are of necessity Anglophone so that the vast majority of Indians who do not know English and stay at home do not impinge on the consciousness of non-Indian observers; and that ever since the rise of Salman Rushdie, several Indian writers in English, especially those relocated in the diaspora, have commanded the kind of international recognition that has tended to eclipse the fact that over 90% of all literary production in India even now continues to be in the Indian languages.

In the above context, I propose to explore in this essay three distinct kinds of semiotic encounters which however are all in a way intermeshed. Firstly, I examine the claim that writing transnationally in English is in itself a form of translation, i.e. a transaction between two languages, though the writing is all in only one language. Secondly, I wish to examine in particular the case of one diasporic Indian writer in English, Jhumpa Lahiri, who has herself made the strongest and most eloquent claims for being a translator in this intermediary sense. And lastly, I proceed to look at her novel *The Namesake* and also at the film based on it with the same title, to revisit the question of how books and films relate to each other and, more specifically, the means and resources available to each of these mediums for representing the double codes of translation as well as explicit bilingualism. The first of these encounters is located across the interstitial space between the home and the diaspora, the second in the subterranean processes of one language subtly shaping and informing another, while the third and last is a double encounter between two radically contrasted forms of artistic representation, the novel and the film, where my focus still remains on the use of two alternating verbal (as opposed to cinematic) languages and the modes of representing each in relation to the other.

Translation and 'Cultural Translation'

Translation, the rendering of a text in one language into another language, was given a new and peculiarly diasporic meaning when Salman Rushdie claimed, on his own behalf and on the behalf of other migrant writers: "We are translated men" (Rushdie 17). He was here invoking the etymological sense of the word, of being carried across, presumably from his location in native India to a desired destination elsewhere, in his case England. He was in the process endowing migrancy with added value, for being 'translated' implies and subsumes an authentic originality of location, while at the same time devaluing translation as the term has been traditionally understood by divorcing it from the knowledge of two different languages, which makes verbal translation a harder task to attempt and accomplish than merely boarding an aeroplane. The self-serving glibness of his formulation was underlined when Ngugi wa Thiong'o, the Kenyan novelist who had gone into exile also in England but only after having served one year in a Kenyan prison in a solitary cell with the threat of worse to come, distanced himself from Rushdie by saying: "No, I don't think of myself as a translated man [...]. I think of myself as a *transported* man" (wa Thiong'o, 337; emphasis in the original), evoking poignantly the historical sense of 'transport' as the practice of banishing criminals to a far-away penal colony.

It has been pointed out that Rushdie's *Midnight's Children* is not in fact much of a 'translated' work for it is not easy to determine in which language his characters may be 'originally' speaking; indeed, "Rushdie's own comments reveal ultimately that he evaded the issue of the underlying languages the characters are speaking" (Gane 569). It has also been suggested that Rushdie's own knowledge of Hindi/Hindustani, from which he somewhat ostentatiously strews occasional words and phrases throughout his narrative, is no more than 'skin-deep' and in certain cases demonstrably wrong (cf. Trivedi 1999). On the other hand, though Rushdie did become a much-translated man even in the familiar sense after the success of *Midnight's Children* when his novel was promptly rendered into numerous languages of the world, there seemed to have been no need felt, paradoxically, to translate this work into any of the Indian languages until a Hindi publisher commissioned and brought out a translation eighteen years later, to coincide with the fiftieth anniversary of Indian independence: *Adhi Rat ki Santanen* (1997). One vital aspect of the original that was certainly lost in this translation, and perhaps could not but be lost, was the authenticating effect produced in English through the use of Hindi words, for unlike the English reader who knew no Hindi, the Hindi reader had reason to wonder what all the fuss was about in using a few words of Hindi. This translated text served in fact to deconstruct the original and its originality, for it gave the lie to Rushdie being a translated man in any literary sense.

The supposition that postcolonial writing is a form of translation thus cannot be granted as readily and positively as many practitioners and critics of such writing have claimed. However, this has not prevented an even larger claim being made more recently that all diasporic Anglophone writers are 'cultural translators'. Again, as 'cultural translation' is not a concept or term current in Translation Studies and not to be found in any major encyclopaedia, reader or survey of the field, it must be regarded as a postcolonial invention and an even more blatant or – in an exculpatory and expedient euphemism from postcolonial discourse itself – catachrestic attempt to appropriate the term 'translation' to its own purposes. And it is also insidious, for no attempt is made to suggest that cultural translation has any kind of underpinnings in another 'original' language or that anything specifically to do with language is at all involved. Indeed, it is difficult to imagine why the term 'translation' is here deployed at all, except possibly to retain some residual notion of an umbilical cord which connects this writing (in terms of its content) to where the writers come from.

In another broad and even less literary connotation, the term 'cultural translation' has been extended to mean, in effect, existence as a migrant in a foreign country. The arch-theorist of this new term would appear to be Homi Bhabha and one of the most self-consciously assertive of its practitioners as a diasporic writers is Jhumpa Lahiri. To begin with Bhabha, he offers his most sustained discussion of the term, which seems hardly to have been used in this sense before, in the penultimate chapter of his book *Location of Culture*, titled "How newness enters the world: Postmodern space, postcolonial times and the trials of cultural translation". Seeking generally "to negotiate narratives where double-lives are led in the postcolonial world" (213) and "the transnational character of contemporary culture" (214), he narrows in on the controversy that surrounded *The Satanic Verses* and proceeds to offer "[his] theoretical description of blasphemy as an act of cultural translation" (226) while he also defends 'heresy' as virtually a function of migrant hybridity. Thus viewed,

> Rushdie performs the subversion of its [the Koran's] authenticity through the act of cultural translation – he relocates the Koran's 'intentionality' by repeating and reinscribing it in the locale of the novel of postwar cultural migration and diasporas. (Bhabha 226)

This comes close to suggesting that heresy and blasphemy are a prerogative of the migrant – as if non-migrants could not possibly commit blasphemy and heresy on home ground. This is elaborated and reinforced a little later in a passage of wider significance:

> If hybridity is heresy, then to blaspheme is to dream [...] it is the dream of translation as 'survival' as Derrida translates the 'time' of Benjamin's concept of the after-life of translation, as *sur-vivre*, the act of living on borderlines. Rushdie translates this into the migrant's dream of survival; an *initiatory* interstices; an empowering condition of hybridity; [...]. (Bhabha 226f.)

There is a suggestion elsewhere by Bhabha, in an earlier chapter of his book, that 'cultural translation' is inherent in other kinds of hybridity as well: "the object of linguistic science is always already in an enunciatory process of cultural translation, showing up the hybridity of any genealogical or systematic filiation" (Bhabha 58). But it is firmly on the terrain of the necessarily hybrid *migrant* that Bhabha locates this practice in its most potently political manifestation, and that would appear to be the crux of his pioneering conceptualisation of the term 'cultural translation' – so much so that this is the sense in which he often uses the term 'translation' as well.

Of all the contemporary creative writers, Jhumpa Lahiri seems to identify most closely with the idea of the migrant writer as translator, in a sense uncannily close to Bhabha's. Lahiri was born in London to Indian Bengali parents who moved to the U.S.A. when she was three and was brought up in Rhode Island. She obtained a B.A. in English Literature from Barnard College, M.A. degrees in English as well as Creative Writing, and a Ph.D. in Renaissance Studies. Her first book of fiction, *The Interpreter of Maladies: Stories of Bengal, Boston and Beyond* (1999) won her the Pulitzer prize the following year, a distinction even more remarkable for the fact that the prize has seldom been awarded for collections of short stories. Her first novel, *The Namesake* (2003) was made into a film with the same title (2007), and her third book, *Unaccustomed Earth* (2008), another collection of short stories, opened at number 1 in the *New York Times* bestseller list instantly upon publication. Of all the Indian diasporic writers, she would appear to have the biggest reputation and readership in the U.S.A.

Shortly after she had won the Pulitzer, Lahiri published in 2000 a short article titled "My Intimate Alien" which could be regarded in many ways as her manifesto as a writer. Countering the criticism in the Indian press that she did not seem to know her India well enough, she said: "I am the first person to admit that my knowledge of India is limited, the way in which all translations are" (Lahiri 2000, 120). To compound what might seem a gratuitous deprecation of all translations, she asserted that her representation of India was in fact her "translation of India" (118). Not only was she a translator, it turned out, but the characters she created were translators no less: "Almost all of my characters are translators, insofar as they must make sense of the foreign to survive" (120). This would seem directly to allude to Bhabha's formulation, in the passage cited above, of the Derridean-Benjaminian "*survivre*" and his formulation of "the migrant's dream of survival", nor can one put it entirely beyond the realm of possibility that Lahiri may actually have read Bhabha before she wrote this, as someone who has a Ph.D. degree in English literature from a major American campus. Anyhow, Lahiri concluded this meditation on herself as a diasporic writer by drawing herself to her full creative height and by grandly declaring: "And whether I write as an American or as an Indian, about things American or Indian or otherwise, one thing remains constant: I translate, therefore I am" (120).

One may note here the repeated prioritisation of 'American' over 'Indian', for if Lahiri were not American by nationality and passport but Indian, she would not qualify to be even considered for the Pulitzer – just as Rushdie is British by nationality, or else Margaret Thatcher's government might have considered deporting him in the face of the Iranian *fatwa* rather than protecting him at enormous expense to public funds (– though he could still under the rules have won the Booker prize for which only publication in England is required). But to return to Lahiri, in what sense precisely does she claim that being a translator is the *raison d'etre* of her being? She certainly cannot translate from Bengali into English or vice versa, for when one of her short stories was published in Bengali translation, she did not even have the linguistic competence to read it – or, as she herself put it, the Bengali version remained "inaccessible to me" (Lahiri 2000, 120), as if it were the fault of the Bengali language.

The Double Semiotics of Book and Film

In this context, I propose to discuss, in the rest of this essay, the more specific issues of diasporic bilingualism and 'translation' (either implicit, as claimed by Lahiri, or explicit, as in actual literary translation), with Lahiri's own novel *The Namesake* and the film made on it as a case-study. Before analysing these works, however, it may be appropriate to reflect briefly on the relationship between books and films generally. For about a century now, the new medium of film has contested with the form of the novel (itself eponymously the last 'new' form) the vast space of popular story-telling and has effectively outstripped the novel, at least in terms of mass appeal and consumption as well as financial rewards. What is still very much at issue in repeated academic discussions, however, is whether the film can tell a story as well as the novel in terms of artistic resourcefulness and nuance. The debate comes to a head, of course, when a direct comparison is possible, as in the cases of novels which have been turned into films. But the very idea of comparing the two is in itself a bone of contention, as many film theorists have argued that films have an idiom and indeed a *language* of their own and are thus to be judged entirely on their own autonomous terms and not as versions or appendages of another medium such as the literary (For a fuller discussion especially in the Indian context, see Trivedi 2006, 51-53.).

The matter is made more complex by the historical circumstance that the mode of narration in films is believed in many crucial ways to be indebted to older forms of narrative such as the novel, and that verbal language still forms a significant constituent of it. As Christian Metz, perhaps the most thoroughgoing and influential theoretician of the view that cinema is a distinct and independent art-form and has a language of its own, has nevertheless acknowledged, the cinema's

> strength, or its weakness, is that it encompasses earlier modes of expression: some, truly languages (the verbal element), and some languages only in [a] more or less figurative sense (music, image, noise). Nevertheless, […] [s]peech, noise, and music were annexed at a later time, but film was born with *image discourse*. (qtd. in Elliott 2004, 3)

Among the several other distinctive features of each artform that Seymour Chatman highlights in his essay "What Novels Can Do That Films Can't (and Vice Versa)", one is that "the camera depicts but does not describe" and another that though it can show an act, it cannot always indicate the degree of intentionality behind the act, as in the film sequence which renders the phrase in a Maupassant story, "she showed her limbs up to the knee", where one can see what is shown without being able to discern whether it was meant to be so shown (Chatman 440, 443). It may be added that films cannot render similes or metaphors that literary language often deploys to great effect, and that the omniscient narratorial exploration of the subconscious psychological processes of the minds of characters with which novels often deepen the visible action is usually lost in films. Another larger and more basic consideration is that in visualising a character in a definite and defining way by having of necessity a certain actor play it, "[i]mages are scrambling the function of language which must operate out of the imaginary to function properly", as Wlad Godzich has put it (qtd. in Beller 68). What the novel leaves to the imagination of the reader is already imagined for the viewer in film, and thus given a fixity which serves to close off further possibilities of imagining.

For example, in Roman Polanski's astonishingly (and therefore perhaps somewhat disappointingly) faithful film version of Thomas Hardy's novel *Tess of the d'Urbervilles*, the title role was played by the German actress Nastassja Kinski (who won a Golden Globe award for it) and though (at least to my untutored Indian eye) she looked English enough, she certainly did not look like a milkmaid with rounded arms and with the indomitable physical strength of a country girl in the way that Hardy repeatedly prompts the reader to imagine her. On the other hand, few who watched Kinsky in that role could have been unaware of her elfin appearance and her screen reputation as "the enigmatic seductress" (Suzie Mackenzie) – while Tess in the novel is depicted as an innocent girl who *is* seduced (or in some interpretations raped) but who remains nevertheless 'a pure woman' as the sub-title of the novel has it.

Similarly, in Mira Nair's film of Lahiri's *The Namesake*, the protagonist and his parents, the three major characters, are all played by actors who look Indian enough, but who do not at all look like Bengalis which they are definitely and essentially portrayed as being in the novel. It may be argued that this would hardly have made a difference to the audience in the West, for which this film was primarily intended, but in fairness to Nair, it must be added that she had offered the role of the mother originally to Rani Mukherjee, a superstar of Indian films who is a Bengali, who however turned it down, and subsequently to Konkana Sen, a moderately successful mainstream actress who is a Bengali too, but who turned it down as well. Nair finally settled on the non-Bengali Tabu, mainly an arthouse actress. In the novel, incidentally, Ashima, the character that Tabu played, we are told, "had been compared on more than one occasion to the actress Madhabi Mukherjee" (Lahiri 2003, 9; the novel *The Namesake* is hereafter cited as *N*) – who had what was popularly regarded as an iconically Bengali face and was cast in three of his films by Satyajit Ray. Indeed, at the premiere of the film in Calcutta, Mira Nair felt obliged to say, by way of mitigating her failure to cast a Bengali actress, that though played by Tabu, the character of Ashima had been modelled on how Madhabi Mukherjee had looked and played the female lead in Ray's film *Mahanagar* (1961; i.e., *The Metropolis*, set in Calcutta). (Bhattacharya) In any case, Nair then, as if in compensation, recruited for the smaller roles a number of migrant Bengali non-actors resident in the U.S.A. including some members of Lahiri's own family and indeed, for a fleeting cameo, Lahiri herself cast as 'Jhumpa Mashi [Aunt]'.

We are speaking here, thus, of a basic constituent of cinematic visuality that functions as a fundamental semiotic factor, i.e., what an actor actually looks like, which then has a bearing on yet another kind of expressive language, i.e., body language. Related to this is the consideration that all star actors carry with them the baggage of roles that they have already played, for which some of them have even become typecast. However, to return to the primary or at least predominant meaning of language, as the medium of verbal expression, we find in the novel and the film versions of *The Namesake* a number of examples of what one medium can do and the other cannot which are of special relevance to the diasporic bilingual situation – and perhaps for that reason not often discussed or theorised in mainstream novel/film debates.

The Two *Namesakes* – in Fiction and in Life

The Namesake narrates the story of an Indian engineer, Ashoke Ganguli, who comes to the U.S.A. in the mid-1960s to obtain a Ph.D. in fibre optics from the M.I.T. and then stays on to teach at another university in the Boston area. While still a student, he goes back home to Calcutta to return with a bride, Ashima, also a Bengali. They have a son born in 1968 who is named Gogol but who grows to feel ashamed of his name which he changes to Nikhil (– though this Sanskritic Indian name still echoes the first name, Nikolai, of his detested namesake, the Russian writer Gogol). As they grow up Gogol/Nikhil and his sister Sonia drift further and further apart culturally from their parents. Gogol has a couple of white American girl-friends but then marries disastrously a Bengali while Sonia actually marries, happily enough, a white American. Ashoke now suddenly dies, and Ashima, who has never really felt at home in the U.S.A., decides to sell the house and go back to India, planning to spend six months every year in each country as, it now transpires, her husband and she had always intended to do once he retired.

This intimately domestic novel thus does not take it upon itself to address many of the major problems of migrants: the struggle to find a job (for Ashoke with his Ph.D. appears simply to walk into a cushy one, off-stage), social and cultural insecurity and isolation (for the Gangulis soon enough have a number of other Bengali families to interact with), or any kind of cultural or racial discrimination (for when Gogol is laughed at by his schoolmates, it is solely because of his odd and absurd name). Ashoke continues to do well in his job and is a visiting professor in another university when he dies; Ashima misses her parents and grandparents in Calcutta and is initially lonely in America but distinctly less so after she has children, and when they have grown up and gone away she even takes up a job in a local library. Indeed, the biggest source of distress in this bland and blithe book seems to be the odd name Ashoke has saddled his son with, for eccentrically personal reasons; it is this little one-off individual oddity which Lahiri signals to be the eponymous crux of the novel.

This may seem excessive and quite out of proportion, except that it turns out that Lahiri is thus catharting in art her own private embarrassment and unhappiness at her parents having named her 'Jhumpa' informally (as a *daknam*, or a name by which one's intimates call one), whereas her formal name (or *bhalo-nam*, the good name), was the sonorous mouthful 'Nilanjana Sudeshna' (Her good name got erased when her American primary school-teacher, quite understandably, preferred the shorter and simpler version.). This distinction and indeed disjunction between two spheres of one's cultural existence or even two identities, the one proper and official and presentable to the external world and the other private and informal and confined to the intimate circle of one's family and friends, is an acknowledged cultural practice among the Bengalis, more so than among other Indians where quite often, as indeed universally, the pet name is a diminutive of the formal one. But the gap is polarised in the case of Bengali names, where the informal name is utterly nonsensical and chosen mostly for the sound, while the formal name is full of grand and ambitious signification. In Lahiri's own case, 'Jhumpa' has no meaning at all, while 'Nilanjana' means lightning, or alternatively, a woman adorned with blue (or dark) eye-kohl, while the rarer 'Sudeshna', the name of a minor queen in the *Mahabharata*, means a good looking woman and possibly also one born in a good place or a good country. (This may seem odd for, as noted above, Lahiri was born not in India but in England.)

One may thus imagine, and even sympathise with, Jhumpa Lahiri's personal discomfiture at having been reduced to the nonsensical and babyishly silly name 'Jhumpa' for the rest of her days. But she may appear to have botched the artistic possibilities inherent in such rightly resented infantilisation when, unlike in her real life, she chose to go for the distinctly fanciful and thoroughly un-Bengali pet-name 'Gogol' in the case of her fictional protagonist. This was perhaps to be too clever by half, with the result that what could have been potentially developed as a migrant's shame arising from retaining a home-grown cultural practice now hinges on just individual idiosyncrasy. Mira Nair's film does the right thing by comparatively downplaying the 'namesake' business, for it is obvious that the novelist needs to be rescued from an autobiographical obsession which she has not been quite able to subsume or transform into art.

Two Languages in the Two *Namesakes*

But it would be unfair to judge Jhumpa Lahiri, the self-proclaimed translator of diasporic experiences, by her rendering of the excessively personal and over-invested case of the namesake, despite her own eponymous insistence on it. After all, Bengali pet-names are meant to be, and indeed are "frequently meaningless, deliberately silly, ironic, even onomatopoetic" (*sic*; *N* 26), and thus willfully overdetermined to be so non-semantic as to be utterly untranslatable, as 'Jhumpa' genuinely is and as alas 'Gogol' artificially is not. A far fairer index of just how well Lahiri is able to represent the alien experience of the migrant would be to see how she goes about representing the publicly translated as well as the privately untranslated mother-language of the migrant on alien ground.

The Namesake does much better in this regard from the start; in fact, it could hardly have done better. In the last month of her pregnancy, after she has prepared quietly in her kitchen with makeshift American ingredients an approximation of the Bengali dish she really craves for, Ashima speaks the first words in the novel, to her husband who is studying in the bedroom, addressing him not by his name but indirectly and obliquely as it is only right for a traditional Indian wife to do: "And so, instead of saying Ashoke's name, she utters the interrogative that has come to replace it, which *translates* roughly as: 'Are you listening to me?'" (*N* 2; my emphasis) On the next page, already driven to a hospital to deliver her first child and in the throes of birthing, she sees her husband momentarily go away, saying to her "in Bengali": "I'll be back." (*N* 3) But this doesn't ring as true, for clearly what he must have said is the utterly untranslatable (*Ami*) *ashi*, which literally means 'I'm coming', while what it idiomatically means is: I must go but since saying farewell is not something regarded as happy or auspicious, let me say instead that I'm coming, which I will be sooner or later. Lahiri gets it right the next time she uses this collocation when she also adds, belatedly, a minimal cultural gloss: "'I'm coming,' Ashima had said, for this was the phrase Bengalis always used in place of good-bye." (*N* 37)

More significant perhaps are the situations in the novel where Bengali and English are seen to jostle each other in an implicitly bilingual situation and sometimes openly to contest the same space of articulation. Ashima, who has studied English in college and recited from memory Wordsworth's "The Daffodils" to prove that she is a girl suitable for someone already living abroad like Ashoke to marry, finds her English coming unstuck at the most elementary level in America and is acutely discomfited. As she is undergoing labour pains, the American nurse asks her if she is hoping for a boy or a girl. "As long as there are ten finger and ten toe", Ashima replies – omitting to add "I don't mind" and not even realising it, for syntax in an Indian language like Bengali would not require it. But she has, she does realise, made a more basic mistake.

> Patty smiles, a little too widely, and suddenly Ashima realizes her error, knows she should have said "fingers" and "toes." This error pains her almost as much as her last contraction. English had been her subject [in college, and she knew] the difference between Aristotelian and Shakespearian tragedy. But in Bengali, a finger can also mean fingers, a toe toes. (*N* 7)

A similar anxiety of linguistic performance afflicts Gogol, and to some extent Ashoke as well, on Gogol's first day in school. When the principal asks the father, "Mr Ganguly, does Nikhil [i.e., Gogol] follow English?", Ashoke responds, "Of course he follows" (omitting the object, again in a characteristic syntactical deviation in the Indian use of English), and adds, "My son is perfectly bilingual". But Gogol refuses to say a word in either language when Ashoke, addressing his son for the first time in English, and "in careful accented English" at that, asks him to speak, or even when he later cajoles the child "in Bengali, calmly and quietly" to do so (*N* 58f.). As the novel progresses, the parents speak in Bengali and the children don't, despite being sent on alternate Saturdays to Bengali language and culture classes (*N* 65f.), and as a grown-up Gogol realises that though he can follow and speak his mother tongue, "he cannot read or write it with even modest proficiency" (*N* 118).

Gogol later has a Bengali girl-friend, Moushumi, who at age twelve had already decided not to marry a Bengali man and then staged a further 'rebellion' against her heritage by majoring in college in French: "Immersing herself in a third language, a third culture, had been her refuge – she approached French, unlike things American or Indian, without guilt, or misgiving, or expectation of any kind" (*N* 214). Such deep double denial and desperate escapism are not perhaps what 'the interstitial third space' celebrated in upbeat postcolonial theory is supposed to be, but they do appear to add up to an all too likely scenario in which the conflicted migrant seems able to resolve or at least break through her dilemma only by migrating yet again and even further afield, for another unknown and strange 'refuge'. It is not only reckless, identity-obliterating escape that we witness here but also a betrayal of all that a person has ever been. Reflecting this perhaps at another level, Moushumi, who has despite her pubescent vow married Gogol, soon after betrays and leaves him, for a white academic whose "name alone" is "enough to seduce her," Dimitri Desjardins, who has a Ph.D. in German literature (*N* 256f.), and who thus promises a fourth migrant heaven to her, even beyond the French third.

To many book addicts and literary scholars, the turning of a novel into a film is a kind of betrayal as well. In the case of narratives of migrant lives, with the retention or not of one's mother tongue being deliberately deployed as an indicator and measure of one's identity, the novel seems a particularly apt form in which to embody the battle of languages, for like other literary forms and unlike film, a novel itself operates through language. The medium is the message here – except that it might have been rather more fully so, or at least more interestingly so, one may speculate, had this particular novel, *The Namesake,* been written not in English but in Bengali.

Anyhow, while most films of novels reach a wider audience, the apprehension still attaches to them that they do so by making the novel simpler and cruder, so that what is gained in terms of popular circulation is at the cost of artistic sophistication and nuance. A corollary to this is the widespread belief that it is the more traditional and less experimental or artistic novels that lend themselves better to being adapted into films. Thus, as Kamilla Elliott has shown, the Victorian novel, with its realism as well as melodrama, has proved to be a bigger source than any other body of literature (including Shakespeare) for being adapted into twentieth century films: "I have located over 1500 film and television adaptations of British Victorian prose fiction [...]. Numerous Victorian novels have been filmed more than 20 times – some over 100 times" (Elliott 2003, 3). On the other hand, as George Bluestone has remarked, "Proust and Joyce would seem [...] absurd on film" (qtd. in Elliott 2004, 21 n. 67). The popular prejudice in the matter seems to run to the effect that one can't make a good film from a good book, either because the medium of film is not as fine or because, as the distinctly artistic director Francois Truffaut argued, "a masterpiece is something that has already found its perfection of form" (qtd. in Elliott 2003, 12). The fact that the film *The Namesake* was at least as big a success as the novel may thus be aptly juxtaposed with a review of the novel in *The Daily Telegraph,* prominently and approvingly quoted in the preliminary pages of the paperback 'film tie-in' edition: "Spurning [...] wordplay [...], she writes with journalistic precision. Like a Victorian urban chronicler, she loves to amass inventories" (qtd. in Lahiri 2006, n.p.).

Like many films of books, Mira Nair's film of necessity cuts out a lot of the detail and goes for a tidier coherence of plot. It does not introduce any significant new scenes or episodes or take any major so-called liberties. And yet, just by being a film and exploiting its technological potential, it adds a new dimension to the representation of the theme of the migrant's bilingualism that the novel did not possess and apparently could not possibly possess: it lets us hear and even see the Bengali language, not once but repeatedly as a significant motif running through the film. To represent the migrant's language, the novel either had to transcribe isolated Bengali words into the Roman script, with or without italics, or resort to the equally common device of explicitly and intrusively signalling that a certain character at a certain moment was not speaking in English, the language the novel is written in (e.g., "'I'll be back,' Ashoke says to her in Bengali" *N* 3). But a character in the film simply goes ahead and says it in Bengali for all of us to hear loudly and clearly – and, what is more, to understand as well with the help of English subtitles.

Bilingualism and Double Enunciation

This duality of articulation or doubleness of enunciation is hardly possible in a printed text, and then only cumbersomely and often wastefully, as in some bilingual editions of selections of poetry. In a film, on the other hand, it seems like the most natural thing to happen, especially when a character who looks different in colour, features and dress speaks in a different language as well. The bilingual effect here must be distinguished of course from the very different experience of watching a 'foreign' film in which there is no code-switching and all the characters all the time speak in an unfamiliar language, which then is made transnationally intelligible through (necessarily selective) subtitling, or from films that are dubbed from one language into another (as most notably in the case of Hollywood films shown in some of the major European countries).

To return to the kind of selective and indeed strategic bilingualism that marks the double life of migrants and is significantly present in both the book and the film *The Namesake*, the film has Ashima, even after migrating to America, speaking a fair bit of Bengali throughout her stay there of nearly three decades. As a woman, she is thus shown to be the custodian of "the inner domain of national culture", a space which is not penetrated and contaminated in the same way as the public sphere under colonial role, according to Partha Chatterjee (9) and that retains, it may be extrapolated, a similarly impermeable integrity under the conditions of transnational migration (Incidentally, in a kind of in-joke, Partha Chatterjee, who teaches for part of the year at Columbia University, is cast in *The Namesake* as one of the guests at Ashima's last party, who appears briefly to sing a few lines of a comic song which has alternating lines in Bengali and in English, thus playfully embodying linguistic hybridity.).

Mira Nair's film not only has Bengali actually spoken in it where so signalled in Lahiri's text but it decides in this regard to go beyond the novel on its own by turning from English into Bengali some other passages as well. For example, where the book has: "Rickshaw drivers [in India] dress better than professors here [in America], Ashoke [...] thinks frequently to himself" (*N* 31), the film has Ashoke not merely thinking so – which could hardly be shown – but actually saying so to Ashima, and in Bengali, at which they share an intimate and reassuring laugh together at the richest nation in the world which in this particular respect is apparently not able to stand comparison with poor India.

Probably the most effective example of the film taking recourse to Bengali in a moment of utmost familial intimacy where the book had done no such thing occurs late in the narrative when Ashoke suddenly dies in an unfamiliar campus and Gogol is sent by Ashima to claim his body and to dispose of his belongings while she herself stays at home, according to Indian convention. As Gogol is flying back to Ashima, he remembers, in a moment of deep cultural recall, that when Ashoke had received the news of the death of *his* father in India years back, he had gone into the bathroom and shaved his head clumsily with a disposable razor for, as Gogol had later come to understand, "it was a Bengali son's duty to shave his head in the wake of a parent's death" (*N* 179). In the novel, a silent remembrance of this ritual at this moment is poignant enough as the American-born Gogol has in general grown increasingly alienated from his home culture, but the film proceeds truly to raise the stakes here. It shows Gogol going to a barber shop and actually having his own head shaven similarly (to the background accompaniment, inexplicably, of a loud rap song) before he returns to Ashima, so that when she sees him, she is stunned and moved by this unexpected but gratifying act, and says to him in Bengali: "*Etar kono dorkar chhilo na, Baba*". (There was no need for this, son.) This is a rare occasion when she instinctively speaks to the grown-up Gogol in Bengali and in an even rarer act, he now shyly answers her in Bengali saying simply that he wanted to do it. Mother and son are united at this moment not only by grief but by their mother-tongue.

A film can achieve these synaesthetic effects as print cannot because (as we may remind ourselves) quite early in its development as a new medium, cinema attained a technological break-through by which it progressed from being a 'movie' to (also) becoming a 'talkie'. The polarised emphasis on films being primarily a visual medium and the novel being a verbal medium – as typically in the chapter-title "Novels, Films, and the Word/Image Wars" (Elliott 2004 1-22) – is thus exaggerated if not basically flawed, for in all films and especially perhaps in films with a literary provenance, words, speech and dialogue are used to as much effect as the visual image itself. Several exponents and theorists of the novel including notably Henry James had spoken metaphorically about how a novel can *tell* as well as *show*. In contrast, films can show as well as make us *hear* in a way novels cannot, and they do so in a strictly physical and non-metaphorical sense. In Sanskrit poetics, drama was regarded as a medium which had two equally important components, the *drishya* (the visible) and the *shravya* (the audible), and it could be argued that films too exploit equally both these resources for their expressive effect.

Finally, a film cannot merely make us hear bilingually, it helps us also make sense of what we hear in an alien language by taking recourse, paradoxically, to what is the medium of the novel, the printed word – as used in a film in subtitles. Again, Mira Nair, who had earlier in her *Monsoon Wedding* (2001) creatively exploited the inherently bilingual situation of upper-class English-educated Indians, and has at the same time shown an exceptionally keen desire to succeed in Hollywood (cf. Trivedi 2008, 205-8), seeks to go innovatively further in this regard in *The Namesake* than most film-makers may have attempted to do. She introduces a scene in which Ashima is writing a letter home to her family, and writing it in Bengali – as we see in a tight close-up which fills the whole screen with the unfamiliar script. Furthermore, what Ashima is writing is not subtitled, perhaps so that the effect of the Bengali script being shown so prominently may not be diluted or diminished through the simultaneous display of the Roman script; instead, we have here a voice-over by Ashima in English in a distinctly Indian accent.

Right from the start of the film, in fact, as soon as the credits begin to roll, Nair strikes a bilingual keynote in a rare and innovative manner, by presenting the title of the film and the names of the major actors as scripted in a kaleidoscopic medley of orthography combining letters from both the scripts, Bengali and Roman. Thus, the word NAMESAKE written in Roman capitals has the two 'A's in an inbetween lettering which makes them look on the one hand like pseudo-gothic small 'a's in Roman while they clearly are, on the other hand and for those who can read the Bengali script, the Bengali vowel 'ai' which is pronounced as in 'pain' and therefore accurately represents the sound of the two 'A's in NAMESAKE. More imaginative still is the lettering that begins to form the name of Kal Penn (who plays Gogol), with a Bengali

'K' followed by a Roman 'A' and a Bengali 'L', and a Bengali 'P' followed by a mirror-image Roman 'E' (which still does not look like any Bengali letter), a Bengali 'N' and then, following the Western spelling rather than the sound, a Roman 'N' as well. Tabu (who plays Ashima) has too short a name to be amenable to full treatment in this regard but she still gets a Bengali soft 'T' followed by a Roman 'A', a Bengali 'BU' (for one must write B and U joined together in Bengali and not separately) and then a Roman 'U' as well for good measure. Irrfan Khan (who plays Ashoke) presents more possibilities and gets seven Bengali letters (including, it may be noted, one error) with Roman representing only the 'A' in his first name and the 'HA' in his last name. The "Titles and Graphic Design" for the film are credited to Divya Thakur – in straight Roman lettering, alas, for the bilingual treatment is reserved only for the actors playing the major parts, including Jacinda Barrett and Zuleikha Robinson. If there were an Oscar for this category, as indeed there is for numerous other ancillary skills, Thakur would certainly deserve a nomination.

Such hybrid scripting may serve to remind us that films, however visual, must have a *script*, so called, and a screen*play*, even in cases where they are not based on literary works. Various film directors, some of whom are significantly called *auteurs* so as to honour their artistic seriousness and distinction, have held widely varying views on this non-visual but necessary element of a film. For example, when an interviewer put it to Wim Wenders that "Alfred Hitchcock said scriptwriting was his favourite part of filmmaking; the shooting was almost a chore he had to do afterwards", Wenders responded, "Writing is the worst. I hate that like the plague" (Wenders 475). But there is no escaping the fact that films must be written before they can be shot (barring the familiar but now diminishing practice in Bollywood where constant improvisation often prevailed over the script, or even added up to a script *post facto*), and this again goes to narrow the supposedly unbridgeable divide between films and novels as art forms.

Indeed, to go against the grain of the debate so far on films and novels, in which they have been seen as not only radically different from each other but as serving opposed ends, there may be a case for arguing, on the basis of some of the factors discussed above, that they also share vast areas of overlap and similarity. The early impulse, wholly understandable, on the part of the theorists of cinema to locate the new medium as far away from the good old novel as they possibly could has abated, the anxiety of disambiguating cinema from the pre-existent and predominant literary form of the novel seems to have lost its edgy sharpness and, perhaps more importantly, the snobbish sense of artistic superiority that the champions of the novel claimed for it has also shed some of its shine as a consequence of the greater acceptability of cinema as the chief narrative medium of our age and the inversely corresponding periodic announcements on the other hand that the novel is dead.

For all these reasons, it may be time now to re-view film and the novel in terms of their many affinities and similarities. They are often nominally the same, in the sense that nearly all films of the book are named after the book and so are the fewer books of the film. In this sense, books and films may be said to be – ahm! – namesakes, and even the chicken-or-egg debate as to which has priority has examples adducible on either side. Before the film *Slumdog Millionaire* (2008) earned a huge amount of box office money and also won eight Oscars including one to Simon Beaufoy for the screenplay, or indeed for '*Writing* (Adapted Screenplay)' as distinct from '*Writing* (Original Screenplay)' [my emphasis], as these awards are officially called, the novel by Vikas Swarup on which it was based, titled *Q&A* (2005), had already been reviewed widely and had sold well internationally. But after the film and the Oscars, it has been reissued under the title "*Slumdog Millionaire: Originally Published as Q&A*" (Swarup 2009). And this is not merely *post facto*; this novel seems to have been born dreaming to be a film when it grew up. As the review extracts reprinted in the 'film tie-in edition' put it, this novel is "[g]loriously fantastical" (*The Times*), and it "reels [!] from farce to melodrama to fairytale" (*You Magazine*). And as an uncannily proleptic review said: "When it is turned into the movie it wants to be, *Q&A* will be a delight" (*New York Times Book Review*; Swarup n.p.). What proves to be a double delight quite often, as in the cases of both *The Namesake* and *Slumdog*, is the way in which films have begun to bear the doubled semiotic burden of not only implied but explicitly enunciated bilingualism, especially in locales which are either migrant-transnational or destitute-postcolonial.

Works Cited

Beller, Jonathan L. "Kino-I, Kino-World: Notes on the Cinematic Mode of Production." *The Visual Culture Reader*. Ed. Nicholas Mirzoeff. 2nd ed. London: Routledge, 2002. 60-85.
Bhabha, Homi K. *The Location of Culture*. London: Routledge, 1994.
Bhattacharya, Roshmila. "Ashima was modelled on Madhabi Mukherjee in Mahanagar" [interview with Mira Nair]. *Screen Weekly* 30 March 2007. 23 April 2009
<http://www.screenindia.com/old/fullstory.php?content_id=15307>.
Chatman, Seymour. "What Novels Can Do That Films Can't (and Vice Versa)." *Film Theory and Criticism: Introductory Readings*. Eds Leo

Braudy and Marshall Cohen. 5th ed. New York: Oxford UP, 1999. 435-51.
Chatterjee, Partha. *The Nation and Its Fragments: Colonial and Postcolonial Histories*. Delhi: Oxford UP, 1995.
Elliott, Kamilla. "Novels, Films and the Word/Image Wars." *A Companion to Literature and Film*. Eds Robert Stam and Alessandra Raengo. Malden MA: Blackwell, 2004. 1-22.
—. *Rethinking the Novel/Film Debate*. Cambridge: CUP, 2003.
Gane, Gillian. "Postcolonial Literature and the Magic Radio: The Language of Rushdie's Midnight's Children." *Poetics Today* 27: 3 (2006). 569-96.
Lahiri, Jhumpa. "My Intimate Alien." *Outlook* (special issue on "Stree" [Woman]), 2000. 116-120.
—. *The Namesake* [Paperback "film tie-in edition"]. New Delhi: HarperCollins, 2006. [orig. published 2003]
Mackenzie, Suzie. "Daddy's Girl" [interview with Nastassja Kinski]. *The Guardian* 3 July 1999. 26 April 2009
<http://www.guardian.co.uk/theguardian/1999/jul/03/weekend7.weekend3>.
Nair, Mira. *Mira Nair's The Namesake*. DVD: "Collector's Edition" with "Bonus Features." Mumbai: UTV Software Communications Ltd., 2007.
Rushdie, Salman. *Imaginary Homelands: Essays and Criticism 1981 – 1991*. London: Granta/Penguin India 1991.
Swarup, Vikas. *Slumdog Millionaire: Originally Published as Q&A*. London: Black Swan "film tie-in" edition, 2009.
Trivedi, Harish. "The Anglophone Shakespeare: the non-Anglophone Shakespeare." *Shakespeare without English: The Reception of Shakespeare in non-Anglophone Countries*. Eds Sukanta Chaudhuri and Chee Seng Lim. Delhi: Pearson Longman, 2006. 192-208.
—. "All Kinds of Hindi: The Evolving Language of Hindi Cinema." *Fingerprinting Popular Culture: The Mythic and the Iconic in Indian Cinema*. Eds Vinay Lal and Ashis Nandy. New Delhi: Oxford UP, 2006. 51-86.
—. "From Bollywood to Hollywood: the Globalization of Hindi Cinema." *The Postcolonial and the Global*. Eds Revathy Krishnaswamy and John C. Hawley. Minneapolis: U of Minnesota P, 2008. 200-210.
—. "Salman the Funtoosh: Magic Bilingualism in *Midnight's Children*." *Rushdie's Midnight's Children: A Book of Readings*. Ed. Meenakshi Mukherjee. New Delhi: Pencraft, 1999. 69-94.
wa Thiong'o, Ngugi. "Ngugi wa Thiong'o with Harish Trivedi." *Writing across Worlds: Contemporary Writers Talk*. Ed. Susheila Nasta. London: Routledge, 2004. 327-39.
Wenders, Wim. *On Film*. London: Faber 2001.

Renate Brosch

Migrating Images and Communal Experience

Starting from the assumption that images are adapted to different contexts more easily than texts, since they seem to require less cognitive effort, I discuss the way images migrate through different media and cultures. I hold that they become agents in so far as they contribute to the shaping of identity and difference in the process of travelling through different medial and cultural contexts. However, their impact or "performativity" is not exhausted in providing an aid to self-fashioning and othering, as it were, but extends into the world of cultural practice as migrating images can provide the basis for the formation of interested communities of readerships.

Images and Agency

In an older essay, W.J.T. Mitchell gave a rather wide and inclusive definition of images as ranging from the concrete and graphic to the mental and visionary (Mitchell 1990, 20). This wide-ranging understanding apparently necessitated a distinction he made in his more recent *What do Pictures Want?*, where he described the "meta-picture" or in more common usage "icons" as "living images" present in a collective imaginary as a verbal and/or visual trope (Mitchell 2005, 10). For the present purpose "image" should be understood in the sense of Mitchell's definition, i.e. as reaching towards a symbolic compression of visual events. In contrast to "picture", as illustration, photograph, painting and on screen display, the term "image" carries connotations of visual ideas beyond a particular realisation. Such ideas can be triggered or produced by pictures, by films, and other visual media, but also and very effectively by literature. The reaction they cause in the reader – a term I will use in the following discussion in the sense of the receiver of any medium – builds on other earlier images and ideas. Powerful response to an image depends on many things; it does not depend on mimetic effect. Dinosaurs, creatures which no human being has ever seen, are a powerful image in Western culture, and so are vampires. Robin Hood and Cinderella have become images in this expanded sense, beyond any individual representation. Obviously, these are examples of images that have become mythical and stereotypical constructions because their repeated occurrence in cultural production has made them part of the collective imaginary, i.e. meta-pictures or global icons.

In these latter images, but also in any single act of realisation (whether in producing or reading an image), pre-conditioning by the visual world encountered up to this point takes place. Hence, images cannot be narrowly conceived as visual phenomena; rather, they are always the result of an ideologically informed way of seeing. At this point the hermeneutics of vision intersect with problems of authority and power vested in the dominant visual technologies and representations (Heywood and Sandywell x). Meta-pictures of nations or ethnicities, for instance, are much more complicated and complex phenomena whose emotional impact is not as easily determined as in those iconicities mentioned above.

While images of the destruction of the World Trade Center have gone around the world and become global icons of the 9/11 terror attack, pictures of the collapse of parts of the Pentagon building are almost unknown. Dimitri Liebsch chooses this example to illustrate a distinction between visibility and invisibility which is central to Visual Culture Studies, since the relative invisibility of the Pentagon pictures compared to the Twin Tower pictures is due to political, economic and aesthetic reasons (Liebsch 22). More recently, the video document of a shoe hitting former US president George W. Bush on the head at a press conference in Bagdad was circulated so widely on the internet that it achieved cult status within a short period of time and a small company selling the type of foot-wear in question suddenly faced commercial success with thousands of buyers demanding similar products.

Cultural articulations are produced and received in the context of extensive unconscious associations as well as deliberate acts of connecting to prior knowledge, memory and circumstance, all of which constitutes informational material with which readers and viewers invest the represented world. The reception of cultural productions whether in the form of literature, pictures or films is not simply a recognition of meaning which occurs when all the details of text, context and circumstance have been clarified; "reading" always means blending the "given" with a framework of knowledge, ideas and images, a process which in turn impinges on the latter. "Blending" is a term suggested by Mark Turner for any act of cognitive interpretation which necessitates the correlation of different elements (Turner 16).

As Winfried Fluck puts it:

> We do not encounter an image 'for the first time' in the act of reception, then. Rather we see it in the context of a cultural imaginary that plays a crucial part in determining what different viewers actually see in looking at one and the same picture. The image always already precedes the picture. It is the virtual background for the actualization of the meaning of the picture. Images are already there as part of the imagination before we 'see' them in representation. Or, more precisely: What we actually see is shaped by the store-house of images in our imagination with which we approach the pictures. (Fluck 2007, 72)

The intentionality of acts of seeing automatically connects what is seen to the cultural imaginary in which each individual participates. The "store-house of images" Fluck refers to, is shaped by visual events in all sorts of media, including descriptions and metaphors in literary texts which evoke a visualisation on the part of the reader, constituting an unconscious resource for mental schemata from memory which in turn determine forms of representation and reception. This store-house of images is subject to modifications and transformations so that a cultural imaginary of oneself and others is constantly being reshaped, a process of transformation which takes place on an individual and a collective scale. Hence, in these processes of reception identities are constructed for oneself as well as for those entities represented. From this, the theoretical conception of *imagines agentes* or 'the image as agent' in current art historical theory gleans added meaning (cf. Bredekamp, Böhme 21).

The question of meaning in images has been thoroughly explored by hermeneutics and semiotics with the result that everyone finds some residue or surplus value in images that goes beyond communication, signification or persuasion (Mitchell 2005, 9). This "power of images" (Freedberg 1989) lies beyond any particular meaning that can be attributed to them in their ability to transmute and to transcend disbelief. This special power may be attributed to the fact that images are more intimately connected to the pre-Oedipal world of primary processes, the semiotic in Julia Kristeva's terms, and the unconscious. An image can coexist in unconscious and conscious parts of the mind, and hence imagery is closer to mood and affect (Pajaczkowska 2000, 20). The experience and the reading of an image is never completely translatable into verbal utterance (Haustein 13). The direct access that images have to emotional response is also part of their power and magic and therefore of their impact on the viewer. They have since antiquity been known to precipitate memory and to engage the affections. In his groundbreaking discussion of the working of the mind, Mark Turner argued that "image schemas" are fundamental to the understanding of sequences of narrative (Turner 18). Hence, "activities" or effects of images are often unconsciously absorbed by readers: because of the lack of propositional articulation in iconic signs, their sense or form has a kind of subversive access to cognition.

But it is not only in a subconscious or automatic way that images contribute to understanding. Recent cognitive studies have emphasised that thinking takes places in visual rather than verbal forms confirming the distrust of logocentric interpretations of cognition and consciousness that was voiced in Visual Culture Studies. Mitchell stated rather cautiously that "we create much of our world out of the dialogue between verbal and pictorial representation" (Mitchell 1994, 161), and before him Rudolf Arnheim made a similar point in *Visual Thinking* (1969). Lakoff's famous studies of metaphor came to the conclusion that human understanding depends on the visual form of knowledge which metaphors offer. They supplement propositional knowledge with a knowledge that is "embodied, imaginative and gestalt" (Lakoff 235). The spatiality of images is apparently a conceptual necessity for imagining all sorts of abstract things. Bergson explained the interdependence of the verbal and the visual as follows: "We have but two means of expression, the concept and the image. It is by means of concepts that a system develops; it is via images that it intensifies, when the system is pushed back towards the intuition from which it descended" (Bergson, cf. Shusterman 92). This interesting statement on the intensifying effect of images provides a starting point for considering the endurance and tenacity of images, which can be observed to remain even when the framework of knowledge has changed, a tenacity which must be seen as partly responsible for their transformation into global icons.

But it also makes clear, that the idea of the agency of images cannot remain ideologically innocent. It is an agency that works in two directions from both sides of the equation: readers and images generate new ideas when at the same time rendering them compatible with those previously accepted. Readings of images cannot therefore consist only of an analysis of their structural properties or their iconic strategies but must include some account of their function as agents of mental and social processes. Therefore explanatory frameworks must try to avoid the rigid binaries of earlier structuralism by attempting to explain processes of signification. Thus by focusing on the dynamics of sign production and sign interpretation, interpretive examinations of images transcend the level of materiality and mediality of the image. It is apparently in the ontologically indefinite space of interaction between text and reception that meta-pictures or icons, which appeal beyond their immediate site of origin, are created.

Transmedia Migration

As is well known since Lessing's time, images are spatial while narrative is temporal. Thus when we read an image we are imposing a consecutive narrative structure onto it, a procedure which was made obvious in classical ekphrastic descriptions which aimed to energise the stasis of the image, i.e. infuse it with *enargeia* (cf. Hagstrum 12). Yet, in traditional narratological analysis, description was understood as a relatively static impediment to the temporal succession of narrative. This notion may have been a legacy of modernist preferences for an imagist break-up of narrative sequence, which celebrated "spatial form" in literature (Frank). This preference demonstrates the ability of images occurring in verbal texts to be received as 'halting places' in the temporal succession where attention is suspended. In other words, this chiastic polarity of images and texts becomes fraught with surplus meaning as it is an opportunity for each medium to disturb its boundaries and to insinuate meta-medial commentary (Brosch 2002). In each case, images serve as intensifiers in verbal discourse, and the text-image-interaction clearly holds the promise of a multiplied semantic and emotional effect.

The migration of images through different media was traditionally a domain of interart studies or text-image studies. However, these discussions do not adequately take into account the enormous changes in the perceivable world and in cultural production since the arrival of the 'new media' and the 'pictorial turn'. Not only did they often concern themselves exclusively with high art but they also tended to employ concepts which were developed in the context of art history's understanding of images as pictures. Neither Peter Wagner's idea of 'iconotext', nor the venerable concept of ekphrasis, nor that of a semiotic code is adequate as an explanatory paradigm for the transmedial migration of images in the "global manifold" (Brosch and Kunow 2005). More productive for looking at globalised images is the work that has been done in the cross-over area of intermediality. In this field efforts were made to supplement the traditional approaches of art history with its long history of iconographic interpretation in order to appreciate the surplus value and magic of the combined activity of images and words.

Another problematic implication can be avoided by discussing migrating images as intermedial phenomena: a study of influences and adaptations tends to introduce an implicit or covert hierarchy, because of the temporal difference and therefore precedence, which a 'pretext' seems to possess over a later adaptation. Most adaptation theorists nowadays warn against the 'fidelity fallacy', i.e. the tendency to evaluate an adaptation in terms of its veracity to the original source. This search for faithful representation only leads to unproductive evaluations in terms of verisimilitude to an original source (McFarlane 22). The inadequacy becomes immediately apparent, when we consider rewritings of legends and myths whose point of origin and reliance on prior sources can no longer be ascertained. Comparing under these paradigms can only mean to consider structural change from one to another, an interesting observation, but one that does not reach far enough in a global cultural situation where it becomes impossible and often undesirable to authenticate origin.

The concept of 'intermediality' seems to provide a solution to the problems posed by these earlier attempts to fathom the interaction of different sign systems, since it replaces the concept of 'art' with the neutral term 'medium'. Werner Wolf defines "intermediality" as the crossing of boundaries between media of communication, conventionally perceived as being distinctively different (Wolf 170, 172). However, this is only one of a variety of definitions available. In contrast to Kristeva's 'intertexuality', the concept of intermediality operates on several levels and therefore must incorporate the interaction, fusion or multiple usage of two or more sign systems (Paech 18). In spite of the emerging differences and even incompatibilities between definitions, a productively fuzzy concept has been arrived at which is satisfactory in the face of a proliferating hybridity of medial and generic forms.

Forms like the internet cannot be cast as either textual or visual, they make obsolete a protectionist attitude towards pictorial or textual purity. But like genres, which are freely adopted conventions, media impose certain limitations and possibilities on the user. The crossing of media-boundaries becomes a crucial issue when images migrate through different media and become exposed to different audiences in the process, because the channel of communication significantly shapes the message which is constructed by the receivers' mental image (Ryan 6). The fact that responses are shaped though not completely determined by their presentational formats necessitates the consideration of the kind of experience engendered by transmediation. Intermedial articulations are not simply a matter of the relationship between different sign systems or media but a matter of different modes of subjectivity and sociability.

In order to resolve this dilemma, migrating images must be understood as a receptive phenomenon as well as one of mediality. A recent study of today's new digital media by Jay David Bolter and Richard Grusin manifests a greater awareness of the participation of readers in what they call "remediation", i.e. "the representation of one medium in another" (Bolter and Grusin 45). Bolter and Grusin maintain that what is new about the current media situation is the extent to which it enables and encourages borrowing and the refashioning of earlier cultural products. Instead of privileging a "before and after" standpoint, taking properties from one medium and introducing them into another should be seen as "reuse", according to Bolter and Grusin. This reuse can be an occasion for immediacy, as in computer games where references to the medium itself are eliminated, as well as for "hypermediacy" when mediation is made explicit and self-referential. With "reuse comes a necessary redefinition, but there may be no conscious interplay between the media. The interplay happens, if at all, for the reader or viewer" (Bolter and Grusin 45) who happens to know the images alluded to or referred to in intertextuality.

When considering phenomena of media transfer, we therefore have to take the changing aesthetic experience into account. The increasing amount of dynamic and mobile media has led to a more dynamic understanding of "image" in the sense of visual event (Mirzoeff 5). However, it is only when an aesthetic attitude which has a transformational effect is introduced into the encounter with a visual event, that symbolic meaning can be achieved. A reminder may be necessary that, as Winfried Fluck puts it, "the aesthetic describes not a quality of an object – so that some objects, called art, possess this quality and others do not – but a possible function of an object, so that, by taking an aesthetic attitude toward an object, any object for that matter, any spatial representation – building, subway map, landscape or a picture – can become an aesthetic object" (Fluck 2005, 26). In insisting on the relevance of the aesthetic experience, I emphatically do not want to imply that we should ignore or neglect the political and social circumstances that determine production and reception. The aesthetic as an intentional attitude may in fact produce symbolic value in a political and ideological sense.[1]

Obviously images are ideologically productive, or acquire agency, because of the way they constantly break up and reassemble, cut across and connect ideas of individual and collective identity. Images nourish and sustain cultural life by taking part in the circulation of ideas, whether this takes place in the form of acknowledged or unconscious influence, creative borrowing, or wholesale appropriation, this migration from one place or period to another and from one medium to another is "a useful and enabling condition of intellectual activity". In this reuse, however, as Said noted about travelling concepts in general, intellectual gain or loss may be involved (Said 226). Images are prone to misapprehensions and distortions in these intermedial processes, but these can turn out to be productive, precisely because images carry a great potential for transformation into symbolic icons (Haustein 13).

Applying these ideas to travelling images brings to the foreground the obvious fact that transfer into another medium opens up new audiences by bringing into play a different aesthetics for whatever is represented. Hence, an image which occasions a great amount of intermediality can become a meta-picture and thus responsible for shaping further reception processes. The cultural imaginary peculiar to a region and period is made up of a fund of images with strong appeal and visibility from its history. As cultural production continues, new images become participants in this collective imaginary constantly feeding into already established images and icons of communal identity as well as modifying or undercutting these, so that a continuous shape-shifting of visual identity construction is taking place. Reme-

---

[1] The notion of mental images which accompany any reception process is a complicated matter which literary and cultural studies preferred to ignore until quite recently. Though early reader response aesthetics already drew attention to the central role images play in the mind of readers during the experience of fiction, even this theoretical approach tended to concentrate on the appellative textual strategies rather than the receptive imaginative accompaniment of the act of reading. It was only with the introduction of cognitive science into literary studies that such considerations of the visualising process could be recovered for narrative analysis. (cf. Brosch 2007)

diation and adaptation have always played a major role in these processes of change, but in the era of the 'new media' there has been an accelerated dissemination beyond the confines of national cultures. Thus processes of 'image migration' encourage the emergence of global icons.

Transcultural Migration

Although Western hegemony has hitherto served its dominance in the production of images; the West will not remain the only source of global appeal. Globalisation has already produced a complex network of capitalist-inspired social relations which depends on and encourages a transnational imaginary which – as Graham Huggan puts it – "shuttles continually between local and global perspectives" (Huggan vi). The increasingly global context in which any cultural articulation is produced and received makes it necessary to recognise this interplay between local and more international concerns. In this sense a transnational reading informed by the theoretical premises of postcolonialism and derived from a multiplied awareness of a nation's various engagements with other nations and with the wider world is more advisable and also more relevant than a strict interest in the confines of national culture and its peculiarities. In the words of Huggan again, the

> postcolonial approach [...] has the advantage of linking the local and the global; few approaches, after all, are more attuned to the shifting politics of location or to the intricate global circuitry within which cultural identities – regional, national, transnational – are strategically refashioned and commercially deployed. (Huggan ix)

But this approach can also profit from an exchange with the ideas generated around visual culture.

Electronic and digital media are the main sources for a global transmission of images. In a globalised culture, readers and viewers are more likely to encounter fictions from elsewhere or to see adaptations of well known images and narratives into new cultural contexts. Taking its cue from the constant stream of images in the media, current art projects make prominent use of strategies which insert existing images and icons into new contexts seeking to disclose the processes of transformation inherent in this 'migration'. Obviously, the effect on readers and viewers alters when cultural productions are adapted into different forms or disseminated into new locations. Such alterations require an adaptation of ways of seeing which would take into account an implied reciprocity of the gaze or an awareness of the Other in the act of looking (Haustein 164).

The prominent intermediality of the majority of contemporary cultural productions in a global market must presuppose an imaginary reception which is more projective, i.e. more tolerant and creative in its dealing with unfamiliar details. Such a reading would have to be prepared to accommodate what is new to the framework of the already known, perhaps by making far-fetched analogies. Of course, this is nothing new in processes of understanding cultural articulations. However, global appeal demands increased blending of the particular encountered in a fiction with a frame-work of wider knowledge and memory, and on the interaction of information given with preexisting knowledge and assumptions.

Encountering deterritorialised images thus consists of a successful negotiation of two opposite impulses: on the one hand, there is the rationalising intercultural effort at reading the image and bringing to it as much as we can provide from contextual knowledge as seems appropriate. On the other hand, reading an image entails the screening of the picture (or decoding the visual strategy of a fiction) in terms of the images and preconceptions with which we approach it and then (often unconsciously) producing hypotheses about it. The productive part in the process seems to be that we "decorporealize" the image in order to link it with the new context and to make it "our own" (Fluck 2007, 72, Belting 21).

It seems, as many Visual Culture scholars have pointed out, that the proliferation of images is generating contradictory potentialities for reception: an iconophilic succumbing to the seductive power of images and simultaneously an iconoclastic effort to resist and reinterpret them. Both are a tribute to the fertility and vitality of images, qualities quite distinct from aesthetic (in the traditional sense) or commercial value, because this vitality is a value played out in a social and communicative context (Mitchell 2005, 90, 92).

The vast amount of visibility produced in the various visual media has led to changes in the reception of images. But what happens to images in the process? Through the media's making available of images the viewers' imagination is no longer dependent on an intimate knowledge of the thing represented. Description of settings, localities and landscapes, a textual feature which used to be one of the strongest incentives to reading, is steadily becoming less elaborate as today's media-educated readerships are less dependent on verbal descriptions. Many fictional narratives also refuse to participate in the discourse of mapping or rationalising space which is discredited by the colonial effort to which its humanist epistemological basis belongs. Gaps and omissions in the narrative description of setting or the spatial design of a film again are particularly relevant in a global postcolonial perspective, as this lack of detail will inevitably lead to more structural readings: a more structural reading will also lead to an emphasis on difference and distinction.

Due to the joint effect of migration and the new media, a new quality of the cultural imaginary seems to be emerging. As Arjun Appadurai has argued, their joint effect on the work of the imagination is a destabilising influence.

> As moving images meet deteritorrialized viewers, these create diasporic public spheres that confound theories which depend on the continued salience of the nation-state as the key arbiter of important social changes. In this context of circulating images and audiences, where neither image nor audience is easily bound within local, national or regional spaces, the consumption of media is growing in audience agency, whether it be acted out in resistance, irony, selectivity, or other acting. [...] These sodalities are often transnational, even postnational, and they frequently operate beyond the boundaries of the nation. (Appadurai 177)

Against predictions of more global regimentation through the media, he sees "growing evidence that the consumption of mass media throughout the world provokes resistance, irony, selectivity, and in general, audience agency" (Appadurai 176). Thus, according to this line of argumentation, there is an active, creative element in media consumption which produces imaginative communities beyond the national. At the same time, an increased potential for resistant readings and ironical misapprehensions, which are tolerated or even encouraged by migrating fictions, seems to offer a creative antidote to the visual power of display exercised in societies of spectacle, surveillance and simulacra.

Concluding from these positions, one could claim that the increasing globalisation of markets and distribution of images and texts necessitates a new criticism which pays due attention to the semantic shifts and layerings occasioned by the deterritorialisation of audience and image. Attention to the aesthetic experience involved could be a remedy for the tendency of postcolonial criticism which has, despite its relatively recent provenance, become stale and "ossified", tending to constantly fall back on "standard rhetorical manoeuvres and paradigms" (Huggan x). It is here that my redefinition of aesthetic experience as a performative communality comes in.

Aesthetic Experiences – Reading Communities

Media culture has significantly changed the way we make sense of things. It seems that criticism which describes and explains finite texts based on a linear model of information and a one-way textual communication is less relevant to this cultural situation. Instead we need to look at migrating images from the perspective of the experience involved, an approach which means employing performative and processual explanatory models rather than essential and static ones. The circulating images in global media cultures have increased audiences' visual understanding and simultaneously decreased the attention span for passive reception. Today's readerships obviously encounter fictions in situations often very different from the solitary immersive reading posited by traditional literary criticism. The new media have largely shifted reception attitudes from passive consumption of media to participatory screen activities. As our newest technologies favour iconicity for events not necessarily visual (e.g. windows desktop, medical and biological representation), they encourage connective (rhizomic) receptional processes. The computer's ability to provide random rather than linear access to information and images may have already changed the way we perceive and imagine. Computer formats enable readers to break up narrative continuity and reorganise them spatially. A fluid, roaming visualisation is legitimised by these media. It stands to reason that the random and digressive readings encouraged by the World Wide Web promote different forms of attention and different forms of vying for attention. Undeniably, media culture encourages analogical projections and adaptive readings which are in turn promoted by conspicuous gaps in representations or slippages of attention. Irregularities of reception have become common which defy any conventional readings often based on binary constructions of 'us and them'. An active and creative appropriation of images by transnational communities can create surprising connections.

Barbara Stafford recently insisted on the need for recuperating the creative potential of "analogy, the art of sympathetic thought", which was predominant in early modernist thinking (Stafford 10). Analogy speaks to the need to make connection, to our experience of feeling "near, even interpenetrated by, what is distant, unfamiliar, different". This form of analogical or projective thinking seems particularly productive and promising in a global, postcolonial context, where cultural articulations need to find means to engage readers with the unknown and to enable them to adapt their local, ethnic specifics to particular reading situations. What Stafford calls a "web working creative act" is increasingly at work in intermedia communication, and can prove a welcome creative potential that discovers and yokes together similarity in difference (Stafford 8). Apparently, according to Stafford, analogy works through visualisation; in other words, the dominance of images helps to reinforce the productivity of the imaginary, and can thus increase empathy and understanding and contribute to a new ethics of reading.

Migrating images in a global context tend to produce a kind of reception which is less closely bound to the intended meaning of a cultural product. At the same time as viewers have come to rely on the media for supplementary information as a framework to the processing of images and texts, the receptive attitude to both has apparently diminished considerably in respect. Considering Stafford's proposal, this may not be a deplorable lack but an enabling condition for the emergence of meta-images or global icons for a transnational imaginary. In general, this occurs when images with a high degree of visual narrativity and a low degree of closure are presented, i.e. images which are sufficiently ambiguous to appeal to the imagination and to accommodate divergent convictions and narratives so that they transmute themselves in changing circumstances, and, most importantly, so that they lend themselves to receptive processes of transfer. The expansion of images into symbolic icons seems to take place with greater intensity in periods of anxiety when the community which fashions itself through the imaginary feels threatened. But a conflict of cultures does not necessarily promote a "clash of images" as icons are not a barrier but a challenge for intercultural understanding (Haustein 16).

The speed and extent of communication make it possible to generate images from creatively 'misapprehended' or reworked sources which develop a transnational appeal around which an interpretive community will rally and so gradually elevate an image into a meta-picture. The image of the shoe flying in the face of President Bush mentioned at the beginning of this essay carried connotations of wide emotional impact: a relatively harmless practical joke humiliating the powerful appealed with its inversal of hierarchies not only to those present at the event. The shoe became an iconic object of added symbolic meanings. Even more remarkable is the readiness of Western audiences to adopt symbolic value and semantic readings from an Islamic background. Shortly after, in the beginning of the year 2009, a demonstration against the military action of Israel in the Gaza strip could depend on the ability of the public to decode the image, when hundreds of demonstrators in London threw their shoes at the door of Downing Street No. 10.

Thus the current cultural situation is opening up boundaries in terms of epistemology and intercultural affiliation. It is my thesis that images nowadays can produce a transnational imaginary in an inventive negotiation of the local and the global, making the local particularities reach out to other communities and embedding these within a cosmopolitanism which finds intercultural resonance especially under circumstances of impending crisis, i.e. disaster threatening from global warming or a global financial crash. They achieve this transnational appeal, I would suggest, when they invite a projection beyond the particulars presented and encourage a blending of these with transnational connecting narratives and myths.

As the emphasis in culture moves away from the fixed text to visual events like moving images and performances, we can find that aesthetic value results not so much from a structure or property of an image, but from its interaction with the audience, an interaction which constitutes interpretative communities "providing the possibility of discussion, negotiation, intervention" (Hunter 2), and an interaction which rests on developing common moral agendas. Images should therefore be conceived of as performative not only in constituting identity and difference but in shaping reading communities beyond the national, because of their power to unite readers into communities of reading by demanding of them to neglect particulars for common concerns and purposes, in the course of which aesthetic attitudes and symbolic images are again generated.

Works Cited

Appadurai, Arjun. "Here and Now." *The Visual Culture Reader*. Ed. Nicholas Mirzoeff. London: Routledge, 2000. 173-79.
Arnheim, Rudolf. *Visual Thinking*. Berkeley: U of California P, 1969.
Belting, Hans. *Bild-Anthropologie: Entwürfe für eine Bildwissenschaft*. München: Fink, 2001.
Bolter, Jay David and Richard Grusin. *Remediation: Understanding New Media*. Cambridge, Mass: MIT Press, 1999.
Böhme, Hartmut. "Imagologie von Himmel und Hölle. Zum Verhältnis von textueller und bildlicher Konstruktion imaginärer Räume." *Bilder-Denken: Bildlichkeit und Argumentation*. München: Fink 2004. 19-43.
Bredekamp, Horst. "A Neglected Tradition? Art History as Bildwissenschaft." *Critical Inquiry* 29 (2003): 418-29.
Brosch, Renate. "The Curious Eye of the Reader: Perspective as Interaction with Narrative." *Seeing Perception*. Eds S. Horstkotte and K. Leonhard. Newcastle: Cambridge Scholars Publishing, 2007. 143-65.
—. "Verbalizing the Visual: Ekphrasis as a Commentary on Modes of Representation." *Mediale Performanzen: Historische Konzepte und Perspektiven*. Eds Jutta Eming, Annette Jael Lehmann and Irmgard Maassen. Freiburg i.Br.: Rombach, 2002. 103-23.
— and Rüdiger Kunow, eds. *Transgressions: Cultural Interventions in the Global Manifold*. Trier: WVT, 2005.
Fluck, Winfried. "Imaginary Space; Or, Space as Aesthetic Object." *Space in America: Theory, History, Culture*. Eds Klaus Benesch and Kerstin Schmidt. Amsterdam: Rodopi, 2005. 25-40.
—. "Playing Indian: Media Reception as Transfer." *Intermedialität/ Transmedialität*. Gundolf S. Freyermuth. Köln: Böhlau, 2007. 67- 86.
Frank, Joseph. "Spatial Form in Modern Literature." *The Widening Gyre: Crisis and Mastery in Modern Literature*. Ed. Joseph Frank. New Brunswick, N. J.: Rutgers UP, 1963. 3-62.
Freedberg, David. *The Power of Images: Studies in the History and Theory of Response*. Chicago: UCP, 1989.

Hagstrum, Jean. *The Sister Arts: The Tradition of Literary Pictorialism and English Poetry from Dryden to Gray*. Chicago: CUP, 1958.

Haustein, Lydia. *Global Icons: Globale Bildinszenierung und kulturelle Identität*. Göttingen: Wallstein, 2008.

Heywood, Ian and Barry Sandywell, eds. *Interpeting Visual Culture: Explorations in the Hermeneutics of the Visual*. London: Routledge, 1999.

Huggan, Graham. *Australian Literature: Postcolonialism, Racism, Transnationalism*. Oxford: OUP, 2007.

Hunter, Lynette. *Literary Value/Cultural Power: Verbal Arts in the 21st Century*. Manchester: MUP, 2001.

Lakoff, George and Mark Johnson. *Metaphors We Live By*. Chicago: CUP 1980.

Lakoff, George and Mark Turner. *More than Cool Reason: A Field Guide to Poetic Metaphor*. Chicago: CUP, 1989.

Liebsch, Dimitri. "Pictorial Turn and Visual Culture." *Visual Culture Revisited*. Eds Ralf Adelmann et al. Köln: Halem, 2007. 12-26.

McFarlane, Brian. *Novel to Film: An Introduction to the Theory of Adaptation*. Oxford: Clarendon Press, 1996.

Mirzoeff, Nicholas. "The Subject of Visual Culture." *The Visual Culture Reader*. Ed. Nicholas Mirzoeff. London: Routledge, 2002. 3-23.

Mitchell, W.J.T. *Picture Theory: Essays in Verbal and Visual Representation*. Chicago: U of Chicago P, 1994.

—. "Was ist ein Bild." *Bildlichkeit: Internationale Beiträge zur Poetik*. Ed. Volker Bohn. Frankfurt a.M.: Suhrkamp, 1990. 17-68.

—. *What Do Pictures Really Want? The Lives and Loves of Images*. Chicago: U of Chicago P, 2005.

Paech, Joachim. "Intermedialität: Mediales Differenzial und transformative Figuration." *Intermedialität: Theorie und Praxis eines interdisziplinären Forschungsgebiets*. Ed. Jörg Helbig. Berlin: Erich Schmidt Verlag, 1998. 14-30.

Pajaczkowska, Claire. "Issues in Feminist Visual Culture." *Feminist Visual Culture*. Eds Carson, Fiona and Claire Pajaczkowska. Edinburgh: EUP, 2000. 1-24.

Ryan, Marie-Laure. *Possible Worlds, Artificial Intelligence, Narrative Theory*. Bloomington: Indiana UP, 1991.

Said, Edward. "Travelling Theory." *The World, the Text and the Critic*. Cambridge, Ma.: Harvard UP, 1983. 226-47.

Shusterman, Raymond. "Aesthetics and the Literary Mind: Some Thoughts from a Thought Experiment." *REAL (Yearbook of Research in English and American Literature)* 24. Tübingen: Narr, 2008. 195-214.

Stafford, Barbara Maria. *Visual Analogy: Consciousness as the Art of Connecting*. Cambridge, MA.: MIT Press, 1999.
Turner, Mark. *The Literary Mind: The Origins of Thought and Language.* Oxford: OUP, 1996.
Wagner, Peter, ed. *Icons-Texts-Iconotexts. Essays on Ekphrasis and Intermediality*. Berlin: Walter de Gruyter, 1996.
Wolf, Werner. "Das Problem der Narrativität in Literatur, bildender Kunst und Musik: Ein Beitrag zu einer intermedialen Erzähltheorie." *Erzähltheorie transgenerisch, intermedial, interdisziplinär*. Eds Vera and Ansgar Nünning. Trier: WVT, 2002. 23-104.

Textual Encounters

Caroline Lusin

Encountering Darkness: Intertextuality and Polyphony in J.M. Coetzee's *Dusklands* (1974) and Matthew Kneale's *English Passengers* (2000)

In the course of literary history, Joseph Conrad's *Heart of Darkness* (1899/1902) was repeatedly adapted to other contexts, which proves the unvarying relevance of its topics. This article examines two complex literary texts referring to Conrad's novella, J.M. Coetzee's *Dusklands* (1974) and Matthew Kneale's *English Passengers* (2000). In an approach reminiscent of Francis Ford Coppola's Conradian film *Apocalypse Now* (1979), Coetzee focuses on an American expert writing about the Vietnam War and on an 18th- century Dutch adventurer in South Africa, while Kneale gives a multiperspective account of events set mainly aboard a ship and in 19th- century Tasmania. In rewriting these colonial projects – and *Heart of Darkness* – *Dusklands* and *English Passengers* subvert the imperial 'master narrative', but deny any authoritative account. This article explores the ways in which Coetzee and Kneale functionalise intertextuality, taking into account the use of language, parody, the issues of 'otherness' or 'alterity' as well as the question of truth and authenticity.

The propensity of a work of art to engage in a semiotic dialogue with others might well be regarded as one of the touchstones of its aesthetic significance. From this vantage point, Joseph Conrad's novella *Heart of Darkness* (1899/1902) holds an eminent place within literary history, since it was adapted to other contexts time and again.[1] In fact, its literary status is such that writers addressing similar issues as Conrad in *Heart of Darkness* can hardly avoid echoing this key text of colonial discourse in one way or the other. As one critic has put it, "Conrad's novella is such a pervading master narrative that writers may respond to it indirectly, even unconsciously" (Farn 31).

In postcolonial discourse, *Heart of Darkness* is a particularly frequent referent due to its profound engagement with questions concerning imperial power and colonial order. Among others, postcolonial rewritings of this novella include Chinua Achebe's *Things Fall Apart* (1959), V.S. Naipaul's *A Bend in the River* (1979), Paul Theroux's *The Mosquito Coast* (1981), David Dabydeen's *The Intended* (1991), Timothy Findley's *Headhunter* (1993) or Abdulrazak Gurnah's *Paradise* (1994). Perhaps most prominently, *Heart of Darkness* has provided the plot and central motifs for Francis Ford Coppola's award-winning movie *Apocalypse Now* (1979), which is set in the Vietnam

---

[1] This concerns not only high literature, but also popular culture (cf. Dryden).

War. Like *Heart of Darkness*, Coppola's film features a journey into the heart of the jungle, where the protagonist encounters a sinister former trade agent, respectively an officer, called Kurtz. In a complex interplay of various intermedial allusions,[2] Coppola transposes *Heart of Darkness* to a new genre and century, highlighting the perpetuation of a primeval impulse to violence and power, which is already inscribed in Conrad's novella.[3] This instance of rewriting *Heart of Darkness* is revealing in several ways. On the one hand, semiotic encounters like this confirm the unvarying relevance of the topics addressed in *Heart of Darkness*. On the other hand, this example testifies to the more general fact that "[r]e-writing literary texts is a way of translating one historical period into another, one culture into another, gender or class perspectives into another social perspective" (Reif-Hülser 80).

This also holds true for J.M. Coetzee's *Dusklands* (1974) and Matthew Kneale's *English Passengers* (2000), which constitute the focus of this article.[4] Different as they may seem at first glance, *Dusklands* and *English Passengers* have several things in common. Both translate *Heart of Darkness* to another historical and cultural context, offering new perspectives on the issues Conrad discusses in his novella. Like *Heart of Darkness*, both refer to events in colonial history that are marked by brutal inhumanity. Coetzee relates the topics Conrad addressed to the American bombing of Vietnam and Cambodia in the 1960s and 70s as well as to the inhuman exploits of white hunter-adventurers in 18th-century South Africa, while Kneale centres on the brutal treatment and near-extinction of the aborigines in 19th-century Tasmania. These colonial settings give both authors the opportunity to draw back on Conrad in focussing on encounters with a multifaceted 'darkness' in man as well as in human history. In both cases, a pronounced historical background thus forms the starting point for reflecting the issues *Heart of Darkness* has raised, such as the nature of history and colonialism, the meaning of civilisation, the precarious encounter between a 'self' and an 'other', the connection of language and authority as well as the questions of epistemological certi-

---

[2] In both cases, Kurtz has obviously gone mad and indulges in ancient, savage rituals. Significantly, *Apocalypse Now* opens with several uncanny lines from a song by The Doors, "The End", which in turn seem to hark back to Conrad's novella: "Lost in a Roman wilderness of pain/ And all the children are insane/ All the children are insane/ Waiting for the summer rain." Read as a condensed version of *Heart of Darkness*, these lines blend the novella's central mystery, the madness of Kurtz, with its initial setting. Right at the novella's beginning, Conrad, too, establishes a link between Roman and modern-day colonialism, when his narrator Marlow envisions how a young Roman must have experienced Britannia in ancient times.

[3] For the relation between *Heart of Darkness* and *Apocalypse Now* cf. Cahir and Stewart.

[4] All references to the editions named below will in the following be abbreviated with *D* for *Dusklands*, *EP* for *English Passengers* and *HD* for *Heart of Darkness*.

tude, (mis)representation and truth. Applied to *Dusklands* and *English Passengers*, the term 'semiotic encounters' therefore has a double meaning: it refers to encounters between texts or discourses as well as to encounters between cultures.

In order to address the topics at issue, Coetzee and Kneale have chosen a textual structure that fosters ambivalence and incertitude. *Dusklands* consists of two closely interrelated novellas, "The Vietnam Project" and "The Narrative of Jacobus Coetzee". "The Vietnam Project" focuses on a US defence ministry propaganda expert writing about the war in Vietnam, whereas "The Narrative of Jacobus Coetzee" tells the story of an 18th-century Dutch adventurer in South Africa. Similarly, Kneale's *English Passengers* is composed of many interrelated stories and gives a multiperspective account of events set mainly aboard a smuggling vessel, ironically called "Sincerity", and in 19th-century Tasmania. As *Dusklands* and *English Passengers* are both composed of more than one narrative, they provide multiple voices on the topics they centre on, whose effect is intensified by intertextual references to *Heart of Darkness* and to other texts. The aim of this paper is to explore how in reconfiguring *Heart of Darkness*, Coetzee and Kneale subvert the imperial 'master narrative' and test the very limits of knowability. This includes taking into account their use of intertextuality and language as well as the question of truth and authenticity.

Suppressing the Voice of the Other:
J.M. Coetzee's *Dusklands* (1974)

When J.M. Coetzee's debut *Dusklands* was published in 1974, critics hailed it as marking the advent of (post)modernism in South African literature. Indeed, this literary dialogue with Conrad flaunts a number of characteristically postmodernist topoi and narrative devices. While other contemporary South African writers at this time still clung to the conventions of realist fiction, Coetzee self-reflexively transgressed its norms. In *Dusklands*, this is particularly apparent in the way in which Coetzee both stresses and undermines its allegedly authentic historical framework, accentuating the novel's fictionality.

In both novellas of *Dusklands*, Coetzee introduces the allegedly authentic 'voice' of history into the fiction by means of one or several (purportedly) historical documents, but ultimately, he subverts it. The epigraph of "The Vietnam Project" links Eugene Dawn's report about propaganda and psychological warfare in Vietnam to existing papers, the Collection of Hudson Institute Reports, which were published in 1968 under the title *Can We Win in Vietnam? The American Dilemma* (cf. Head 29). In the repelling and brutal

"Narrative of Jacobus Coetzee", Coetzee proceeds similarly, introducing a whole range of supposedly authentic historical accounts, which provide different perspectives on Jacobus' story.[5] A bogus translator's preface and purportedly scientific notes to the afterword further underline the narrative's claim to historical authenticity and accuracy. A number of formal devices that "disrupt the realistic surface of the writing" (Attridge 2004a, 655), however, destabilise this claim, among them a pronounced degree of intertextuality. From the beginning, Coetzee highlights the tension between fact and fiction by drawing on a whole range of intertextual allusions, which both stress certain themes and set off the novellas' fictionality. Critics have identified references to John Berryman, William Carlos Williams, T.S. Eliot, Franz Kafka (cf. Watson 24) or Daniel Defoe and compared *Dusklands* to the works of Jorge Louis Borges and Vladimir Nabokov (cf. ibid.).[6] As Watson (ibid.) has put it: "Quotation is basic to his fictional practice". References to Joseph Conrad, however, have in this context never been thoroughly investigated, though his name is frequently mentioned.

In the narrator of "The Vietnam Project", Eugene Dawn, the effect of intertextual allusions comes particularly clearly to the fore. Coetzee disturbs the novella's allegedly documentary character by modelling his narrator and protagonist closely on two other literary characters, the nameless, unreliable first-person narrator of Fyodor Dostoevsky's *Notes from Underground* (1864) and Conrad's infamous Kurtz. Significantly, Dawn works underground, in the cellar of the library, which can be read as a distinct allusion to Dostoevsky's proverbial 'underground man'. Just like the 'underground man', Eugene Dawn embodies what Hegel in *The Phenomenology of Spirit* (*Phänomenologie des Geistes*, 1807) termed the 'unhappy consciousness': both protagonists have a deeply disturbed relationship to their surroundings and lack any awareness or recognition of the 'other'. Living beyond any healthy social relations, they are centred exclusively on themselves. As Dawn puts it: "My true ideal [...] is of an endless discourse of character, the self reading the self to the self in all infinity" (*D* 38). Not unlike Dostoevsky's protagonist, Eugene Dawn as well as Jacobus Coetzee try to assert the reality of their own ego against a stereotyped, mute 'other' (cf. Rogez 43):

> Why could they not accept us? We could have loved them: our hatred for them grew only out of broken hopes. We brought them our pitiable selves, trembling on the edge of inexistence, and asked only that they acknowledge us. [...] Our nightmare was that

---

[5] Apart from the actual narrative, these comprise an afterword (which, as the fictional editor claims in his preface, was the introduction of an earlier edition) and a translation of what is claimed to be Jacobus Coetzee's 1760 deposition, that is, his recorded official statement.

[6] See Gardiner for a comprehensive analysis of the links between *Dusklands* and *Robinson Crusoe*.

since whatever we reached for slipped like smoke through our fingers, we did not exist; that since whatever we embraced wilted, we were all that existed. (*D* 17)[7]

Significantly, both Dawn and Jacobus Coetzee rely on the very mechanism Achebe (210f.) criticised in *Heart of Darkness*: the 'other' is reduced to a mere foil to the 'self'. An all-pervasive misanthropy, sadism and solipsistic brutality are the dominant character traits of both Eugene Dawn, his Russian counterpart and his 19th-century doppelgänger Jacobus Coetzee.

The juxtaposition of Coetzee's characters with Dostoevsky's is geared at drawing the reader's attention precisely to those aspects of *Heart of Darkness* that form the core of *Dusklands*, as the aforementioned traits tie in closely with the intertextual references to Conrad's novella.[8] In *Heart of Darkness*, Conrad uses the voyage into the Belgian Congo in order to show how the thin veil of civilisation only cloaks a deeper underlying ferocity. Coetzee, drawing back on Conrad, uses the colonial setting of *Dusklands* to uncover a very similar truth about human nature. As Dawn declares, "Vietnam, like everything else, is inside me, and in Vietnam, with a little diligence, a little patience, all truths about man's nature" (*D* 14). Dawn and Jacobus Coetzee are similarly out of touch with their surroundings as is Conrad's Kurtz, whose mental state Conrad's narrator Marlow describes as follows:

> I had to deal with a being to whom I could not appeal in the name of anything high or low. [...] He had kicked himself loose of the earth. [...] But his soul was mad. Being alone in the wilderness, it had looked within itself, and [...] gone mad. [...] I saw the inconceivable mystery of a soul that knew no restraint, not faith, and no fear [...]. (*HD* 135)

In Kurtz' case, this dehumanisation is brought about by the actual colonial experience in the Belgian Congo. For Dawn, writing his report does precisely the same. He boasts about "the insights into man's soul that [he has] evolved since [he] began to think about Vietnam" (*D* 9), and the people close to him – particularly his wife Marilyn, who is a bleaker version of Kurtz' bride, his 'Intended' – seem to suspect that Dawn is emotionally crippled: "I am still the captain of my soul. Marilyn and her friends believe that everyone who approaches the innermost mechanism of the war suffers a vision of horror which depraves him utterly" (*D* 10). The echo of *Heart of Darkness* – Kurtz'

---

[7] Cf. the Cartesian dualism between the ego and the external world. Watson (19) therefore concludes: "In *Dusklands* [...] the reader would be far from mistaken in coming to the conclusion that colonialism is primarily the projection of a certain mental aberration located exclusively in the divided consciousness that is a special feature of Western humanity." Canepari-Labib (163ff.) also pays close attention to what she calls "The Struggle for Recognition" in *Dusklands*.

[8] For a detailed account of the issue of solipsism in *Heart of Darkness* cf. Rudrum.

deathbed exclamation "The Horror! The Horror!" (*HD* 139) – is unmistakable.

Although the voyage into the 'heart of darkness', into the recesses of man's soul, is in Dawn's case entirely internalised, Dawn's truth about Vietnam reiterates Kurtz' statement concerning the colonial 'Other' – "Exterminate all the brutes!" (*HD* 117) –, which concludes Kurtz' initially idealistic dossier about the colonial endeavour in the Belgian Congo. In his Vietnam report, Dawn, too, finally dismisses psychological warfare in favour of complete extinction:

> There is only one problem in Vietnam and that is the problem of victory. The problem of victory is technical. [...] Victory is a matter of sufficient force, and we dispose over sufficient force. [...] I dismiss Phase IV of the conflict. I look forward to Phase V and the return of total air-war. (*D* 28)

What this means in practice is illustrated by Dawn's doppelgänger Jacobus Coetzee, who at the end of his narrative embarks on a brutal revenge expedition into the land of the indigenous Namaquas, killing the whole tribe and a number of his former servants in a most ferocious massacre. The only difference between the two protagonists is that Jacobus Coetzee sets into practice what the theoretician Dawn only claims (cf. Rogez 43). With hindsight, Jacobus Coetzee therefore unwittingly characterises Dawn – and himself – as the true savages, when he states: "Savagery was a way of life based on disdain for the value of human life and sensual delight in the pain of others" (*D* 97). Dawn's allegedly scientific report, which claims to be based on Enlightenment rationality, as well as Jacobus Coetzee's actions thus unveil the ostensibly civilising enterprise as motivated by a desire for complete domination and oppression (cf. Gallagher 51ff.). In this sense, *Dusklands* can be read as a sequel to and a comment on *Heart of Darkness*.

This connection between *Dusklands* and *Heart of Darkness* is strengthened by the fact that apart from reinforcing crucial topics and motifs of Conrad's novella, Coetzee develops the implications of Conrad's narrative techniques. In using first-person narrators and juxtaposing different versions of events in the diverse documents that make up "The Narrative of Jacobus Coetzee", Coetzee distinctively foregrounds the fact that stories can never give a truly objective, authentic account of events, but may be distorted or even consciously manipulated. Numerous "glaring inconsistencies" (Attridge 2004a, 658) between the documents of which this part of *Dusklands* consists undermine the verisimilitude of these texts, impairing their claim on authenticity and truth severely. This insight into the subjectivity and potential unreliability of every narration is in nuce already contained in *Heart of Darkness*. Conrad, too, both stresses and undermines the issue of authenticity and truth by amalgamating the stories of up to three different narrators. While most of the story is narrated by Marlow, the main character, this Marlow also gives voice to what he was told by the enigmatic Kurtz. Marlow's narrative, in turn, is transmitted by the nameless narrator of the frame story, who listens to Marlow's story and afterwards reports it to the reader. As Marlow's voice is distinctly the most prominent, this narrative strategy, on the one hand, creates the impression of immediacy and a certain ontological authenticity, which led one critic to state that of all narrators in novels "perhaps none combines caring with impartiality more zealously than Conrad's Marlow" (Hardy 154). The reader feels as though he were told the story by Marlow himself. On the other hand, though, an attentive reader must be susceptible to what this narrative structure suggests epistemologically: in addition to the fact that Marlow is himself implicated in colonialism,[9] the story is doubly mediated and, consequently, doubly undergoes the potentially falsifying process of the selection, ordering and foregrounding of events that are part of every narration.[10]

Coetzee, however, takes the implications of Conrad's narrative technique decidedly further, stressing the opaque character of language as a means to manipulate and distort the truth. "The Narrative of Jacobus Coetzee" focuses not only on Jacobus' hunting expedition, but also on his relationship to his Hottentot servant, Jan Klawer. In the course of the story, it becomes obvious that the terms in which Jacobus talks about Klawer are but tropes and commonplaces of fictional discourse, like the cliché of the 'faithful servant' (cf. Attridge 2004a, 658ff.). The language in which the relationship is described is the master's; the servant and racial 'Other' is expressed entirely in terms of Western discursive conventions and has no voice of his own. That this leads to gross distortion becomes particularly apparent in a scene in which Jacobus and Klawer cross a river. The latter incidentally steps into a hippopotamus hole and is swept away:

> With horror I watched my faithful servant drawn struggling downstream, shouting broken pleas for help which I was powerless to render him [...], until he disappeared from sight around a bend and went to his death bearing the blanket and roll and all the food. The crossing took all of an hour, for we had to probe the bottom before each step for

---

[9] Cf. Greaney 66ff.
[10] In a classically self-reflexive commentary, even Marlow himself highlights the shortcomings of narration: "No, it is impossible; it is impossible to convey the life-sensation of any given epoch of one's existence – that which makes its truth, its meaning [...]. It is impossible" (*HD* 90). This notion is further supported by leitmotifs like the tension between delusion and truth as well as by the unreality or dream-like character of Marlow's experiences, which is stressed again and again. For an overview of divergent evaluations of Marlow in Conrad criticism, cf. Greaney 57ff. Greaney (65) also questions Marlow's reliability, drawing attention to the fact that "Marlow's presence is no guarantee of determinate meaning; he proves to be, as it were, an obscure, ambiguous, illegible speaker".

fear of slipping into a hippopotamus hole and being swept off our feet. But sodden and shivering we finally reached the South bank [...]. (*D* 94)

This at first irritating passage ultimately reveals the fact that Jacobus does not seek to represent the events of his story authentically, but manipulates them to his own ends. While the end of the first paragraph betrays Jacobus' true anxiety, the loss of his provisions, the second paragraph suddenly represents the reader with an entirely different version of the events: according to this second account, both Jacobus and Klawer have crossed the river unscathed. In this way, language is exposed as a convention distorting reality and as a means of constructing and asserting your own – the master's – version of events. *Dusklands* thus faces the reader with "an agonizing encounter both with colonialism's violence, and with the discursive legacy it leaves to its heirs" (Attwell 7).

At the end of both novellas, Coetzee fully develops this connection of language, manipulation and power. Both conclude with scenes in which the 'masters' brutally assert their power: Jacobus achieves this by inflicting a massacre on the Namaquas, and Dawn by stabbing his young son with a knife, just as the police come to the boy's rescue. In a highly improbable Richardsonian 'writing to the moment', Dawn pretends to record his being overpowered by the police straight away: "Amazing. I have been hit a terrible blow. [...] I am utterly out of control" (*D* 42). In a classic metafictional comment, however, Dawn disrupts the illusion of immediate and truthful recording in almost the same breath: "A convention allows me to record these details" (ibid.). The relationship between language and reality proves to be based not on any actual correspondence, but on mere convention, which uncovers the essentially fictional character of Dawn's autobiographical account. The discursive power of language, which also becomes obvious in the river scene, is therefore at once foregrounded and undermined. Ultimately, *Dusklands* thus serves to carry the Enlightenment discourse of modern rationality ad absurdum (cf. Attridge 2004a, 655) as well as to radically question discourses of power. (cf. Huggan and Watson 3f.)

Giving the issue of the unreliability of language and narration a final turn, Coetzee even introduces himself, the author J.M. Coetzee, into the fiction and thus "exposes his own role as the constructor of discourse" (Gallagher 73). The "Narrative of Jacobus Coetzee" was purportedly translated from the original Dutch by one J.M. Coetzee, and in "The Vietnam Project", Eugene Dawn has to face a severe manager called Coetzee, who is modelled on the trivial, absurdly powerful manager from *Heart of Darkness*. Conrad's manager is described as follows:

> He had no learning, and no intelligence. His position had come to him – why? Perhaps because he was never ill [...]. Because triumphant health in the general rout of constitutions is a kind of power in itself [...]. He originated nothing, he could keep the routine going – that's all. But he was great. He was great by this little thing that it was impossible to tell what could control such a man. (*HD* 83)

This hidden reference to *Heart of Darkness* can be read as an ironic, self-reflexive comment on the power of authors. Far from being a self-sufficient postmodernist play with literary conventions, this device serves to accentuate the author's controlling presence in his text. It draws attention to the fact that the narrative is shaped by the idiosyncrasies of its author/narrator, or, to put it more strongly, manipulated by him. Particularly in view of the many 'voices' incorporated into the discourse, it is impossible to discern any definite truth beyond the fact that language is a distorting means of asserting power. The questioning of (colonial) language as a means of domination and manipulation thus proves to be the dominant concern of *Dusklands*. Although this high degree of metafictional self-reflexivity is not to be found in *English Passengers*, Kneale proceeds like Coetzee in several other respects.

Giving Voice to the 'Other': Matthew Kneale's *English Passengers* (2000)

In an interview, Matthew Kneale explained rather simply what he intended to achieve with *English Passengers*: "My first interest was in the craziness of the Victorian British mind. I had written about Victorians being disastrously wrong-headed at home (in London) and so it seemed only right to look at them being disastrously wrong-headed overseas". Actually, however, *English Passengers* is far more complex and universal than Kneale's playful description suggests. Not unlike *Dusklands*, this novel consists of two parallel plots, which in this case converge in the course of the novel: one depicts the crimes against humanity committed during the colonisation of Tasmania in the 1820s and 30s, and the other describes a voyage of the eponymous passengers to Tasmania 37 years later.

At first glance, *English Passengers* appears to be an old-fashioned seafaring adventure novel. This seafaring part of *English Passengers* refers back to the tradition of Victorian adventure fiction, above all to the works of Captain Marryat. With novels like *Peter Simple* (1832/33), *Jacob Faithful* (1834) and *Mr Midshipman Easy* (1836), sea stories for an adult audience, or his children's stories, *Masterman Ready* (1841/42), Marryat set the pattern for seafaring writers of imperialist adventure fiction, looking back "nostalgically to an age of youthful adventure when heroic action was almost routine" (Brantlinger 48). In the 20th century, this tradition was taken up by C.S. Forester's

Hornblower novels (1937-67), which Kneale named as an important influence on *English Passengers*.[11] *English Passengers* can thus be said to prolong the tradition of Victorian adventure fiction into the 21st century. At the same time, though, Kneale subverts, adapts and even parodies this tradition. His protagonist Captain Illiam Quillian Kewley and his crew are not heroic British characters, but smuggling Manxmen from Peel caught in the act by her Majesty's Royal Customs. The Manxmen's funny portrayal, good common sense, shrewdness, warm humanity and almost inexhaustible resourcefulness cannot fail to engage the reader, but they certainly do not quite fit the pattern of classic Victorian adventure fiction. In granting these Manxmen the status of heroes, Kneale gives voice to characters that would in view of the conventions of classical adventure fiction seem entirely unsuitable for this position. This subversion of the formula of adventure fiction is symptomatic of the central concern of Kneale's novel, a desire to voice the concerns of the 'Other' in search of historical truth.

With regard to these issues, the historical background of the plot is crucial. Significantly, the first plot (and the novel) starts in 1857, the year of the so-called 'Indian Mutiny'. Just before the passengers set off, news of the fall of Delhi reaches Great Britain, and when Captain Kewley and his passengers have to defend themselves against pirates later on, they virtually get a taste of what was alleged to have provoked the mutiny in the first place: the greasy paper in which the cartridges of a new kind of rifle were wrapped and which had to be ripped open with the teeth.[12] The fact that the Indian soldiers thus had to swallow a certain quantity of animal grease was said to have been irreconcilable with Muslim and Hindu belief. This initial focus on the 'Indian Mutiny', a traumatic experience for the British that marks the beginning of British Crown rule in India, immediately prepares the reader for one of the novel's central subjects, the nature and effects of racial and imperial domination.[13] These subjects gain even more prominence by the fact that the 1850s plot centres on the fight between the creationists and evolutionists that erupted during the 19th century. The ludicrously self-righteous and hypocriti-

---

[11] In these novels, Forester follows the career of Horatio Hornblower, who is modelled on heroic figures like Lord Nelson, from simple midshipman to Admiral of the Fleet and peer.

[12] As one of the passengers describes it: "First there was the biting into the cartridge, which gave one a mouthful of grease, and the pouring in of the powder. Next came the fiddly business of placing the ram into the end of the long barrel, so one could push home the cartridge and its bullet" (*EP* 129).

[13] In order to stress his care for historical accuracy, Kneale modelled a number of characters on historical personages, among them a fierce aborigine woman called Walyer and an aborigine boy, George Vandiemen, who was sent to England for his education, but died soon after his return to Tasmania. Underlining the novel's factual aspects, Kneale even includes this boy's original school report in the novel's epilogue.

cal Reverend Geoffrey Wilson initiates the voyage in order to prove his belief that the Garden of Eden can be found in Tasmania, which parodies 19th-century attempts to use geology to prove the literal truth of the Bible. The sinister and evil Dr. Potter, by contrast, prefigures social Darwinism. He is obviously modelled on Robert Knox (cf. Wallhead 24), who in *The Races of Men* (1850) provided his own pseudo-scientific theory of imperialism and explained why some races just have to be 'imperialised'. According to Knox, some races are physically and mentally inferior and doomed to perish, while others, above all the Saxon, are destined to reign and dominate their supposed inferiors.[14] Dr. Potter's diary and his pseudo-scientific work "The Destiny of Nations", excerpts of which are reproduced in the novel, clearly emulate Knox' racist book:

> The Celtic Type (instance: *Manx*) is altogether inferior in physique to the Saxon [...].
> Cranial type: G.
> As to his general character, the Celt is wanting in the industriousness of spirit of his Saxon neighbour, his *dominating characteristic* being *indolence* [...].
> In conclusion, the Celt has his place at the *lowest station* within the European division. This is indicated [...] also in his dismal history, which is typified by *disorder*, *disunity* and *decline*. It may be assumed that within the womb the development of the Celtic embryo is arrested [...] a full three weeks sooner than the Saxon. (*EP* 119f.)

Needless to say that Dr. Potter's aim in travelling to Tasmania is to be able to study the in his opinion most inferior of races, the Aborigines, and to collect what he calls 'specimens', that is, their bones. In order to get these, preferably whole skeletons, Dr. Potter shows absolutely no scruples, shying away neither from exhumation nor from theft or dismemberment of corpses. Consequently, the historical setting of the novel enables Kneale both to focus on colonialism's brutality – like wilful massacres on innocent aborigines – and to hint at its eventual effects, the breakdown of the British Empire, which was foreshadowed by events like the 'Indian Mutiny'.

Dr. Potter's quest for 'specimens' as well as the journey in general form the core of Kneale's engagement with *Heart of Darkness*, which gives additional prominence to the topics *English Passengers* addresses. In fact, the use of intertextuality corresponds to the constellation of characters: the parodying references to Victorian sea stories primarily concern the crew of Manxmen, whereas the English passengers are associated with the more sinister aspects

---

[14] "What a field of extermination lies before the Saxon Celtic and Sarmatian races! The Saxon will not mingle with any dark race, nor will he allow him to hold an acre of land in the country occupied by him; this, at least, is the law of Anglo-Saxon America. The fate [...] of the Mexicans, Peruvians, and Chilians, is in no shape doubtful. Extinction of the race – sure extinction – it is not even denied" (quoted from Brantlinger 153).

of intertextuality. When they finally arrive in Tasmania, the English, a number of mule drivers and a guide, the half-caste Aborigine Peevay, set off into the jungle in search of the Garden of Eden. This journey into the heart of the country, however, ultimately leads them into the 'heart of darkness'. The deeper the English passengers penetrate into the jungle, following a river for quite a while, the more they shed the thin veil of civilisation. As Peevay remarks:

> In truth they got more hateful now we were all alone in the world, away from other num [= white people]. One time *mule men* came in the night after they drank secret *rum*, laughing at me that my ones were all dead now – which was some hateful joke – and telling that I would soon be likewise. (*EP* 355)

Secret grudges erupt, and as in the case of Kurtz in *Heart of Darkness*, savage impulses come to the fore; the group disintegrates. Unable to face reality, or rather because he has to face the reality into which he has been misled, completely on his own and almost starved to death, the Reverend even runs mad. Far from finding the Garden of Eden, he ironically ends up in the 'heart of darkness'. On a larger frame, Dr. Potter's whole macabre enterprise corresponds to the exploitative colonial quest that is criticised so harshly in Conrad's *Heart of Darkness* by means of the imagery playing on 'light' and 'darkness'. Instead of bringing the light (Enlightenment and civilisation), the colonisers in *Heart of Darkness* take the light away (in hunting for and exporting ivory). Principally, Dr. Potter does the very same: he, too, unscrupulously takes away bones in order to draw profit from it, i.e. to become an established scientist. Through the intertextual allusion to *Heart of Darkness*, Kneale encourages his readers to consider Dr. Potter's brutal endeavour in a broader context. It cannot be dismissed as the aberration of a single individual. On the contrary, it illustrates the very principle of colonialism, which is shown to be marked by ignorance, inhumanity, exploitation and an utter lack of awareness for the dignity of the 'Other'.[15]

While Coetzee completely suppresses the voice of the 'Other', Kneale stimulates the awareness of it by incorporating the voices of more than twenty very different first-person narrators of diverse origin and social standing into the novel's narrative structure. More importantly, he gives what might be called 'subaltern' voices the opportunity to speak, too, whether it be the Aborigine Peevay, the farmer Ben Hayes or the convict Jack Harp (cf. Wallhead 7). The resulting multiperspective account of persons and events

---

[15] It perfectly fits this aspect of the novel that Dr. Potter and his followers leave one of their companions, the botanist Timothy Renshaw, injured in the jungle, and that it is the Aborigine Peevay who saves him.

serves to question notions of alterity, knowledge and truth. The novel consists of various letters, diaries or documents which are all characterised by the peculiar style and idiosyncrasies of their writer, like the hypocritically unctuous language of Reverend Wilson, the colourful Manx dialect of Captain Kewley or the strangely hybrid English of the aborigine Peevay. In this way, Kneale provides both coloniser and colonised with distinct voices and enables us to see and evaluate the same things from different perspectives (cf. Nünning 378f.). A short dialogue between the Governor of Van Diemen's Land and Mr Robson, allegedly a benefactor of the Aborigines, for instance, shows how the colonisers tend to denigrate the colonised to mere things or irresponsible children: "'Whom have we mislaid?' 'Merely a couple of aborigines, your Excellency. They can be so naughty'" (*EP* 264). At the same time, the English are portrayed to a significant extent from the perspective of what they might consider their 'Others'. Thus, the smuggling Manxman Captain Kewley effortlessly sees through the various hypocrisies of his passengers and understands perfectly well why the Indians should have rebelled against the British. Even central items and concepts of Western society are thus defamiliarised and questioned. This becomes particularly apparent in the language of the anglicised Aborigine Peevay. In Peevay's parts of the novel, some expressions are capitalised in order to signal a distance between the speaker, his language and the concepts or commodities it serves to express, as in his description of certain concepts or commodities introduced by the British in the ill-famed Aborigine colony Flinders Island:

> By and by he [Peevay's half-brother Tayaleah] became Robson's best blackfellow [...]. He did CRAFTS and he was FARMER. Then he did GIVING THINGS FOR COINS, whose name was MARKET, and got a hat called STRAW. When MARKET finished – which it did very soon – he did NEWSPAPER, [...] which stopped quicker even than MARKET. Mostly, though, he was a TEACHER. (EP 256)[16]

On the one hand, this creates a defamiliarising effect. Viewed from the perspective of the 'Other', the capitalisation makes these innovations appear perfectly absurd and useless. On the other hand, it means that Peevay cannot establish a sensible connection between signifier and signified. In this re-

---

[16] This is also particularly obvious when Peevay finally rebels against British rule and its commodities and destroys his own cottage and household: "First I lit candles so I could see. Then I took TEAPOT and made it fly like a bird to wall [...]. Next I broke legs off STOOLS and TABLE and hit these against SHELVES, so they fell down, very loud. After I put pieces of TABLE and STOOLS, together with BOOK and TOP HAT all in a big PILE, just beside CURTAINS. Finally I took CANDLES and lit PILE, so it became a fire, very beautiful, that burned down COTTAGE" (*EP* 343).

spect, the capitalisation of certain expression creates an intense awareness of language and foregrounds its conventional referentiality.

This problem of referentiality is crucial to the whole novel. The plot of *English Passengers* hinges on a problem of reference, an act of 'mistranslation'. Intending to locate the Garden of Eden and to prove the literal truth of the Bible, the Reverend identifies rivers named in the Bible with existing rivers in Tasmania:

Biblical Name:	Aboriginal Name:
Euphrates	Ghe Pyrrenne
Gihon	Gonovar
Pison	Pewunger
Hiddekel	Liddywydeve (*EP* 22)

The exploration plot only comes into existence because the Reverend believes to have 'translated' the names of the rivers correctly. Like Coetzee, Kneale thus parodies scientific discourse, creating awareness for the relativity of normative standards and the precarious character of language and referentiality.

Conclusion

In both *Dusklands* and *English Passengers*, intertextuality proves to be part of an intense engagement with notions of truth, authenticity and knowability. Both novels take up the discursive legacy of colonialism and subvert the imperial master narrative in multiple ways, using *Heart of Darkness* as a point of reference. Establishing analogies to Conradian characters, topics, motifs and narrative techniques, Coetzee and Kneale underline the ongoing relevance of the topics Conrad addressed and simultaneously adapt these to support the concerns that are central to their own works. Drawing on pseudo-scientific and historical documents rooted in a colonial context, they address the complex relationship of 'Self' and 'Other', which is also central to *Heart of Darkness*. In both cases, this concern with 'otherness' or 'alterity' is closely linked to language. Coetzee and Kneale undermine the discourse of hegemonic culture, showing a particular interest in language or, more specifically, in the precarious relationship of language and power as well as of language and reality. In this respect, however, they each adopt a different approach. While Coetzee thematises the 'Other' in bluntly suppressing his/her voice and focussing on the 'Self', Kneale grants both their distinct voice(s) and deconstructs the 'Self' from the perspective of the 'Other'. Similarly, Coetzee exposes the mere conventionality of (fictional) language, whereas Kneale shows a concern for and a certain belief in authenticity by granting each narrator his or her distinct voice.

Ultimately, *Dusklands* and *English Passengers* therefore also partake of a specific ethical force, which is supported by the references to Conrad's *Heart of Darkness*. This concerns not only the creation of an awareness for 'otherness' or 'alterity', but also the epistemological implications of the novels. As Attridge (2004a, 669) states, "literature's distinctive power and potential ethical force resides in a testing and unsettling of deeply held assumptions of transparency, instrumentality and direct referentiality".[17] The 'darkness' to be encountered in the works of Conrad, Coetzee and Kneale thus comprises not only the dark forces and motives of man, the antithesis of civilisation, but also a certain semiotic or referential opacity. Both *Dusklands* and *English Passengers* deny any ultimately authoritative account, albeit in different ways. Instead, they draw attention to the problem of subjectivity, referentiality and 'mistranslation', which Conrad poses implicitly and explicitly in *Heart of Darkness*. Coetzee at once foregrounds and undermines the discursive power of language and carries the Enlightenment discourse of modern rationality ad absurdum. Kneale, though, does not deny the possibility of at least approaching some kind of truth through narrative, but questions the reliability of any single narrative. As in the case of *Heart of Darkness*, the implications of the issues addressed in *Dusklands* and *English Passengers* thus go far beyond the colonial context of the novels.

Works Cited

Achebe, Chinua. "'An Image of Africa': Racism in Conrad's *Heart of Darkness*." 1975. *Postcolonial Discourses: An Anthology*. Ed. Gregory Castle. Oxford: Blackwell, 2001. 210-20.
Attridge, Derek. "Ethical Modernism: Servants as Others in J.M. Coetzee's Early Fiction." *Poetics Today* 25.4 (2004a): 653-71.
—. *J.M. Coetzee and the Ethics of Reading*. Chicago: U of Chicago P, 2004b.
Attwell, David. "'The Labyrinth of My History': J.M. Coetzee's *Dusklands*." *Novel: A Forum on Fiction* 25.1 (1991): 7-32.
Brantlinger, Patrick. *Rule of Darkness: British Literature and Imperialism, 1830-1914*. 1988. Ithaca and London: Cornell UP, 1990.
Cahir, Linda Costanzo. "Narratological Parallels in Joseph Conrad's *Heart of Darkness* and Francis Ford Coppola's *Apocalypse Now*." *Joseph Con-*

---

[17] For a thoroughgoing analysis of the ethical implication of 'otherness' as it is presented in *Dusklands* cf. also Attridge 2004b, 1-21.

rad's *Heart of Darkness: A Casebook*. Ed. Gene M. Moore. Oxford: OUP, 2004. 183-96.

Canepari-Labib, Michaela. *Old Myths – Modern Empires: Power, Language and Identity in J.M. Coetzee's Work*. Frankfurt/Main: Peter Lang, 2005.

Coetzee, J.M. *Dusklands*. 1974. London: Vintage, 2004.

Conrad, Joseph. *Heart of Darkness*. 1899/1902. Ed. D.C.R.A. Goonetilleke. Peterborough: Broadview Literary Press, 1995.

Demory, Pamela. "Apocalypse Now Redux: *Heart of Darkness* Moves into New Territory." *Literature Film Quarterly* 35.1 (2007): 342-4.

Dryden, Linda J. "'To Boldly Go': Conrad's *Heart of Darkness* and Popular Culture." *Conradiana: A Journal of Joseph Conrad Studies* 34.3 (2002): 149-70.

Farn, Regelind. *Colonial and Postcolonial Rewritings of* Heart of Darkness: *A Century of Dialogue with Joseph Conrad*. Boca Raton, Florida: Dissertation.com, 2005.

Gallagher, Susan VanZanten. *A Story of South Africa: J.M. Coetzee's Fiction in Context*. Cambridge, MA: Harvard UP, 1991.

Gardiner, Allan. "J.M. Coetzee's *Dusklands*: Colonial Encounters of the Robinsonian Kind." *World Literature Written in English* 27.2 (1987): 174-84.

Greaney, Michael. *Conrad, Language and Narrative*. Cambridge: CUP, 2002.

Hardy, Barbara. *Tellers and Listeners: The Narrative Imagination*. London: Athlone Press, 1975.

Head, Dominic. *J.M. Coetzee*. Cambridge: CUP, 2004.

Huggan, Graham and Stephen Watson. Introduction. *Critical Perspectives on J.M. Coetzee*. Eds Graham Huggan and Stephen Watson. Basingstoke: Macmillan, 1996. 1-12.

Kneale, Matthew. *English Passengers*. 2000. London: Penguin, 2001.

McDonald, Sean. "A Conversation with Matthew Kneale." *Boldtype*. 13 July 2008 <http://www.randomhouse.com/boldtype/0400/kneale/>.

Nünning, Vera. "Ethics and Aesthetics in British Novels at the Beginning of the 21st Century." *Ethics in Culture: The Dissemination of Value through Literature and Other Media*. Eds Astrid Erll and Herbert Grabes. Berlin: De Gruyter, 2008. 369-92.

Reif-Hülser, Monika. "Translating Cultures – Translating Histories: Stories of Africa." *Xenophobic Memories: Otherness in Postcolonial Constructions of the Past*. Eds Monika Gomille and Klaus Stierstorfer. Heidelberg: Winter, 2003. 77-100.

Rogez, Mathilde. "Variations on a Frontier: J.M. Coetzee's Novel *Dusklands* in Context." *Commonwealth: Essays and Studies* 28.1 (2005): 40-52.

Rudrum, David. "Living Alone: Solipsism in *Heart of Darkness*." *Philosophy and Literature* 29.2 (2005): 409-27.
Stewart, Garrett. "Coppola's Conrad: The Repetitions of Complicity." *Critical Inquiry* 7.3 (1981): 455-74.
Wallhead, Celia. "To Voice or Not to Voice the Tasmanian Aborigines: Novels by Matthew Kneale and Richard Flanagan." *Revista Alicantina de Estudios Ingleses* 16 (2003): 283-95.
Watson, Stephen. "Colonialism and the Novels of J. M. Coetzee." *Critical Perspectives on J.M. Coetzee*. Eds Graham Huggan and Stephen Watson. Basingstoke: Macmillan, 1996. 13-36.

Georgiana Banita

Affect, Kitsch and Transnational Literature: Azar Nafisi's "Portable Worlds"

Azar Nafisi's *Reading Lolita in Tehran* eloquently expresses the grievances of women living in the Islamic Republic of Iran, but has often been regarded as an extension of American imperial hegemony. While the extreme ideological suppression in some Islamic cultures is undeniable and unpardonable, in her book Nafisi portrays the West as an arbiter of truth and dismisses non-Western cultures as regressive and evil. Several scholars have criticised the book's selective memory, which glosses over the history of the Iranian nation and caters to the neo-orientalist fantasies of a Western audience. This essay seeks to reveal how visual and textual practices of reframing bring Nafisi's memoir in the proximity of cultural kitsch, undermining the non-ideological, transformative function she ascribes to fiction. Taking my cue from theories of kitsch espoused by Jean Baudrillard and Milan Kundera, particularly in connection with totalitarian regimes, I argue that the cumulative effect of the book's insistence on the transnational validity of Western fiction is a spurious glorification of universal values and sentiment at the expense of political engagement and critical thinking.

> We are surrounded by "beautifying lies" [...] – a "spread of democracy" that often bolsters its opposite, a "march of freedom" that often liberates people to death, a "war on terror" that is often terroristic, and a trumpeting of "moral values" often at the cost of civil rights. [...] The blackmail that produces our "categorical agreement" operates through its tokens. (Foster 17)

In a review quote on Azar Nafisi's *Reading Lolita in Tehran*, included on the publisher's website, NPR correspondent Jacki Lyden notes:

> When I first saw Azar Nafisi teach, she was standing in a university classroom in Tehran, holding a bunch of red fake poppies in one hand and a bouquet of daffodils in the other, and asking, 'What is kitsch?' Now, mesmerizingly, she reveals the shimmering worlds she created in those classrooms, inside a revolution that was an apogee of kitsch and cruelty. [...] You will be taken inside a culture, and on a journey, that you will never forget.

Indeed, Nafisi's memoir of her intense literary discussions with seven female students in Tehran, all of whom she coached in adopting the wisdom of Western classics as ultimate knowledge and enlightenment, is not likely to fade from its readers' memory. The reasons for this staying power might, however, have more to do with kitsch than the reviewer cited here would have suspected. Azar Nafisi's memoir, published by Random House in 2003, blends a harrowing portrayal of the life of women in post-revolutionary Iran with a powerful personal testimony about the timeless global purchase of

Western literary classics. The book found a wide audience, and its success made Nafisi a celebrity in the United States partly due to the timely publication of the memoir to coincide with a proliferation of female book clubs and reading groups under the lasting impact of Oprah Winfrey's groundbreaking achievements in this field. Itself a very apt and indeed widespread choice for such reading groups across the U.S. (cf. Abbott 106), *Reading Lolita in Tehran* has spent over 117 weeks on the *New York Times* bestseller list to date, has been translated into 32 languages and has won diverse literary awards.[1] Since the publication of Nafisi's book in 2003, other autobiographical accounts of tormented life conditions under Iran's Islamic regime, such as Azadeh Moaveni's *Lipstick Jihad* (2005) or Marjane Satrapi's *Persepolis* (2003, adapted for the screen in 2007), have nurtured the interest of wide audiences in the region and its relations to the U.S.

Azar Nafisi is a Visiting Professor and director of the Dialogue Project at the Foreign Policy Institute of Johns Hopkins University's School of Advanced International Studies in Washington, D.C., where she teaches aesthetics, culture and literature, with a focus on the relationship between culture and politics. Nafisi also held a fellowship at Oxford University, where she conducted a series of lectures on culture and the important role of Western literature and culture in Iran after the revolution of 1979. She taught at the University of Tehran, the Free Islamic University and Allameh Tabatabai before her return to the United States in 1997 – earning national respect and international recognition for her advocacy work on behalf of Iran's intellectuals, youth and especially young women. More importantly, Nafisi has been consulted on issues relating to human rights in the Islamic world, both by policy makers and various NGOs in the U.S. and elsewhere. She is also invested in the promotion of not just universal literacy, but of reading books of global literary relevance. Such a concept is inevitably fraught with ideological tensions and potential criticisms about the imperialist undertones of Nafisi's approach still loom large, despite the obvious value of a transnational perspective in the production and reception of literature, especially within the particularities of our global historical moment.

In the following, I will focus on the visual and cultural transplants effected by Nafisi's subversive efforts as a professor of Anglo-American literature in Tehran against the background of the publicity surrounding the promotion and reception of the book. Both the memoir itself and its cultural afterlife hinge to a large extent on what may be called 'transnational projec-

---

[1] These include the 2004 Non-fiction Book of the Year Award from Booksense, the Frederic W. Ness Book Award, the 2004 Latifeh Yarsheter Book Award, an achievement award from the American Immigration Law Foundation, as well as being a finalist for the 2004 PEN/Martha Albrand Award for Memoir.

tion'. Specifically, Iranian culture is seen as displaying or aspiring towards American traits through its seditious adulation of classic American literature and what Nafisi unabashedly describes as the "dogged desire for life, liberty and the pursuit of happiness by young Iranians today" (Nafisi 341). At the same time, American literature is seen as not only germane to a radically different cultural environment, but also as the propagator of global cultural literacy and the purveyor of a transnational empathetic consciousness that the book seeks to invoke in its readers. My purpose here is thus twofold. First, I want to address several arguments that castigate Nafisi's project as ideologically misguided and politically counterproductive. Secondly, on the basis of the book's visual allegories in the form of illustration and ekphrasis, I want to propose the concept of kitsch as a way to begin thinking about how *Reading Lolita in Tehran* imagines connections between two civilisations on a starkly hegemonic basis that employs a relatively simple apparatus of sentimentalism and cultural voyeurism. Kitsch, I argue, can function as a heuristic for Nafisi's stance, often resting on ideological shorthand and shortcuts, which produce truth claims in the absence of apposite evidence or argument. Throughout, I seek to reveal what strikes me as the book's most valuable trope, namely the practice of translating one "portable world" (Nafisi 341) into the idiom of another in a further instance of (to retain the intermedial metaphor) cultural ekphrasis. In her teaching, for instance, Nafisi often encounters students who read Western literature through the prism of Islamic doctrine and thus reject it as decadent, immoral and godless. Conversely, Nafisi filters her perception of her students and the academic environment in Tehran through an ideal of subversiveness and counter-revolution imbued with Western ideology and frequently misconstrued ideas about the so-called clash of civilisations.

Prominent *New York Times* reviewer Michiko Kakutani is quoted in the book's blurb with the statement that Nafisi's memoir "is an eloquent brief on the transformative power of fiction – on the refuge from ideology that art can offer to those living under tyranny, and art's affirmative and subversive faith in the voice of the individual" (Kakutani E6). The claim that art can exist outside ideology is questionable to say the least, as Nafisi's own blend of fiction, pedagogy and political engagement patently demonstrates, despite her repeated attempts to extricate specifically female modalities of subversion through reading and discussion from the more aggressive forms of political militancy that is a prerogative of masculinity. In a rare recourse to Oriental literature, Nafisi illustrates this gender-oriented contrast by invoking Scheherazade, the heroine of *A Thousand and One Nights*:

> Scheherazade breaks the cycle of violence by choosing to embrace different terms of engagement. She fashions her universe not through physical force, as does the king, but

through imagination and reflection. This gives her the courage to risk her life and sets her apart from the other characters in the tale. (Nafisi 19)

In keeping with this stark differentiation of ideological resistance – one that paradoxically reflects what critics of Muslim societies call the "gender apartheid" of the Islamic revolution – *Reading Lolita in Tehran* focuses on the story of Nafisi and her exclusively (and deliberately) all-female book club after Nafisi's resignation from the University of Allameh Tabatabai.[2] Every week teacher and students convene over tea and pastries to discuss masterpieces of the Anglo-American canon, which also provide the structure of the book: Nabokov's *Lolita*, Fitzgerald's *The Great Gatsby*, James' *Daisy Miller* and *Washington Square*, as well as Jane Austen's *Pride and Prejudice*. What the studious women seek in these works are literary "epiphanies of truth" (Nafisi 3) that resonate with their lives in the Islamic Republic of Iran, a place whose "absences were more real than its presences" (Nafisi 5). In reading these books, Nafisi and her disciples thus embark on the double project of giving "a different color to Tehran" by immersing themselves in the 'riches' of Western thought, on the one hand, and of helping to redefine that thought in light of their own experience, on the other hand. The result is "this Lolita, our Lolita" (Nafisi 6), a mongrel creature with a foot in both worlds – East and West – yet believable in neither.

To preempt potential rejoinders that my reading of the book highlights its foibles while underplaying its strengths, I should begin by saying that Nafisi's is a timely, exceptionally interesting book delving into the substrata of a region we certainly ought to be more informed about. In elegant and eloquent prose, the memoirist proffers readings of Nabokov, Fitzgerald, James and Austen that baffle even the most seasoned critic in their transcultural astuteness. To be fair, the insight remains rather one-directional: while we certainly recognise that Islamic culture gains added dimension and becomes more easily translatable into Western terms as a result of Nafisi's insightful comments, it nevertheless remains unclear how the texts themselves profit from these topical readings. In other words, while they may seem revolutionary to Nafisi's reading group – who, like Lolita, create their little pockets of freedom and take every opportunity to flaunt their insubordination (Nafisi 25) – the novels fail to shed their conventionality in the eyes of their Western read-

---

[2] The reasons why Nafisi relinquishes her academic position have to do with draconian practices that imposed sartorial and ideological codes: "how well could one teach when the main concern of university officials was not the quality of one's work but the color of one's lips, the subversive potential of a single strand of hair? Could one really concentrate on one's job when what preoccupied the faculty was how to excise the word wine from a Hemingway story, when they decided not to teach Emily Brontë because she appeared to condone adultery?" (Nafisi 11).

ers. The only exception may be Nafisi's interpretation of Nabokov's *Lolita* as a study of authoritarianism, a reading that chimes with recent approaches to the novel in terms of its focus on what may be called 'hyper-authorship' – i.e. an overbearing authorial presence and its effects on the narrative. More often than not, however, Nafisi refashions the texts to fit the context of the Islamic Republic,[3] restaging them in the spirit of contemporary performances of classic Shakespearean plays, exoticised and upgraded in keeping with whatever cultural worlds they have been transplanted into. Yet this liberal handling of the textual material should not detract from Nafisi's critical acumen and the astonishing ease with which she juggles the multiple levels of her memoir, one that switches dexterously among her life story on three continents,[4] the personal trajectories of her students, political developments within and outside Iran, as well as the plots of the texts she subjects to literary scrutiny.

Having said that, it appears that by restricting her otherwise empathetic narrative to an ideologically biased perspective susceptible of political attachment to the Bush Doctrine and its interventionist policies in the Middle East, Nafisi has made herself vulnerable to vitriolic attacks from several quarters (cf., among others, Rowe). Some of these zero in on issues that might seem extraneous to the book's achievement or lack thereof, such as the fact that both before and after the publication of her bestselling memoir, Nafisi was promoted alongside proponents of anti-Muslim sentiments by Benador Associates, a neo-conservative agency that arranges influential and lucrative speaking engagements or prominent newspaper publication for such champions of total war with the Middle East as Richard Perle and James Woolsey.[5] Other points of criticism pertain to the textual paradoxes of the book rather than to the contested persona of its author. On the "new luminosity" of her life as a result of the intimacy fostered by the reading group, Nafisi writes: "We had to reveal aspects of ourselves to one another that we didn't even know existed. I constantly felt I was being undressed in front of

---

[3] About Fitzgerald's Gatsby she writes: "He wanted to fulfill his dream by repeating the past, and in the end he discovered that the past was dead, the present a sham, and there was no future. Was this not similar to our revolution, which had come in the name of our collective past and had wrecked our lives in the name of a dream?" (Nafisi 144). Khomeini's hubris is likened to Humbert's ambitions: "Like all great mythmakers, he had tried to fashion reality out of his dream, and in the end, like Humbert, he had managed to destroy both reality and his dream" (Nafisi 246).
[4] Nafisi's education spans several countries: England, Switzerland, the US, and Iran.
[5] A consistent point of criticism against Nafisi pertains to her associations with highly influential neoconservatives such as Paul Wolfowitz, Fouad Ajami and British Orientalist Bernard Lewis, all of whom Nafisi mentions in the acknowledgements to her book (Nafisi 345-47). Cf. also DePaul 78f.

perfect strangers" (Nafisi 60). Indeed, one of the most intensely studied tropes in the book is that of unveiling, understood as a transgressive practice of identity formation that amplifies the liberating effect of reading forbidden or suppressed literature.[6] This occurs especially in conjunction with the effortless or even enthusiastic acceptance of decorative Western paraphernalia (such as bright red lipstick), as the female students become more confident and somewhat less discriminating in their choice between high and mass Western culture. In an article that investigates the pedagogical issues at work in Nafisi's intellectual defiance of a repressive political system, Simon Hay contends that the book

> follows these young women through a gradual progression of disrobement, accompanied by the application of Western accoutrements, and we are taught to understand this as a voyage of self-discovery; at a more abstract level, the book disrobes Iranian – and Islamic – culture for Western eyes, and by implication teaches us to understand this looking not as what Freud would call *scopophilia*, voyeuristic desire and desire-for-power, but as a healing, caring, *freeing* exercise. [...] But the covering and uncovering of Eastern women's bodies for the benefit of Western audiences, Western viewers and readers, has a long history. A long colonial, orientalist history. (Hay 11f.)

While Nafisi and her students may wish to manifest their right to be free of clothing in an act of resistance to the Islamic view of the female body as inherently and unredeemably sinful, the sartorial statement loses its edge and is trivialised by an uncritical adoption of exoticist paradigms that Nafisi does not fully succeed in detaching herself from. Further, Hay points out Nafisi's insistence that "true transgression and rebellion are neither political nor ideological" (Hay 15); in other words the apolitical alternative to the oppressive Islamic regime is nothing but a highly idealised consumerist dream of a bourgeois Western existence. One of Nafisi's students, Yassi, waxes sentimental on what she regards as a rebelliously romantic lifestyle, "long walks holding hands with someone she loved, even a little dog perhaps?" (Nafisi 32) – which harks back to contemporary advertising jingles and the visual tropes of matchmaking services, i.e. the capitalist products of a liberal society that could not be more at odds with Yassi's own upbringing.

In her discussion of the book, Amy DePaul goes as far as to liken the occasionally raunchy (by Islamic standards) exchanges among the members of the book club to the American series *Sex and the City*, set against the backdrop of the Islamic capital rather than the postmodern, sexually liberated

---

[6] As Nafisi briefly explains, "Fitzgerald and Hemingway were very difficult to find. The government could not remove all of the books from the stores, but gradually it closed down some of the most important foreign-language bookstores and blocked the distribution of foreign books in Iran" (Nafisi 91).

New York City (DePaul 73). Our sympathy for the women's yearnings is premised on our unequivocal acceptance of a liberal lifestyle model; the sentimental appeal of the book thus bifurcates into compassion for the young women of Iran on an individual level, and the unambiguous knowledge that Western culture is infinitely superior to their own. In other words, if they could simply adopt the freedom of the West, these helpless and subjugated but otherwise very moving Eastern urchins would lead much more enjoyable lives. Such a eulogy of mass products of the Western world, reduced here to the global common denominator of free romance and pet ownership, supports the claim I want to make that Nafisi inadvertently employs the aesthetic mode of kitsch in an effort to universalise Western lifestyles and their depictions in literature.

One of the most irresistible attractions of the books that Nafisi and her students pore over is their emphasis on individual struggles, whether or not they are, as in Gatsby's case, doomed to fail. Especially at a time when tyrannical ideologies in Iran banish individualist thinking, young women are seduced by the democratic individualism and critique of power relations perpetrated by such writers as Fitzgerald and James. Yet, despite this apparent investment in the values of privacy and self-determination, in the eyes of some critics Nafisi herself can be found guilty of an identity confiscation or "solipsization" (Nafisi 37) very similar to the depersonalising strategies of the Islamic regime. By extrapolation, not only does she, according to these detractors, divest her students of their individual personalities, but by overlooking the individuality of Persian culture itself she threatens to duplicate Humbert Humbert's emotional crime – "the confiscation of one individual's life by another" (Nafisi 33) – by affirming the superiority of Western culture over its Iranian counterpart, thus indirectly furthering the neo-conservative policy goals of the Bush administration.

The most passionate proponent of this critique is Hamid Dabashi, Professor of Iranian Studies and Comparative Literature at Columbia University, who sees the book as an "extension of American imperial hegemony" (Dabashi, "Lolita and Beyond"). Dabashi chastises Nafisi as being a 'Native Informer' or 'Comprador Intellectual' (Dabashi, "Native Informers") at the service of the American empire, sustaining the momentum of the current Middle Eastern conflict and the war on terror. To Dabashi, this explains Nafisi's refusal to engage with Persian history and culture,[7] preferring, in an orientalist tradition, to gloss over the invasive influence of Western values by describing it as universal enlightenment or epiphanic truth. Dabashi's de-

---

[7] Such omissions contradict Nafisi's statement that "we in ancient countries have our past – *we obsess over the past*. They, the Americans, have a dream: they feel nostalgia about the promise of the future" (Nafisi 109, my emphasis).

scriptions of Nafisi herself ("the Fox News anchorperson of Western Literature" and so on) often sound defamatory and unjustifiably personal. Their value and detriments have already been discussed at length (DePaul 76f.). Suffice it to say that many of Dabashi's claims revolve around aspects similar to those that have suggested to me the idea that Nafisi may be producing something much less harmful than she has intended, and as such in profound contrast to the liberating and transformative function she ascribes to literature. Namely, Dabashi speaks of the "pedophilic pathologies of an Orientalized imagination" invoked in the book to prove the superiority of Western culture (Dabashi, "Lolita and Beyond"), a metaphor that presupposes a pattern of streamlined cultural consumption by which simplified images of Iran become available as commodities on a predatory Western mass market.

Dabashi does not shy away from comparing Nafisi with Lynndie England, implicitly relating the undemanding view of Iranian damsels-in-distress waiting for the West to come to the rescue to the kitschy mise-en-scène of England's poses with Iraqi detainees at the Abu Ghraib prison near Baghdad. While unreasonably harsh, the analogy has the virtue of pinpointing the perils of any endeavor to discuss Middle Eastern conditions from a perspective colored by Western ideology, considering the potential traps set by the growing media depository of conflictual propaganda, such as the inflammatory iconography of Abu Ghraib. Moreover, in Dabashi's view Nafisi confirms to Americans that they are the measure of civilisation and that the rest of the world is only tolerable to the degree that it approximates Western ideas and aspirations. Iranian people are belittled in the process and reduced to stereotypes or fictional figurines inspired by the author's love of reading, which degenerates into a knack for character diminishment and narrative manipulation. While the book does harbor fictional treasures and never fails to enthrall as a narrative, the cumulative effect of such reductive narrative portrayal is not to amplify the universal value of literature by showing that it resonates with people of all cultural castes, as the author would have it, but to increase the marketability of the Iranian stories she depicts by insisting that they are, like fiction itself, easy to relate to.

Nafisi's contested position as a mediator between cultures is deeply inflected by her status as a highly educated, upper-middle-class woman that has already displayed considerable interest in issues of feminism in the Muslim world. Since the events of September 11, 2001 and the outset of the war on terror, the media and public opinion have established frequent connections between Islamic fundamentalism and the situation of women in Muslim countries. These associations revolve mainly around the simple theme that Muslim women are victimised by religious dogma. Before the American intervention in Afghanistan, for instance, feminist advocacy on behalf of oppressed Afghan women was used to drum up support for Western military action. To give a literary example that functions on a similar level as Nafisi's book, Khaled Hosseini's second bestseller *A Thousand Splendid Suns* (2007) emphasises in melodramatic fashion the plight of women persecuted by the Taliban.

It is this opportunistic condemnation of the position of Muslim women for the purpose of war propaganda that has been criticised, among others by Parvin Paydar, as a fatal combination of Orientalist feminism and feminist Orientalism (cf. Paydar). Historically, the former term denotes the efforts of Orientalists to invoke women's rights as a means of legitimating their colonial presence; the modern equivalent contained in the term 'feminist Orientalism' refers to the aforementioned attempts by prominent neoconservatives to raise support for the war in defense of women's rights. As Roksana Bahramitash compellingly argues, while Nafisi's memoir purports to defend women's rights, it remains steeped in classic Orientalist stereotypes (cf. Bahramitash). First, it assumes a binary opposition between East and West, between misogynist backwardness and human rights progress, as well as a clash of civilisations. Second, it regards Oriental women as victims rather than transformative agents, thus ignoring their potential for social empowerment, despite Nafisi's manifest interest in her students' education through literary enlightenment and the acquisition of basic critical thinking skills. Third, notwithstanding the diversity of her students' individual life stories, Nafisi hardly ever distinguishes among them in terms of their capacity for political resistance or their allegiance to antifeminist religious dogma. Many Iranian women certainly felt uncomfortable with the female dress code, yet devout women often welcomed it and experienced the constraint as liberation. While she does elaborate on the religious leanings of one of her students, Razieh, Nafisi tends to essentialise the religion of Islam and retains a pessimistic view of women's lives in post-revolutionary times, failing to acknowledge women's progress since the revolution and after Nafisi's own departure from Iran.

Nafisi's representation of Iranian women has also come under heavy criticism in light of Gayatri Spivak's critique of the voices who claim to represent subaltern women (cf. Spivak). Whereas Nafisi writes extensively about herself and her middle-class students, she accords little attention to less privileged women such as her nanny, who is mentioned only briefly when the revolutionaries use Nafisi's house to capture an armed drug dealer. Such conspicuous absences demonstrate that Nafisi's claim as a well-educated and sheltered academic to represent all women of her country is highly biased toward her own position as member of a social and literary elite. Women at the other end of the social scale also disprove her dim views of female helplessness in post-revolutionary Iran. Since at least the early 1990s, Iran has witnessed the presence of activist women who engage in political resistance on a more concrete and transformative level than the literary subversion Nafisi praised and practised in her book and in her teaching. Most prominent among these figures is Shirin Ebadi, a human rights lawyer who was honored with a Nobel Peace Prize in 2003 in recognition of her work promoting the rights of Muslim women. Instead of doing justice to the nuances of Iranian feminism, which certainly did not start with the publication of *Reading Lolita in Tehran*, Nafisi resorts to comedic jibes at the misbalanced gender relations that persist in Muslim societies, loosing some of the credibility of her critique through the kitschy triviality of such comments as:

> "It is a truth universally acknowledged that a Muslim man, regardless of his fortune, must be in want of a nine-year-old virgin wife." So declared Yassi in that special tone of hers, deadpan and mildly ironic, which on rare occasions, and this was one of them, bordered on the burlesque. "Or it is a truth universally acknowledged," Manna shot back, "that a Muslim man must be in want not just of one but of many wives?" (Nafisi 257)

The intertextual and intercultural use of Austen's famous opening sentence in the novel *Pride and Prejudice* epitomises the way in which Nafisi's book seeks to create channels of conversation between two nations that she, however, does not treat equally or with the same degree of interest. More a parody of Muslim traditions from a Western perspective than a credible critique of their consequences and authority, such passages detract from Nafisi's otherwise intriguing methods of transcultural mutation, culminating in the fascinating narrative behind the book's cover.

Before discussing the cover image it should be noted that images, visual recollections, photographs and illustrations permeate the textual fabric of Nafisi's memoir, whose style has clearly been inspired by Nabokov's pictorial writing.[8] The book opens with a comparison between two photographs of Nafisi's female students, one in which all are represented in Muslim garb, while the other depicts them in unveiled splendor, full of vital color and natural freshness: "In the first photograph, standing there in our black robes and scarves, we are as we had been shaped by someone else's dreams. In the second, we appear as we imagined ourselves. In neither could we feel completely at home" (Nafisi 24). One subchapter begins with the visually beguiling sentence: "I wonder if you can imagine us. We are sitting around the iron-and-glass table on a cloudy November day; the yellow and red leaves reflected in the dining room mirror are drenched in a haze" (Nafisi 39). Im-

---

[8] Nafisi herself has authored an academic study of Nabokov's works entitled *Anti-Terra: A Critical Study of Vladimir Nabokov's Novels* (1994).

ages of all kinds form a strong undercurrent to the book,[9] but they are veiled, restricted, prohibited, or metaphors for the power of the imagination. Following the example of a painter friend, Nafisi sets out, for instance, to use her teaching activity as a means of expressing "the colors of [her] dreams" (Nafisi 11) – the shiny spots of pigmentation still allowed by a regime that is bent on discoloration, personal and ideological, private and public.

The most disputed image of the book, however, is also one whose genealogy seems to suggest that the victim may perhaps have learnt something from her oppressors, and is now engaging in very similar acts of censorship. The cover of *Reading Lolita in Tehran* presents a cropped image from a larger photograph that contains an explicit political theme. The full image depicts two young girls involved in the election of the reformist Iranian President Khatami, reading a newspaper in anticipation of the election results. The cover image excises the newspaper, leaving two young faces with downcast eyes framed by black scarves. In Dabashi's interpretation, the full and cropped images send contrasting messages about Iranian women to the reader; critics have likened the book itself to its cover image as it omits those contextual details which show that Iranian women can also be active agents of progress and feminist emancipation. By contrast, the jacket of *Jasmine and Stars: Reading More than Lolita in Tehran* (2007), a book written by Fatemeh Keshavarz[10] partly in response to Nafisi's memoir, shows two Iranian women in a demonstration outside the University of Tehran in 2005, holding signs which say that they object to antifeminist oppression and that they demand equal rights with men. Their smile and relaxed attitude, complete with oversized sunglasses in the style of Hollywood starlets, project open self-confidence rather than subversive gloom. Of course, it is the intolerant regime that makes such demonstrations and the signs the two women carry necessary in the first place; yet the image illustrates the resilience of Muslim women in the face of suppression and their agency in the public sphere, where they shed their victimised status and take up essential democratic initiatives. It is precisely this agency and presence of Iranian women in the intellectual domain that Nafisi fails to capture, which is ironic to the extent

---

[9] Dabashi, who has written extensively on Iranian film, takes particular note of Nafisi's portrayal of film in the book, including the use of a blind Iranian film censor as a metaphor for the colorlessness of Iran's culture. As Dabashi points out (and Nafisi fails to observe), Iran has produced one of the most fascinating national cinemas of the last half-century, with creations that emerge from a consistent artistic tradition.

[10] Fatemeh Keshavarz is a Professor of Persian and Comparative Literature at Washington University, St. Louis. Unlike Nafisi, Keshavarz has pursued a more conventional academic career, with studies at University College, London and a number of scholarly works on classic and modern Persian literature. It is from the perspective of her background as a Persian scholar that Keshavarz objects to the cultural lacunae in Nafisi's book on the Iranian side.

that Nafisi's claim is to reveal the secret lives of women in post-revolutionary Iran.

The duplication of images involved in *Reading Lolita*'s book cover, coupled with the book's unselfconscious sentimentality vis-à-vis the rituals of salvation that Western literature provides, leads me to conclude that Nafisi's memoir conforms to a cultural pattern of kitsch, one that Nabokov's own *Lolita* can be said to anticipate. The concept of kitsch is central not only to Nabokov's portrayal of Lolita, but also to the self-image of Nafisi's female students who absorb the consumerist trends of Western popular culture, and functions as a filter through which they regard the world. Nabokov describes kitsch – or, to use his own term, "poshlost" – as

> corny trash, vulgar clichés, Philistinism in all its phases, imitations of imitations, bogus profundities, crude, moronic and dishonest pseudo-literature – these are obvious examples. Now, if we want to pin down *poshlost* in contemporary writing, we must look for it in Freudian symbolism, moth-eaten mythologies, social comment, humanistic messages, political allegories, overconcern with class or race, and the journalistic generalities we all know. *Poshlost* speaks in such concepts as "America is no better than Russia," or "We all share in Germany's guilt". (Nabokov 12)

In its insistence on the humanising mission of the Western canon at the expense of Iran's own existence as an independent nation with its traditions and specific ideologies, *Reading Lolita in Tehran* appears to fit the description of colonial poshlost. Yet it also calls to mind definitions of kitsch as the reduction of aesthetic objects or ideas into easily marketable forms, partly deriving from postmodern consumerism.[11] According to Jean Baudrillard, "to the aesthetics of beauty and originality, kitsch opposes its *aesthetics of simulation*: it everywhere reproduces objects smaller or larger than life; it imitates materials (in plaster, plastic, etc.); it apes forms or combines them discordantly; *it repeats fashion* without having been part of the experience of fashion" (Baudrillard 111). Nafisi's book borders on kitsch in its tendency to simplify and trivialise the complex underpinnings of Islamic culture and of the East-West dichotomy by reducing them to black-and-white stereotypes. Written primarily for a Western readership and geared in particular to an American audience, *Reading Lolita in Tehran* aims to find a common denominator that would help its readers perceive the world it sets out to denounce and relate to it. Despite the elitist titles discussed in the book,

---

[11] When kitsch becomes especially self-conscious, it tips over into what Susan Sontag has defined as "camp" ("Notes on Camp", 1966). Although the shower scene that opens Nafisi's memoir might qualify as camp in its intertextual allusions to products of American culture such as Alfred Hitchcock's *Psycho*, little of the book's content can easily be subsumed to the aesthetics of camp.

ultimately Nafisi seeks to engage the attention of lay readers, the kind of moderately cultured people that take a genuine pleasure in the act of reading but regard it as a hobby rather than as a serious political pursuit. In this, the book is tied more to Western mass consumption and thus to profit-making entertainment than to the earnest objective of reviving the spirit of literary subversion, both for Muslim culture and for enlightened readers in the West.

Nafisi's elaborations on the gratefulness of her Iranian students for the aesthetic blessings of Anglo-American literary works contain elements of kitsch, while stopping short of becoming metafictional. Although Nafisi looks for ways to dedoxify both Muslim dogma and Western traditions by bringing them in tense intertextual proximity – along the lines of what Linda Hutcheon commends as the refreshing repoliticisation of interpretation through the subversive strategies of modern parody – she accomplishes the exact opposite (cf. Hutcheon). Rather than questioning ideological positions, Nafisi attributes to Western literature a claim for ultimate truth. Her invocations of literary texts belonging to diverse literary epochs and written in starkly different styles, all of which she collates under the umbrella of Western art, recall what Fredric Jameson has called "blank parody" or pastiche (Jameson 17). Despite cannibalising a number of heterogeneous discourses of Western thought in literary discussions that display an overt political awareness, Nafisi's memoir fails to mount a credible critique of any political system. Paradoxically, its political bite is neutralised both by a too radical and simplistic parody of Western tropes – such as the humorous dictum borrowed from Austen – and by the book's failure to elevate its acerbic take on Muslim culture beyond the level of mimicry and commoditisation.

This lamentable absence of irony is most visible in the characters' naivety and unselfconscious acceptance of received wisdom as rebellious provocation capable of destabilising (or emasculating) a tyrannical regime. Indeed, what strikes the reader as the book's most kitsch-sounding quality is the pose struck by the female readers and their professor in absorbing the morals and lessons of Western novels and feeling their own intellect elevated in the process. While they do take a step back from the books they read to meditate on the act of reading itself, they gain little critical distance from the cultural position of subordination they find themselves in – despite Nafisi's statements to the contrary:

> Those of us living in the Islamic Republic of Iran grasped both the tragedy and absurdity of the cruelty to which we were subjected. We had to poke fun at our own misery in order to survive. We also instinctively recognized poshlust – not just in others, but in ourselves. This was one reason that art and literature became so essential to our lives: they were not a luxury but a necessity. What Nabokov captured was the texture of life in a totalitarian society, where you are completely alone in an illusory world full of false

promises, where you can no longer differentiate between your savior and your executioner. (Nafisi 23)

It is on a more subtle level that a truly metafictional technique can be observed which, rather than freeing the book from its ideological double-bind, only deepens its artificiality. Nafisi's cultural and literary exegeses not only embody a kind of prepackaged sentiment (about morality, the redeeming power of fiction and the supremacy of individualist thought), but the book also conveys the message that such sentiments are universally shared. As Marita Sturken observes, "when this takes place in the context of politically charged sites of violence, the effect is inevitably one that reduces political complexity to simplified notions of tragedy" (Sturken 22). While Sturken refers primarily to the sites of punctual aggression (such as the settings of terrorist attacks and their commemoration), Nafisi's book can be said to apply a similar method in its unnuanced and Manichean morality, as well as in its paradoxical effort to battle totalitarianism by means that are themselves doctrinaire. Kitsch has often been described as the dominant mode of totalitarian regimes, which often use kitsch to advertise the idea of a universal consensus. In an oft-quoted passage from his novel *The Unbearable Lightness of Being*, dissident Czech writer Milan Kundera writes:

> Kitsch causes two tears to flow in quick succession. The first tear says: how nice to see children running on the grass! The second tear says: how nice to be moved, together with all mankind, by children running on the grass! It is the second tear which makes kitsch kitsch.The brotherhood of man on earth will be possible only on a base of kitsch. (Kundera 251)

The first tear would correspond to the enthusiasm prompted by Nafisi's book club in herself and in her students, while the second tear appears when Nafisi extends her insights into literature to a cultural critique that results in an ecstatically egalitarian vision of the world, sacrificing all reflection so as to glorify feeling. "A novel is not an allegory", Nafisi remarks, "it is the sensual experience of another world. If you don't enter that world, hold your breath with the characters and become involved in their destiny, you won't be able to empathize, and empathy is at the heart of the novel" (Nafisi 111). The value of literary masterpieces, Nafisi suggests, rests not only in their universal and absolute quality but, through their potential for cultural reenactment, also in their capacity to enlist the admiration and acquiescence of foreign audiences.

In the current political climate this interpretation allows U.S. culture to appear both distanced from and deeply implicated in the troubled strife of the Middle Eastern region. Informed by Nafisi's memoir, the reader may ultimately come to perceive the temporal and spatial coordinates that define the profound alterity of Persian culture as yet another stage in the reception history of such global icons as Lolita and Jane Austen. At best, what Nafisi leaves out in terms of religious and cultural specificities of Muslim civilisation will incite the reader to historical reflection and political engagement. At worst, the American public will be inured to its government's political strategies by the comforting illusion that the same patterns of consumption and consumerism reign supreme where the military machine has yet to tread. *Reading Lolita* might inadvertently have smoothed the rough edges of an ideological conflict which now appears as light-hearted and agreeable as a literary roundtable among liberated women of fetching beauty and a common passion for Mr. Darcy.

Works Cited

Abbott, Charlotte. "Book Lovers of the World Unite: Will *Reading Lolita in Tehran* Become One of the Year's Biggest Book Club Reads?" *Publishers Weekly* 26 Jan. 2004: 106.

Bahramitash, Roksana. "The War on Terror, Feminist Orientalism and Orientalist Feminism: Case Studies of Two North American Bestsellers." *Critique: Critical Middle Eastern Studies* 14 (2005): 221-35.

Baudrillard, Jean. *Consumer Society: Myths and Structures*. London: Sage, 1998.

Dabashi, Hamid. "Lolita and Beyond: Foaad Khosmood Interviews Hamid Dabashi." *ZNet* 4 Aug. 2006. 12 Dec. 2008
<http://www.zmag.org/znet/viewArticle/3442>.

—. "Native Informers and the Making of the American Empire." *Al-Ahram Weekly On-line* 1-7 June 2006. 12 Dec. 2008
<http://weekly.ahram.org.eg/2006/797/special.htm>.

DePaul, Amy. "Re-Reading Reading Lolita in Tehran." *MELUS* 33.2 (2008): 73-92.

Foster, Hal. "In New York." *London Review of Books* 20 March 2003: 17.

Hay, Simon. "Why Read Reading Lolita? Teaching Critical Thinking in a Culture of Choice." *Pedagogy: Critical Approaches to Teaching Literature, Language, Composition, and Culture* 8.1 (2008): 5-24.

Hutcheon, Linda. *The Politics of Postmodernism*. New York: Routledge, 1989.

Jameson, Fredric. *Postmodernism, or, the Cultural Logic of Late Capitalism*. Durham: Duke UP, 1991.

Kakutani, Michiko. "Book Study as Insubordination under the Mullahs." *New York Times* 15 Apr. 2003: E6.

Keshavarz, Fatemeh. *Jasmine and Stars: Reading More than Lolita in Tehran*. Chapel Hill: U of North Carolina P, 2007.

Kundera, Milan. *The Unbearable Lightness of Being*. Trans. Michael Henry Heim. New York: Harper and Row, 1984.

Moaveni, Azadeh. *Lipstick Jihad: A Memoir of Growing Up Iranian in America and American in Iran*. New York: Public Affairs, 2005.

Nabokov, Vladimir. "Interview with Herbert Gold." *The Paris Review* 41 (1967): 1-19.

Nafisi, Azar. *Anti-Terra: A Critical Study of Vladimir Nabokov's Novels*. Tehran: Tarheh Now, 1994.

—. *Reading Lolita in Tehran: A Memoir in Books*. London: HarperCollins, 2004.

Paydar, Parvin. *Women in the Political Process in Twentieth Century Iran*. Cambridge: CUP, 1995.

Rowe, John Carlos. "Reading *Reading Lolita in Tehran* in Idaho." *American Quarterly* 59 (2007): 253-75.

Satrapi, Marjane. *Persepolis*. New York: Pantheon Books, 2003.

Sontag, Susan. *Against Interpretation, and Other Essays*. New York: Farrar, Straus & Giroux, 1966.

Spivak, Gayatri Chakravorty. "Can the Subaltern Speak?" *Marxism and the Interpretation of Culture*. Eds Cary Nelson and Larry Grossberg. Chicago: U of Illinois P, 1988. 271-313.

Sturken, Marita. *Tourists of History: Memory, Kitsch, and Consumerism from Oklahoma City to Ground Zero*. Durham: Duke UP, 2007.

Walter Göbel

Washington Irving's "Rip van Winkle", A Postcolonial Reading or: In Search of a Usable Past

Washington Irving's "Rip van Winkle" is undoubtedly one of the most famous, but also one of the most enigmatic short stories of the nineteenth century. Part of the enigma is due to the multiple search for a usable past in the story and in the *Sketch Book* itself. The glorification of traditional and even medieval English culture in the spirit of Edmund Burke, the idealisation of an idyllic Dutch past in New York state and the fascination of Native American myths seem equally to have inspired the romantic poet's mind. While decoding this plethora of cultural intertexts, most critics have, however, not paid any attention to the postscript which Irving added in 1848. Approached from a postcolonial point of view, the postscript calls the entire tale in question and deconstructs the Dutch and German legendary intertexts by adding an older layer of myth and fable. Native American culture takes over, most obviously in the symbolic remapping of places, and dislocates white mythologies as much as European romanticism, conceding – possibly against the author's intentions – a cultural precedence to the expropriated Native Americans, while the centre of poetic inspiration moves from the old to the new world.

Introduction

There have been so many excellent interpretations of Irving's "Rip van Winkle", whether mainly biographical, intertextual, mythic, psychological, political or feminist, that a new approach seems to demand some explanation.[1] Or does it? Isn't it a commonplace that complex and paradoxical texts, especially those with an enigma at their centre, require periodical reinterpretation according to the shifting horizon of the present and its mediation with the

---

[1] Some of these approaches can be found in *1860-1974. A Centenary Commentary on the Works of Washington Irving*, ed. Andrew B. Meyers, which includes Philip Young's famous psychological approach, and in *Critical Essays on Washington Irving*, ed. Ralph M. Alderman. Among more recent interpretations I would like to mention Jeffrey Rubin-Dorsky, "The Value of Storytelling: 'Rip van Winkle' and 'The Legend of Sleepy Hollow' in the Context of The Sketch Book" – especially for Irving's search of a mythic England; Richard J. Zlogar, "'Accessories That Covertly Explain': Irving's Use of Dutch Genre Painting in 'Rip van Winkle'"; Peter Kuczynski, "Intertextuality in Rip van Winkle: Irving's Use of Büsching's Folk-Tale Peter Klaus in an Age of Transition"; Deanna C. Turner, "Shattering the Fountain: Irving's Re-Vision of 'Kubla Khan' in 'Rip van Winkle' (one of the few contributions to mention the postscript, which perhaps addresses "criticisms that he had clung too closely to European models", 14); Colin D. Pearce, "Changing Regimes: The Case of Rip van Winkle" for a philosophical-theological approach; and Jutta Zimmermann, "Exemplarisches Erzählen in Washington Irvings 'Rip van Winkle'". Zimmermann emphasises the importance of the, albeit playful, creation of national myths for the story, anticipating some of my postcolonial argument.

horizon of the past? The criticism of the "Rip Van Winkle"-story is exemplary for this hermeneutic truism: questions about the many possible pretexts[2] influencing Irving – Sterne, Fielding, Goldsmith, German legends, Dutch genre painting have been among the main intertextual sources –, about moral messages, about hidden psychological or psychoanalytical agendas, about symbolism, myth and politics have in their turn illustrated the history of literary fashions and theories and allowed for the discovery of ever new keys for the central enigmas of the text and its many intertexts. And the present age offers a new set of questions within the framework of postcolonial studies, which I will reduce to two: how did the postcolonial American situation affect the question of cultural identity and how is the colonial situation of the Native American nations inscribed into the story? There is, however, an additional, more simple reason why a new reading of "Rip van Winkle" is offered here: a dissatisfaction with the way in which the postscript from the year 1848 – a 'peritext' according to Gerard Genette – has commonly been interpreted or rather, more often than not, been completely disregarded. A typical example of this is Helmbrecht Breinig's remark that the postscript should not be taken into account, because it was added much later (Breinig 1971, 151).[3] In the second part of the interpretation offered here, however, the postscript will move to the centre of attention, as it deconstructs or rewrites the entire story.

Framing Rip with Irving's own Paratexts and Intertexts: The *Sketch Book* and *Knickerbocker's History*

The openness of the "Rip van Winkle"-story may to some extent be due to Irving's concept of the *Sketch Book*, which presents itself as a somewhat haphazard collection of various kinds of texts. Side by side we find essays on aspects of English culture ("Rural Funerals", "London Antiques") and detailed quasi-ethnological descriptions of rituals and festivities (e.g. Christmas), parts of a travelogue presenting famous locations (Stratford-Upon-Avon, Westminster Abbey), sentimental tales reminiscent of Sterne's *A Sentimental Journey* ("The Widow and her Son", "The Pride of the Village"), sketches of celebrities met or imagined (William Roscoe, James I of Scotland), essays on poetry and criticism ("English Writers on America", "The Art of Book Making") and two depictions of Native American life and history ("Traits of Indian Character" and "Philip of Pokanoket"), which were written earlier (in 1814) and added to the collection. Irving presents himself

---

[2] The term is throughout used in the sense of 'antecedent text'.
[3] Especially for a German critic such a positioning is unusual, because critical editions are traditionally based upon the author's final version of a given text.

as a virtuoso collector and as a wanderer and loiterer in the Sketch Book, feeling – as his persona Geoffrey Crayon has it – like a "homeless man, who has no spot on the whole world which he can truly call his own" (Irving 1978, 209).[4] Little wonder then that the haphazard collector's attitude should also reflect upon the lack of unity in specific stories.

On his 17-year tour of Europe Washington Irving seems to have conducted a twofold quest: for his own identity as a poet and for a more poetic past. For a dilettante artist on a never-ending grand tour, the *Sketch Book* provides the appropriate literary form: a cornucopia of random tales, full of fascination and imaginative appeal, but without a clear message. The prevailing tone is one of nostalgia for a better, more poetic past. England, its old customs and rituals, its monuments and venerable architecture, its graveyards and abbeys are admired in the true romantic spirit and opposed to a more prosaic America. As Irving has it in "The Author's Account of Himself":

> Europe held forth the charms of storied and poetical association. There were to be seen the masterpieces of art, the refinements of highly cultivated society, the quaint peculiarities of ancient and local custom. My native country was full of youthful promise; Europe was rich in the accumulated treasures of age.
> Her very ruins told the history of times gone by, and every mouldering stone was a chronicle. I longed [...] to tread as it were in the footsteps of antiquity – to loiter about the ruined castle – to meditate on the falling tower – to escape in short, from the commonplace realities of the present, and lose myself among the shadowy grandeurs of the past [...]. I will visit this land of wonders, thought I, and see the gigantic race from which I am degenerated. (*SB* 9)

The poetic and the prosaic worlds are here opposed, much in the spirit of Tocqueville a few decades later.[5] Entranced equally by history, old customs and fables as well as by graveyards, churches and tombs, as many a 'dark' romantic then was, Irving, the connoisseur and collector of British texts and icons of bygone ages, echoes the idealisation of the past to be found in Edmund Burke's *Reflections*, in S.T. Coleridge's *On the Constitution of the Church and State* or later in Thomas Carlyle's *Past and Present*. He even goes as far as to admire the feudal past:

> In proportion as people grow polite they cease to be poetical. [...] Society has acquired a more enlightened and elegant tone; but it has lost many of its strong local peculiarities, its homebred feelings, its honest fireside delights. The traditionary customs of golden-hearted antiquity, its feudal hospitalities and lordly wassailings, have passed

---

[4] All quotations in text (abbrev.: *SB*) refer to this edition.
[5] Cf. Part II,1, Chapter 11 of *On Democracy*, where Toqueville maintains that the utilitarian spirit predominates in the U.S. and that the aesthetic faculties are neglected.

away with the baronial castles and stately manor houses in which they were celebrated. (*SB* 114 and 151)

Like many American Romantics, Irving was allured by the spell of gothic architecture and literature, by tales of the supernatural, by myths and fables and he was led to explore what he envisioned as a more poetic world. Somewhat in the spirit of Henry James a few years later, he was a precursor of the lost generation and an ardent admirer of everything ancient and awesome. No wonder the British public welcomed *The Sketch Book* most warmly, as it was no less than a eulogy to England and its traditions and full of British lore.

> Nothing in England exercises a more delightful spell over my imagination, than the lingerings of the holyday customs and rural games of former times. They recall the pictures my fancy used to draw in the May morning of life, when as yet I only knew the world through books, and believed it to be all that poets had painted it; and they bring with them the flavour of those honest days of yore, in which, perhaps with equal fallacy, I am apt to think the world was more homebred, social, and joyous, than at present. I regret to say that they are daily growing more and more faint, being gradually worn away by time, but still more obliterated by modern fashion. They resemble those picturesque morsels of Gothic architecture, which we see crumbling in various parts of the country [...]. Poetry, however, clings with cherished fondness about the rural game and holyday revel, from which it has derived so many of its themes – as the ivy winds its rich foliage about the gothic arch and mouldering tower [...]. (*SB* 148)

To create idealised versions of the past was a common feature of much of romantic literature, for example of Sir Walter Scott's historical novels. Irving follows the fashion prescribed by the Scottish bard whom he visited at Abbotsford in 1817, and with whom he concurred in admiring everything ancient and hoary. It is remarkable, however, that after the revolutionary wars which led to the founding of the United States, Irving should have turned back to Europe and joined such authors as Burke and Coleridge in emulating aspects of the feudal past. Irving spoke of his own age as degenerated, a term which implies that the past was a better and especially a more poetic age. This holds true for England as much as for the States: according to Washington Irving's *Knickerbocker's History of New York* (1809), New York's Golden Age also lies in the past, specifically in the 17th century, when New York was still known as New Amsterdam.

> In these good times did a true and enviable equality of rank and property prevail, equally removed from the arrogance of wealth, and the servility and heart-burnings of repining poverty; and, what in my mind is still more conducive to tranquillity and harmony among friends, a happy equality of intellect was likewise to be seen. [...] The province of the New Netherlands, destitute of wealth, possessed a sweet tranquillity that wealth could never purchase. There were neither public commotions nor private quarrels; neither parties, nor sects, nor schisms; neither persecutions, nor trials, nor punish-

ments; nor were there counsellors, attorneys, catchpolls, or hangmen. [...] In this dulcet period of my history, when the beauteous island of Mannahata presented a scene, the very counterpart of these glowing pictures drawn in the golden reign of Saturn, there was, as I have before observed, a happy ignorance, an honest simplicity prevalent among its inhabitants, which, were I even able to depict, would be but little understood by the degenerate age for which I am doomed to write. (Irving 1893, 242 and 261)[6]

Knickerbocker's History of New York, a covert intertext in "Rip van Winkle", tells a story of decline from the Golden Age. The Yankees, who finally took over New Amsterdam and introduced the spirit of gain, unrest and improvement are, it appears, mainly to blame for the destruction of what Martin Roth has simply called Irving's *Land of Cockaigne* (Roth 122). Both the *History of New York* and "Rip van Winkle" tell stories of bygone days before the dream of success became pervasive, before Benjamin Franklin's ideology and the Puritan work-ethic transformed the Dutch tranquillity and strife and warfare with the Yankees began to prevail. According to Roth, the *History of New York* "as a whole is a burlesque version of the fall of man" (Roth 123). The *History* presents a story of decline from a former state of paradisal innocence. And this theme affects the very form of Knickerbocker's history: it turns against the bellicosity of traditional historiography and offers instead, especially in the first volume, an idyllic description of an American domestic paradise. Irving's parodic and burlesque tone turns against official historiography and supplants it with the domestic felicity of a pastoral Dutch colony:

What are the great events that constitute a glorious era? – The fall of empires; the desolation of happy countries; splendid cities smoking in their ruins; the proudest works of art tumbled in the dust; the shrieks and groans of whole nations ascending unto heaven! (*HNY* 318)

Rip van Winkle is a descendant of the more happily situated Dutch ancestors by name and he encounters them during his adventure in the Kaatskills in person, especially Hendrick Hudson, the founder of New Amsterdam with his crew of the Half Moon. Rip thus has a glimpse of what Knickerbocker, who tells the tale and who also wrote the *History of New York*, has interpreted as the Golden Age. And here the Kyffhäuser-myth mentioned in the 'Note' which is appended to the story as a 'peritext' gains special significance: if it suggests the return of the reign of the good king Barbarossa, then Knickerbocker similarly seems to hope for the return of a Golden Age in what is described as "a little village of great antiquity, having been founded by some of the Dutch colonists" (*SB* 29). And Hendrick Hudson becomes, as it were, another good king and also the representative of a more poetic past.

---

[6] All subsequent quotations from this edition, abbrev. as *HNY*.

The "Rip van Winkle"-story adds mythic and poetic dimensions to the prosaic Yankee life which Irving calls 'degenerate'. It also adds an epic dimension, because the founding fathers are presented as demi-gods, apparently with everlasting life and, as in the Golden Age, a tendency to associate with mortals. The Dutch past thus becomes an idealised location for communal memories in Irving's nostalgic view. At the same time, the story turns against and questions everything that appears today to be most American: the revolutionary wars and the declaration of independence as well as the Yankee go-getter spirit and the dream of success. Instead, a mythic past is projected which, however, is not part and parcel of the United States at all, because, according to Knickerbocker's version of history, the Yankees destroyed the Dutch Golden Age. It may appear that in *The Sketch Book* Irving turns away from modern America twice: towards a mythic Golden Age of the Dutch and – in most of the other sketches – towards the myth of a *Merry Old England*. Both of these moves can be understood as attempts to find one's roots in a poetic version of history, and both suggest a deep-seated unease concerning anti-federalist politics and life in the modern United States.

This unease is emphasised by the opposition between the poetic and the prosaic. The former seems to be associated with the past only and with orality, the latter with modern materialist culture – oppositions which were widespread in nineteenth-century thought, e.g. in Burke's and in Carlyle's works. Rip van Winkle can himself be seen as a bard who envisions the more perfect past: he retells his story again and again while adding to it, embellishing it and thus forming communal memory through poetry and myth. Rip the dreamer is the type of the inspired poet who can contribute to national identity by providing somewhat nostalgic energising myths. At the end of the story he passes his tale on and it becomes part of the common lore of the villagers:

> He used to tell his story to every stranger that arrived at Mr. Doolittle's Hotel. He was observed at first to vary on some points, every time he told it, which was doubtless owing to his having so recently awaked. It at last settled down precisely to the tale I have related and not a man or woman or child in the neighbourhood but knew it by heart. (*SB* 41)

Diedrich Knickerbocker knows about the power of oral tale-telling and mythical projections, for he is a collector of legends and stories, not a bookish man. His research testifies to the importance of orality and of legends for a young nation. They contribute to what Knickerbocker calls 'true history', that is oral history which has stayed alive in the communal memory of the people, not the unromantic scholarly versions of the past which are to be found in academic versions of history:

His historical researches, however, did not lie so much among books, as among men; for the former are lamentably scanty on his favourite topics; whereas he found the old burghers, and still more, their wives, rich in that legendary lore so invaluable to true history. Wherever, therefore, he happened upon a genuine Dutch family, snugly shut up in its low roofed farm house, under a spreading sycamore, he looked upon it as a little clasped volume of black letter, and studied it with the zeal of a bookworm. (*SB* 28)

The Postscript, a Belated Peritext

The postscript was added to the story in 1848. It mainly concerns Indian traditions and a whole pantheon of Indian spirits, including Manitou, who supposedly also dwell in the Kaatskill mountains. On the one hand, this postscript adds to the mysterious and haunting atmosphere of the story.[7] On the other hand it enhances the ambiguous nature of the tale: are the supernatural elements Rip encounters of German origin – as the appended note about 'Frederick der Rothbart' suggests and various other implicit intertexts, such as the folktale of Peter Klaus the goatherd – or are the Kaatskills haunted by the Dutch founding fathers – or are they possibly a site of Indian mythology? Superimposing one possible origin, one possible mythical intertext upon the other seems to endanger the unity of effect, while, as it were, reflecting the eclectic nature of *The Sketch Book* as much as the haphazard way in which the footloose, rambling Irving would collect any kind of folklore, myth, tall tale indiscriminately, whether Scottish, French, German, Native American or Spanish. The overlapping intertexts which seem to fight for precedence suggest a postmodern indeterminacy concerning national identity, which the multiple paratextual bracketing of the narrative – by introduction, frame tale, note and postscript – appears to endorse. However, I would like to offer an alternative reading from a more postcolonial point of view.

From a postcolonial vantage-point Irving can first of all be seen as the typical alienated intellectual. Educated in the culture of the mother country and fascinated by its aesthetic and intellectual dominance, he spent most of his creative life in Europe, anticipating the lost generation. His admiration for the mother country, its profusion of ruins, ancient buildings, monuments and its splendid history let him even long for an undemocratic past which, after the shock of the French Revolution, was idealised in the romantic age, especially by Scott, whom Irving met and admired. In "Westminster Abbey" Irving/Knickerbocker's retrospective imagination comes alive:

---

[7] This aspect has been emphasised by Deanna C. Turner, who talks of "another myth from the mountains [...] a more ancient and authentic one" (13). Jutta Zimmermann also takes the postscript to merely provide an extra emphasis for the main story and points out some parallels (262).

> On looking around on the vacant stalls of the knights and their esquires; and on the rows of dusty and gorgeous banners that were once born before them, my imagination conjured up the scene when this hall was bright with the valour and beauty of the land; glittering with the splendour of jewelled rank and military array; alive with the tread of many feet and the hum of an admiring multitude. All had passed away […]. (*SB* 139)

Don't we hear nostalgic reverberations of Burke: "But the age of chivalry is gone […]"? Irving's eclectic search for roots and for a usable past, his antiquarian collecting of British, Dutch, German and Native American stories and myths, can be interpreted as symptomatic for many a contemporary member of the alienated postcolonial elite. V.S. Naipaul, in *The Enigma of Arrival*, shows a similar fascination with the mother country, only slowly giving way to a disillusionment which can, however, provide no alternative identity: once cut loose from your post-colony and at the same time disillusioned by the mother country you are adrift on the Atlantic or, referring to the de Chirico-Painting which provides the title of Naipaul's novel, lost in a faraway harbour. The travelling spirit, which Knickerbocker criticises in the restless and unsatisfied Yankees, is also the plight of the homeless intellectual, torn between a colony which lacks a modern culture and a fascinating mother country teeming with old cultural artefacts. At best such a homeless intellectual will become polyglott like Irving or Naipaul and acquire a thorough intercultural competence. For the construction of a national identity, however, he has lost his bearings. According to Martin Roth, "Irving (like Knickerbocker) desperately needs a spiritual ancestor in order to sustain his alienation in the present. Yet, like Rip van Winkle trembling before the stony figure of Hendrick Hudson, he cannot bring Peter Stuyvesant fully to life", that is, in the *History of New York* (Roth 154).

For, poetical as it is, a usable Dutch past can be revived in poetry and fiction only, and Knickerbocker's interest in it is nothing but antiquarian and nostalgic. On the other hand, English culture can surely not serve as the main guideline for the newly emancipated republic. As for German legends, they will merely inspire poetry – and perhaps that is all Irving actually aimed at: poetic inspiration from whatever source, though Knickerbocker's *History of New York* seems to convey more definite political messages and Irving's flight from the U.S. and his criticism of the Yankees also seem to voice a deep dissatisfaction with the current state of politics in the United States.

Where now do Manitou and the Native American pantheon of spirits come in? In a postcolonial reading, Manitou could provide an alternative to the nostalgic projection of a deified Dutch past on the one hand and the search for roots in European folklore (Barbarossa, Peter Klaus) on the other. Daniel F. Littlefield comments: "The romantic associations which Irving had for the Indian in his aboriginal state are much like those he had for the European past." (Littlefield 141) Nevertheless, Manitou could represent an indigenous American spiritual power which is to invigorate the poetic and mythic heritage of the new America, and help to transform and to poeticise the materialistic United States. Manitou stands for the ability of what will later be termed the Native American First Nations to provide the U.S. with an authentic and poetic cultural heritage and with inspiring pretexts. Such an interpretation would make the postscript postcolonial in the fullest sense of the term, anticipating a renaissance of Native American culture. The Native American population gained attention in the romantic age not only as noble savages – there is much of that in Irving and Cooper[8] – but also as the original owners of the land, who were unjustly expropriated or even gruesomely exterminated, as Knickerbocker has it in the *History of New York*:

> Think you the first discoverers of this fair quarter of the globe had nothing to do but go on shore and find a country ready laid out and cultivated like a garden, wherein they might revel at their ease? No such thing: they had forests to cut down, underwood to grub up, marshes to drain, and savages to exterminate. (*HNY* 71)

Even more explicit are the critical remarks in "Traits of Indian Character":

> [...] should [the poet] venture upon the dark story of [the eastern tribes'] wrongs and wretchedness; should he tell how they were invaded, corrupted, despoiled; driven from their native abodes and the sepulchres of their fathers; hunted like wild beasts about the earth; and sent down with violence and butchery to the grave; posterity will either turn with horror and incredulity from the tale or blush with indignation at the inhumanity of their forefathers. (*SB* 233)

The awareness of the injustices and atrocities committed towards the First Nations was continually spreading, last not least because of Irving's own *A Tour on the Prairies* in 1832, the year he returned from Europe. J.F. Cooper's singular success with his *Leatherstocking Tales* will also have had an effect upon Irving, who knew *The Pioneers* in any case. Much of the *Tour on the Prairies* – to the hunting grounds of the Pawnees, the Osages and the Comanches – may appear somewhat superficial: Irving offers more picturesque details than ethnographic facts, comparing the Native Americans to cavaliers, gentlemen or banditti (Irving 1979, 12, 28, 42), but nevertheless he is well aware of the "wrongs and insults that the poor Indians suffered in their intercourse with the rough settlers" (Irving 1979, 92). In *The Adventures of Captain Bonneville* (1837), Irving shows the detrimental effects of white

---

[8] And Irving is quite aware of this danger of idealisation. In *A Tour on the Prairies* he observes: "As far as I can judge, the Indian in poetical fiction is like the shepherd of pastoral romance, a mere personification of imaginary attributes" (Irving 1979, 27).

colonisation on Native American populations. Tours of Indian territory were popular in the early 19th century. John Treat Irving, Washington Irving's nephew, went on a tour to the hunting grounds of the Pawnee Tribes in 1833 and wrote about the decline of the First Nations:

> But where are the braves of the nation? They have come within the blighting influence of the white man. They have been swept away, even as is the grass of their own prairie before the fire of the hunter. A spring may come, again to revive the drooping face of nature; but to them there is no spring, no renovation. It is probable, that ere two centuries shall elapse, there will be but a very remnant of their race; a few wretched beings, lingering about the then abodes of civilization, unheeded, unnoticed; strangers in the land of their fathers. (Irving 2001, 16)

The belated postscript can be interpreted as Knickerbocker's or even as Irving's bad conscience awakening. The culture of the repressed Other is at last taken into account and finally supersedes the claims of an early Dutch colony which was nostalgically projected as the lost Eden. Native American myths come to question the power of European myths and intertexts which are receding slowly. The repressed Native American voices are to be heard in *The Sketch Book* in the form of two interpolated tales which were published earlier and which seem somewhat unaccommodated in this new version of a *Sentimental Journey* through England and Germany with its folk-tales and legends. The added native American tales ("Philipp of Pokanoket" and "Traits of Indian Character") in *The Sketch Book* appear formally and thematically just as awkward as the postscript to "Rip van Winkle". But in this formal oddity the suppressed culture surfaces and makes itself felt as the subversive Other culture demanding recognition. These two tales, though more romanticised than the postscript, which approaches an ethnographic discourse, give the postscript additional weight and show how Native American voices are fighting for recognition. To sum up: the postscript can be interpreted as adding ambiguity to the main tale, but it can also be interpreted as a total rewriting of the white construction of cultural heritage, communal memory and of the poetic past. Whether this second level of meaning was consciously aimed at or not is not of prime interest here.

There are many factors which could have contributed to Irving's change of heart concerning the representation of the Native Americans, for example the *Indian Removal Act* and the atrocities which were reported after 1830, e.g. about the Seminole Wars in Florida and the deceitfulness of the U.S. Army and General T.S. Jesup, who seized the Seminole leader Osceola when he came under a flag of truce to negotiate peace in 1837. Then there was the Treaty of New Echota (1835), which led to the removal of the Cherokees and the *Trail of Tears*. Many Native American Tribes were continually harrassed, persecuted and deported after 1830.

Whose Kaatskills?

"Rip van Winkle" begins with a presentation of the Kaatskill mountains, "a dismembered branch of the great Appalachian family" – perhaps cut off like the Dutch people from the mainstream of American history. The Kaatskills are liable to change with the light and the weather, producing the "magical hues and shapes of these mountains" (29); they are called "fairy mountains". Straightaway the setting seduces the reader to let his imagination wander into the realms of magic and of fairy-tales, that is, to wax poetical and mystic. Later Peter Vanderdonk tells the villagers that "the Kaatskill mountains had always been haunted by strange beings" and this is again confirmed in the postscript, which introduces two typographical variants, thus stressing the accuracy of the ethnographer:

> The Kaatsberg or Catskill mountains have always been a region full of fable. The Indians considered them the abode of spirits [...] there was a kind of Manitou or Spirit, who kept about the wildest recesses of the Kaatskill mountains, and took a kind of mischievous pleasure in wreaking all kinds of evils and vexations upon the red men. (42)

The 'Note' then alludes to another possible meaning: the Kaatskills may be coloured by legend to become a second kind of "Kypphauser Mountain", in which the once and future king is supposedly immured.

The Kaatskills are difficult to perceive clearly, they change shape and colour continually and add mystery and suspense to the story, while also stimulating the reader's imagination. They are mysterious and difficult to interpret, as a number of cultures are successively called upon to provide various meanings and to help unriddle the mystery of the Kaatskills. In their metamorphic character they allow for many poetic appropriations and for the multiple meanings the American reader will find in his new continent. In their vagueness and ambiguity they appear modernist, a focus of connotations without clear signification. Such multiple superimposed meanings can be interpreted, as we have seen, as a sign of disorientation, of a frantic casting about for a usable past and for usable national myths. On a metaphorical level, however, the Kaatskills can also be seen as the site of poetic inspiration, as a modern mixture between Parnassos and Mount Olympos: in this context the multiple legends surrounding the Kaatskills, the Kyffhäuser legend, the Hendrick Hudson legend and the Manitou legend could be interpreted as an ongoing battle for inspirational and mythic precedence, an ongoing search for the adequate mythic pretext. Is there, first of all, an authentic American myth, such as that of Hendrick Hudson, which would allow for a birth of indigenous poetry or does the American artist still depend upon the import of legends from Europe, in this case from Germany, to transform a materialist culture into a romantic and imaginative one? And then, finally, the postscript, an afterthought after 30 years: may not, perhaps, the Native Americans, the original inhabitants be the natural inheritors of the American Mount Olympus and may not their ancient myths be the best source for the birth of a new poetic American culture?

Native Americans have the last word in this story, their myths concerning the magical weather in the Kaatskills, the fertility of the valley, the tales of many a hunter and the birth of the Kaaters-kill stream proliferate and supply ethnographic detail in the postscript, suggesting a number of interlacing observable geographic facts suffused with mythic elements. In these tales and legends places (Garden Rock) and a stream (the Katers-kill) are named and thus (America is) symbolically taken possession of: naturally the oldest myths and names would belong to the Native American languages. Irving's afterthought acknowledges the most obvious indigenous source of myth and poeticality and with the postscript he rewrites and even erases much of the former story and along with it the younger mythical pretexts. European romanticism and invented white mythologies must give precedence to the older culture and its mythology, while the language of ethnography comes to supersede that of poetry. The postscript is a subversive statement which displaces the postcolonial conundrum of the English-American cultural conflict as much as the old Dutch-Yankee conflict and allows for the voices of those people to be heard again who have suffered from extermination, expropriation and materialism much more than the former Dutch settlers. Whether Irving fully realised what the implications of his postscript were, is not particularly relevant: the postscript questions the former version of the "Rip van Winkle" tale and of white mythology by its very existence and allows for some of the silenced Native Americans to find a voice.

Terminological Postscript: The Concept of the Postcolonial

Postcolonial Studies traditionally focus on texts which oppose colonialist or imperialist ideologies and Western structures of knowledge and power. The term 'postcolonial', when interpreted in this way, comes to share much common ground with the term 'anti-colonial' or, as Elleke Boehmer has pointed out, with critique and subversion (Boehmer 3). Like many postcolonial critics, Boehmer implicitly turns against Bill Ashcroft's too expansive use of the label and emphasises the need to clearly define its various meanings. Padmini Mongia has observed that "confusion and criticism often attend" the uses of the term postcolonial, which has come to mean different things in different parts of the world – e.g. in settler colonies as opposed to invaded colonies (Mongia 2f.) and similarly Ania Loomba has demanded a specification of its meaning in every single instance (Loomba 12).

If we take 'anti-colonial' elements to be central to the concept of the postcolonial, it cannot be applied to the "Rip van Winkle"-story – nor to *The Sketch Book* itself. Like the other famous 'cultural aristocrat' of the early 19th century, James Fennimore Cooper, Irving was deeply impressed by the apparent superiority of the mother culture. Both authors remained indebted to European romanticism and chose to spend many years in exile in Europe. Both were afraid of the uncontrollable nature and the possible excesses of mass democracy and sceptical about the spirit of the go-getter, while admiring classical gentlemanly ideals of civic virtue and subscribing to conservative republican attitudes (Clark 187f.). In Irving's case the disillusionment with the ethics and politics of the new nation was directed against Yankee materialism first and foremost, in Cooper's case we have a general emulation of the landed gentleman and a fear of the masses and of Jacksonian democracy. Both authors illustrate attempts at the mediation and hybridisation of transatlantic cultural influences and ideals – much in the spirit of Walter Scott's Waverley-hero, who vacillates between a number of political parties – but also give voice to a deep scepticism towards modern forms of mass democracy; they can thus hardly be seen as representative postcolonial writers according to the definition offered above. Irving's emulation of the Middle Ages and his love of old customs and legends make him somewhat of a nostalgic exiled idealist, who is overwhelmed by and deeply sceptical of the revolutionary wars and their final economic and cultural effects. His repeated rejections of the Yankee present in favour of European pasts, e.g. of the poetic projection of an idyllic Dutch-American New York state and of the myths and legendary lore of many nations, mimic colonial cultural influences more than they allow for postcolonial gestures of U.S. self-assertion. When Rip returns from his journey, he is much disturbed by the changes he witnesses: the political canvassing, the substitution of George Washington's image for George IV's or the hectic pace of modern Yankee life.

However, between the first version of the story and the postscript a significant change seems to have occurred. Irving had returned to the States and though still sceptical of the Yankee spirit and economy, he finds new poetic inspiration in Native American culture and now offers a postcolonial message transcending European-American cultural and political strife. In the "Postscript" some myths and legends of the marginalised Native American cultures surface and offer poetic inspiration. Undoubtedly, nostalgia for a more poetic past still predominates, but the author/narrator – unwittingly perhaps – becomes the defender of elements of the ostracised Native American culture, which comes to assume a position of aesthetic superiority and is liberated from the traditional stereotypes of the barbaric and the uncouth. On the one hand, this shift was surely also triggered by European romanticism – Irving's Native Americans, e.g. the noble Philipp of Pokanoket and Scott's highlanders have some features in common, both representing a nobility of behaviour paired with poetic creativity – on the other hand a postcolonial message is transmitted as we move from the nostalgic assimilation to the former 'centre', which is found in much of *The Sketch Book*, to the subversion of the Yankee go-getter mentality from within the United States.

But Irving's fascination with the cultures of the First Nations was never straightforward. While somewhat romantically admiring the poetical and mythical elements of Native American culture and hoping for a transformation of new world materialism, he just as much admired the spirit of the trappers and the fur trading companies. His *The Adventures of Captain Bonville* was published in 1837 and was a memorial to the

> courage, fortitude and perseverance of the pioneers of the fur trade, who conducted these early expeditions, and first broke their way through a wilderness where every thing was calculated to deter and dismay them. They had to traverse the most dreary and desolate mountains, and barren and trackless wastes, uninhabited by man, or occasionally infested by predatory and cruel savages. (8)

Among these "predatory and cruel savages" are the Blackfeet Nation, which is presented in the blackest of colours by Irving, though he later in the volume admits that they were quite often justified in fighting against the white traders because these, more often that not, proved untrustworthy and deceitful, e.g. twice attacking members of the tribe who approached them with the pipe of peace in their hands. Irving's loyalties were curiously split. His love of adventure led him to admire the bravado of Captain Bonville's adventures in native territories, which were financed by the affluent fur trader John Jacob Astor. That traders and trappers were inevitably followed by settlers and thus contributed to the expropriation and finally the extermination of the First Nations, is not clearly admitted by Irving. In *The Adventures of Captain Bonville* he assumes that white culture will never advance to the "irreclaimable wilderness" of the Rocky Mountains "where there is nothing to tempt the cupidity of the white man" (269). For the more accessible plains, however, he accepts the neccesity of establishing "a mounted force to protect our traders in their journeys across the great western wilds and [the policy] of pushing the outposts into the very heart of the singular wilderness we have laid open, so as to maintain some degree of sway over the country" (270).

Such an inclination to idealise some of the native Americans and some of the heroic trappers side by side may appear prevaricating if not paradoxical and prove how the romanticising vision of the poet, which will glorify outlaws of any kind, glosses over deep cultural and economic conflicts. But in any case such paradoxes and conflicts are also inscribed into the poetic text: in "Rip van Winkle" the tension between the heroic and mythic father figure of Hendrik Hudson, propagator of the Hudson Bay Company which in 1821 extended its dominion to the Pacific and the love of Native American myths and fables creates fissures in the narrative, which appears not homogeneous, but rather a conglomerate of main text, note and postscript, vying for precedence in their turn. In this formal aesthetic tension the dilemma of romantic idealist art in a materialist phase of nation-building is reflected.

Works Cited

Alderman, Ralph M. *Critical Essays on Washington Irving*. Boston: G.K. Hall, 1990.

Boehmer, Elleke. *Colonial and Postcolonial Literature*. 2nd ed. Oxford: OUP, 2005.

Breinig, Helmbrecht. *Irving's Kurzprosa: Kunst und Kunstproblematik im erzählerischen und essayistischen Werk*. Frankfurt: Peter Lang, 1971.

Clark, Thomas. "'The American Democrat' Reads *Democracy in America*: Cooper and Toqueville in the Transatlantic Hall of Mirrors." *Amerikastudien* 52.2 (2007): 187-208.

Irving, John Treat. *Indian Sketches: Taken During an Expedition to the Pawnee Tribes in 1833*. Santa Barbara, Cal.: The Narrative Press, 2001.

Irving, Washington. *The Adventures of Captain Bonville*. Ed. Robert A. Rees. Boston: Twayne, 1977.

Irving, Washington. *The Crayon Miscellany*. Ed. Dahlia Kirby Terrell. Boston: Twayne Publishers, 1979.

Irving, Washington. *Knickerbocker's History of New York*. 2 vols. New York: G.P. Putnam's Sons, 1893.

Irving, Washington. *The Sketch Book of Geoffrey Crayon, Gent*. Ed. Haskell Springer. Boston: Twayne, 1978.

Kuczynski, Peter. "Intertextuality in 'Rip van Winkle': Irving's Use of Büsching's Folk-Tale 'Peter Klaus' in an Age of Transition." *British Romantics as Readers: Intertextualities, Maps of Misreading, Reinterpretations*. Eds Michael Gassenmeier et al. Heidelberg: Carl Winter, 1998. 295-315.

Littlefield, Daniel F. Jr. "Washington Irving and the American Indian." *American Indian Quarterly* 5.2 (1979): 135-54.

Loomba, Ania. *Colonialism/Postcolonialism*. 2nd ed. London: Routledge, 2005.
Meyers, Andrew B., ed. *1860-1974. A Centenary Commentary on the Works of Washington Irving*. Tarrytown, N.Y.: Sleepy Hollow Restorations, 1976.
Mongia, Padmini, ed. *Contemporary Postcolonial Theory: A Reader*. London: Arnold, 1996.
Pearce, Colin D. "Changing Regimes: The Case of Rip van Winkle." *Clio* 22.2 (1993): 115-28.
Roth, Martin. *Comedy and America: The Lost World of Washington Irving*. Port Washington, N.Y.: Kennikat Press, 1976.
Rubin-Dorsky, Jeffrey. "The Value of Storytelling: 'Rip van Winkle' and 'The Legend of Sleepy Hollow' in the Context of *The Sketch Book*." *Modern Philology* 82 (1985): 393-406.
Turner, Deanna. "Shattering the Fountain: Irving's Re-Vision of 'Kubla Khan' in 'Rip van Winkle.'" *Symbiosis: A Journal of Anglo-American Literary Relations* 4.1 (2000): 1-17.
Zimmermann, Jutta. "Exemplarisches Erzählen in Washington Irvings 'Rip van Winkle.'" *Exempla: Studien zur Bedeutung und Funktion exemplarischen Erzählens*. Berlin: Duncker und Humboldt, 1995. 249-67.
Zlogar, Richard J. "'Accessories That Covertly Explain': Irving's Use of Dutch Genre Painting in 'Rip van Winkle.'" *American Literature* 54.1 (1982): 44-62.

Irina Bauder-Begerow

Echoing Dickens:
Three Rewritings of *Great Expectations*

Charles Dickens' *Great Expectations* enjoys masterpiece status in the history of English literature. This paper discusses two twentieth-century novels which use Dickens as a central pretext. Peter Carey's *Jack Maggs* (1997)[1] is a postmodernist rewriting of Dickens. The novel reconstructs the text from the returning convict's point of view and adds a metafictional aspect with the introduction of Dickens' 'alter ego'-character Tobias Oates. Lloyd Jones' *Mister Pip* (2006)[2] thematises the recipient's role in a totally unliterary context – depicting the response to *Great Expectations* of mostly illiterate South Pacific islanders in the context of political upheaval in the early 1990s. With Carey's splitting up of Pip's original autobiographical tale into multiple plotlines and Jones' bringing in a female protagonist to narrate an iconoclast reading of *Great Expectations*, these texts share the concentration on formerly marginalised foci. Employing a postcolonial narratological stance, my paper outlines the different narrative techniques these novels use to provide an audible counter-voice to Dickens' 'hegemonic master text'.

Introduction

Charles Dickens' *Great Expectations* is undoubtedly the epitome of a literary classic. A student of English literature is sure to find this masterpiece mentioned in any textbook on Victorian fiction: young Pip telling the story of his traumatic childhood darkened by his tyrannical sister and his encounter with the convict in the marshes. The reader witnesses Pip's efforts to leave his marginalised social background behind, observes him developing feelings for the supercilious Estella and learns to see Pip's convict benefactor Magwitch in a certain light – as insinuated by the autodiegetic narrator Pip himself. As the plot unfolds, the reader unawares absorbs the events through the protagonist's lens: Pip emplots his autobiography as the suffering orphan's social rise and his inner growth from egocentrism to altruistically taking responsibility for his patron.[3]

In this paper, two recent rewritings of *Great Expectations* will be analysed with respect to the challenges they present to the 'natural givens' of their pretext. Peter Carey's *Jack Maggs* gives priority to the formerly ostracised convict figure, assigning both protagonist status and the narrator role to the – slightly renamed – Australian outcast Jack Maggs. Dealing with a late

---

[1] Carey's novel will be referred to as *JM* in the following.
[2] The abbreviation *MP* will be used to denote Lloyd Jones' novel in this essay.
[3] Morris (1987) problematises Pip's depiction of his moral character.

twentieth-century war-ridden village's reading of *Great Expectations*, Lloyd Jones' *Mister Pip* – shortlisted for the Booker in 2007 and winner of the Commonwealth Prize in the same year – is about an illiterate setting as incompatible with the fictional world of a Victorian classic as can be. Although these novels are set in different time frames, they both relate to Australia or its immediate geographical vicinity and present a new image of this formerly peripheral colonial place. As a result, these texts are situated in the wider context of the "writing back" paradigm, which was fittingly devised by Australian scholars.[4] Carey and Jones, however, transfer London's importance as the central hub to formerly antipodal places.

This essay will investigate the interplay of form and content and their functions with respect to their shared Dickensian pretext. Furthermore, it deals with the epistemological implications of narrating in regard to the undermining of absolutist claims of storytelling. I will begin with a short survey of what postcolonial narratology has to offer for a fruitful analysis of the texts. In the analytical chapters, I will explain how both texts cite themes from *Great Expectations* and renegotiate central issues of the pretext. I shall look into the question which characters are granted an audible voice and whether there are shifting narrative 'power balances'. I will point out what plot motifs of *Great Expectations* are echoed in the rewritings and in what ways the rearrangement of both character constellation and conception reevaluates Dickens' work. In the final part, I will shift the discussion to another level and ask in what way Carey's and Jones' novels go beyond a mere rewriting, thus questioning the legitimacy of the concept of a literary 'classic' as such.

Postcolonial Narratology

Postcolonial narratology offers a useful theoretical framework for an analysis of what Carey's and Jones' rewritings do with their Dickensian pretext. This approach is productive for my interpretation as it combines the systematic analytical tools of structuralism with more context-concerned variables. Postcolonial narratologists interpret narrative forms as conveyor of semantic implications in that they inform the primarily text-immanent narratological approach with the discernment of postcolonial thought.[5]

Both *Jack Maggs* and *Mister Pip* play with the narrative situation of the pretext. They confer the narrative authority upon the 'colonial other' who thus obtains a hearing. In *Great Expectations,* Pip as the sole narrator deter-

---

[4] Ashcroft, Griffiths and Tiffin (1989).
[5] The idea behind the contextualisation of narratology does not suggest, however, that there is such a thing as *the* theory of postcolonial literature (cf. Birk and Neumann 116).

mines and controls the dominant mode of perception: he monopolises the narrative mediation of what happens in the text, of what he choses to tell and in what ways he depicts the other characters. At the same time, Australia as colonial space only functions as offstage edge of the world and is primarily connoted as the destination of convict transportations. Nevertheless, it also serves as the source of Magwitch's wealth and so as the economic basis of Pip's social rise in England.

Carey's and Jones' rewritings democratise the autodiegetic narrative power by putting further narrators and focalisers alongside the protagonist's voice. A side-effect of this multi-perspective structure is the reinterpretation of the 'imperial view': While Carey emphasises the author's quasi-imperialistic role in shaping his fictional worlds, Jones reads Dickens against the grain by offering a peripheral outlook on the 'imperial' text. Both novels reconstruct the ideologically charged spatial structure of the Victorian classic by a new centre-periphery semanticisation and so reveal it as a carrier of meaning.

Turning Dickens Down Under: *Jack Maggs*

Dickens' *Great Expectations* is the main intertextual reference point for *Jack Maggs*. With the central character constellation of the renamed convict and his protégé, however, Peter Carey retains only the very kernel of the original story and spins new plotlines around it. This parallel pairing must not deceive the readers about the fact that the respective mates Maggs/Magwitch and Henry Phipps/Pip are not the 'same' characters. Carey's figures and their Dickensian models are not even situated on the same narrative level: the reader rather finds himself in the London of 1837 when the ambitious young author Tobias Oates (i.e. the alter-ego of the younger Charles Dickens, who has not yet become 'the bearded eminence', *JM* 325), is in desperate need of inspiration for a new novel. Carey's novel virtually translates the possible genesis of *Great Expectations* into fiction, inserting a new metafictional frame between the historic reality of the author and his fictional work.

It is evident that the fictional world of *Jack Maggs* differs essentially from Dickens' creation. Carey not only discards the story line featuring Estella, Miss Havisham and Mr Jaggers. In his rewriting, the remaining acquaintances also have gone through a personality change. Comparing the two books, the sophisticated reader becomes immediately aware that the character constellation itself is rewritten. The convict and his protégé have changed places with respect to the allocation of sympathy and central character traits.

Unlike Dickens' Magwitch, who after his return yields passively to Pip's and Herbert's plans for him, Carey's Maggs actively pursues his aims. He controls the spatial movements and virtually abducts the author to help him search for Phipps in the country. Apart from Maggs' new drive, this convict is a complex character who is psychologically much more convincing than Dickens' Magwitch.[6] He is depicted as an attractive man with an obvious sex appeal for other figures. The character Mercy Larkin as well as his homosexual fellow footman Constable delevop a crush on him. Furthermore, in his apologetic autobiographical account Maggs emphasises that he wants Phipps to like him. The convict understands that his protégé was "frightened to hear Jack Maggs was finally on his way into your polite and educated life" and tries to explain how his criminal career started when he was forced by his foster mother to work as a child thief.[7] He proves to be a delinquent with a very humane side when he vividly outlines the memories of his first love and fellow thief Sophina who was sentenced to death – a loss he was never able to recover from.

Phipps, on the other hand, is a handsome but cowardly and ungrateful young man. Pip's weak twin does not share his fictional ancestor's generosity in helping his returned benefactor but sneaks off when Maggs lands in England and waits according to his own phrasing "like a rabbit hiding in its hole" (*JM* 267). The character of Phipps does not enter the stage until the very end of the book – similar to Magwitch's late reappearance in *Great Expectations*. The convict is a multi-dimensional enigmatic personality, whereas the adolescent Phipps is a worthless spendthrift totally lacking Pip's moral sense. In a dramatic showdown, Phipps even attempts to kill his benefactor to get rid of his unwelcome guest.

In *Jack Maggs,* new female characters enter the stage. Most prominent among these is Mercy, a maid servant. Despite her low social rank, Mercy functions as one of the several narrators telling Jack about her sad story: after the social demise of her family and her father's suicide she briefly works as a child prostitute before she is 'saved' by Mr Buckle, who makes her his mistress.[8] Along with Mercy, women's plight and the servant's perspective are

---

[6] See Meinig 118: "the omniscient narrator of *JM* endows the convict figure with a potential for power and development which is unthinkable in the fixed narrative set-up of *Great Expectations* with its dominating first-person narrator". On the other hand, Renk rightly points out that in the cast of the minor characters, Carey creates characters "as Dickens would with exaggerated, singular characteristics" as the "humble" Percy Buckle and the Fagin-like character of Silas (Renk 62).

[7] This demimonde-motif and the depiction of the back lanes of London implies that *Great Expectations* is not the only pretext. Generally speaking, the whole body of Dickens' oeuvre functions as pretext for *JM*, especially *Oliver Twist*.

[8] Mercy has an intertextual model of her own whom she wants to emulate: she reads Richardson's *Pamela* (1740) hoping "that she, like Pamela, might one day be mistress of the house wherein she had been called to serve" (151). Unlike Pamela, of course, Mercy yields to her master's sexual desire to achieve this end.

introduced into the novel: the atrocities which were part of female Victorian working class biographies – (child) prostitution, abortions[9] and exploitation – are not passed over. The more realistic and inclusive treatment of these themes goes along with a new representation of female characters as opposed to Dickens' rather stereotypical rendering of women: while "a series of evil and unnatural dominatrices – Miss Havisham, Mrs Joe, and Magwitch's wild mistress" (Mukherjee 114) feature in *Great Expectations*, Carey reinvents the gender roles when he grants Mercy a new role pointing beyond the traditional 'helpmate' – which is impressively underlined by Mercy's saving Jack Maggs' life and her losing a finger in the attempt (cf. *JM* 327). Interestingly enough, it is this 'fallen' woman who actively courts Maggs and eventually becomes his wife, thereby bringing about a change for the better in the convict's life and finally managing her own social rise down under: although Jack Maggs stubbornly claims that he would "rather be a bad smell here than a frigging rose in New South Wales" (*JM* 230), Mercy fosters his eventual "self-liberation from a dominating and discriminatory English frame of mind" (Meinig 122). Maggs comes to realise that neither England, which he has idealised in retrospect, nor his self-bred English gentleman are idols worth striving – or risking one's life – for.

With this variation of Dickens' closure Carey reserves the happy ending for the outcast Maggs and his anti-'Angel in the House' wife – accordingly "claiming the story as an originary Australian narrative" (Hassall 128). The exconvict becomes a happy and well-off patriarch with a growing family in Australia. In this paradisiacal setting, Jack Maggs had already grown rich and acquired gentleman status before his return.[10] Having been "twice president of the shire" (*JM* 327), Maggs finally dies a peaceful death – unlike Oates fictional plans for him to die at the stake.

> The first chapters [of Oates' novel] did not appear until 1860, that is, three years after the real Jack Maggs had died, not in the blaze of fire Tobias had always planned for him, but in a musty high-ceilinged bedroom above the flood-brown Manning River. Here, with his weeping sons and daughters crowded round his bed, the old convict met death without ever having read 'That Book'. (*JM* 328)

In England, however, neither such a cosy family idyll nor social mobility seem to be possible. Rather, the English characters are only granted quite

---

[9] Both Sophina's baby and the child Tobias Oates fathers in the adulterous relationship with his sister-in-law are aborted.

[10] "I am a vermin who made ten thousand pounds from mucky clay. I have a grand house in Sydney town. There is a street named for me, or was when I sailed. I keep a coach, and two footmen. I am Mr Jack Maggs Esquire, and I left all that so I might end up here today." (*JM* 280)

horrid prospects towards the end of the book: Tobias Oates' marriage is on the rocks after he has commited adultery with his wife's sister (who dies in the attempt of aborting their baby). The effeminate Pip ends up as a soldier after he has broken with Maggs. Both Phipps and Oates struggle to retain their social status and to cope with their precarious finances. While Phipps' genteel lifestyle is built on the shaky grounds of Maggs' money, the author struggles to provide for the respectable life he "invented [...] for himself" (*JM* 182). The notion of what a gentleman embodies, which is of course of central importance in *Great Expectations,* is a shifting concept in *Jack Maggs.* Offering multiple versions of the gentleman in the form of the grocer would-be gentleman Buckle, who inherits the financial means to enjoy a leisured life, the ambitious young author Oates and the debauched Phipps, the book at the same time deconstructs the gentleman ideal (cf. Meinig 117). Ironically enough, it is the convict who comes closest to being a gentleman in the end – albeit not an English one.

It is not least because he is a central narrator in *Jack Maggs* that the convict appears in a more positive light. As autodiegetic chronicler offering an expiatory account of the hardships he endured, he assumes the narrative authority Pip exerted in the pretext (cf. Thieme 109). The reader is invited to share the convict's memories of *his* traumatic childhood. In this novel, the 'colonial other' is given the opportunity to take control of his story. Sitting at the absent Phipps' desk (which is reminiscent of the character Susan Barton sitting at Daniel Defoe's desk in Coetzee's *Foe*), Maggs writes an epistolary memoir of his childhood and adolescence with Henry Phipps as addressee since he "cannot bear him to think me a common criminal" (*JM* 228). Maggs' narration occupies a considerable part of the novel. At any rate, his narration is much longer than Magwitch's oral account at the end of the second volume in *Great Expectations*. In his letters, Maggs explains that he is writing "a different type of story, by which I mean – mine own" (*JM* 74). The distinct nature of his tale – which is, in fact, a counter-discourse to the pretext, is illustrated by the fact that he uses invisible ink and writes from right to left. Maggs sends Phipps a lemon and a mirror to decipher the message. Thieme compares Maggs' way of writing to that of a Chinaman and argues that the convict hereby reverses Western norms "which is arguably necessary for the expression of subaltern utterance" (Thieme 115).

The discursive transmission in *Jack Maggs* contrasts with *Great Expectation's* narrative situation. In Carey's novel, a whole set of narrators tell diverse stories: the frame narrative set in 1837 is told by a heterodiegetic narrator, who often delegates his authority to the individual perspectives of several focalisers. The heterodiegetic narrative frame is also interspersed with Mercy's drastic autobiographical account, Maggs' longish letters to his foster son and Oates' first drafts for his novel project "The Death of Maggs". The polyphonic perspective structure of this "narrative hybrid" (Savu 129) results in competing and complementary accounts of central events. The reader is presented with a whole mosaic of narratives as opposed to the unitary storyline of *Great Expectations*. The fact that these segments are not necessarily given in chronological order increases the tension and provides unforeseen twists. The multiperspectival structure also produces sympathetic (self-)portraits of several characters. As a result, the novel gives lenient description of the antagonists Oates and Maggs.

While the novel, technically speaking, is written in a realistic style, the conglomeration of stories and different perspectives indirectly comments upon the novel's own fictional status and hence adds an implicit metafictional level to the text.[11] Furthermore, the Victorian author Tobias Oates' appearance in the fictional world generates an implicit autoreferential level: when introducing the author (or at least his fictional doppelgänger) as a character within the text, Carey adds a genuine postmodern feature by foregrounding the textual nature of literature and the production process of literary works – including great English novels. It is of crucial importance, however, that the author does not make his appearance as the celebrity Dickens has become for posterity. Rather we meet a struggling young father and husband in dire straights (the author here has not yet become "the bearded eminence", *JM* 325). In this way, Carey implicitly controverts the romantic concept of the ingenious author. *Jack Maggs* thus challenges the readers' notions "about how 'great' English novels are written" (Meinig 115).

The iconoclast portrait of the author Tobias Oates and his lack of inspiration emphasise that literature is not only generated through the muse's kiss but that its creation is mostly determined by coincidence and subjectivity (cf. Meinig 139) and pecuniary needs which become evident when the author sells the copyright even before he has written a single sentence of the novel. In *Jack Maggs* it is no longer the convict who embodies the abject criminal: rather, the author appears to be the real thief. When Tobias Oates realises that Maggs suffers from a tick doloreux, he quickly grasps that he might exploit this man's obviously interesting past as a goldmine for his new novel project. However, he does not ask for Maggs' consent but decides to extract under hypnosis from the convict's mind what is useful for his fictional purposes. The author turns the convict's biography into a romantic tale:

---

[11] See also Meinig 122, who queries *Jack Maggs*' metafictional quality but argues that the text "fulfils the cognitive function of stirring epistemological and poetological thought. The novel problematizes particularly the question of stories, versions, histories, and their condensation into 'story' or 'history'".

> He soon had himself immersed deep in the details of Jack Maggs' birth. He had learned, by medium of his magnets, that the infant Maggs had been thrown off London Bridge. Now he began to play with the notion that the convict was [...] a bastard son of noble parents. (*JM* 206)

Oates does not even shrink from writing his version of the convict's life while they are travelling together and "the subject of his tale [is] seated staring at him" (*JM* 223). When Maggs realises the extent of Oates' invasion into his private sphere, he violently fights against becoming a character in Oates' work. Their quarrel almost culminates in the 'death of the author'.

> Maggs took the dagger in his right hand and he placed his left arm tight around the other's [the author's] chest.
> "You're a thief," said he quietly. "A damned little thief." [...] "Don't kill me, Jack." [...] "You stole my Sophina, you bastard." [...]
> "You read my note book, Jack? You read my chapter, is that it?"
> "Oh, you wrote a chapter did you? With my name in it?"
> "It is a memorial I am making. Your Sophina will live for ever." [...]
> "You are planning to kill me, I know that. Is that what you mean by painful? To burn me alive?"
> "Not you, Jack, a character who bears your name. I will change the name sooner or later."
> "You are just a character to me too, Toby." [...] (*JM* 279)

Even if Maggs indisputably remains a law-breaker, this character appears almost to be tender-hearted and "as more sinned against than sinning" (Savu 142) through the psychological realism of his letters. On the other hand, Tobias Oates is a rather dubious character: apart from his cheating on Maggs, he commits adultery and is indirectly guilty of both his sister-in-law's and the butler's deaths. Giving priority to his professional success over the personal dignity of others, Oates is demonised as one of "the worst megalomaniacs of all, controlling their self-created fictional worlds and characters in a quasi-colonial exercise of authority" (Thieme 114).

Mister Pip

Unlike *Jack Maggs*, which to a large extent maintains the spatio-temporal scene of the pretext, both setting and plot of *Mister Pip* are totally removed from the context of the original. Lloyd Jones' novel is situated near Australia in Bougainville on the Solomon Islands. The plot is set in the early 1990s, when the teenage narrator Matilda's almost prelapsarian island[12] world turns into hell as it is upset by a brutal civil war.

Mister Pip's intertextual relations with *Great Expectations* are marked intratextually. The most prominent aspect here is the fact that the book as material item plays a crucial role when its sudden disappearance causes catastrophic consequences.[13] Furthermore, the heroine Matilda finds numerous parallels between her own life and Pip's tale. She finds hope in the Victorian orphan's story about the promise of a better life. Pip's socially marginalised background finds a strong echo in the heroine's secluded island life. Using Dickens' character as an escapist identificatory foil in her search for identity, the imaginative adolescent protagonist relates to Pip's character when she imagines to "hear Estella" (114) in her mother's scolding or remembers Pip's approaching Satis' House when she visits her teacher's home (*JM* 115).[14]

Just as the character constellation in *Mister Pip* is only slightly reminiscent of the pretext, the thematic dichotomies dealt with in the novel represent modern variations of the Victorian pretext: for example, the binary opposition of town and country, which is of major importance in the Dickensian text, translates into the tensions between the local islanders and their relatives who have emigrated to the mainland. Accordingly, the notion of being white or participating in Western culture (*JM* 130) replaces Dickens' motif of Pip's striving to become a gentleman. Matilda puts down the failure of her parents' marriage to her father's yielding to the lure of Western life after he left the island to seek work in Australia: "This is one of the reasons why my mum refused to move from the village. She did not want to move to Arawa to see my father turn into a white man" (*MP* 130). The islanders have almost no contact with the Western world. When Matilda finally escapes the chaos of war to live with her father, she realises that he effectively left his origin behind:

---

[12] See *MP* 12: "Bougainville is one of the most fertile places on earth. Drop a seed in the soil and three months later it is a plant with shiny green leaves. Another three months and you are picking its fruit."
[13] Nevertheless, the text should not be read as a fictionalisation of Samuel Huntington's 'clash of cultures'.
[14] See *MP* 21 (both Matilda and Pip don't really know their fathers), 49 (Matilda becomes aware of similarities between Mum and Miss Havisham "who cannot move on from the day of her greatest disappointment"); 126 (the children worry that Mr Watts "would not come out of his house again [...] like Miss Havisham" after his wife's death); 131 (Matilda uses Dickens' England "as a guide" to imagine her father's life in Australia); 196 (for Matilda and Pip "there is no going back" to their old lives, both feel ashamed when thinking of home).

> A black man is easily spotted in Townsville, especially at the airport, and there he stood in the door of the terminal, waving both arms, his face one big shining smile. [...] His transformation into a white man was near complete. He wore shorts, and boots that rose no higher than his ankles. A white shirt did little to hide his bulging stomach. (*JM* 192)

In an intriguing inversion, being white and being English represent 'the other' in this text while 'being normal' connotes black.[15] Matilda recounts that her ancestors thought "they were looking at ghosts or maybe some people who had just fallen into bad luck" on their first encounter with Europeans. Even the dogs "opened their jaws to await the spectacle" (4) of arriving Englishmen. The spatial dimension also shows a different semantics with the reversal of the antipodean quality: when the teacher Mr Watts speaks of England the pupils feel he "might as well have said the moon" (*MP* 24). At the same time, the children struggle to come to terms with Dickens' language. The children also have no idea whatsoever of the concept of a distant 'metropolis' or 'London' (*MP* 73). They have difficulties with several English signifiers which virtually have no signified counterpart in their insular world.[16] The pupils have a hard time translating these foreign concepts into their world knowledge.

With Mr Watts being the only white character on Matilda's island, the West is represented through a one-man white diaspora.[17] Married to an indigenous woman, Mr Watts appears as a special case of a go-between. According to the teacher himself, being white in these surroundings feels a "bit of what the last mammoth must have felt, I suppose. Lonely at times" (*MP* 81). Mr Watts is a rather queer bird: he is a deplorable eccentric suffering from an unknown stroke of fate. He is dressed in the same white linen suit every day and does not object to his nickname Pop-Eye. He is notorious for wearing a clown's red nose and pulling his mad wife through the village on a trolley.

Although the teacher declares that he wants his classroom "to be a place of light" (*MP* 14), he does not embody Western cultural imperialism. Mr Watts is far from following in the footsteps of "benign white men bringing enlightenment to young indigenes" (Reid); nor are his pupils "passive receptors of imposed cultures" (Reid). Ironically enough, Mr Watts is a rather helpless teacher since his comprehension of Western science and intellectual

---

[15] When Mr Watts asks the children how it feels to be black they shrug their shoulders and answer that they believe it is "normal" (*MP* 81).

[16] Mr Watts' pupils have no idea what marshes, wittles and leg irons are (*MP* 21), what a rimy or a frosty morning (*MP* 29), a lawyer or a benefactor (*MP* 45) could mean.

[17] This could be read as an ironic mirroring of the depiction of an individual black character representing the 'other' in the traditional canon of Western literature, most famously of course in Defoe's *Robinson Crusoe* (1719).

history is quite incomplete and he fails to justify its importance to his pupils.[18] The teacher also has large gaps in local cultural knowledge which he compensates by inviting adult natives to instruct his pupils. As a result, "[i]ndigenous values are more robust and meaningful than the sparring at first suggests" (Reid). Without condescension he listens to magical beliefs, hunting instructions and information about the local flora and fauna. Despite Mr Watts' efforts to integrate the adults in his pedagogy, there are conspicuous feelings of inferiority among the uneducated parent generation. They do not approve of the kind of lessons Mr Watts offers as they do not see any value in reading a Victorian classic.[19] The fact that the children become acquainted with Western Literature and share some knowledge about Dickens (although their education remains as sketchy and superficial as can be) distinguishes them from their parents.[20]

Through these parental visits in class, Matilda's god-fearing mother Dolores becomes the antagonist of the rather secular Watts (*MP* 66). With a peripheral female preaching to a basically atheist Englishman, the hackneyed cliché of Christian missionary and heathen natives is given an ironic twist. Dolores abhors Matilda's fascination with literary worlds – and Mr Watts as their messenger.[21] Matilda's mother disapproves of merely reading a text and argues for a didactic function of story-telling: "Stories have a job to do. They can't just lie around like lazybone dogs. They have to teach you something" (*MP* 74). She has no sympathy for the "make-believe person" Pip, who for Matilda has more meaning than the line of her ancestors,[22] which according to her mother also comprises fish and birds. It is evident that both women cling to different narratives they draw meaning from. While Matilda's mother criticises Matilda for befriending a fictional character, the women quarrel over the ontological status of the devil, who, according to Matilda, is still more unreal than Pip because one cannot hear his voice (*MP* 77f.). Unlike her

---

[18] "He knew the word 'chemistry' but could not tell us much more than that. He handed on the names of famous people such as Darwin, Einstein, Plato, Archimedes, Aristotle. We wondered if he was making them up because he struggled to explain why they were famous or why we had to know them." (*MP* 24)

[19] Initially, the islanders hope that Mr Dickens – to whom the new teacher wants to introduce the kids – could help them fix their generator or bring anti-malaria tablets, aspirin, fuel, beer or candles (*MP* 17).

[20] "Although she didn't say so, I knew she thought I was showing off and that I was biting off a bigger piece of the world than she could handle with language [...]. She didn't want to encourage me by asking questions. She didn't want me to go deeper into that other world" (*MP* 30).

[21] Matilda concludes that "[s]he could not see what us kids had come to see: a kind man" (*MP* 41).

[22] "Well, no, Pip wasn't a relative, I explained, but I felt closer to him than the names of those strangers she made me write in the sand" (*MP* 66).

mother, who sticks to her traditional normative ideas of the narrative functions and abhors Dickens' "fancy nancy English talk" (*MP* 195), Matilda has begun to receive and interpret stories according to Western aesthetics – a development Dolores dreads.[23]

Mister Pip is characterised by a plurality of stories and narrators. In Spivak's terms, as a woman and as the colonial 'other', Matilda lives in fact a doubly subaltern life.[24] Nevertheless, she – contrary to Spivak's prediction – finally does speak and creates a 'narrated self': Matilda is the narrator of the frame plot. Like Pip, she tells her story retrospectively as an autodiegetic narrator. The narrator Matilda moulds her experiences into a female Bildungsroman which becomes an effective means of identity formation. The more sophisticated she gets, however, the more she comes to question her teenage idolisation of *Great Expectations*.

The process of Matilda's disillusionment with Mr Watts and his favourite text is accompanied by her discovery that there are a plurality of versions of *Great Expectations*. Mr Watts' class gets in touch with Dickens' text via their teacher's reading of the text aloud. Matilda comes to realise that Mr Watts has only read from a simplified children's version when she finds another copy in the school library which is a full-length version.

> On my second day I went to the school library to see if it had *Great Expectations*. [...] It was a hardback. [...] It was more wordy than I remembered. Much more wordy, and more difficult. But for the names I recognised on the pages I might have been reading a different book. Then an unpleasant truth dawned on me. Mr Watts had read a different version to us kids. A simpler version. He'd stuck to the bare bones of *Great Expectations*, and he'd straightened out sentences, adlibbed in fact, to help us to arrive at a more definite place in our heads. Mr Watts had rewritten Mr Dickens' masterwork. (*MP* 193)

Mr Watts does not only 'rewrite' the novel when using it during his lessons. When the allied rebels occupy the village, Mr Watts entertains the village with a collage of autobiographical elements and motifs from *Great Expectations* – with only his class being aware of the Dickensian influence. Interestingly enough, the teacher introduces himself as Pip. As a consequence, the limits of fiction and real life become indistinct. Still, this "Pacific version of *Great Expectations*" comes down to a defamiliarisation of Dickens tailor-made for the horizon of the jungle fighter's world knowledge – especially because he enriches his account with his pupils' and their parents' oral con-

---

[23] "Although she didn't say so I knew she thought I was showing off and that I was biting off a bigger piece of the world than she could handle with language [...]. She didn't want to encourage me by asking questions. She didn't want me to go deeper into that other world" (*MP* 30).

[24] Spivak 1988.

tributions in class. An additional filter alienating the listeners from the Dickensian original is the fact that Matilda has to translate his narration for the rebels who speak only the island's vernacular.

The textual contours of *Great Expectations* dissolve even more rapidly after the only copy is finally lost in the political turmoil. The text becomes a plaything in the minds of its recipients when Mr Watts encourages his class to reconstruct the text from their memories. The children quickly realise that they are not able to retrieve all the words but rather create a new piece of art by telling the story with their 'voice' – a new version of the text tinged with Pacific colours emerges.

> Mr Watts announced a special task. We would retrieve *Great Expectations*. Some of us were not sure what Mr Watts meant by the word 'retrieve'. Then when it became clear – thanks to Daniel's question – we still wondered if we understood. *Great Expectations* had gone up in flames and could not be retrieved from the ashes. [...] Mr Watts instructed us to dream freely. We did not have to remember the story in any order or even as it really happened, but as it came to us. [...] "We need words, Matilda, We need to remember what Estella actually says to Pip." [...] As he said this he appeared overtaken by a separate thought. "However, if we can get the gist of what is meant, that will be something, at least." [...] Gist. This needed explaining. Mr Watts put it this way. "If I say tree, I will think English oak, you will think palm tree. They are both trees. A palm and an oak successfully describe what a tree is, but there are different trees." So this is what gist means. We could fill the gaps with our own worlds. (107ff.)

Matilda realises that the class' attempt to retrieve Pip's story was doomed from the very beginning when she comes across the 'real' book. Her own autobiographical narrative eventually proves to be a much more effective rewriting. Matilda detaches herself more and more from her fascination with *Great Expectations* as her educational horizon widens. Having finished her university degree, the protagonist decides to do a thesis on Dickens only to finally unmask her former idol as deficient in providing guidance and orientation: "They love his [Dickens'] characters. Well, something has changed in me. As I have grown older I have fallen out of love with his characters. They are too loud, they are grotesques" (*MP* 217). The protagonist manages to channel her enthusiasm for Dickens into a catalyst for writing her own story. She finally puts her scholarly paper aside and begins her own narrative: *Mister Pip* here becomes a 'self-begetting novel' when Matilda describes how she came to write down its first sentence in an attempt to process her traumatic experiences and fight her growing depression (*MP* 216).

The existence of numerous parallel, competing and floating stories in *Mister Pip* evokes a metafictional semantic level: the novel plays with the poststructuralist realisation of the instability of textual meaning. Initially, Matilda deplores the fact that "the trouble with *Great Expectations* is that it's a one-way conversation. There's no talking back" (39). In reality, however, the story's content is continuously altered by its reading and listening audiences. In *Mister Pip,* this indeterminacy is carried to an extreme when there is no longer such a thing as the text as concrete physical item and fixed set of words: after the loss of the only copy Mr Watts' class generates a totally different 'retelling'. With Mr Watts mixing up some plot motifs into his autobiographical account, the text really disintegrates into a 'verbal fluid' which changes its form all the time. In the island's dominantly oral culture and therefore non-European aesthetics, it is no longer the tale which is important. The teller is of particular standing here as mediating negotiator of content and form.

Just as Pip does, the grown-up Matilda undergoes a process of disillusionment after she finally arrives in London. Unlike her fictional friend, however, she decides to find her way home: "Pip was my story, even if I was once a girl, and my face black as the shining night. Pip is my story, and in the next day I would try where Pip had failed. I would try to return home" (219). Eventually, the periphery-centre dialectic loses its grip for the protagonist after she has managed to venture into the capital: having once reached the centre, she is able to chose to return.

Conclusion

The implementation of postcolonial narratology is a fruitful concept for the analysis of the structural relations of intertext and pretext: rewritings direct the attention to the perspective structure of the original and its implict value system. Both Carey's and Jones' novel acknowledge *Great Expectations* as an outstanding literary reference text to which they respond "[c]ritiquing the imperial mindset of the writer" (Renk 69).[25] The texts point to the semantic and hidden ideological tenets of the pretext. At the same time, both rewritings create a new semantics for the spatial structure offering a literary re-mapping of the centre-periphery dichotomy. Both Maggs and Matilda have to free themselves from their fixation on London as a place of longing. Furthermore, these texts go beyond Dickens' point of departure by providing a narrative platform for formerly marginalised perspectives and they playfully discard traditional clichés.

In *Jack Maggs* and *Mister Pip* different techniques are used for a renegotiation of the pretext. Carey's novel only implicitly plays with the pretext in a way that is merely visible for an extradiegetic observer. The characters are not aware of the intertextual nature of their fictional world. In this "postmod-

---

[25] For a differentiated discussion of Dickens' reception in colonial studies see Thieme 104-107.

ern pastiche" (Thieme 112), Carey does not make use of experimental stylistic devices.²⁶ Rather, he transfers twentieth-century epistemological tenets and thematic foci on a realistically transmitted nineteenth-century setting and closed ending.²⁷ *Jack Maggs* thus gives a tongue-in-cheek rewriting of Dickensian plot kernels under the auspices of postmodernist views on the bygone epoch.

Reshifting the focus on the ostracised convict figure and proffering biographical details in the autodiegetic epistolary form, Carey invites the reader to commiserate with his sympathetic rendering of Phipps' benefactor. Conversely, the young beneficiary is not more than a helpless minor character who makes his appearance only in a negligible part of the narrative. The voices of the 'other' resound in the form of rounder characters with a working-class background. The Victorian novel – which as such is also Carey's intertext – ²⁸ would not regard this class in their own right but only as accessory to the bourgeoisie. Furthermore, the spatio-semantic connex differs from the Dickensian pretext in that it sketches Australia not only as abstract projection of a hellish destination of convict transports. Instead, it appears as the promised land where the ex-convict Maggs and the 'fallen' woman Mercy belong to the dignitaries and and are granted private bliss. Australia thus no longer functions merely as a literary backstage in relation to the mother country.

Jones explicitly touches upon the reception of peripheral readers of the Victorian classic *Great Expectations*. At first, *Mister Pip* seems to take an affirmative approach towards the intertextual pretext with the protagonist Matilda using *Great Expectations* as an identificatory text.²⁹ Finally however, the doubly subaltern female protagonist Matilda gradually emancipates herself from Dickens as she more and more comes to question his narrative.

---

[26] Like David Lodge's university novels, the book is also a good read for a less sophisticated reader who is unaware of the intertextual allusion. Nevertheless, Savu is right when arguing that the novel "relies on the reader's familiarity with both Dickens' *Great Expectations* and some key events from his biography" (144).

[27] This structural device is reminiscent of John Fowles' *The French Lieutenant's Woman* (1969) except for the latter's explicitly breaking through the fictional illusion.

[28] See Meinig 116: "Interestingly, intertextuality in *JM* thus links a fictional with a non-fictional intertext [...]. The fictional intertext *Great Expectations* is evoked by the relationship between Maggs and Phipps, while the biographical, non-fictional context of Dickens's life and work is represented by Tobias Oates and his environment, in particular his wife, sister-in-law, and son. The Victorian age and culture can be seen as a third, cultural intertext taken up and subverted in the novel, for example in the female character Mercy with regard to the role of women or in the description of the 'hellish' side of London."

[29] "As we progressed through the book something happened to me. At some point I felt myself enter the story. I hadn't been assigned a part – nothing like that; I wasn't identifiable on the page, but I was there, I was definitely there. I knew that orphaned white kid [...]" (40).

Lloyd Jones' characters stand for readers who apparently were not even taken into account as a contingency when Dickens wrote his masterpiece. In a final twist, Dickens' text comes virtually face to face with this recipient from the outer edge. When visiting a Dickens museum in England, Matilda fixes her gaze on a dummy representing Miss Havisham:

> The tour ended back at Eastgate House. I followed the others up the stairs, and there I encountered Miss Havisham in her white wedding gown. She was stuck behind glass, her back turned to us sightseers. There for all eternity, I wished she could turn, just for half an instant, to find a black woman staring at her. (*MP* 218)

Mister Pip deals with the potential incompatibility between eurocentric aesthetics and the antipodean space, questioning the notion of the inferior nature of the latter's literary traditions. The English classic here does not necessarily function as the awe-inspiring cultural authority. In this context, the text's presence rather causes friction and leads to drastic conflicts.

Jack Maggs and *Mister Pip* challenge the validity of the concept of the literary classic as such – albeit in different ways. Carey and Jones go beyond the normal scope of an affirmative, neutral or critical analysis of the model book. These texts run through problematic aspects of the notion of the (space and) timeless masterpiece with the example of *Great Expectations,* which Mr Watts speaks of as "the greatest novel by the greatest English writer" (*MP* 18). Like Coetzee's *Foe*, *Jack Maggs* sheds light on the production of a literary piece of art, the selection of plot motifs and narrative perspectives, thus revealing the artificiality in the exclusive concept of the literary classic – which may have come into being due to coincidental events (Carey) or is only spatially restricted in its appeal and comprehensibility (Jones). In this sense, these rewritings of *Great Expectations* "are also unwritings" (Mukherjee 130).

Works Cited

Ashcroft, Bill, Gareth Griffiths and Helen Tiffin. *The Empire Writes Back: Theory and Practice in Post-Colonial Literatures.* London: Routledge, 1989.
Birk, Hanne and Birgit Neumann. "*Go-between*: Postkoloniale Erzähltheorie." *Neue Ansätze in der Erzähltheorie*. Eds Ansgar und Vera Nünning. Trier: WVT, 2002. 115-152.
Carey, Peter. *Jack Maggs*. 1997. London: Faber and Faber, 1998.
Clayton, Jay. *Charles Dickens in Cyberspace: The Afterlife of the Nineteenth Century in Postmodern Culture*. Oxford: OUP, 2003.

Dickens, Charles. *Great Expectations*. 1861. Ed. Margaret Cardwell. Oxford: OUP, 1998.
Hassall, Anthony J. "A Tale of Two Countries: *Jack Maggs* and Peter Carey's Fiction." *Australian Literary Studies* 18.2 (1997): 128-35.
Herwig, Henriette. "Literaturwissenschaftliche Intertextualitätsforschung im Spannungsfeld konkurrierender Intertextualitätsbegriffe." *Zeitschrift für Semiotik* 24 (2002): 163-76.
Jones, Lloyd. *Mister Pip*. 2006. London: John Murray, 2007.
Laing, Olivia. "Pip Pip." *The Guardian* 7 July 2007. 8 Dec 2008 <http://www.guardian.co.uk/books/2007/jul/07/featuresreviews.guardianreview21/print>.
Meinig, Sigrun. *Witnessing the Past: History and Post-Colonialism in Australian Historical Novels*. Tübingen: Gunter Narr, 2004.
Morris, Christopher D. "The Bad Faith of Pip's Bad Faith: Deconstructing *Great Expectations*." *Journal of English Literary History* 54 (1987): 941-53.
Mukherjee, Ankhi. "Missed Encounters: Repetition, Rewriting, and Contemporary Returns to Charles Dickens's *Great Expectations*." *Contemporary Literature* XLVI.1 (2005): 108-33.
Reid, Nicholas. "Island in the Sun." *New Zealand Listener* 7-13 Oct 2006. 8 Dec 2008 <http://www.listener.co.nz/issue/3465/artsbooks/7177/island_in_the_sun_.html> 2008>.
Renk, Kathleen J. "Rewriting the Empire of the Imagination: The Post-Imperial Gothic Fiction of Peter Carey and A.S. Byatt." *Journal of Commonwealth Literature* 46.1 (2005): 108-33.
Savu, Laura E. "The 'Crooked' Business of Storytelling: Authorship and Cultural Revisionism in Peter Carey's *Jack Maggs*." *ARIEL. A Review of International English Literature* 36 (2005): 127-63.
Spivak, Gayatri C. "Can the Subaltern Speak?" 1988. *Colonial Discourse and Post-Colonial Theory*. Eds Laura Chrisman and Patrick Williams. New York: Harvester Wheatsheaf, 1993. 66-111.
Thieme, John. *Postcolonial Con-Texts: Writing back to the Canon*. London: Continuum, 2001.

Sarah Säckel

What's in a Wodehouse?
(Non-) Subversive Shakespearean Intertextualities in P.G. Wodehouse's *Jeeves and Wooster* Novels

P.G. Wodehouse's use of intertextual references in his popular comic novels achieves several effects. Most quotations from canonised texts create incongruous, humorous dialogues and scenes. Frequent repetitions of the same quoted material turn it into a part of the 'Wooster world', achieve a certain 'monologic closedness' and heighten the effect of readerly immersion. On the other hand, the intertexts also open up the novels to an intertextual dialogue which triggers comparative readings. The usage of mainly English intertexts, however, creates a 'monocultural' dialogue which emphasises the texts' portrayal of 'Englishness' and 'English humour'. The intertextual references thus work as pillars of English cultural memory; pillars on which the *Jeeves and Wooster* novels' reception itself is built. This paper shall concentrate on the predominating intertextual dialogue between P.G. Wodehouse's *Jeeves and Wooster* novels and a selection of William Shakespeare's plays.

Introduction and Theoretical Approach

What's in a Wodehouse? – Shakespeare and much more. Various forms of intertextual reference such as allusion, imitation, rewriting, parody and quotation abound in P.G. Wodehouse's comic *Jeeves and Wooster*[1] novels. Possibly one of the most quoted sentences in secondary texts concerned with the analysis of P.G. Wodehouse's comic novels is the following statement in which the author describes his style:

> I believe there are two ways of writing novels. One is mine, making a sort of musical comedy without music and ignoring real life altogether; the other is going right deep down into life and not caring a damn.[2]

---

[1] None of the novels is actually called *Jeeves and Wooster*. I chose this umbrella term for the series of novels, which is in fact the title of the successful BBC *Jeeves and Wooster* comedy series starring Stephen Fry and Hugh Laurie.

[2] As mentioned above, these words are quoted frequently, e.g. in the blurb to all Penguin editions (cf. *Jeeves and the Feudal Spirit*, n.p.) and in Mooneyham (119), which shows that the novels were not only produced, but are also read as musical comedies. According to Robert Kiernan "the three-act economy of musical comedy shaped Wodehouse's sense of narrative development" (Kiernan 99) and his "characters [...] correspond to stock types of the musical stage" (Kiernan 99).

This describes both his anti-intellectual and critical attitude towards modernist writing and emphasises that the novels, which are written in a realist mode, are in fact very fictitious intertextual and intermedial creations. Thompson aptly describes his plots as a combination of the "Holmesian detective-story structure with an inverted romance plot" (Thompson 159). This description, however, mainly scratches the surface of Wodehouse's multifaceted and numerous uses of intertextual quotation, allusion and rewriting. The novels' protagonists Bertram Wilberforce Wooster, the narrator, and his personal gentleman's gentleman, Reginald Jeeves, can be linked to many literary predecessors. Bertie Wooster's quixotic reading of detective fiction often worsens the 'scratch he is in' and necessitates a solution from Jeeves, who is a mixture of the clever servant from Greek and Roman comedy, the classic detective and Dickens' Sam Weller (cf. Mooneyham 124). Being Bertie's intellectual superior, the presentation of Jeeves inverts social class prejudices but can also be linked to a long tradition of clever servants (cf. Smith 206, Frye 173). Whereas Bertie Wooster's favourite readings are detective and ghost stories, Jeeves reads Spinoza, Marc Aurelius and, of course, Shakespeare and his language is infused with quotations from these authors and philosophers. Bertie Wooster, on the other hand, learns these quotations from Jeeves and frequently takes them as Jeeves' own words, as in the following example, which is a quotation from Shakespeare's historical play *Julius Caesar* (Act 4.3.217-220):

> "Yes, sir. There is a tide in the affairs of men which, taken at the flood, leads on to fortune. Omitted, all the voyage of their life is bound in shallows and in miseries." "Oh, rather. Quite. No argument about that. But –" (*Joy in the Morning* 174f.)

Numerous canonical and popular texts, biblical quotations, English proverbs, idioms and songs are rewritten in a similar way. Wooster for example refers to himself as "a pretty good silver-lining spotter" (*Joy in the Morning* 181) and Dame Daphne Winkworth's entrance is narrated by Bertie Wooster as follows: "[h]er eye, swivelling round, stopped me like a bullet. The Wedding Guest, if you remember, had the same trouble with the Ancient Mariner" (*The Mating Season* 185). The intertexts are taken from so many diverse texts that for Thompson Wodehouse "does not parody any one particular literary work; he parodies nineteenth-century literature itself" (Thompson 5).

In this paper I shall argue, though, that besides its element of parody, P.G. Wodehouse's use of intertextual references achieves several effects. As shown above, most quotations from or references to canonised and popular texts are used for the creation of humorous dialogues and scenes. Frequent repetitions of the same quoted material, however, turn it into a part of 'Wooster's world', achieving monologic textual closure and strengthening readerly immersion,[3] whereas at the same time opening up the novels to an intertextual dialogue, which triggers comparative readings. So both subversion and containment, which, as some critics maintain, are both always features of comedy, are mirrored by those reinscriptions. Even though the Wooster novels are far from being subversive sociocritical texts, "the duality enabled in joking and comic scenarios opposes any univocal interpretation of the world" (Stott 14).

The usage of mainly English and partly American intertexts, however, furthers a 'monocultural' dialogue which emphasises the texts' portrayal of 'Englishness' and 'English humour'. On the level of production, this may be due to the fact, that Wodehouse wrote most of his works in the 'American diaspora', which both enabled him to portray Britain as an Edwardian and Arcadian world and at the same time heightened his sensitivity for the English language (cf. Smith 221). According to Smith, "he had a vast American public to please and he might have been motivated to give the Americans the foreigner's view of the English, butlers, castles and all" (Smith 220). Here I shall concentrate on the intertextual dialogue between P.G. Wodehouse's *Jeeves and Wooster* novels and a selection of William Shakespeare's plays.

The concept of intertextuality which I am going to apply in my analysis is mainly grounded in Broich and Pfister's study of the phenomenon and employs the concept and terminology of dialogue and dialogism. Furthermore, I shall employ Koestler's bisociation model to explain the creation of the comic through intertextual reference and quotation. My concept of intertextuality as a dialogue is twofold: firstly, it describes a simple communication model, a dialogue between the author/narrator, the text and the reader and disassociates itself from poststructuralist readings in defining intertextuality mainly as a feature predominating in certain texts and not a feature of texts in general. Doing that, I still adhere to Broich and Pfister's intermediatory model which negotiates between poststructuralist, structuralist and hermeneutic approaches in adopting a poststructuralist model of the 'global intertextuality of texts', but differentiating between different degrees of intertextual intensity (cf. Pfister 1985, 25). Employing Broich and Pfister's criteria for intertextual intensity, one can say that the intertextual relationship between Shakespeare's plays and the *Jeeves and Wooster* novels is intense (cf. Pfister 1985, 26-29). For instance, the fact maintained by many sources (cf. Mooneyham 121, Smith 214) that Wodehouse repeatedly read the works of Shakespeare is an evidence for the intertextual relationship which presents

---

[3] Readerly immersion is an important aspect to be taken into account when e.g. analysing the *Jeeves and Wooster* novels' visuality and visual comedy; I analyse it in depth in *Jokes Don't Jump from Nowhere: Intertextual and Intermedial Dialogism in P.G. Wodehouse's Jeeves and Wooster Novels and Beyond* (forthcoming).

itself readily to even 'less knowing' audiences. Thus Pfister's criterion of 'communicability' which says that a maximum intensity is achieved if the author has employed the intertext consciously, has marked it in the text and can presuppose the reader's familiarity with the 'pretext' (cf. Pfister 1985, 27), is given. According to Broich, intertextual references that are presented in a way which facilitates their recognition by the reader are described as 'marked' in opposition to unmarked intertextual references whose recognition solely depends on the reader's familiarity with the pretext (cf. Broich 31-47). In the *Jeeves and Wooster* novels both marked and unmarked references to Shakespeare occur.

Secondly, intertextuality/intermediality as a dialogue here describes the dialogue between text and text/text and image. The latter presents another vital aspect of Wodehouse's comic novels: having been written as 'musical comedies', they often make the reader "picture" (*The Mating Season* 141) a slapstick scene or a metaphorically described person, object or situation. This, however, will be analysed elsewhere.

Conceptionalising intertextuality as a form of dialogue between author/narrator and reader is also in accordance with one of comedy's most crucial features, namely the fact that comedy is an inherently social genre which relies on a shared cultural memory and social conditions that determine to a high degree what can be perceived as comic (cf. Pfister 2002, vi). This might explain Wodehouse's persistent popularity in Great Britain, America and its former colony, India, in contrast to his rare reception in Germany. Moreover, the humorous scenes created through intertextual dialogue can be described in terms of Koestler's bisociation model which conceptualises the creation of the comic as "a thing [...] seen in a dual light; a mental concept [...] simultaneously perceived under two different angles [...] which serves two masters at the same time; it is 'bisociated' with two independent and mutually exclusive mental fields" (Koestler 36). For Koestler there is "a quick oscillation of the bisociated concept between its two contexts, these quick oscillations accounting for the presence of both [...] in consciousness" (Koestler 37). The most straightforward example would be the pun, which triggers two opposed associative streams in the reader but according to Koestler more complex instances of humour can also be explained by this model. He maintains that implicitness is important, as it stimulates the reader's associative flow and compels him for once to listen, to fill in the gaps and to recreate the witticism or humorous scene (cf. Koestler 33). In my opinion, the reading of intertextual references creates exactly the same kind of bisociation process in the reader; the reader's associations flow in two different directions, which meet at a certain juncture, where they are dialogised and create new meaning; and in the case of humorous intertextual reference, first of all a bodily reflex, laughter.

Broich and Pfister's differentiation between specific references (Einzeltextreferenzen) and system's references (Systemreferenzen) can also be applied to intertextual references in Wodehouse's novels. Shakespearean intertextual references mainly consist of specific references like quotation and allusion but also include system's references, namely the features of romantic comedy, the theatrical dialogues and slapstick scenes, and further reworkings of predominant Shakespearean topics like the difference between appearance and reality, meta-narration, eavesdropping, mistaken identities, intertextual rewriting itself and the use of biblical and proverbial quotation and metaphor. Considering the novels within the context of various intertextual linkings besides Shakespeare, not all of them can be termed particular rewritings of Shakespeare's works. So theatricality and intermediality should rather be analysed as features of an intertextual dialogue with Wodehouse's musical comedies and within the context of Dickens' theatrical novels. In the following I shall therefore confine myself to the dialogic linkings which interconnect with Shakespeare's plays and will thus begin with specific textual references.

Reinscribing 'the Romeo': Specific References

> "[...] He moons broodingly to and fro, looking like Hamlet. [...]" I saw her point, of course. No hostess wants a Hamlet on the premises. (*Jeeves and the Feudal Spirit* 64)

> I could see now what I had failed to spot before, that in thinking of him as a Romeo I had made an incorrect diagnosis. The bird whose name ought to have sprung to my mind was Othello. In this Cheesewright, it was plain, I had run up against one of those touchy lovers who go about the place in a suspicious and red-eyed spirit, eager to hammer the stuffing out of such of the citizenry as they suppose to be or to have been in any sense matey with the adored object. (*Joy in the Morning* 26)

The *Jeeves and Wooster* novels are peopled with Shakespearean characters but rewrite the tragic heroes as comic character types in referring to them in the plural and using them as metaphorical descriptions. According to the interaction theory of metaphor, vehicle and tenor are in interaction, they are in a dialogue and both the meaning of the vehicle and the tenor is changed by the interaction. Bisociating this allusion or metaphor makes most readers laugh as it shows the narrator's comic incapability of reading the classics adequately and/or reverently. Wodehouse has always been praised as a stylist and the clash of styles, here a slangy reference to Shakespeare, chiefly creates a bisociation process in the reader. Furthermore it contrasts the light reading of Wodehouse's comic novels with the 'seriousness of canonised texts' while turning the established hierarchy upside-down: Shakespearean characters are used for the description of Wodehousean character types. Tellingly, the Shakespearean characters which are referred to in the *Jeeves and Wooster* novels are those characterised by a preeminent flaw, like Othello's jealousy, and thus readily lend themselves to a comic reinscription. Being part of English cultural memory, the Shakespearean characters not only describe Wodehouse's characters, but are themselves reread, which helps to prolong their longevity in cultural memory as well as connecting the novels to the cultural background, emphasising their 'Englishness' and affirming the social bonds of the laughing community. The transformation of Shakespeare's individual, Romeo, into 'a Romeo' takes away the halo of the canonised and works as a means of comic inversion. According to Smith, "Wodehouse is not so much laughing at the writer[ ] [himself] but at the stained-glass attitudes adopted towards [him]" (Smith 214), which can especially be seen in the multiple system's references, that do not parody, but imitate Shakespearean comedy.

While reinterpreting the Shakespearean characters and opening up the novels to a comparative reading, the Shakespearean quotations and allusions are also integrated into the *Jeeves and Wooster* novels and become a part of them through frequent repetition. Repetition with variation is one of the main features of Wodehouse's novels and he once answered a severe critic as follows:

> A certain critic…made the nasty remark about my last novel that it contained "all the Wodehouse characters under different names." He has probably by now been eaten by bears, like the children who made mock of the prophet Elisha: but if he still survives he will not be able to make a similar charge against *Summer Lightning*. With my superior intelligence, I have outgeneralled the man this time by putting in all the old Wodehouse characters under the same names. Pretty silly it will make him feel, I rather fancy. (qtd. in Mooneyham 120)

The same applies to his use of quotation. One of the very frequently repeated Shakespearean quotations is the following from *Macbeth*: "*Macb.* If it were done, when 'tis done, then 'twere well / It were done quickly" (1.7.1f.). Wooster first takes the sentence as one of Jeeves 'gags', as he often calls them:

> "Yes, sir. If it were done when 'twere done, then 'twere well it were done quickly," he [Jeeves] said, making for the door and I thought, as I had so often thought before, how neatly he put these things. (*Stiff Upper Lip* 171)

Later on he learns that this is a quotation from Shakespeare and misquotes it for his own purposes.

> Feeling, therefore, that if the thing was to be smacked into, 'twere well 'twere smacked into quickly, as Shakespeare says, I treacled the paper and attached it to the window. All that now remained to be done was to deliver the sharp. And it was at this point that I suddenly came over all cat-in-the-adag-y. (*Joy in the Morning* 110)

Again the singularity of the event, Macbeth's murder, is exchanged with a repetitious experience, it is "another of those cases of if it were done, then 'twere well 'twere done quickly" (*Much Obliged, Jeeves* 129). The repetitious use of the same quotations is not only a characteristic of the running gag in comedy, but detaches the words more and more from their original source, reduces comparative readings and furthers a reception of the texts as closed and monologic, a 'fun-for-fun's-sake' reading. It creates that popular 'Wooster world' in which audiences are immersed easily without being distracted by 'too subversive' intertexts. Still, Catherine Belsey's words on reinscription can be applied to a reading of Shakespearean quotations in Wodehouse:

> Re-inscription represents a process of discovery. The new is constructed out of old materials to produce a text that modifies the possibilities for the future. In this respect, it surely constitutes one instance of cultural memory which puts on display the process of remembering. Texts, like cultures, have a past. Intertextual memory does not simply recover this, as if it had been stored away in a trunk and could now be brought to light just as it was. Instead, as memory revitalizes previous texts, it brings the past into the present, and thus alters or expands the options for the future. Instead of displaying what was, cultural memory uncovers what *will have been* the case. By that means it modifies both past and future. (Belsey 15f.)

Reinscribing Shakespeare in light comic novels is not only an example for Wodehouse's constant subversion of authority figures, but also – especially as concerns the system's references (see below) – rereads the bard's 'high brow' works as popular entertainment in their own time. Further, these reinscriptions achieve a deep embeddedness of P.G. Wodehouse's novels in English culture and literature and *can* trigger comparative readings.

Both the characters and quotations from Shakespearean tragedy create hyperboles and their psychological, philosophical and/or political depth is translated into a more earthy and bodily (everyday) literality. Shakespearean sexual allusions, however, have not been recreated in the *Jeeves and Wooster* novels. Wodehouse's novels and Bertie Wooster as a narrator have often been described as 'innocent'; the characters' problems and needs resemble those of school boys and Wooster's school-boyish reading of the classics pushes the bard himself off his pedestal.[4]

> I groaned a hollow one. The heart had sunk. One has, of course, to make allowances for writers, all of them being more or less loony. Look at Shakespeare, for instance. Very unbalanced. Used to go about stealing ducks. Nevertheless, I couldn't help feeling that in springing Joke Goods on the guardian of the girl he loved Boko had carried an author's natural goofiness too far. Even Shakespeare might have hesitated to go to such lengths. (*Joy in the Morning* 56)

> I nodded. His meaning had not escaped me. If you analysed it, it was the old Bacon and Shakespeare gag. Bacon, as you no doubt remember, wrote Shakespeare's stuff for him and then, possibly because he owed the latter money or it may be from sheer good nature, allowed him to take the credit for it. I mentioned this to Jeeves, and he said that perhaps an even closer parallel was that of Cyrano de Bergerac. (*Joy in the Morning* 204)

This is not mere comic inversion, but also a 'humanisation' of Shakespeare, the icon. For Wooster, Shakespeare is one of "those poet Johnnies" (*Carry On, Jeeves* 45) and a "brainy bird" (*Carry On, Jeeves* 46) and he associates literature in general with Shakespeare, so that he takes most quotations Jeeves uses as Shakespearean quotations. In always applying the quotations from Shakespeare to his life, the fictitiousness of the novels is stressed and the novels' decisive 'anti-intellectualism' is preserved. The representation of Shakespeare and his works is far from being satirical (cf. also Smith 214) and only shares some features with parody. A benevolent comicality is created which is emphasised by the system's references to Shakespearean comedies. Specific references to Shakespearean comedies are rarer than references to his tragedies, but exist as well. Tellingly, the words of 'tragedy in comedy', the words which Viola uses for telling Orsino indirectly about her unrequited and unspoken love for him (cf. *Twelfth Night* 2.4. 111-16), are recreated in a humorous way but the title of the last chapter in *The Inimitable Jeeves* is called "All's well" (*The Inimitable Jeeves* 214) and aunt Dahlia says "[s]till, all's well that ends well" (*The Code of the Woosters* 476). Thus Bertram Wilberforce Wooster could in one respect be interpreted as a character who has migrated: like Shakespeare's Bertram in *All's Well that Ends Well*, he does not want to marry certain women, but unlike the Shakespearean Bertram, he never has to, because Jeeves always rescues him.

---

[4] cf. Mary Lydon (23), who enjoyed reading those rewritings as a school-girl.

All's Well that Ends Well Whenever Love's Labours are Lost: System's References

One of the predominant themes of Shakespearean comedy is thus reversed: for the protagonist, Bertram Wooster, a happy ending does not mean marriage but the escape from an engagement and marriage. Most of the plots, which are structured like criminal cases, centre around an unlucky engagement from which Jeeves needs to rescue Wooster, who, aiming to be a *preux chevalier*, would never break an engagement. The usually parental and unjust law which forces the hero at the beginning of a Shakespearean comedy to marry out of duty and not love, is exchanged with the self-imposed law of being a perfect English gentleman. Englishness is here exaggerated, parodied and subverted. The self-imposing of a law which is hard to keep and the happy ending, which is not, or not yet, marriage, however, links Wodehouse's comic novels to his favourite Shakespearean comedy, *Love's Labour's Lost*, in which according to Berry, the division of the lovers' minds and internal, self-imposed obstacles keep them as much apart as parental law (cf. Berry 9).

In contrast to Shakespeare's Benedick, who at least presents himself as a scorner-of-love, Wooster's engagements sometimes 'just happen', because women mistake his wooing on behalf of another man for his own wooing. He also falls in love, before realising that the women he falls in love with are "a pippin" (*The Mating Season* 36) concerning their "outer crust" (*Much Obliged, Jeeves* 25) but are otherwise either bossy or sentimental. Those frequently repeated instances of 'appearance versus reality', which might be read as a rewriting of this major Shakespearean topic, lose their twisted subtleness in *Jeeves and Wooster* and become more positivistic. In *Much Ado About Nothing*, Beatrice and Benedick seem to note a 'nothing', but the audience remains wondering if this nothing hasn't really been something from the beginning. In *Twelfth Night*, Viola, disguised as Cesario tells Olivia "I am not what I am" (*TN* 3.1.143), but in the performance reality of Elizabethan theatre, the actor is a man. In *Jeeves and Wooster* the discrepancy between appearance and reality is merely used to create fun for fun's sake. People are not what they appear to be but the reader sees what they are 'really' like. As in popular detective fiction, the 'good guys' and the 'bad guys' exist and when Wooster prides himself in his intelligence, for instance, the reader recognises the incongruity between Wooster's words and 'reality', namely that what he prides himself in, is something obvious:

> The response was not what you would call lyrical, but we Woosters can read between the lines. His eyes were rolling in their sockets, and his face had taken on the colour and

expression of a devout tomato. I could see that he loved like a thousand of bricks. (*Joy in the Morning* 24)

However, this quotation also shows the incongruous relationship between Wooster, the character, and Wooster, the narrator. According to Gerd Dose narrator and character are not congruent because the latter's intellectual weakness is disclaimed by the former's ability to structure the narration, in which associations and digressions are all employed for a purpose (cf. Dose 29). Wooster, the narrator, interestingly employs 'sprezzatura' which, lying at the heart of Beatrice's and Benedick's witty repartees and at the heart of Shakespeare's own work, is defined by Greenblatt as "a technique for the manipulation of appearance, for masking the hard work that underlies successful performances" (Greenblatt 522).[5] Witty repartees like Beatrice's and Benedick's, however, are absent in the *Jeeves and Wooster* novels as Wooster, the character, and all the other characters, despite Jeeves, are not quick-witted.

There is usually a movement from peace and order to confusion and back to peace and order in Shakespeare's comedies, and this applies to the *Jeeves and Wooster* novels as well. The title *Joy in the Morning* sums up Wooster's 'boomps-a-daisy'-feeling at the beginning and end of the novel (*Joy in the Morning* 3, 272). In Wodehouse, though, Shakespeare's "green world is usually the country estate" (Mooneyham 121) and the movement from peace to confusion and back to reconciliation and peace is certainly a comic device which is shared by the majority of comic works.

Although the *Jeeves and Wooster* novels never end with a wedding, only with engagements, which can be broken again for the creation of the sequels' plots, the fact that every novel ends with at least one or two couples pairing off and Wooster being 'saved from the doom of marriage', link them to Shakespearean romantic comedy which usually ends with several weddings (cf. Frye 163). At the end of *The Mating Season,* Wooster lists the sundered and reunited hearts as follows:

---

[5] The title *Much Ado About Nothing* is an example for Shakespeare's use of sprezzatura. The nonchalant title *Much Ado About Nothing* is resonant with self-reflexive meaning. 'Nothing' in Elizabethan times was pronounced as 'noting' and thus reflects on the several 'notings of nothings' which trigger both the comic and the tragic strands of the plot. (cf. Greenblatt 522f.)

Sundered Hearts	Reunited Hearts
(1) Esmond	(1) Esmond
(2) Corky	(2) Corky
(3) Gussie	(3) Gussie
(4) Madeline	(4) Madeline
(5) Officer Dobbs	(5) Officer Dobbs
(6) Queenie	(6) Queenie
(7) Catsmeat	(7) Catsmeat
(8) Gertrude	(8) Gertrude

It came out exactly square. Not a single loose end left over. (*The Mating Season* 252)

The happy ending's transference into a list presents a metafictional comment on the constructedness of this comic novel, which stresses its artificiality and fictionality. Nevertheless subversion and containment go hand in hand in the Wooster novels and the fact that this list has been written by the narrator, Bertie Wooster, supports a reading which sees this 'technical treatment' of relationships as simply in line with his eccentric character. Metafictional comments, which can be seen as a further link to Shakespearean comedy, are used differently in Wodehouse. I here concur with Mooneyham, who says "that Wodehouse's self-reflexivity has more links to the nineteenth century practice of the intrusive author than to modernism" (Mooneyham 128). Whereas the audience in Shakespearean drama is made aware that they are watching a play through metadramatic devices like the play in the play, the fool's songs and epilogues or comments by the characters whose double meaning works as a metadramatic comment, Wooster's metafictional comments are rather used in order to stress the realist content of his 'autobiographical narrative'. He sums up parts of earlier novels for 'newcomers', gropes for the right words, which Jeeves always finds, and sometimes addresses the reader.

Both Shakespeare's and Wodehouse's works hark back to the Greek and Roman tradition. As mentioned before, Jeeves can be linked to the Greek and Roman stock character of the clever slave, the 'servus callidus'. Whereas his predecessors' task is to smoothe the way for "sexual gratification of a young man of no great abilities" (Creaser 82), Jeeves' main task is to disentangle Wooster from that. Furthermore, Wodehouse rewrites Plautus', Terence's and Shakespeare's 'parallel plots'; like the latter he uses "rich varieties of plot doubling, repetition, contrast, and counterpoint" (Miola 28).[6] As shown above, *The Mating Season* presents the intertwined relationships of nine characters (Wooster included), which 'result' in four final pairings.

---

[6] Miola names e.g. the two gentlemen of Verona and their beloved, the two sets of twins in *The Comedy of Errors*, the two sisters and courtships in *The Taming of the Shrew*, the two love affairs in *Much Ado About Nothing* and the two households in *The Merry Wives of Windsor* (cf. Miola 28).

148 Sarah Säckel

Instead of crossdressing, only men are disguised, like in the classical comedies of Terence and Plautus (cf. Berry 81) and Shakespearean play with gender uncertainties and homoeroticism is not recreated in *Jeeves and Wooster*. Gender roles are simplified and women are mostly bossy, sometimes oversentimental and always suppress Wooster, which this example amongst others shows:

> To me the girl was simply nothing more or less than a pot of poison. One of those dashed large, brainy, strenuous, dynamic girls you see so much of these days. She had been at Girton, where, in addition to enlarging her brain to the most frightful extent, she had gone in for every kind of sport and developed the physique of a middleweight catch-as-catch-can wrestler. (*The Inimitable Jeeves* 44)

This stereotyping of female characters is closer to Shakespearean tragedy than comedy. According to Schülting, women in Shakespeare's tragedies are either 'saints' or 'whores' (Schülting 532). In the *Jeeves and Wooster* novels they chiefly fall into the following categories: aunts, (ex-)fiancées and women who want to marry men that went to school with Wooster and whom (according to his gentlemanly code of behaviour) he must therefore help to overcome the impediments against their marriage. Aunt Agatha can be said to substitute the Shakespearean patriarchs (e.g. Egeus from *A Midsummer Night's Dream*) as she insists on Wooster' marriage to women he detests. Wooster describes her repeatedly as

> cold and haughty, though presumably unbending a habit of conducting human sacrifices at the time of the full moon, as she is widely rumoured to do, and her attitude towards [him] has always been that of an austere governess, causing [him] to feel as if [he was] six years old and she had just caught [him] stealing jam from the jam cupboard [...]. (*Much Obliged, Jeeves* 45)

These aunts, who are also substitute parents, conform to the conservative female roles, which predominate the history of comedy[7] and can also be depicted in the silent slapstick films of the 1920s and 1930s (cf. Stott 97), the time in which the *Jeeves and Wooster* novels were first written. Referring to British comedy series, for which the conservative, one-dimensional role of women also holds true, Stott describes female characters as having "repeatedly been given the role of joyless authority figures [...], wives who are simultaneously mothers to their infantilized husbands" (Stott 81).[8] This holds

---

[7] "As we look back over comedy's treatment of gender and sexuality, we must conclude that versions of female sexuality that explore the configuration of women's identity and desire beyond a handful of stereotypes are still severly lacking." (Stott 82)

[8] Stott lists e.g. *Steptoe and Son* (1962-74), *Porridge* (1973-77), *Dad's Army* (1968-77), *Yes, Minister* (1980-88) (cf. Stott 81).

true for the *Jeeves and Wooster* novels, whose school-boyish protagonist fears to be 'moulded' by his aunts and fiancées:

> I had been engaged to Honoria Glossop nearly two weeks, and during all that time not a day had passed without her putting in some heavy work in the direction of what Aunt Agatha had called 'moulding' me. I had read solid literature till my eyes bubbled; we had legged it together through miles of picture-galleries, and I had been compelled to undergo classical concerts to an extent you would hardly believe. All in all, therefore, I was in no fit state to receive shocks, especially shocks like this. Honoria had lugged me round to lunch at Aunt Agatha's, and I had just been saying to myself, "Death, where is thy jolly old sting?" when she hove the bomb. "Bertie," she said, suddenly, as if she had just remembered it, "what is the name of that man of yours – your valet? [...] When we are married, you must get rid of Jeeves." (*The Inimitable Jeeves* 58)

In this way heterosexual relationships endanger male-male friendships[9] like in Shakespeare's comedies (e.g. *The Two Gentlemen of Verona* or *A Midsummer Night's Dream*) but on top of that, they destroy the male, school-boyish world of play. Even Wooster's favourite aunt, Aunt Dahlia, often blackmails him, if he refuses to do what she wants him to.

Because romantic comedy's theme is courtship, "[m]arriage could be described as the main reason for the participation of women in comedy, as well as one of the primary conditions under which men and women are seen to interact" (Stott 77). In fact, the *Jeeves and Wooster* plots mainly deal with tricking Wooster's fiancées into breaking off their engagement and bringing couples at strife together again or convincing the father or legal guardian, who is against the marriage, to accept it. The latter point again resembles Shakespeare's comedies.

Despite the parallels in plotting romantic comedies, a comparative reading of Shakespeare's and Wodehouse's female characters has to criticise the

---

[9] Jeeves and Wooster's relationship is not homoerotic, but could be classified under what Emily Eells calls 'Anglosexuality'. The latter refers to male-male relationships that, although not physically homosexual, describe a psychological androgyny of close male friendships or working partnerships, as in the case of Sherlock Holmes and Doctor Watson (cf. Berberich 40). Wodehouse's "fictions are chaste in the extreme. [...] There is no sex or obscenity, adultery or guilty love, in Wodehouse at all. Wodehouse knew his limitations; in a letter written in 1960 he called attention to the very sort of subject which could be fatal to his fiction: 'I've just finished my new novel. Fairly good, I think, but what does it *prove*? I sometimes wish I wrote that powerful stuff the reviewers like so much, all about incest and homosexualism' (*Yours* 161)." (Mooneyham 125) Although Jeeves and Wooster often act like a couple, they are both explicitly described as heterosexual. As mentioned above, this description is vital for creating this innocent world of school-boyish play and additionally, the familial intimacy shared by Jeeves, Wooster and the reader creates the feeling of 'being at home' which heightens the novels' immersivity, triggers an escapist reception and popularises the novel with this 'sitcom effect'.

conservative representations of women by the latter. Whereas Shakespeare's female characters are presented as competent in their use of language, eloquent, witty and powerful (cf. Magnusson 169) and whereas they "do things with words – to change minds, transform situations, harm others, and help them" (Magnusson 169),[10] Wodehouse's female figures' intelligence is presented negatively and their bossiness creates antipathies in the reader and turns them into butts of the jokes. However, the men (with the exception of Jeeves) are usually presented as rather dumb and clumsy and are similarly made fun of; thus both sexes are presented as stock characters and one can absolve Wodehouse of misogyny. Because of the reversion of the romantic plot, the negative presentation of women seems to have a required function in the plots; in the Jeeves' novel *Ring for Jeeves*, in which the 'Wooster substitute', Bill, actually wants to marry his fiancée, Jill, a very positively portrayed, emancipated woman is presented. Moreover, P.G. Wodehouse makes the reader laugh about almost everything and everyone who seems to take himself too seriously, dictators and communists, patriarchs and matriarchs, masters and servants alike. This creates an indeterminacy as to what or if he criticises anything at all; the laughter created is more a laughter for laughter's sake and the object which is to be laughed at can be compared to the dead body in the classic detective novel; it only holds a function. Shakespearean plays, on the contrary, also include farcical episodes, but otherwise can be read as subverting Elizabethan anxieties and authorities or ridiculing general human vices like Malvolio's hypocrisy (cf. Mangan 240). Wodehouse's novels certainly also have to be read within their historical context and can be described as poking fun at political and literary authorities of the time (and beyond). Nevertheless, as the laughter they evoke is directed at almost everyone and everything, it lacks a decided subversive and (socio-) critical stance. When viewing Wodehouse within the historical context of WWI, WWII and the post-war world, it is rather interesting to see how he e.g. rewrites myths of motifs of Englisness and creates a fictional world that becomes a comic escapist space.

A crucial similarity between Wodehouse's comic novels and Shakespeare's plays lies in their rewriting of their own previous works, other sources and popular culture. Wodehouse's treatment of biblical and proverbial quotations also resembles that of Shakespeare in a way and might be read as a further recreation. Both authors use their audience's common cultural knowledge, twist it and use it for comic metaphoric description and characterisation. In *A Preface to Shakespeare's Comedies: 1594-1603*, Michael Mangan shows how *Twelfth Night* reworks various themes and even

---

[10] Magnusson names Rosalind, Portia, Viola and Beatrice (cf. Magnusson 169).

characters from preceding Shakespearean comedies and, [11] as shown above, Wodehouse was repeatedly criticised for his repetitiveness (cf. Mangan 230f.). Interestingly, however, even the themes of Shakespeare's comedies and tragedies are closely related and thus may be said to precede Wodehouse's comic reinscriptions of Shakespearean tragedy. Furthermore, most Shakespearean plays are rewritings like Wodehouse's *Jeeves and Wooster* novels; this could be one explanation for the writers' great popularity if we apply what Hutcheon says about the audience's pleasure in adaptation, namely, that it simply comes "from repetition with variation, from the comfort of ritual combined with the piquancy of surprise" (Hutcheon 4).

Conclusion

To conclude: specific references to Shakespeare's tragedies (and a few comedies) are mainly used for the creation of humorous scenes through incongruity and bisociation but they also invert the 'seriously taken', canonised literature and work as pillars of cultural memory. Both specific and system's references enhance the novel's evocation of a very fictional 'Englishness', which is taken ad absurdum through the portrayal of a gentleman ideal that can be compared to Shakespeare's 'parental law'. Thus subversion and containment always go hand in hand in the *Jeeves and Wooster* novels' comic rewritings. Further, the (monologic) repetition of the same quoted material creates the popular (and 'closed') 'Wooster world' in which readers are easily immersed.

Depending on the reader's reception, however, the system's references can also trigger comparative readings as the ones presented above. These e.g. show the features of popular literature and culture in Shakespeare's plays or can explain why Shakespeare's plays are today classified as 'high literature', whereas Wodehouse's novels are usually classified as 'popular (low) literature'. System's references like the theme of 'appearance vs. reality' or the presentation of characters show that in contrast to Shakespeare's plays, Wodehouse's novels cannot 'be interpreted endlessly' (cf. Schulte-Sasse 39), which would be an important feature of high literature according to Schulte-Sasse.

However, in an age of cultural studies, this high-low distinction does not justify the continuous exclusion of Wodehouse from literary histories and 'serious analysis' any more, because they thus miss out on a vital aspect of the English literary imagination and cultural memory, which crosses high-

---

[11] E.g. cross-dressing, mistaken identities, identical twins, appearance versus reality, to name but a few of Shakespeare's repeated comic themes.

low boundaries.[12] With its "sweet, melancholy nostalgia for an England of innocent laughter and song" (McCrum 418) the *Jeeves and Wooster* novels fill this gap and so do analyses of them. Therefore more work needs to be done and will be done on these novels. Should you have further questions right now, however, ask Jeeves.[13]

Works Cited

Belsey, Catherine. "Remembering as Re-Inscription – With a Difference." *Literature, Literary History, and Cultural Memory*. Ed. Herbert Grabes. Tübingen: Gunter Narr Verlag, 2005. 3-17.

Berberich, Christine. *The Image of the English Gentleman in Twentieth-Century Literature: Englishness and Nostalgia*. Aldershot: Ashgate, 2007.

Bergson, Henri. *Laughter: An Essay on the Meaning of the Comic*. Champaign: Book Jungle, n.d.

Berry, Edward. *Shakespeare's Comic Rites*. Cambridge: CUP, 1984.

Broich, Ulrich. "Formen der Markierung von Intertextualität." *Intertextualität: Formen, Funktionen, anglistische Fallstudien*. Eds Ulrich Broich and Manfred Pfister. Tübingen: Niemeyer, 1985. 31-47.

Creaser, John. "Forms of Confusion." *The Cambridge Companion to Shakespearean Comedy*. Ed. Alexander Leggatt. CUP, 2001. *Cambridge Collections Online*. CUP. 17 February 2009 DOI:10.1017/CCOL0521770440.006.

Dose, Gerd. "Agatha Christie und nicht P.G. Wodehouse: Beobachtungen und Überlegungen zur wissenschaftlichen und außerwissenschaftlichen Rezeption englischsprachiger Populärliteratur im deutschsprachigen Kulturraum." *Anglistik & Englischunterricht* 17 (1982): 9-49.

Frye, Northrop. *The Anatomy of Criticism: Four Essays*. New York: Atheneum, 1967.

Greenblatt, Stephen. "Much Ado About Nothing." *The Norton Shakespeare. Based on the Oxford Edition*. Oxford: W.W. Norton & Company Inc., 1997.

Hutcheon, Linda. *A Theory of Adaptation*. New York: Routledge, 2006.

"Jeeves." *The New Oxford Dictionary of English*. 1998.

---

[12] According to Schulte-Sasse, the rigid distinction between high and low literature is much more a German than an Anglo-American issue (cf. Schulte-Sasse 3).

[13] The internet engine *Ask* was called *Ask Jeeves* until 2006, which shows the character's longevity and productivity in cultural memory. Furthermore he even has an entry in the *New Oxford Dictionary*.

Kiernan, Robert F. *Frivolity Unbound: Six Masters of the Camp Novel*. New York: Continuum, 1990.
Koestler, Arthur. *Insight and Outlook*. New York: The Macmillan Company, 1949.
Lydon, Mary. "First Love: Reading with P.G. Wodehouse." *Profession* (1994): 21-25.
Magnusson, Lynne. "Language and Comedy." *The Cambridge Companion to Shakespearean Comedy*. Ed. Alexander Leggatt. CUP, 2001. *Cambridge Collections Online*. CUP. 20 May 2009 DOI:10.1017/CCOL0521770440.010.
Mangan, Michael. *A Preface to Shakespeare's Comedies: 1594-1603*. London: Longman, 1996.
McCrum, Robert. *Wodehouse: A Life*. London: Viking, 2004.
Medcalf, Stephen. "The Innocence of P.G. Wodehouse." *The Modern English Novel: The Reader, the Writer and the Work*. Ed. Gabriel Josipovici. London: Open Books Publishing Ltd., 1976. 186-205.
Miola, Robert S. "Roman Comedy." *The Cambridge Companion to Shakespearean Comedy*. Ed. Alexander Leggatt. CUP, 2001. *Cambridge Collections Online*. CUP. 17 February 2009 DOI:10.1017/CCOL0521770440.002.
Mooneyham, Laura. "Comedy Among the Modernists: P.G. Wodehouse and the Anachronism of Comic Form." *Twentieth Century Literature: A Scholarly and Critical Journal* 40.1 (1994): 114-38.
Pfister, Manfred. "Introduction: A History of English Laughter?" *A History of English Laughter: Laughter from Beowulf to Beckett and Beyond*. Ed. Manfred Pfister. Amsterdam: Rodopi, 2002. v-x.
—. "Konzepte der Intertextualität." *Intertextualität: Formen, Funktionen, anglistische Fallstudien*. Eds Ulrich Broich and Manfred Pfister. Tübingen: Niemeyer, 1985. 1-30.
Schulte-Sasse, Jochen. *Literarische Wertung*. Stuttgart: J.B. Metzlersche Verlagsbuchhandlung, 1971.
Schülting, Sabine. "Die späteren Tragödien." *Shakespeare Handbuch*. Ed. Ina Schabert. Stuttgart: Alfred Kröner Verlag, 2000.
Shakespeare, William. *Julius Caesar*. Ed. T.S. Dorsch. London: Methuen, 1955.
—. *Macbeth*. Ed. Kenneth Muir. London: The Arden Shakespeare, 2004.
—. *Twelfth Night*. Eds J.M. Lothian and T.W. Craik. London: The Arden Shakespeare, 1975.
Smith, Sharwood. "The Very Irreverent P.G. Wodehouse: A Study of *Thank You, Jeeves*." *Dutch Quarterly Review of Anglo-American Letters* 8 (1978): 203-22.

Stott, Andrew. *Comedy*. New York: Routledge, 2005.

Thompson, Kristin. *Wooster Proposes, Jeeves Disposes or Le Mot Juste.* New York: James H. Heinemann, 1992.

Wodehouse, P.G. *Carry On, Jeeves*. 1925. London: Penguin Books, 1999.

—. *The Code of the Woosters*. 1937. *Jeeves and Wooster Omnibus*: *The Mating Season*. 1949. *The Code of the Woosters*. 1937. *Right Ho, Jeeves*. 1934. Foreword by Hugh Laurie. London: Penguin Books, 2001.

—. *The Inimitable Jeeves*. 1923. London: Penguin Books, 1999.

—. *Jeeves and the Feudal Spirit*. 1954. London: Penguin Books, 1999.

—. *Joy in the Morning*. 1947. London: Penguin Books, 1999.

—. *The Mating Season*. 1949. *Jeeves and Wooster Omnibus*: *The Mating Season*. 1949. *The Code of the Woosters*. 1937. *Right Ho, Jeeves*. 1934. Foreword by Hugh Laurie. London: Penguin Books, 2001.

—. *Much Obliged, Jeeves*. 1971. London: Penguin Books, 1981.

Ida M. Samperi

"No Text Just Comes out Ex Nihilo, It Always Comes out of Other Texts":[1] Christine Brooke-Rose's *Thru*

Christine Brooke-Rose's *Thru* is a perfect example for the fusion of different signifying systems within a fictional work. The text addresses the manifold theories of the critical debate of the sixties and seventies, fuses them together and transforms them to create a new, subversive *discourse on discourses*. Kristeva's and Bahktin's concepts of intertextuality and dialogue, Lacan's psychoanalytic premises, Derrida's innovative ideas about the *Text*, Barthes' *death of the author*, Greimas' theories of narrativity and Jakobson's diagram are some of the ideas which *Thru* not only addresses directly, but also and most importantly merges together, 'dismantling' and 'reconstructing' them towards metaphorical and power-redistributive directions. The specialised jargons of disparate critical theories are fused, rehandled and played on, so that diverse signifying practices, crossing each other, give life to new meanings and endless interpretations. Stretching across theories, *Thru* plays on their mixture and the dialogue which results is a intertextual, interdisciplinary and parodying discourse, a collage which aims at subverting those very discourses it is made of.

The label of 'difficult' haunts the reputation of Christine Brooke-Rose's experimental fiction, with the effect of marginalising it and hindering its reception by a wide reading public. Her work has not yet been broadly recognised for its groundbreaking contribution to contemporary literary practice.

One of the reasons for her supposed 'obscurity' corresponds precisely to one of the main characteristics of her highly innovative narrative technique, namely the use of specialised jargons for the creation of metaphorical discourse. At the basis of this feature lies Brooke-Rose's intuition that "jargon has great poetry" (Friedman and Fuchs 83), i.e. that the technical language specialists use becomes highly metaphorical, if used literally and it can therefore be employed at the service of creative writing.

An 'incomprehensible' lingo drawn from different semiotic systems and rendered in metaphorical terms starts shaping Brooke-Rose's narrative from the sixties onwards. In *Out* she uses the chemical imagery and the new theories of uncertainty in physics, which undermine the scientific law of causality and foreground a subjective way of experiencing reality. In *Such*, it is the terminology of astrophysics which becomes a metaphor for the relationships between people. In *Between*, it is a wide range of technical discourses and jargons coming from various specialised fields of knowledge such as linguis-

---

[1] Tredell 34

tics, anthropology, history, sociology and genetics. However, it is in *Thru*[2] that the metaphorical use of specialised jargon reaches its highest expression, and it is *Thru* which most of all earned its author the reputation of 'obscure'.

Published in 1974, the work simultaneously addresses and pokes fun at the turmoil of literary theories which were fighting for precedence on the French scene during the sixties and seventies. In this sense, the novel is a perfect example for the fusion of different signifying systems, a semiotic encounter *par excellence*, which blends disparate critical discourses and transforms them to create a new, subversive *discourse on discourses*.

Thru offers neither a conventionally-delineated plot, nor a narrator in the traditional sense of the term: discourses and situations present themselves *objectively* and the narration consists of a flux of utterances coming from numerous sources which continually slide from one to the other, giving the reader no means to distinguish them but (and not always) the context. Nevertheless, a basic situation can be reconstructed throughout the text: we are in a class of creative writing at a university, probably in America; the teacher is Armel Santores, whereas his ex wife, Larissa Toren, is a teacher as well but in another, unspecified university; the students' homework is presented in the text together with their class discussions and events from Armel's and Larissa's private lives, their relationship, their break-up and their respective love affairs with Veronica and Stavro.

Although various themes can be detected throughout the novel (language, love, teaching problems, politics, memory and history among others), the text is most emblematic for the reader in light of the collage of theories it addresses and transforms, the dialogue among them resulting in metaphorical discourse. In *Thru*, *myriads* of critical issues reveal themselves and are inextricably linked with one another. Hence, the over-stressed difficulty for which Brooke-Rose got – in her own words – "rapped on the creative knuckles" (Brooke-Rose 1989, 103).[3]

Barthes, Lacan, Derrida, Kristeva, Greimas, Bahktin, Irigaray, Propp and Jakobson are some of the figures whose theories are 'dismantled' and 'reconstructed' in the text. Their specialised jargons and different theories are fused, rehandled and played on. Crossing each other, different signifying practices give life to new meanings and endless interpretations.

What Brooke-Rose calls the "jargon and discourse that human beings invent to protect their discipline and to keep the outsider out" (Tredell 32),

---

[2] Christine Brooke-Rose, *Thru* [London: Hamish Hamilton, 1975]. *The Christine Brooke-Rose Omnibus*. 577-742. All subsequent references to the text will be from this edition and will be abbreviated as *T*.

[3] "My real fans, however, seem to like this one best. Perhaps my real fans are all narratologists", comments Brooke-Rose (Brooke-Rose 1989, 103).

becomes metaphorical if embedded in a specific context and interpreted literally, often repeated in different contexts and consequently acquiring diverse connotations.[4] Juxtaposition and repetition play a basic role in this process since by juxtaposing separate words or sentences, a link is created between them and a new, unexpected and metaphorical implication is generated. This effect is further enhanced when a word or sentence previously used comes back (often slightly varied) in a different context and suddenly gives life to something new, highlighting the surprising, often hilarious and/or poetical aspect of language.

All the critical theories presented in *Thru* form an integral part of the events its characters seem to experience. In order to better appreciate the way they build up the narrative and how the text reshapes them for its own purposes, I will provide some examples of this practice.

The famous Barthesian question "Who speaks?" is frequently asked in the text in order to highlight and play on the impossibility of distinguishing a steady point of view which filters narration, while Barthes' concept of the *death of the author* ironically becomes the object of discussion between the teacher and one of the students during a class debate,

> But what about the clarity of the message?
> You read what you want into it.
> I see. And what do you read?
> It's not for me to say, I wrote it.
> But the reader is the writer and the writer is the reader. (*T* 608)

If the contemporary trend has utterly dismissed the author from the text in favour of the supreme reader's interpretation, the whole question is here humorously recast: if the reader is the writer, it follows that the writer is the reader and therefore can read into the text what he wants: a paradoxical, unsustainable situation.

Similarly, the Lacanian dialectic of desire is repeatedly used to tackle sex and love themes. The relationships delineated between the characters of opposite sexes continually reflect the subject's/object's lack of heart and are governed by the much discussed castration complex: "in the dialectic of desire, the subject is subverted and the object is from the start an object of central loss" (*T* 594). In this connection, when Armel and Larissa argue, the well-known question "Che vuoi?" jumps back from one to the other,

---

[4] In this respect the author reveals, "I needed to send up the structuralist jargon, also to use it as poetry, to use the very jargon of narratology as a metaphor, in a way, to deconstruct it" (Friedman and Fuchs 88).

> But what do you want?
> Ah! Che vuoi? (*T* 654)

If the coordination of the subject's discourse for Lacan occurs in a mechanic of transfer to and from the locus of the Other, it is always the *Other* who seems to speak in *Thru*. The letter O – varying into A for *Autre* – is a basic pattern throughout the text: "S represents the subject of discourse and O the Other place and o the object of desire $o^1\ o^2\ o^n$." (*T* 669). If it is from the Other that the subject receives the image of itself and its own discourse, in Brooke-Rose's novel we read, "Who speaks? The Other Author" (*T* 705), a sentence which combines Lacan's and Barthes' theoretical implications.

After Larissa receives a marriage proposal by Stavro, the Lacanian dialectic subject/object mingles with Greimas' semiotic square, where contrary concepts are both opposed and equivalent to each other in a direct logic of interrelation, as a way of expanding on the latent modality of desire in a love relationship,

> the dialectic of desire that gravitationally pulls you towards the centre of attention she enjoys as from the start an object of central loss [...] will you stay with me always always please will you marry me. [...] the introduction, into the superficial grammar, of wanting as a modality, permits the construction of modal utterances with two actants united in a proposition, the axis of desire then authorizing a semenic interpretation of them as virtual performer subject and an object instituted as value. Adam wants an apple Adam wants to be good. Such an acquisition, by the subject of the object, seems to occur as a reflex action, which is only a particular case of a much more general structure well known as the diagram of communication represented in its canonic form as an M and a Y of crossed limbs with diagonals from the I to the object

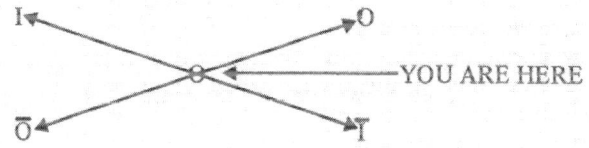

> never believing anything said in moments of passion

(*T* 694f.)

A quotation from Bakhtin is used by Larissa to oppose Armel's denigration of Stavro,

> You have no right to reify him into the voiceless object of an intellect that delimits him. A human being lives to the end on his lack of definition, he always has the last word. Read Bakhtine! Of course he'll have the last word which will be a cowardly silence. (*T* 711)

The basic role played by linguistics within the contemporary cultural panorama is made clear by Larissa conversing with Stavro. The dialogue leads to a highly ironical comment on semioticians,

> […] most of the books of those shelves, which are my corner, are in your field aren't they, all the disciplines have come together through linguistics now it's very exciting every system is being thought out again from top to bottom, even psychoanalysis has taken up from de Saussure.
> Who's de Saussure?
> But. Stavro! I thought you said you taught Linguistics? He's the father of it all.
> Well, I don't know, it's Applied Linguistics I do.
> Oh – I see. I'm sorry, I didn't mean, but why did you come to the Semiotics Congress then?
> Oh just to see and learn.
> And did you?
> Not really, it all struck me as very pretentious.
> Some of it yes. But that's the funny side, *even semioticians don't communicate*. (*T* 721)[5]

At Christmas time, a company of six people sit chatting by an open fire in a cottage. Larissa's perceptions are described by recurring to linguistic terms as she "watches, bored, the imperceptible shrug of scorn functioning like the bar between signifier and signified for ever eluded" (*T* 649).

During a class debate one of the students gets angry and starts criticising the organ isation of the academic syllabus in very violent terms, upon which the teacher remarks,

> You are turning this place into a carnival. Well I have no objection it's a mode of perception as Bakhtine has shown, but you should then be aware that carnival has its own structure at every level all taboos suspended all hierarchy reversed and certain very specific ineluctable processes I forebear to mention. (*T* 635)

Linguistic jokes – which in *Thru* are wide-ranging – humorously address the critical debate as well: the acronym "R.E.M." (*T* 596) which initially stands for Rapid Eye Movement, comes to signify the relationship between Recipient, Emitter and Message: "unrapid eyes movements tampering the Message between Emitter and Recipient so that EMR → REM (REM)" (*T* 610f.). In the same way, the critical concept of "fallacy" is humorously played upon as it becomes the "pathetic fallacy" (*T* 595), whilst Todorov's concept of *porte-récit* is ironically mistranslated as "tale-bearer" and explained while mixed with the Lacanian Other,

---

[5] Emphasis mine.

160 Ida M. Samperi

a tale-bearer, whose life also depends on his narration generated by the surplus value left over from the previous tale and itself generating the next. Read Todorov les homes-récits on this. Each I leads into another I, unless I into O for Other interruption with a point of information? (*T* 618)

Even the typographical arrangements such as columns with binary oppositions or linguistic trees seem to recall structural principles and order. It is not by chance therefore that the figure resembling a linguistic tree has at its basis the word 'order'.

(*T* 615)

This image also seems to represent the outline of a amphitheatrically-shaped university room, where a faculty meeting is being held, miming therefore the confusion of the many participants' voices during the meeting, each expressing their ideas while the president calls for 'order', thus at the same time providing the reader with information on what is being said and describing the arrangement of the room without referring to a conventional description.

Again, Jakobson's model of communication is both printed on the page and variously addressed in different contexts, as for instance when the teacher warns the class,

> we mustn't confuse the levels of discourse. My function here is not to narrate but to teach, or shall we say I am not a function of your narrative, and we are using a metalanguage, so: [...]

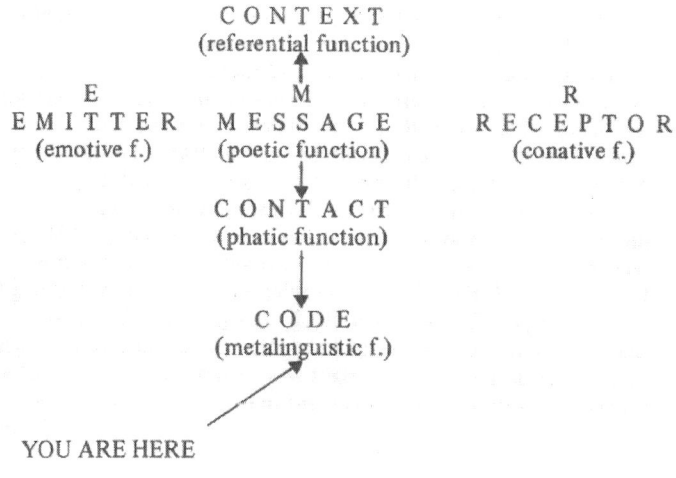

(*T* 628f.)

Rastier's (*T* 658), Irigaray's (*T* 631) and Kristeva's (*T* 647) are some of the other theories played upon in the text, together with the presentation of some elements of Boolean algebra (*T* 699), with musical notations (*T* 619), with lullabies, popular songs, sayings, linguistic jokes and Chinese ideograms. Even an excerpt from a rhetoric manual dating back to 1574 is entirely reported on the page.

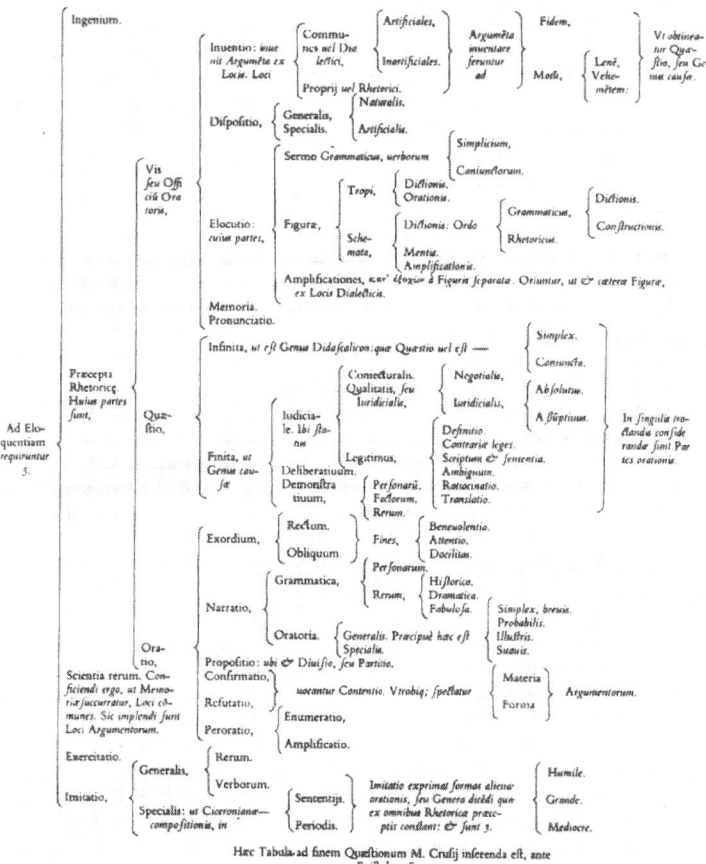

(*T* 601)

Stretching across theories, *Thru* plays on their mixture and their dialogue which results in interdisciplinary and parodying discourse, a collage which aims at subverting those very discourses it is made of. As a matter of fact, the text never fails to *renew* the endless allusions to and quotations from other books, magisterially distorting and blending them in order to let new and sudden relations of meaning emerge between them: a new text, an new solution is created out of the old preexisting ones.

Another case in point is the relationship between Stavro and Larissa, which is interpreted in the light of Derrida's idea of text, of the Lacanian dialectic of desire and of Greimas' notion of attribution and wanting modality,

> [t]hese things do matter in a text like the human body [...]. "The introduction, into the superficial grammar, of wanting as a modality, permits the construction of modal utterances with two actants: the subject and the object. The axis of desire uniting them then authorises a semantic interpretation of them as virtual performer subject and object instituted as a value. (*T* 633)

Later on, after a dialogue between Armel and his 'other' lover (Larissa and Armel both have other lovers but still depend on each other), Jakobson's diagram is used to convey the idea of a quadrangular love relationship:

> the eternal quadrangle or [...] two deixes that are conjoined, because corresponding to the same axis of contradiction, but not conforming, and equivalent, at the fundamental level, to contradictory terms [...]. Thus the circulation of values, interpreted as a sequence of transfers of value-objects. (*T* 667)

A salient example for this theoretical bricolage is to be found in a paragraph that presents Derrida's *différance*, Lacan's unmarked term and Freud's Fort-da, all rehandled in the light of a discourse on the fictionality of the characters and their relationship to each other and to the text when Armel tells Larissa,

> reinvent me [...] I shall then be different (and language consists of difference!) but from what unmarked term of your binary conception is harder to determine than in mere linguistics [...] we do not exist. But by all means let's go on pretending we do, going forth da and multiplying the letters (Fort/da). (*T* 631)

All the different discourses reassembled and rehandled within the fictional tissue acquire multimetaphorical meanings. At each reading a multiplicity of new interpretations and combinations of meaning can be discovered. The same author explains, "I've always been fascinated by the fusions effected through metaphor and this can be done in many subterranean ways" (Turner 27).

Along these lines, *Thru* becomes, in Barthes' words, a writing which

> ceaselessly posits meaning to evaporate it, carrying out a systematic exemption of meaning [and which], by refusing to assign a 'secret', an ultimate meaning, to the text (and to the world as text), liberates what may be called an anti-theological activity, an activity that is truly revolutionary since to refuse to fix meaning is, in the end, to refuse God and his hypostases – reason, science, law. (Barthes 1977, 147)

Thru challenges and subverts, in line with Derrida's deconstruction, the supposed transparent relation of meaning and thing represented, i.e. the metaphysical notion of being as "self-presence of the subject" (Derrida 1976, 12), for which meaning is instituted once and for all. The deferral of meaning ensures that meaning can never be definitively present. Since the sign always refers to other signs *ad infinitum*, in a process where no ultimate referent or foundation can be established, meaning is ultimately undecidable: *Thru* produces a proliferation and a dissemination of meaning.

What is more, such a multiple fusion of discourses acquires a peculiar poetical value which is underlined by the teacher on various occasions,

> you've done linguistics haven't you no well you must every poet must it's wildly poetic, the binary polarity in any field phonic or semic [...] white versus black or white versus non-white. But that's logic it's as old as Socrates it comes in the Protagoras. (*T* 661)

> Generative grammar's the thing it's the grammar of the universe and it's wildly poetic why they have rules called it-deletion and psych-movement subject-raising and object-raising and head-noun chopping can you imagine the object of central loss being raised read Hegel on Aufhebung it becomes wildly funny. (*T* 662f.)

In this light, the language of *Thru* exemplifies the poetic language Kristeva theorised, a "signifying practice" (Kristeva 1984, 15) which counters formalist structures and attests to the limits of ideological constructs for the interpretation of the text. Poetic language shakes the border between 'true' and 'false', undermines meaning, it is "polyvalent and multi-determined" (Kristeva 1980, 65), it does not permit identification with one single meaning, it always escapes the definition of one unique truth and offers multiple connotations and interpretative possibilities.

Thru is a dialogic, revolutionary text, a polyphonic novel where discourse reads itself, enters into dialogue with itself and "constructs itself through a process of destructive genesis" (Kristeva 1980, 77). In its subversive and rebellious carnivalesque structure, "two texts meet, contradict, and relativise each other" (Kristeva 1980, 78), thus subverting binarism, destroying the order of the law, the 0-1 logic, God, the authority, the univocal and dogmatic structure of society.

Being a dialogic, polyphonic novel, *Thru* has remained on the edge of official culture as it tends to explode the structure of bourgeois society, its system of signification. *Thru*'s polyphony entails a logic *other*, which is the reason why, to use Kristeva's words, it has been "declared unreadable, ignored [because it] embodies the effort [...] to break out of the framework of causally determined identical substances and head toward another modality of thought that proceeds through dialogue" (Kristeva 1980, 89). Brooke-

Rose's novel is thus "a practice that pulverises unity, making it a process that posits and displaces theses" (Kristeva 1984, 208), a struggle which dissolves the bond between subject and society, creating the conditions for renewal.

If, as Kristeva saw, a dialogic novel is necessarily intertextual – "dialogism identifies writing as [...] intertextuality" (Kristeva 1980, 68) – in that the text inserts itself into the chain of "exterior" texts and the chain of texts is inserted within the text, then intertextuality as subversive strategy becomes the very structuring principle of *Thru*. The intertextual dialogue is introduced by the very first image of the novel: four eyes which stare back through the rearview mirror of a car, two of them real, the other two generated by an optical illusion. The movement of looking forward and seeing one's own reflection coming back initiates the practice of the text looking at itself and reflecting what is behind, reflecting other texts and thus positing itself within their chain. In *Thru* indeed, we read that the "text within the text [...] generates another text" (*T* 631) and that the new solution generated is "a text which in effect is a dialogue with all preceding texts" (*T* 621).

Intertextuality is subversive in that it opens up a dialogue between the discourses of the critical debates of the time and the present text, reshaping theories into metaphor. It becomes, however, the more subversive as it inserts those discourses into the wider chain of the *entire culture* and its *fictional* production. In point of fact, the endless network of quotations, the texts and subtexts *Thru* is made up of, are both the 'real' critical texts of narratology and the fictional texts of literature.

Thru addresses the *whole* textual tradition, from Cervantes to Rabelais, from the Bible to the contemporary literary debates on fiction, from e.e. cummings to David the psalmist, from Scheherazade to *I Promessi Sposi* and Beckett, from Sterne's *Tristram Shandy* to Didcrot's *Jacques*. Literary references, echoes and quotations are spread all over the novel and used by the characters in their conversations to express their feelings or comment on the situations presented: T.S. Eliot, Dante, Shakespeare, E.M. Forster, Wallace Stevens and so on, "[w]ithin each text is another text, within each myth another myth" (*T* 608), like a "show within the show" (*T* 587). References are endless and structured as a *regressus ad infinitum*, a process which can be summarised in the pseudo-formula, "F(bo(lo(bo(lo(books)oks)oks)oks)oks)n" (*T* 684), reinstated as "Books within books, looks within looks, looks within books, books within looks" (*T* 678), or in the principle of "Once upon a time laid out in rectangles into which you enter as into a room saying once upon a time" (*T* 605), a play on the classical beginning of a fairy tale which infinitely leads onto other tales. The text is said to be "in its moment [...] of dialogue with all preceding texts" (*T* 699). Since "[n]o text just comes out ex nihilo, it always comes out of other texts" (Tredell 34), each book is in communication with all preceding books, each book looks back, like in a rear mirror, for its predecessors, it must confront its antecedents, it is impossible to elude what came before, for a book is the result of the history of culture and narration. To look back is absolutely necessary to go forward, just like looking back in the rear mirror of the car is necessary for us to drive safely. Like Barthes' 'inter-text', *Thru* embodies "the impossibility of living outside the infinite text" (Barthes 1975, 36), referring to other texts in a never-ending movement of intertextuality and becoming "a multi-dimensional space in which a variety of writings, none of them original, blend and clash [...] a tissue of quotations drawn from the innumerable centres of culture" (Barthes 1977, 146).

In a text where one of the characters states "we've used almost everything from Phaedrus to Freud" (*T* 653), Kristeva's theory on the relationship between (the dead) author, characters and reader is presented as a discussion between Diderot's master and his Jacques. Explaining this dialectic the master tells Jacques "You should read Kristeva that's what she says", and then he paradoxically reinstates "I am in fact dead, Jacques" (*T* 647).

Another salient example of the mix of discourses is to be found when we read, "Che vuoi? [...] Votre demande is not an askable question. Veuillez appeller ultérieurement. Freud Freud why persecutest thou/me" (*T* 675). Lacan's question is here followed by the typical answer of a busy telephone line, to which follows a biblical quotation, the question Christ asks Saul (Acts 22, 7), rehandled with Freud as its addressee. The bar between "thou" and "me" recalls de Saussure's signifier/signified as well as Lacan's subject/object.

Again a lover's request of staying for the night is preceded by a mix of bits of discourses taken from Genette, Barthes, Jakobson and Diderot,

> within the grammar of that narrative the roles can be interchanged and textasy multiplied until punctually at a fixed hour all the forged orgy ceases. For the deep structure of I am your slave is undoubtedly you will be mine and yet there is no transformational rule in any grammar which explicitly effects this since it is written up there that all deletions, reflexivisations dative movements object-raisings and other transformations be recoverable so that here it is merely a question of conjugality which comes under the lexicon and the morphophonemic rules as for example in please don't go Armel it's so nice having breakfast together. (*T* 665)

The names of the characters become the cause for an excursus on the meaning and role of proper names in literature, touching on Barthes, Propp and ending up with a direct question to Jacques the fatalist,

> I should have stuck to pronouns as in late twentieth century texts which refuse biographies since a name must have a civic status [...]. That's the rule. Written up there. In the

grammar of narrative. Like attributes–states, properties and statuses. Iterative as opposed to actions. But any agent can enter into relationship with any predicate […] no need to talk like Propp et al of hero villain lawbearer these are predicates. The agent is not the one who can accomplish this or that action but the one who can become subject of a predicate […]. So there have to be proper names after all, Jacques, Jacques why are you asleep? (*T* 647)

Similarly, the dialectic of desire becomes a topic of discussion between Jacques and his master (*T* 595). Again, Barthes' *death of the author* is readdressed and mixed with the mistranslation of Todorov's *porte-récit* and a quotation from Lewis Carroll's Queen of Hearts: "There's no more private property in writing, the author is dead, the spokesman, the porte-parole, the tale-bearer, off with his head" (*T* 607).

By referring simultaneously to the preceding fictional texts and to the contemporary corpus of critical theories, blending together 'real' and fictional texts, intertextuality becomes extremely subversive. *Thru* becomes the centre of dialogism and intertextuality, inscribing itself, as Kristeva explains, at the intersection of two axes: horizontally, it belongs to writing subject and addressee and refers to a specific cultural context, while vertically, it refers to the whole amount of literary works preceding the text (cf. Kristeva 1980, 65). The dialogic text becomes a discourse involving the totality of relationships between the individual, the unconscious and culture, in a movement of confrontation and appropriation which becomes destruction and construction, "productive violence" (Kristeva 1984, 16) and both revolution and *jouissance*.

By dialoguing both with its preceding *fictional* texts and with its contemporary theoretical texts and by inserting the whole amount of discourses into the broader 'text' of our culture, *Thru* perfectly illustrates Derrida's concept that "[t]here is nothing outside of the text" (Derrida 1976, 158), that *everything is text*, that the 'text' is what is broadly inscribed within culture and society, what is both outside and inside it. This very notion is indeed taken up in *Thru* and reworked into several instances: we read of "a text like love" (*T* 660), "a text like the human body or society" (*T* 685), "a text like love and three beautiful illegitimate children" (*T* 660), or again "a text like the world or the human body that merely engenders itself in to writing" (*T* 592-3). The entire culture becomes a *text*, a liminal space between the binary oppositions, which produces endless meaning and possible interpretations.

Clearly stating that "anyone has a right to subvert a text with any other" (*T* 643) and positing "textuality as subversion of society" (*T* 670), *Thru* is a text which deconstructs the concept book and "denudes the surface of the text" (Derrida 1976, 18), "lighting up the commonplaces from the other place to generate a text" (*T* 722), laying bare the system of binary oppositions which supersedes our culture, "white versus non-white […] it's as old as Socrates" (*T* 661), "the war between man and woman, day and night, the city and the tomb" (*T* 678), "the potion and the holy grail the pen and the paper" (*T* 687). In sexual relationships, binary oppositions show the double standard: female adultery is "non-prescribed", whereas male adultery is "non-forbidden" (*T* 661), "the double standard is rampant everywhere one is amazed" (*T* 636). By showing the underlying binarism at the heart of each of these stories and by presenting critical theories as stories themselves, their status of illusion is laid bare. As a 'text' like any other, religion is introduced into the intertextual chain by means of several ironical biblical misquotations. Religion is just another fictional text and even the dogma of Jesus' incarnation is wittingly treated as we read, "did Christ have an Oedipus complex?" (*T* 723). If everything is text, everything is fiction, a trope which can be subverted to show the basic illusion which generates it: love, family, history, society, politics, religion, literary and psychological theories are all 'stories' to be narrated; life is made up of stories.

In this vein, the processes of juxtaposition and repetition which *Thru* enacts are strictly related to Derrida's deconstructive strategy, for which repetition is not the mere return to and of the same, but rather the production of difference within the same, a generative act. It is a continual referral, rather than reference, to other traces. The repetitive and deferring movement of memory constitutes the present as an infinite stratification and rearrangement of "'signs' of memory" (Derrida 1978, 258). Repetitions in *Thru* are the same but different (slightly varied in content or context) inscribing the text into a spiral movement of space and time: everything comes back but it is different at the same time. Repetition becomes the trace, the différance which deconstructs a notion of closed off present-to-itself and for itself – a movement strictly linked to the intertextual theme: literature is a text in which everything comes back again and again to generate new life out of the old to create a new text out of its intertextual remainders. The present is both a return and the possibility of a return, of repetition. Presence is only possible by means of the différance, the trace, the operation of signification which endlessly links past and future. Signification does not depend on presence as origin (the author, the speaker, meaning), it is independent from the absence, because arche-writing is at work at the origin of sense. Meaning is never simply present, but *always already* engaged in the movement of the trace.

If each text bears in itself other texts *ad infinitum*, the juxtaposition of texts, basic to Derrida's approach, lays bare the text within the text and produces subversion. By means of juxtaposition, *Thru* carries on the deconstructive strategy within and by itself, becoming a "blue lacuna of learning and unlearning a text within a text" (*T* 585).

Christine Brooke-Rose's Thru   169

A perfect illustration for the fusion of real and fictive texts is constituted by Larissa being presented as a "dompna soisebuda", made up of the parts of different women. The dance of the seven veils becomes the dance of her twenty-seven selves,

> composed of femme-reine, femme-enfant femme-fatale, grey eminence Cleopatra's nose Musset's Muse a bit of Heloise old and new the charming scatterbrain Georges Sand Mme de Merteuil George Eliot Antigone Elizabeth Barrett Browning Elinour of Aquitaine Mrs. Pankhurst Circe Julia Kristeva Joan Baez Penelope Virginia Woolf Helen of Troy la princesse lointaine Scheherezade Pallas Athene la belle indifférente the man with the blue guitar.

The dance of the twenty-seven veils/

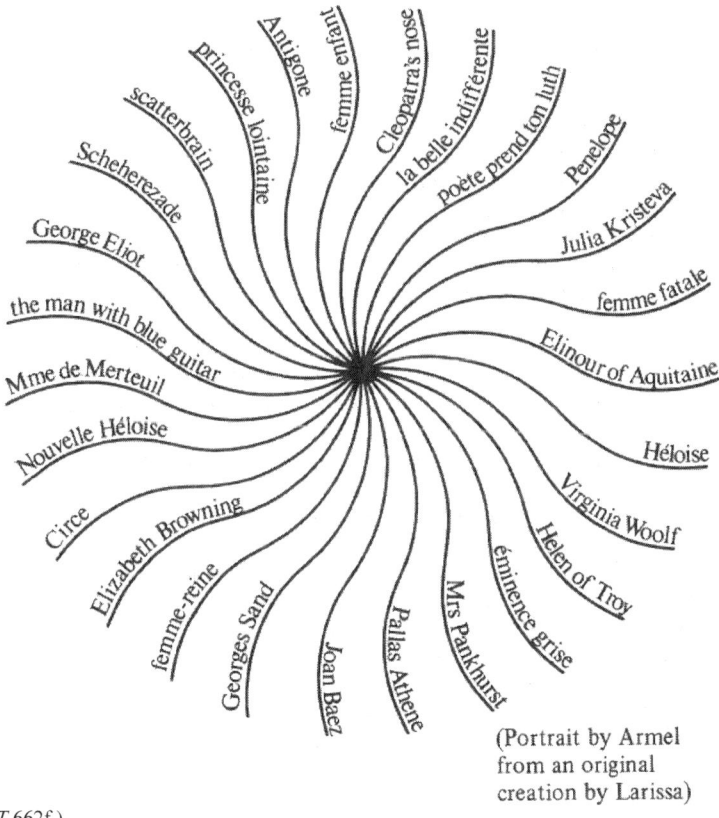

(Portrait by Armel from an original creation by Larissa)

(*T* 662f.)

Larissa is a fictional character made up of parts from both 'real' and fictive personae. The boundary between reality and fiction is blurred as 'reality' is shown to be only a construct.

Another case in point is the very special sort of bibliography which lists on the same footing both real and fictive personalities,

> See Bibliography*
> *retrogradiens
> Wallace Stevens John Dryden Umberto Eco Daniel Defoe Sigmund Freud Moses Ezra Pound Wallace Stevens T.S. Eliot (or Guido Cavalacanti) Dante Alighieri Alexander Pope William Shakespeare Saroja Chaitwantee S. Eliot Snoopy Hegel Ali Nourennin and the occidental discourse of Westerns.
> **retroprogradiens
> The retrovizor 1001 Nights Ezra Pound Lewis Carroll Robert Burns Lewis Carroll Robert Graves Louis Hjelmslev Ali Nourennin Paul Stradiver oh her Georges Bataille William Shakespeare Jacques Derrida A.J. Greimas Noam Chomsky Plato Ezra Pound the voters Ruth Veronica his reflection Diderot Roland Barthes Edward Fitzgerald Francis Bacon Sophocles W.K. Wimsatt Robert Greene Daniel Defoe Moses Wallace Stevens Sigmund Freud Wallace Stevens the folk Barbra Streisand Jesus Christ Frank Kermode Jacques Lacan Denis Diderot the institution Ezra Pound the chairman of the hour Jeremy Roland Barthes Francis Bacon Jeremy Armel Tzvetan Todorov e.e. cummings the short plump demagogue Bertrans de Born James Joyce Wayne C. Booth Homer Roman Jakobson Julia Kristeva Ali Nourennin at al W.B Yeats Northrup Frye Umberto Eco John Cage Jane Austen a Victorian old maid Julia Kristeva Dr. Santores the Institution Saroja Chaitwantee Traditional Wisdom Gertrude Stein William Shakespeare Peter Brandt Christopher Isherwood Ali Nourennin Anton Chekov the chairman of the hour hagiography Armel? The lanky henchman Julian Claire Olivier the chairman of the hour Charles at al Homo Scholasticus Lawrence Sterne Choto Rustaveli Scheherezade Tzvetan Todorov the Student Body Karl Marx Plato Tristram Shandy Alessandro Manzoni thus meeting up with the occidental discourse of the Western. (*T* 622-3)

This peculiar inventory also presents characters from *Thru*, (Ali Nourennin, Saroja Chaitwantee or Dr. Santores), thus strengthening the link between preceding (fictional and 'real') texts and figures and the present text.

The binarism fiction/reality is played upon throughout the text: the relationship between the inner reality of the text and the outer, 'real' world it refers to, is blurred. With an apparently contradictory dynamics, the text seems to dismantle the idea of fiction as representation of an "outer world reality", "this being a text, not an imitation of life" (*T* 657), focusing the attention of both the reader and the characters on the process which shapes the chimera of writing, endlessly referring to the "optical illusion" it creates. At the same time, however, the text shows how the supposed authenticity of the 'real' withdraws behind layers of narration, how reality is an illusion and 'everything is text'. The 'real' level outside the narrative game is undermined.

In this way, the text utterly denies the prospect of discerning between 'internal' and 'external' reality, also by means of a continuous and purposeful shift of focalisation which shakes the whole logic of narrative representation. The hierarchy of narrative levels collapses into absolute reversibility, suggesting that there might be no reality apart from the text ('there is nothing outside of the text').

Thru is "text of radical ontological hesitation" (McHale 200), which utterly abolishes the border between real and fictional. It is impossible to separate 'truth' from 'falsehood', because this very distinction crumbles. The once steady border between reality and representation collapses as reality becomes fiction and *vice versa*. This absolute blurring is carried on in order to subvert the real/fictional dichotomy and to reaffirm the latter. We are unable to distinguish what is 'true' from what is 'false' and indeed we are not meant to, because it all is 'just narration', narration being neither true nor false, but 'simply' narration.

If the opposition truth/falsehood, reality/fiction, real/imitation is subverted, *Thru* reaffirms the fictionality of fiction, because "this is the text we are creating it verbally we are the text we do not exist either we are a pack of lies" and because after all "as you said yourselves or was it Armel, it's only a semiotic castle" (*T* 733).

Works Cited

Barthes, Roland. *The Pleasure of the Text*. Trans. Richard Miller. New York: Hill and Wang, 1975.
—. *Image Music Text: Essays Selected and Translated by Stephen Heath*. London: Fontana, 1977.
Brooke-Rose, Christine. *Between*. 1968. *The Christine Brooke-Rose Omnibus: Four Novels: Out, Such, Between, Thru*. Manchester: Carcanet, 1986. 391-575.
—. *Out*. 1964. *The Christine Brooke-Rose Omnibus: Four Novels: Out, Such, Between, Thru*. Manchester: Carcanet, 1986. 7-198.
—. *Such*. 1966. *The Christine Brooke-Rose Omnibus: Four Novels: Out, Such, Between, Thru*. Manchester: Carcanet, 1986. 199-390.
—. *Thru*. 1975. *The Christine Brooke-Rose Omnibus: Four Novels: Out, Such, Between, Thru*. Manchester: Carcanet, 1986. 577-742.
—. "Illicitations." *The Review of Contemporary Fiction* 9.3 (1989): 101-9.

Derrida, Jacques. *Of Grammatology*. Trans. Gayatri Chakravorty Spivak. Baltimore: Johns Hopkins UP, 1976.

—. *Writing and Difference*. Trans. Alan Bass. Chicago: CUP, 1978.

Friedman, Ellen G. and Miriam Fuchs. "A Conversation with Christine Brooke-Rose." *The Review of Contemporary Fiction* 9.3 (1989): 81-90.

The Holy Bible: King James Version. London: Collins Clear Type Press, 1957.

Kristeva, Julia. "Word, Dialogue, and Novel." *Desire in Language: A Semiotic Approach to Literature and Art*. Ed. Leon S. Roudiez. Trans. Thomas Gora, Alice Jardin and Leon S. Roudiez. New York: Columbia UP, 1980. 64-91.

—. *Revolution in Poetic Language*. Trans. Margaret Waller. New York: Columbia UP, 1984.

McHale, Brian. "'I Draw the Line as a Rule between One Solar System and Another': The Postmodernism(s) of Christine Brooke-Rose." *Utterly Other Discourse: The Texts of Christine Brooke-Rose*. Eds Ellen G. Friedman and Richard Martin. Normal (IL): Dalkey Archive Press, 1995. 192-213.

Tredell, Nicholas. "Christine Brooke-Rose in Conversation." *P. N. Review* (1990): 29-35.

Turner, Jenny. "Reclaim the Brain." *Edinburgh Review* (1990): 19-32.

Visual Encounters

Nicola Glaubitz

Transcribing Images – Reassembling Cultures: Kazuo Ishiguro's Japan

Ishiguro's 1986 novel *An Artist of the Floating World* engages with processes of constructing and ascribing identities in a transcultural and intermedial perspective. Its painter protagonist Masuji Ono narrates his experience of cultural transition during the American occupation of Japan immediately after the Second World War, trying to cope with the loss of an unquestioned sense of cultural, personal and political identity. The essay introduces the notions of 'transcription' and 'translation' of cultures in order to argue that Ishiguro identifies, not the presence of cultural differences as such, but the absence of reliable frameworks of reference as problematic effects of a culture on the brink of globalisation. In so far as Ishiguro's writing is indebted to Japanese film and consciously addresses an audience familiar with mass media images of other cultures, the question of how cultural differences are constituted remains virulent but, as the essay argues, finally unresolved for the novel as a whole.

I

Kazuo Ishiguro's relation to his place of birth, Japan, has been an issue in the critical discussion of his books ever since the surprising success of his first novel, *A Pale View of Hills,* in 1982. His Japanese name and the (partly) Japanese setting he chose for his first two books suggested an outsider's view on British culture as it is portrayed, for example, in *A Pale View of Hills* and in *The Remains of the Day* (1989). Moreover, the success of writers like Salman Rushdie and Timothy Mo coincided with the publication of Ishiguro's first books and contributed to critical interest in postcolonial literature, and this label was tentatively applied to Ishiguro, too. But Ishiguro is not writing from a postcolonial perspective and Japan, itself a colonising nation, has no history of colonialism. One may even argue if and to what extent Ishiguro writes from an immigrant's point of view (Cheng 9), having left Japan with his family at the age of six and having received a "very British" education (Bigsby 16) in the south of England. The issue of cultural difference nevertheless plays a major role in his novels. If cultures "may be said to be the invention, manufacture, and partial implementation of 'fictitious' (in Bentham's sense) cores and differences under pressure" (Pfeiffer 198), this essay will argue that the pressures Ishiguro engages with are those of globalisation rather than imperialism (Sim 25). The conditions and processes of (cultural) identity construction are addressed, in this context, through the issues of visual entertainment culture and visual stereotypes in *An Artist of the Floating World* (1986). The historical period to which Ishiguro kept returning in four of his novels[1] – the decades from the 1930s through the Second World War into the 1950s – are significant in this context as a period of transition from imperialism to globalisation and one of its palpable symptoms, the growing worldwide influence of American popular culture (Ashcroft 11).

In *An Artist of the Floating World*, first-person narrator Masuji Ono, an elderly and retired painter, is looking back on episodes of his life. He lives in an unspecified Japanese city and tries to adapt to the new social and political order characterised increasingly by elements of American culture. The book's four sections are set in 1948, in April and in November 1949, and in 1950. In the narrated present, family affairs prompt Ono to come to terms with his past: his younger daughter's (Noriko) marriage plans have failed because her future husband's family unexpectedly pulled out of the marriage negotiations. Another opportunity comes up for her, but she and her sister Setsuko are apprehensive that Ono's support for Japanese militarism in the Second World War (he painted propaganda images) will again prove an obstacle for her marriage plans. Ono thinks over his career and finally even apologises for his mistaken political allegiances to his prospective in-laws. At least, this is how Ono perceives the situation: once Noriko is married, she and her sister deny ever having urged him to apologise, or to come to terms with his past (*AFW* 191, 193), and the narrative gives no clue whether they tell the truth, whether they want to protect him from further self-doubts or whether they have acted from selfish motives, taking advantage of Ono's failing memory and trying to disclaim responsibility for his embarrassing act of apology (cf. Petry 77). Ono, throughout the book, is debating with himself whether he remembers episodes from his past correctly. In his encounters with former colleagues, friends and with his family, a sense of his past as well his personal identity emerge as a result of constant reaffirmation, correction and renegotiation. As a consequence, it remains tantalisingly impossible for Ono to assign any unquestionable – and that means socially shared – significance to many episodes of his life. A similar search for and subsequent slippage of significance characterises his artistic career. The ascription of meanings to visual representations, and the always provisional quality of such ascriptions, mirrors Ono's search for the significance of his life's work. Visual stereotypes, or 'visiotypes', and culturally specific painting styles are a recurring topic of debate between the novel's characters.[2] The processes of

---

[1] The decades before and after the Second World War serve as backdrops for *A Pale View of Hills* and *An Artist of the Floating World* (hereafter quoted as *AFW*), the *The Remains of the Day* (1989) and *When We Were Orphans* (2000).

[2] Uwe Pörksen has introduced the term 'visiotypes' for images which have come to stand for concepts in certain discursive contexts (Pörksen 27), as for example the image of the 'blue

meaning construction that Ishiguro describes are located between visual and verbal semiotic systems, on the level of the narrated as well as that of narrative strategy. In the following considerations, Ludwig Jäger's terms 'transcription' or 'transcriptivity' will be introduced to describe this intermedial relation.

II

Ono's very first employer, the Takeda firm, plunges him into the production of visual stereotypes. The firm manufactures paintings for export and the paintings Ono is asked to produce are supposed to look 'typically Japanese'. The apprentice painter senses that he and his colleagues are involved in an act of self-orientalisation (cf. Lewis 18f., 25f.):

> We were [...] quite aware that the essential point about the sort of things we were commissioned to paint – geishas, cherry trees, swimming carps, temples – was that they look 'Japanese' to the foreigners to whom they were shipped out, and all the finer points of style were quite likely to go unnoticed. (*AFW* 69)

The 'Japanese look' of paintings will become a central concern for Ono, who develops the vision of a socially and politically engaged art in order to alleviate social injustice and to overcome Westernisation. One of the major conflicts the book stages is that between Ono and his teacher Seiji Moriyama, whose position can be characterised as aestheticist. Moriyama (or Mori-san, as he is nicknamed by his students) is determined to make his pupils appreciate the world of socially marginalised itinerant actors and musicians, whom he frequently invites to his country house-cum-studio for drinking bouts. Moriyama's celebration of the ephemeral beauty and the passing moments of melancholy he finds in the actors' lives and performances reads like a continuation of central ideas of Edo aesthetics (Lewis 55). Without having developed into a philosophical discipline and without constituting an institution of 'art' in the Western sense, Japanese discourses on aesthetics from the Edo period (1600-1868) have singled out certain situations, embedded in mundane practices like tea-drinking, music, calligraphy or poetry, as art-like (Parkes 2005). Japanese aesthetic terminology describes moods and situa-

---

planet' has come to stand for the earth's fragile ecological balance, or as the double helix has come to stand for the DNA and consequently for the human genome. Pörksen is mainly concerned with the political implications of visiotypes within political discourses (in the wider sense of the term) and argues that visiotypes are more resistant to change and negotiations than language-based stereotypes. For those images discussed here that evoke a cluster of sometimes unspecific meanings, I will continue to use the somewhat awkward term 'visual stereotype'.

tions rather than objects and forms, for example *mono no aware*, standing for the transience and 'pathos' of things, or *yugen*, standing for the impression of profundity and mystery (Parkes 2005, Odin 3f. and passim). The fictive painter in Ishiguro's book continues this tradition of capturing the so-called 'floating world', the world of entertainment, prostitution and night life in Japan's capital as depicted in the *ukiyo-e* woodblock prints of Hishikawa Moronobu (1618-1694), Kitagawa Utamaro (1753-1806), or Ando Hiroshige (1797-1858).[3]

In the book, Moriyama is praised as a "modern Utamaro" (*AFW* 140) and his programme is described as a conscious attempt "to 'modernize' the Utamaro tradition" (*AFW* 140). From Ono's perspective, this is achieved mainly through Westernisation: Moriyama "had, for instance, long abandoned the use of the traditional dark outline to define his shapes, preferring instead the Western use of blocks of colour, with light and shade to create a three-dimensional appearance" (*AFW* 141). His main concern, Ono reports, was to "capture the feel of lantern light" (*AFW* 141). This description, however, is close to the aesthetic position formulated by Japanese novelist Junichiro Tanizaki in his well-known 1933 essay *In praise of shadows* (*In'ei raizan*), which is certainly not in favour of Westernisation. Quite on the contrary, Tanizaki sets out to demonstrate the significance of traditional Japanese aesthetic categories for the present. Not always avoiding essentialist arguments, he argues that Eastern art can be distinguished by its mastery of shadows, that is, its subtle, implicit, allusive and subdued modes of expression, from a general tendency towards clarity and explicitness inherent in Western art. He also praises the morbid and mysterious appearance of women when they keep hidden in the darkness of traditional Japanese houses or in sparsely lit rooms at night (Tanizaki 50-52, 59-62). When Moriyama's mastery in evoking "a certain melancholy, nocturnal atmosphere around his women" (*AFW* 141) in lamp-lit darkness is described in Ishiguro's novel, the parallel to Tanizaki is obvious.

Ishiguro's references to Japanese art begin with evocations of a well-known visual repertoire of woodcuts which became popular in Europe in the context of late 19th-century *japonisme* (and encouraged Claude Monet and Vincent van Gogh to rethink and change traditional European modes of organising pictorial space). The descriptions of Moriyama's style, however, encourage readers to imagine a combination of styles normally considered as typically Japanese and characteristically European, and the allusions to aes-

---

[3] *Ukiyo* is a term from Buddhism referring to the transience of all things; *e* means 'picture' (Lewis 55). Katsushika Hokusai's (1760-1849) 'Great Wave off Kanagawa', depicting a small boat about to be submerged by a tsunami wave with Mount Fuji in the background, is perhaps the best known and most widely reproduced woodblock print motif.

thetic positions add further complications: Moriyama combines the European avant-gardes' spirit of new departures in art with an allegiance to aesthetic ideas of the Edo period. The larger historical and cultural context in which the artist's work is one of constant exchange between Japan and Europe. Any attempt to identify national or cultural styles and to align them with specific aesthetic positions is bound to fail. The importance both Ono and Moriyama ascribe to stylistic differences, therefore, seems exaggerated and the school's constant discussions about 'heresies' and 'treason' suggest that the complexity of subtle aesthetic issues – but maybe also their banality – is not really at stake and in fact serves as a screen for the actually virulent questions of loyalty and hierarchy.

This suspicion of banality overshadows Ono's final break with Moriyama and will continue to haunt the aging painter. In the 1930s, Ono still firmly believes that artists should directly engage with social and political issues and correspondingly adapts his style: in rejection of Mori-san's 'decadent' and Westernised manner of painting, he returns to the graphic outlines of Japanese woodcuts (*AFW* 168, 174). As a description of one of his paintings suggests, he also returns, unawares, to the easily decipherable stereotypes of Japan that he had despised so much at Takeda's, using the mythical image of the samurai warrior as an eye-catching signifier of Japan's heroic past: three impoverished, ragged boys are wearing "the manly scowls of samurai warriors ready to fight. It is no coincidence [...] that the boys in my picture held their sticks in classic kendo stances" (*AFW* 168). Ono even enhances the immediately recognisable message of the image with "bold red characters" (*AFW* 168). This strategy of endowing an image with an unmistakable meaning can be read as a final act of rebellion against Moriyama, who had rejected any such instrumentalisation of art. The narrative, however, remains impartial and plays down the importance of these contrary aesthetic positions: a closer look at Ono's development reveals the similarities rather than the differences between the two artists. As an old man, Ono finds he has internalised many of Moriyama's ideas and even gestures (*AFW* 137, 151). Mori-san, on the other hand, shares his pupil's fear that the depiction of the 'floating world' might be a waste of talent and energy, and shows sympathy for Ono's ideas about a more socially meaningful 'art engagée'. Ono, in the end, feels he has wasted his talent for a political cause that nevertheless helped him build his career and ensured his fame well into the postwar era. Moriyama's dilemma is not much different: it lies in the discrepancy he perceives between his (intellectual and political) powers and the relative triviality of the artistic horizon he has chosen to restrict himself to (*AFW* 150). Ono's next teacher, Shigeo Matsuda, illustrates the point from another angle: he is an advocate of socially engaged art but almost cynically denies that art can have any influence on society at all.

III

The narrative undermines all attempts to clearly distinguish between Japanese and European art, or between traditional and progressive art. It also implies that such distinctions are created and held in place – not so much by the images themselves – but by their adjacent discourses. The structural equivalents Ishiguro brings to notice in Moriyama's and Ono's aesthetic and political attitudes suggest that aesthetic traditions as well as their 'key images' are reinvented, reworked and reappropriated rather than blindly continued, and that exchange across cultures is the rule and not the exception. This depiction of tradition as an ongoing process is close to Hobsbawm's and Ranger's concept of 'invented traditions'. Its media-specific dimension, however, can be captured in more detail with Ludwig Jäger's concept of 'transcription', informed by linguistic, semiotic and cognitive approaches. Transcription or transcriptivity refers to the process of semiosis and at the same time to fundamental processes of cognition (Jäger 2007, 2). Cognition, according to Jäger, is an act of establishing reference by repetition and difference. Reference is established in a fundamental way each time a thought or perception becomes conscious: when bodily affection is perceived, or when a thought is visualised, silently verbalised or voiced and thus repeated in a slightly different mode. Reference is therefore always established to a *trace* of something preceding, and hence involves its *mediation*. Transcription can be intra-medial, for example when a verbal thought is remembered or reformulated verbally; it can also be inter-medial, for example when a conceptual thought is visualised. This 'logic' of reference, or transcriptivity, Jäger argues, also holds for semiotic processes on a larger scale, such as those involved in cultural transmission. Cultural elements are constantly 'made readable', they are reactualised and in this process rewritten and transcribed.[4] The difference established between the underlying 'script' and its 'transcription' allows for interventions, changes and new interpretations (Jäger 2002, 33). A narrative representation of a historical event, for example, is a transcription of historical sources which, as an act of selection from a variety of sources, constitutes the historical event as such (Jäger 2002, 30).

The term 'transcriptivity' denotes an ongoing process of meaning constitution comparable to Derrida's concept of an endless semiosis that cannot be traced back to any origin or fixed reference. In that respect, it differs from

---

[4] Although the term 'transcription' is derived from theories of writing, Jäger explicitly intends it to cover other media as well (2002, 30, 33).

'translation' which at least implies the existence of an original meaning or definite cultural characteristics that can be transferred into another language or semiotic system.[5] This is not to say that the concept of transcription is in any way superior to or less problematic than the concept of translation. 'Transcription', however, captures the mechanisms of discursive modification and purification of images described in Ishiguro's novel in a more precise way and also encompasses its concern with complex transcultural 'semiotic encounters'. Acts of transcription (of images as well as of verbally transmitted memories, beliefs, etc.) are shown to result in fragile and temporary constructions of national or personal identities, and Ishiguro is more interested in production contexts of stereotypes than in their referential truth values. This line of argument is inherent in Rebecca Walkowitz' observation that national stereotypes, in Ishiguro's books, are locally produced as cultures are lived from day to day, and are as much a "product of the local imagination as they are an imposition of foreign scrutiny" (Walkowitz 1055). She argues further that stereotypes are "invented not only to maintain a boundary from the outside but also to erect boundaries in the face of new, perhaps internal estrangement" (Walkowitz 1054). As a consequence, national stereotypes of Japan cannot be treated exclusively as orientalist impositions (Walkowitz 1063), and Edward Said's postulate that orientalism is by necessity an effect of European domination over 'the East' needs to be qualified. As early as 1980, Richard E. Minear has pointed out that the study of Japan eschews the concept of orientalism and suggests to place its dynamics within the wider framework of "cross-cultural perception in general, rather than European or American perceptions of the 'non-Western' world" (Minear 516).

Minear's call for cross-cultural perspectives, Walkowitz' reference to locally produced stereotypes, and Jäger's concept of cultures as processes and practices of transcription are ideas that circulate, explicitly as well as implicitly, in the recent debate on globalisation. Bill Ashcroft, one of the most prominent scholars of postcolonial studies, observes that 'globalisation' has to some extent superseded notions of imperialism and cultural hegemony with their clear-cut opposites of oppressor and oppressed, centre and periphery, progress and primitivism, or colonisers and colonised, which were central to earlier postcolonial discourse (Ashcroft 9-11). The effects of globalisation, he writes, must be sought in phenomena like mass production, mass communication, mass consumption and the mass-marketed American

---

[5] When Irmela Hijiya-Kirschnereit characterises Ishiguro's novel as an attempt to translate and to "represent" Japanese culture for British readers (Hijiya-Kirschnereit 25), this implication is deliberate because she scrutinises the accuracy of cultural and historical references in *AFW* – admitting, however, that translation always includes creative and productive aspects.

culture that began to exert a worldwide influence since the 1950s. This new form of cultural-consumerist hegemony, Ashcroft argues, supports and was itself supported by the political dominance of the United States. But like another globalisation critic, Arjun Appadurai, Ashcroft also holds that cultural and consumerist hegemony is only one side of the coin, and that 'globalisation' includes a renewed significance of the sub-national and the local (Ashcroft 11). Local practices of appropriation and consumption of widely circulating cultural materials, for example, may differ from culture to culture, offering options of 'strategic resistance' against dominant US culture. Arjun Appadurai offers a hypothesis why and how the interplay between local and global cultural flows has achieved a new quality. His hypothesis is based on both the significance of images in a wider sense and, as I would argue, on a concept of transcription. Migration and mass media, Appadurai thinks, have made images, role models, fashions, lifestyles and ideas of what the future might look like, available worldwide, creating "a new order of instability in the production of modern subjectivities" (Appadurai 4). Mass media images in particular emerge as "forces [...] that seem to impel (and sometimes compel) the work of the imagination" (Appadurai 4). As a consequence, imagination becomes an everyday activity rather than something confined to myth, entertainment and escapism, a "staging ground for action" (Appadurai 7, 31). Transcribing cultural materials, one could say, is encouraged and guided by the new emphasis on imagining the future which is, according to Anthony Giddens, increasingly replacing an orientation towards the past, e.g. tradition.[6] While pointing out the chances for reassembling cultures from a wide range of practices and materials, Appadurai also draws attention to problematic aspects of a globalised/localised culture: the instable situation cultures face in the highly mediated present, he observes, almost inevitably provokes the hardening of cultural differences into culturalist and polemogenous assumptions (Appadurai 16) – and, one should add, into visiotypes serving these purposes. The new global cultural system, Koichi Iwabuchi seconds, "promotes difference instead of suppressing it" (Iwabuchi 153).

Here, Ishiguro's novel offers a similar perspective on (national) identities which are constantly open to revision: *An Artist of the Floating World* highlights the culturalist and controversial potential that identity constructions can attain, connected with but also independent of orientalist assumptions. The narrative draws attention to the fragility of visiotypes and their constitutive transcriptive processes by featuring a protagonist who struggles to ascribe meaning to but finally fails to glean significance from his artistic work. If Ishiguro's novels engage with globalisation, they offer something different

---

[6] See Anthony Giddens for the notion of an imaginative "colonisation of the future" (117) as a feature of late modernity in his *Modernity and Self-Identity*.

than an overt (and superficial) critique of global capitalism, as suggested by Wai-Chew Sim.[7] Ishiguro undoubtedly ascribes a homogenising influence to American culture but eschews an explicit critique in favour of another concern. It is not so much the *presence* of cultural differences as such which proves disturbing for the book's characters. It is the crystallisation of such differences in national or orientalist stereotypes and visiotypes, and their unquestioned acceptance which causes problems. And finally, the *absence* of reliable points of reference making up the texture of everyday culture proves even more disturbing. The example of art, inhabiting a 'floating world' and provoking but at the same time eschewing any attributions of social, political or personal significance, in this respect mirrors Ono's predicament (cf. Petry 68): his fundamental problem is how to construct and stabilise a viable personal, cultural and social identity out of a range of possibilities (hence his pilgrimage from one teacher to the next), and not how to escape the pressures of dominant cultural forms (hence his unbroken and unreflected fondness for visual stereotypes).

IV

The difficulty of dealing with the absence of cultural references that can be taken for granted is also of central concern in those parts of *An Artist of the Floating World* dealing with the transition from a nationalist-imperialist Japan to a postwar culture, influenced by elements of American popular culture. Introducing Ono's grandson Ichiro as a figuration of Japan after the Second World War enlarges the novel's scope from Ono's personal history and emphasises the narrative's concern with issues of modernisation. Ichiro, aged between five and seven years, is both an agent of change and its victim. His father Suichi is still traumatised by the war and preoccupied with himself. It is Setsuko, the mother, who voices her husband's disapproval of Japanese notions of heroism and his encouragement of Ichiro's interest in cowboys and American cartoon heroes. Ono, on the other hand, unsuccess-

---

[7] See also Petry 64. Sim points out correctly that Appadurai pays too little attention to the culturally homogenising effects of transnational corporations and finance markets (Sim 25) but fails to notice that Ishiguro's treatment of cultural differences as articulated by popular culture does not amount to a one-sided criticism of capitalism itself. The concept of 'globalisation' and its 'cultural flows' is treacherous in so far as it almost automatically conjures up the image of a world of unlimited exchange and unrestricted mobility in which consumer options as well as options of strategic resistance via consumption or appropriation of cultural materials are equally distributed. In order to conceptualise both the hegemony of certain states and cultural spheres and the more or less restricted options of local communities to engage with transnational 'flows' (or to be superseded by them), the term 'transnational' is more useful.

fully tries to familiarise the boy with Japanese folk heroes like Lord Yoshitsune or the famous sword fighter Miyamoto Musashi (*AFW* 30), and attempts to turn him prematurely into a 'real man' by taking him to the monster movie *Godzilla* and urging him to drink sake (*AFW* 78, 156f.). Ichiro, however, remains unruly, greedily soaks up American television series like *Popeye the Sailor* and *The Lone Ranger,* and prefers spinach and ice cream to Japanese dishes. Largely ignorant of the past, he embraces the culture of the new world power fervently but clumsily, still heavily indebted to his Japanese surroundings: when he plays at being the 'Lone Ranger', he adapts the cowboy's famous cheer to his horse 'Hi ho Silver' to Japanese pronounciation ('Hi yo Silver'), and babbles away in sounds he claims to be English (*AFW* 34f.). When he talks of 'Popeye', he calls him 'Popeye Sailorman', possibly a conflation of the common Japanese postwar loanword for 'employee', *salaryman.* These small inaccuracies in picking up English words and American cultural icons are examples of 'transcriptive' acts within the process of appropriating culture. As a child's playful experiment, they exemplify the negotiation processes inherent in cultural practice as such but the narrative leaves open how Ichiro's fondness for US popular culture will develop; if he will finally follow his father's harsh rejection of all things Japanese, if he will fulfil his grandfather's worst fears and become Americanised or if he will continue to handle cultural differences in a playful, flexible manner.

Gregory Mason has shown that this depiction of postwar modernisation in Japan is comparable to the films of Japanese director Yasujiro Ozu from the late 1940s to the early 1960s, for example *Late Spring* (1949), *Good Morning* (1959), *Equinox Flower* (1958) or *An Autumn Afternoon* (1962) (Mason 1989). Many of Ozu's younger characters cherish consumerism, baseball and Western clothing at the expense of social responsibility. The generation that has experienced the war is torn between nostalgia and a rational but not yet emotional acceptance of new roles for young women and the new predominance of the nuclear family. Ono, likewise, regrets the presence of American popular culture and the younger generation's fondness for modern apartments, American-style hotels and entertainment (*AFW* 156) while accepting their presence as inevitable. These parallels in characterisation, plot structure and problem orientation between Ishiguro's first two novels and Ozu's postwar films point, if one follows Mason, to the presence of yet another dimension of transcription. Mason's claim that "Ishiguro's Japan has come to him almost entirely from Japanese films" (Mason 1989, 39) suggests that the narrative transcribes images from popular visual culture instead of pretending to represent, verbally, first-hand experience. His argument is partly corroborated by interviews with Ishiguro in which the author has repeatedly stressed the importance of Japanese movies for his writing, especially the work of

Ozu, Mikio Naruse and Akira Kurosawa. Ozu's films, he states, have "given me the courage and conviction to have a very slow pace and not to worry if there isn't a strong plot" (Vorda and Herzinger 82), and he also admits that the visual details of Japanese films have played an important role for him: "The visual images of Japan have a great poignancy for me, particularly in domestic films like those of Ozu and Naruse, set in the postwar era, the Japan I actually remember" (Mason 2008, 4).

In spite of similarities in mood or plot and Ishiguro's frequent interview references to Japanese films, it is difficult to pin down instances where Ishiguro may actually have transposed visual traces of Japanese films into literature. Descriptions of places or characters in *An Artist of the Floating World* rarely offer visual details (like references to colours or textures), and leave the work of imagining to the reader. When Ono conjures up his traditional Japanese house, for example, he refers in a rather general mode to "the fine cedar gateway, the large area bound by the garden wall, the roof with its elegant tiles and its stylishly carved ridgepole pointing out over the view" (*AFW* 7). This strategy of alluding to vague visual impressions rather than describing them in detail is deliberate, as Ishiguro explains in another interview:

> [...] the average reader comes to any book with so many images. You say something like: an 'ocean liner', immediately lots of images from Titanic movies or whatever, crowd into your head. We now have so many visual images that you don't really have to do very much description. You just manipulate these received images in the reader's head. (Gallix 149)

There is one instance in *An Artist of the Floating World* where Ishiguro actually evokes such an image from film – albeit not from Japanese film. Ono's chance encounter with Jiro Miyake, his daughter's first marriage prospect, in front of a row of "small, seedy offices" (*AFW* 53) evokes the atmosphere of American *film noir*, the haunt of private detectives like Sam Spade or Philip Marlowe, and the clue proves correct because Ono realises, at a later point, that Saito must have been hiring a detective at that moment in order to investigate into his past (*AFW* 95). Other possible transcriptions of Japanese movies, in particular those of Ozu, can ironically be found in aspects of Ishiguro's novel whose historical and cultural accuracy is contested. The gleaming new office buildings Ishiguro places in the novel's setting, the Western-style hotel in which the first meeting with the Saitos takes place, as well as the movie *Godzilla* (1954) date from a period later than 1950, as Irmela Hijiya-Kirschnereit has pointed out. Such architectural and cultural features of modernisation in Japan, however, play an important role in Ozu's movies; lengthy shots of office buildings often serve as transitions between scenes (for example in *An Autumn Afternoon,* 1962), and the contrast between traditional and modern architecture visually underlines the narrated tensions between generations.[8] These examples do not, after all, amount to evidence that Ishiguro's images of Japan are gleaned 'almost entirely from Japanese movies', as Mason argues; but they point, this time symptomatically, to the limits of transcription or, more precisely, to a point where poetic license and the freedom of transcription are indistinguishable from a mistranslation of culture and historical fact.

Ishiguro is aware of this difficulty. He claims to have little regard for historical and cultural documentation when he writes fiction and tries to render the Japan he writes about as "a kind of imaginary world" (Sexton 32), a plausible and at the same time distant world. He means to treat 'Japan' as an object not rendered transparent by verbal description and reference to visual detail. Finding a setting for a novel, for him, has more to do with finding an adequate backdrop for a certain type of conflict situation than with the reworking of historical issues:

> I would search through history books in the way that a film director might search for locations for a script he has already written. I would look for moments in history that would best serve my purposes, or what I wanted to write about. (Ishiguro and Oe 58)

In other comments, the term 'translation' serves a similar argumentative purpose, coming close to the concept of transcription (repetition with a marked difference), introduced above: the effect Ishiguro tries to achieve for his narratives set in Japan is that of a translation clearly recognisable as a translation:

> In a way the language has to be almost like a pseudotranslation, which means that I can't be too fluent and I can't use too many Western colloquialisms. It has to be almost like subtitles, to suggest that behind the English language there's a foreign language going on. (Mason 2008, 13)

Especially for the dialogues, he claims to have developed "a certain kind of translationese" (Mason 2008, 13). The stilted manner of address, suggesting

---

[8] Hijiya-Kirschnereit also detects cultural inaccuracies, identifying elements of British culture in the Japanese setting – washing put out on lines rather than on poles, the eating of oranges and pureed spinach, a statue of the emperor in a public place. The search for the origin of Ishiguro's images (in a sense exceeding the purely visual) results, at least for Hijiya-Kirschnereit, in a diagnosis of failed cultural translation (Hijiya-Kirschnereit 20, 29). Even if the concept of 'cultural translation' and its implication of cultures as stable entities is problematic, her misgivings are difficult to dismiss since the historical and cultural inaccuracies do not fall into the scope of the narrator's (Ono) unreliability, nor are they contained by a meta-narrative dimension.

rather than giving English equivalents for the formulae expressing respect and politeness in Japanese, is a case in point. Setsuko, for example, refers to her father as if she were addressing a third person: "It is very kind of Father to consider Ichiro's feelings so carefully" (*AFW* 157). The formal dialogues evoke a constant awareness of distance between the object and the describing language itself, and this distance is further highlighted in many other descriptions.[9]

In his later novels *The Remains of the Day* and *When We Were Orphans*, Ishiguro also taps a 'cultural imaginary' interwoven with images and narrative elements of popular culture and evokes as well as distances the halo of cultural myths, clichés and ideologies associated with certain places. The country house setting of *The Remains of the Day* (1989) epitomises a notion of Englishness shaped by the landed gentry and the Victorian British Empire as unfolded in novels by Jane Austen, John Galsworthy or Evelyn Waugh. But it also engages with the resuscitation of this particular 'Englishness' as a component of Margaret Thatcher's anti-European rhetoric and as an object of nostalgia in the 1980s campaigns to identify and preserve 'national heritage' (cf. Su 563-565). The country house theme returns in *When We Were Orphans* (2000) where Ishiguro sends his detective protagonist Christopher Banks from the cosy town and country houses of the English upper class in 1930 to the bloody chaos of the 1937 Japanese attack on Shanghai. Banks is modelled on private detectives like Margery Allingham's Peter Campion, and is obviously meant to figure the failings of gentlemanly ideals in the first forebodings of the Second World War (Döring 67f.). In a similar way, Shanghai loses the contours of a real geographical setting in the course of Banks' investigations and becomes indistinguishable from a nightmare in which the protagonist reenacts deep-seated childhood fears (Döring 80, Wong 93).

Like the newer novels, *An Artist of the Floating World* – especially in its references to the interplay of visual and verbal semiotic systems and in its indebtedness to film, memory, and vague but popular images of Japan – is symptomatic of literary writing in the context of globally circulating image flows. It is merely symptomatic because those passages dealing with painterly, orientalist stereotypes of Japan both use and critically reflect processes

---

[9] The narrator frequently indicates that he is remembering or trying to recall a scene as, for example, in the following passage which makes its degree of exactness explicit and implies that other memories might be less 'vivid': "I have, however, a more vivid memory concerning one such night. I can recall walking alone across the central yard, grateful for the fresh air, having for a moment escaped the revellings. I remember I walked over to the entrance [...]" (*AF* 146). Mike Petry has analysed the narrative techniques used in *AFW* in more detail, cf. 81ff.

and consequences of image production while the whole novel's entanglement in the transcriptive logic of mass-mediated culture is not fully contained by this reflexive framework: the historical and cultural inaccuracies in particular can be seen as results of a deliberate but also careless manipulation of those images a late 20th-century reader might have gleaned from her cinematic and mass medial experience. When these images are introduced for effect only, they reduce culture and history to mere decoration – or to a scriptwriter's locations – whose status as results of past (and as materials for future) transcriptive and imaginative work is not acknowledged. Ishiguro's book, therefore, both reflects on a situation where the origins and authenticity of cultures are no longer at stake and where a future-oriented pragmatics of the imaginary gains significance – but is also complicit with this situation.

Works Cited

Appadurai, Arjun. *Modernity at Large: Cultural Dimensions of Globalization*. 1996. Minneapolis: U of Minnesota P, 2000.

Ashcroft, Bill. "The Emperor's New Clothes: Global (Dis)Affections." *Postcolonial (Dis)Affections*. Eds Walter Göbel and Saskia Schabio. Trier: WVT, 2007. 9-23.

Bigsby, Christopher. "In Conversation with Kazuo Ishiguro." 1987. *Conversations with Kazuo Ishiguro*. Eds Brian W. Shaffer and Cynthia F. Wong. Jackson: UP of Mississippi, 2008. 15-26.

Cheng, Chu-Chueh. "Making and Marketing Ishiguro's Alterity." *Post-Identity* 4.2 (2005): 32 p. 2 July 2007
<http://hdl.handle.net/2027/spo.pid9999.0004.202>.

Döring, Tobias. "'Sherlock Holmes – He Dead'. Disenchanting the English Detective in Kazuo Ishiguro's *When We Were Orphans*." *Postcolonial Postmortems: Crime Fiction from a Transcultural Perspective*. Eds Christine Matzke and Susanne Mühleisen. Amsterdam: Rodopi, 2006. 59-86.

Gallix, François. "Kazuo Ishiguro – The Sorbonne Lecture." 1999. *Conversations with Kazuo Ishiguro*. Eds Brian W. Shaffer and Cynthia F. Wong. Jackson: UP of Mississippi, 2008. 135-55.

Giddens, Anthony. *Modernity and Self-Identity: Self and Society in the Late Modern Age*. Stanford: StUP, 1991.

Hijiya-Kirschnereit, Irmela. "Lost in Translation, oder Was vom Japaner übrigblieb." *Schriftlichkeit und Bildlichkeit: Visuelle Kulturen in Europa und Japan*. Eds Ryuzo Maeda, Teruaki Takahashi and Wilhelm Voßkamp. München: Fink, 2007. 17-33.

Ishiguro, Kazuo and Kenzaburo Oe. "A Novelist in Today's World: A Conversation." 1989. *Conversations with Kazuo Ishiguro*. Eds Brian W. Shaffer and Cynthia F. Wong. Jackson: UP of Mississippi, 2008. 52-65.
—. *An Artist of the Floating World*. London: Faber and Faber, 1986.
Iwabuchi, Koichi. *Recentering Globalization: Popular Culture and Japanese Transnationalism*. Durham: Duke UP, 2002.
Jäger, Ludwig. "Bezugnahmepraktiken: Skizzen zur operativen Logik der Mediensemantik." *Transkriptionen* 8 (2007): 2-8.
—. "Transkriptivität: Zur medialen Logik der kulturellen Semantik." *Transkribieren: Medien/Lektüre*. Eds Ludwig Jäger and Georg Stanitzek. München: Fink, 2002. 19-42.
Kelman, Suanne. "Ishiguro in Toronto." 1989. *Conversations with Kazuo Ishiguro*. Eds Brian W. Shaffer and Cynthia F. Wong. Jackson: UP of Mississippi, 2008. 42-51.
Lewis, Barry. *Kazuo Ishiguro*. Manchester: MUP, 2000.
Mason, Gregory. "An Interview with Kazuo Ishiguro." 1989. *Conversations with Kazuo Ishiguro*. Eds Brian W. Shaffer and Cynthia F. Wong. Jackson: UP of Mississippi, 2008. 3-14.
—. "Inspiring Images: The Influence of Japanese Cinema on the Writings of Kazuo Ishiguro." *East West Film Journal* 3.2 (1989): 39-52.
Minear, Richard H. "Orientalism and the Study of Japan." *Journal of Asian Studies* 39.3 (1980): 507-17.
Odin, Steve. *Artistic Detachment in Japan and the West: Psychic Distance in Comparative Aesthetics*. Honolulu: U of Hawai'i P, 2001.
Parkes, Graham. "Japanese Aesthetics." *The Stanford Encyclopedia of Philosophy* 2005. 28 October 2008 <http://plato.stanford.edu/entries/japanese-aesthetics/>.
Petry, Mike. *Narratives of Memory and Identity: The Novels of Kazuo Ishiguro*. Frankfurt: Peter Lang, 1999.
Pfeiffer, K. Ludwig. "The Black Hole of Culture: Japan, Radical Otherness, and the Disappearance of Difference (or, 'In Japan Everything Normal')." *The Translatability of Cultures: Figurations of the Space Between*. Eds Sanford Budick and Wolfgang Iser. Stanford: StUP, 1996. 186-203.
Pörksen, Uwe. *Weltmarkt der Bilder: Eine Philosophie der Visiotype*. Stuttgart: Klett-Cotta, 1997.
Sexton, David. "Interview: David Sexton meets Kazuo Ishiguro." 1987. *Conversations with Kazuo Ishiguro*. Eds Brian W. Shaffer and Cynthia F. Wong. Jackson: UP of Mississippi, 2008. 27-34.
Sim, Wai-Chew. *Globalization and Dislocation in the Novels of Kazuo Ishiguro*. Lewiston: The Edwin Mellen Press, 2006.

Su, John J. "Refiguring National Character: The Remains of the British Estate Novel." *Modern Fiction Studies* 48.3 (2002): 552-80.
Tanizaki, Junichiro. *Lob des Schattens*. 1933. Zürich: Manesse, 1987.
Vorda, Allan and Kim Herzinger. "An Interview with Kazuo Ishiguro." 1990. *Conversations with Kazuo Ishiguro*. Eds Brian W. Shaffer and Cynthia F. Wong. Jackson: UP of Mississippi, 2008. 66-88.
Walkowitz, Rebecca L. "Ishiguro's Floating Worlds." *English Literary History* 68 (2001): 1049-76.
Wong, Cynthia F. *Kazuo Ishiguro*. 2nd ed. Horndon, Tavistock: Northcote, 2005.

Joachim Frenk and Christian Krug

Handovers of Empire:
Transatlantic Transmissions in Popular Culture

The essay enquires into a recurrent motif explored by a number of British and American film productions since the Second World War: a 'handover of Empire' from the United Kingdom to the United States. The films in question seem to take pleasure not just in taking up this narrative motif but in dressing it up, turning it into a nostalgic celebration of the past or a cherished vision of the future. The motif has developed its own popular-culture tradition charged with a specific national heritage, and in this it seems to have garnered a fairly stable place, both in a narrative and in an ideological sense, in the cultural (film) imaginary. The case study of the handover of empire is provided by James Bond films of the 1960s and '70s, where a handover of the 'burden of Empire' to the US constantly occurs on various levels, including production, distribution and consumption. In its most visible form, on the level of plot and characters, however, such handovers are alluded to but constantly deferred. In the 1960s, both the need for allusion and deferral is seen in connection with popular political discourses in Britain and the US about a re-evaluation of the political roles of these two nation states. Second, both allusion and deferral can be placed in a context of an emerging popular culture with a perceived potential in the 1960s to transgress the very concepts of nationhood and the power of nation states that seemed to be at the heart of the Bond franchise.

For this paper we would like to take our cue from the last words spoken by a quintessentially British character in a major Hollywood film production, *The League of Extraordinary Gentlemen* (2003). The dying words of Allan Quatermain, "[m]ay this new century be yours, son, as the old one was mine", are indicative of a recurrent motif that has been variously staged, ideologically charged, celebrated or debunked in a surprising number of Anglo-American popular fictions since the 1950s: a handover of the burden of Empire from an old imperial power, Great Britain, to a perceived economic and political successor, the United States of America.

The rationale of *The League of Extraordinary Gentlemen* could be described as an excessive and obsessive *bricolage* of texts from 19th-century popular culture. The film presents an eclectic assembly of characters from canonical 19th-century literature teaming up to save the British Empire by relying on their extraordinary abilities. The founding of this illustrious league takes place in London, the heart of the Empire; the year is 1899. M, the head of the British secret service, gathers together Allan Quatermain, the quintessential literary hero figure of 19th-century British Imperialism, Dorian Gray, Mina Harker (of *Dracula*), Captain Nemo, Rodney Skinner (the invisible man), and Dr Jekyll/Mr Hyde. There clearly is an excess of 19th-century myths of Britishness at the beginning of the film; the movement is from darkest Africa, the retreat of Quatermain where the emissaries of the Empire find him, to rainiest London, where the founding of the league takes place in late Victorian splendour, in a library stacked with old volumes archiving the history of the Empire. The league's task is to prevent the phantom, a ruthless genius, from profiting from the ongoing arms race and from provoking the European powers into starting a world war.

At the first critical moment, when the league has to face the phantom for the first time, another defender of world peace joins them unexpectedly and offers his help. Having ably eliminated a number of the phantom's henchmen, he introduces himself as "Special Agent Sawyer, of the American Secret Service". Tom Sawyer gives the rationale for US interference: "Well, if a war starts in Europe, how long is it gonna take until it crosses the Atlantic?" It is Quatermain who decides that the American Sawyer can become a member of the league, which so far was an exclusive affair of the British Empire. Tom Sawyer, the ur-American figure, comes as an outsider, joins the inner circle and proves his value for the league a number of times, once even saving Quatermain's life. From the beginning, a special relationship is established between the old imperial hero Allan Quatermain and the young newworld daredevil Tom Sawyer.

In a crucial scene on board of Nemo's ship *Nautilus*, Quatermain teaches Sawyer how to shoot – not, as Quatermain insists, the American way ("fire enough bullets and hope to hit the target"), but in superior, imperial, style. As Quatermain tells Sawyer: "You have to feel the shot. Take your time with it. You have all the time you need. All the time in the world". This scene, like a great number of others, self-consciously (and not without a sense of irony perhaps) calls for an allegorical and an ideological reading. Such demands for ideological readings are firmly inscribed into the film and are one part of the meta-fictional pleasures it has on offer. Here, Quatermain's shooting mantra "all the time in the world" indicates that the representative of the British Empire benefits from a long tradition, and he knows that he does not have to hurry to achieve his goals. The over-eager American Sawyer shoots too fast; he cannot hit targets at long range; by contrast, the long British tradition can provide him with a far-sighted approach – it therefore offers security and a more profound imperial self-confidence to the newcomer.

At the same time, it becomes clear that the old Englishman and the young American recognise each other as father and son – true to Rider Haggard's character, the natural son of Quatermain has died – and this patriarchal relationship between the Brit Quatermain and the American Sawyer is constructed as one of the keys to the ultimate success of the league. The old Quatermain needs the abundant vitality of Tom Sawyer because Quatermain himself, like the British Empire, is no longer the young adventurer he used to be. He is rather the Quatermain of *King Solomon's Mines*, a fifty-five-year-old "taking up a pen to try and write a history" (Haggard 7); or, as the phantom tells Quatermain in the film, "You feel yourself to be John Bull – but you're weak". Not only is old Quatermain not as strong as he was, there is a traitor among the British: the amoral dandy Dorian Gray, who of course only *looks* as young as Sawyer, turns out to be a helper of the phantom and openly admits that he is "no loyal son of the Empire".

The phantom, the arch-enemy of mankind and of world peace, who hides his personality and ethnicity behind a mask and affects an east-European accent, in the end turns out to be yet another famous figure from 19th-century literature. He is just a convenient mask for the man who has appeared in London as 'M', and 'M' here spells itself out as Professor Moriarty, Conan Doyle's Napoleon of crime. Even after Professor Moriarty's outlandish weapons factory (in Mongolia) is destroyed, the criminal mastermind is still bent on wreaking further havoc on civilisation, and in a dramatic climax of the film, after having saved Sawyer's life, Quatermain is stabbed by one of Moriarty's henchmen and his glasses are broken. Sawyer now has to shoot the villain at long range, proving that he shoots just as well as the old Brit, who hands over his Elephant rifle to the young American.

But while Sawyer has got all the time in the world, Quatermain has not – he dies, and with him seems to die what he represents in contemporary popular culture: British adventurers of the 19th century and the world-as-Empire they used for their exploits. The handover of a century indicated in the last words of Quatermain, "[m]ay this new century be yours, son, as the old one was mine", is also a handover of an imperial mission – Quatermain has worked for the good of the world by maintaining and enlarging the British Empire in the 19th century; Tom Sawyer is expected to do the same in the 20th century. In the film, the United Kingdom gallantly acknowledges that the time has come for the United States to take over.

This movement of *translatio imperii* has often been rehearsed in popular culture texts since the later 19th century. The action of *The League of Extraordinary Gentlemen* is set in 1899, and the motif of a handover of empire is already present in British texts of that time. A famous example is Kipling's notorious "The White Man's Burden", written in that same year 1899 explicitly to exhort the (not very unwilling) US to more openly embrace the idea and politics of imperialism in the Philippines. For Kipling, the US are about to become an imperial equal who has to subject to "[t]he judgment of your peers" (Kipling 480). Two years before, Bram Stoker's *Dracula* (1897) had offered another glimpse of future American greatness. The English academic Dr. Seward is filled with admiration for Quincey P. Morris, the Texan who has joined the group of friends helping van Helsing hunt down the beast from the east:

> Dr. Seward's Diary
>
> 22 September. – [...] What a fine fellow is Quincey! I believe in my heart of hearts that he suffered as much about Lucy's death as any of us, but he bore himself through it like a moral Viking. If America can go on breeding men like that, she will be a power in the world indeed. (Stoker 156)

Dracula asserts that the rise of America as an imperial world power might be unstoppable due to its masculine virility, and this assessment seems to hold true even after Quincey has died of the wound he received from Dracula's servants – but only after the American has driven his Western democratic Bowie knife through the heart of darkness of the east-European aristocrat, putting an end to Dracula's undead *ancien régime*. Incidentally, in Francis Ford Coppola's *Bram Stoker's Dracula* (1992), Quincey P. Morris appears as Winchester-toting cowboy in Britain, although there is no detailed description in the novel as to Morris' appearance.

The motif of a handover of Empire from the United Kingdom to the United States has developed its own tradition in popular culture charged with a specific national heritage, and in this it seems to have remained fairly stable both in a narrative and in an ideological sense. In the following, we will focus on this motif as it occurs particularly in film productions since the Second World War, where a number of films seem to take pleasure not just in taking up this narrative motif but in dressing it up, turning it into a nostalgic celebration of the past, sometimes even a cherished vision of the future. To inquire into the permutations and into the functions of such a narrative and ideological motif, however, raises some methodological questions, not least with respect to the categories of the 'national' and 'transnational'. There are a lot of uncanny returns of dreams of Empire in popular culture since 1945 – but who is dreaming? If the audience is encouraged to dream, one would have to ask, which audience; is it possible these days to segment the projected audiences of major Hollywood productions into national categories – or not to? If one looks at contemporary large film franchises, it seems that an international pop-culture imaginary informs mostly nostalgic narratives, discourses, and dreams of Empire, but again the question would be which elements of these dreams produce the greatest lust and/or release for whom?

The League of Extraordinary Gentlemen conceptualises transnationalism as a threat in that it depicts a villain whose plans of world domination are specifically directed against a world conceptualised in 19th-century fashion as consisting of nation states destined to fight out the coming world war. But there are also clear intertextual references that point towards the 20th century, and towards another highly successful dream of Empire. When at the first meeting of the league, Quatermain comes to meet M, the fact that Quatermain is played by Sean Connery clearly addresses an obvious subtext of the scene: just like James Bond, Connery's most famous role, who is regularly summoned to be sent on a mission by his superior M, Quatermain faces a late-Victorian, fake 'M' who pretends to protect both the British Empire and world peace. The presence of Sean Connery (on whom the film's marketing was based) gestures towards the Bond series – an intertextual link which the film stresses in a number of ways.[1]

Our case study of the handover of empire as a recurrent motif in major film productions after the second World War will be provided by James Bond films of the 1960s and '70s. We will argue that handovers of the 'burden of Empire' to the US constantly occur on various levels of the Bond films. In its most visible form, however, on the level of plot and characters, such handovers are alluded to but constantly deferred. We will argue that in the 1960s, both the need for allusion and deferral must be seen in connection with popular political discourses in Britain and the US about a re-evaluation of the political roles of these two nation states. Second, both allusion and deferral have to be seen in a context of an emerging popular culture with a perceived potential in the 1960s to transgress the very concepts of nationhood and the power of nation states that seemed to be at the heart of the Bond films.

The 1960s handovers happened (but not quite) at a time when Britain was described as "a nation in decline" and when the United States emerged as a modern 'empire', assuming the attributes of an imperial power and exercising control and influence in both the political and the economic sphere (Street 2002, 187). In the early 1950s, David Cannadine has argued, Churchill could still promote the idea that England was the only country that occupied a central place in the "three great circles among the free nations and democracies", with the three circles defined by England's relationship to America, Europe, and the Commonwealth. By the end of the 1960s, England had moved from the centre to the margins of each of these circles: it was dependent on American military force in the Suez crisis, Britain's application to join the European Common Market had been denied, and she was shorn of Empire except for Rhodesia and Ulster (Cannadine 2003, 280).[2]

---

[1] For instance, Quatermain's "all the time in the world" is a direct quotation from the Bond film (the first without Connery), *On Her Majesty's Secret Service*, where Bond uses the words to address his dying wife.

[2] A similar point is made by Cynthia Baron (136).

Notions that 'Britain had won the war but lost the peace', that there was a shift from 'Rule Britannia' to 'Britannia Overruled', echoed through political discourses and through popular culture in both the US and the UK in the three decades after World War II.[3] Former US Secretary of State Dean Acheson famously said in 1962, the year the first Bond film was released, that Britain had lost an empire but had not yet found a role in the world.[4] Equally resounding are the words Tiger Tanaka hurled at his British counterpart: "You have not only lost a great Empire, you have seemed almost anxious to throw it away with both hands" – this derision occurred two years later, in 1964, in Ian Fleming's *You Only Live Twice*.[5]

At the same time, the British middle classes were enjoying a new feeling of affluence and a diversification of leisure; they generally described their living standard as high, prompting Prime Minister Harold Macmillan to famously proclaim that "most of our people never had it so good".[6] Bond films participate in the promulgation of a 'culture of affluence' by exporting the resulting, new lifestyle of 'Swinging-Sixties England' to the Continent and the US. This paradox of a nation which many perceived to be both in decline and in affluence can be keenly felt in Bond films up to the 1970s: the perceived shift from a culture of austerity to a culture of affluence and consumerism may well be reflected in James Bond's conspicuous consumption and his "penchant for brand-name goods" (Chapman 2005, 135, Cannadine 2003, 280).[7] The theme of a 'nation in decline' informs Bond's dealings with his American CIA counterpart, Felix Leiter, and with the villains.

This, then, is the context in which, on the level of plot and character construction, the handover of Empire does not quite occur between Bond and

---

[3] Cf. David Cannadine 2002, Keith Robbins, Donald Anthony Low, David Reynolds.

[4] Speech at West Point Academy, NY, 5 December 1962. The "special relationship" between Great Britain and the United States was first evoked by Churchill in 1946.

[5] "Now it is a sad fact that I, and many of us in positions of authority in Japan, have formed an unsatisfactory opinion about the British people since the war. You have not only lost a great Empire, you have seemed almost anxious to throw it away with both hands. […] [W]hen you apparently sought to arrest this slide into impotence at Suez [in 1956], you succeeded only in stage-managing one of the most pitiful bungles in the history of the world, if not the worst. Further, your governments have shown themselves successively incapable of ruling and have handed over effective control of the country to the trade unions […]" (qtd. in Bennett and Woollacott 108f.).

[6] Macmillan uttered his most famous phrase during a speech he gave at Bedford, 20 July 1957.

[7] Tim Bergfelder has commented that in the Bond films "Britishness constituted itself less as an identity or as a sense of place, but as an accumulation of consumer products, fashion accoutrements and self-mocking stereotypes" (150; qtd. in Street 2002, 188).

Felix Leiter.[8] In Ian Fleming's novels, Felix Leiter is clearly subordinate to Bond, both in structural and in ideological terms;[9] Kingsley Amis called the novel-Leiter a "nonentity" whose only function was to take orders from Bond – so as to demonstrate how Bond, "the incarnation of little old England with her quiet ways and shoe-string budget[,] wip[es] the eye of great big global-tentacled multi-billion-dollar appropriating America."[10] In the films up to the 1970s, Leiter may still be a nonentity as a character, self-deconstructing in a multiplicity of appearances – seven different actors have played Leiter in eight Bond films. However, Felix Leiter's appearance and function in the first feature film, *Dr No*, are highly significant as they point toward an ideological project of the films of the 1960s. Whereas in the novels, Britain was implausibly constructed as the dominant partner in the Anglo-American alliance, in *Dr No* the United Kingdom and the United States are presented as equals (Chapman 2005, 139).[11]

In the first longer sequence in which he features, Leiter is not only Bond's equal, he is visually almost indistinguishable from Bond – a shared identity constructed mainly through style; again a reminder of the 'culture of affluence' in the films. The fact that in the first feature film Bond and Leiter are close to exchangeable is perhaps best indicated with reference to their very first screen appearance, in the CBS TV adaptation of *Casino Royale*, which was produced as early as 1954. In an act of national appropriation, this TV production does in fact reverse Leiter's and Bond's roles: James "Jimmy"

---

[8] The very presence of both Bond and Leiter in many films (even those where he does not feature in the novels or short stories) shows that what is at stake in the films is often implicitly about Western, and not just British, values.

[9] Cf., for example, Bennett and Woollacott, who argue that in the novels it is always Bond, not Leiter, who "engages in the decisive contest with the villain. Leiter's role is always structurally subordinated to that of Bond. He supplies Bond with technical support and hardware, added muscle where needed and money […]. England is […] imaginarily placed at the centre of the world stage in being chosen as the target of the villain's conspiracy" (98), and "indeed the system of NATO alliances, as represented in the novels, typically functions as a means of placing Bond – and thereby England – imaginarily at the centre of the world stage" (97f.).

[10] "The point of Felix Leiter, such a nonentity as a piece of characterization, is that he, the American, takes orders from Bond, the Britisher, and that Bond is constantly doing better than he, showing himself, not braver or more devoted, but smarter, wittier, tougher, more resourceful, the incarnation of little old England with her quiet ways and shoe-string budget wiping the eye of great big global-tentacled multi-billion-dollar appropriating America" (Amis, also qtd. in Chapman 2005, 143).

[11] Leiter's character did not feature in the novel *Dr No* but was added by the scriptwriters. According to Sarah Street, Bond films "privileged an assumed Western supremacy that was premised on [an] Anglo-American cooperation" which took the form of an "idealized, even mythical, concept of an Anglo-American 'special relationship'" (Street 2002, 187).

Bond is an American; the name of his British pendant (played by Australian actor Michael Pate) is Leiter, "Clarence Leiter" (cf. Chapman 1999b, 40-4).

In the next four feature films, Felix Leiter becomes "a command figure for American power", and Bond's successes in the films frequently rest on him (Bennett and Woollacott 209). This is achieved mainly through a paternal discourse. *Goldfinger* (1964) provides a good example: in contrast to the 1954 novel, where Bond is superior to Leiter, in the film Leiter is given a paternal role (cf. Street 2002, 188). M asks Leiter and the CIA to keep an eye on Bond while he is in the US, a task Leiter successfully takes on and identifies with: "That's my James", he remarks on one occasion. Leiter thus functions as a "surrogate M" (Bennett and Woollacott 209). In *Goldfinger*, both book and film, Bond takes on a threat directed against the US, and while in the film the maintenance of the *Pax Americana* is leased to Britain, in the person of Bond, this only happens in a "context of close American supervision and background control" (Bennett and Woollacott 156).

Such paternalism is still present in *Casino Royale* (2006) where Leiter finances Bond's poker game when he runs out of money. The scene exemplifies the continued form that the 'special relationship' between the UK and the US imaginatively takes: as paternal discourse.[12] Thus it effectively reworks the paternal relationship established in *League of Extraordinary Gentlemen* three years earlier.

This paternal discourse of the films is continued on an economic level in what one might term a 'production-paternalism'. Given the fact that *Casino Royale* deals with how Bond came into existence, the scene can be read as a meta-fictional reference to the financing and production of the first Bond films of the 1960s. The films were American/British joint ventures: while using predominantly British technicians and while filming at Pinewood Studios, the Bond films were financed with US-American money by US and Canadian producers. The British crew had more or less a token function: long-term problems of the British film industry meant that cheap film-making facilities in Britain were increasingly exploited by American studios under laws passed in 1950. These laws made films eligible for government subsidies if they were registered in Britain and mainly used British production staff. *Thunderball* is an extremely successful example of this practice: the film received a subsidy of $2.1 million, more than 20% of its production budget.[13] In this handover of empire, a British studio system willingly ceased

---

[12] In the novel *Casino Royale*, where the scene also occurs, Bond "needs Marshall Aid" (see statement by Fleming biographer Andrew Lycett, qtd. in Chapman 1999b, 32).

[13] cf. Street 2002, 169-72 and Street 1997, 183; Leach 97; Bennett and Woollacott 178. According to Sarah Street, the Bond films are examples of "a cross-cultural and cross-media

control to an American system, which in effect appropriates a British one, subsidised by British taxpayers' money.

On a narrative level, the Bond films are remarkable not so much because they do not affect a handover of empire – after all, there are the generic restraints of formula fiction: a handover would effectively bring the series to an end. What is remarkable is the continued presence of the motif, and that this presence produces a need for it to be deferred. The longer it is deferred, the more the films take it out on the unlucky Felix Leiter. The character is made to leave his job, and he is torn to pieces by a shark (in the novel *Live and Let Die*); his newly-married wife is raped and murdered (in the film *Licence to Kill*). The reasons for this increasingly violent deferral are located on an ideological level. We would argue that Bond films are not just informed by (national) discourses about, for example, a nation in decline. They are also informed by dissolutions of traditional concepts of nationhood in general. This takes two forms.

'Transnational idea(l)s' in Bond films are first located, perhaps not surprisingly, with the villains. If 'transnationalism' is understood in a general sense as an attempt to question, dissolve, transgress or even void traditional concepts of nationhood, while at the same time such attempts remain implicated in these concepts (after all, 'transnationalism' retains 'national' in its name) – then transnational utopias or dystopias emerge in the Bond films of the 1960s and '70s in the constructions of villains, their henchmen, and their organisations.

The first Bond film, *Dr No*, made the villain the titular figure, and it put into place the elements of a mythology that future villains would be patterned on: Dr No is, first, a composite of multiple nationalities which he variously evokes, or between which he oscillates.[14] In Bond films of the '60s and '70s, the villains' evil machinations are often specifically directed against nation states,[15] and their plans to rule the world are transnational in a very radical sense, for they often seek to abolish the very concept of nation states.[16] As far

---

dialogue" as they were influenced by American films, especially on the level of style, and as they in turn influenced American TV (Street 2002, 186).

[14] The same has been argued for the novels of the 1950s and early 60s, where multi-ethnic characters combine ethnic characteristics and stereotypes rather than blending them. According to Vivian Halloran, the villains of the novels are often territorially displaced and very complex ethnic/racial hybrids, but their hybridity remains stable until the very end (which is mostly their deaths). Bond, on the other hand, delivers "various ethnic/national and class performances", but he only half-heartedly assumes identities as masquerade and throws them off in quick succession (158f., cf. 161).

[15] A quintessential scene that has become part of popular mythology is that of the head of SPECTRE directly addressing, via TV link, a congress of heads of state.

[16] Prime examples are *The Spy Who Loved Me* and *Moonraker*.

as geography is concerned, these organisations are almost always located in places that transgress state borders or national boundaries. They are located for instance in the Caribbean, which according to Vivian Halloran provides the films with "an ethnoscape for a discussion of the competing ethnic and national claims to authenticity and/or validity" of "displaced, racially hybrid villains" (Halloran 159).[17] The villains' locations also hover uneasily between their status as former colony and newly-gained independence: Jamaica for example, the setting of *Dr No*, gained its independence in the months between the production of the film and its release. The villains' headquarters are often decentralised or mobile, and are sometimes set in fluid spaces altogether as, for example, in the ocean (*The Spy Who Loved Me*), or in space (*Moonraker*).[18] All this is not to say, however, that the idea of transnational

---

[17] According to Halloran, the Caribbean also constitutes a Prattian "contact zone" "between European, American, Asian and African forces battling for global supremacy in the post-World War II world" (160). The Caribbean provides the setting for four novels, two short stories, and a number of the films in the time in question. The Caribbean has also frequently been imaginatively linked with pirates in popular culture, and we would add that the films use established tropes and visual markers from pirate fiction to flesh out its idea of a transnational deviancy and the perceived threats to established nation states. The novels have already been submitted to a structuralist analysis in their relation to the narrative genre of pirate fiction by Vivian Halloran, who has attempted to uncover an underlying "mythification of piracy" (159) that informs the narrative of many of the novels. She identifies three narrative tropes that are consistently developed into narrative patterns: "the pirate treasure chest" in novels such as *Goldfinger*, "the sea monster" and the "plantation economy" (160). Some of the films even self-consciously acknowledge their debt to literary and popular pirate genres: in *The Spy Who Loved Me*, for example, much of the 'motley crew' mythology of pirate fiction is used in the portrayal of the multi-national crew of henchmen; in the film, a tanker mogul builds a pirate ship with which he captures smaller vessels. In *You Only Live Twice* (1964) a very similar narrative device is used but transposed to space, where a pirate satellite captures other satellites.

[18] Maibaum's screenplay to *Dr No* shows that this decentralisation both of the threat posed by the organisation and of the locality of its headquarters was made a central part of the Bond mythology from the beginning of the franchise. SPECTRE's logic of the 'beyond' is an imaginary identification with a position of omnipotence: "BOND: 'With that sort of disregard for human life you can only be working for the East.' / DR NO (*contemptuously*): 'East? West? Points of the compass, Mr Bond. Each as brutishly stupid as the other. *I* work for SPECTRE.' / BOND: 'Spectre? Never heard of them...and I thought I knew all the nuts.' / DR NO: 'Special Executive for Counter-Intelligence, Terrorism, Revenge, and Extortion.' / BOND: 'They sound a pleasant bunch. (*He looks around and shrugs*). Albeit a little theatrical...if this is their headquarters.' / DR NO: 'Headquarters? Don't talk like a fool, Mr Bond. [...] No, this is not their headquarters. Crab Key is but a microcosm of the organization, syndicate, call it what you will. Do you think that the diversion of a few miserable rockets is the be-all and end-all of all our efforts?' / BOND (*looking at him levelly*): 'I'm calling your bluff. What is?' / DR NO (*after slightest pause, looking at him levelly*): 'Ultimate control...Complete...All-Powerful...of the world...and beyond.'" (Draft screenplay qtd. in Chapman 1999b, 75f.).

villainy is not to some extent contained by the films: in *The Spy Who Loved Me*, the pirate villain, his motley crew, and the fictions of villainous transnationalism are tied to a specific multinational company belonging to one rich individual, and they are made the problems of very national concerns between established nations, specifically Britain and the US.

Next to the villains, there is a second place where concepts of nation states and nationhood threaten to dissolve. Traditional analyses of Bond films have often seen the Bond character as a resilient token of a British Empire whose continued validity and potency is imaginatively reaffirmed, even though (or because) in socio-political terms, this Empire had been lost. We would argue instead that the crisis in James Bond films up to the 1970s runs deeper. The handover of Empire in these films needs to be constantly deferred because there is a structural, ideological problem in the very myth of nationhood at the semantic centre of James Bond films: James Bond.

Bond's Britishness (often implicitly taken to mean his 'Englishness') is usually taken for granted. His nationality in the actual novels and films, however, is somewhat at odds with academic discourse, which has constructed a popular mythology of his *über*-Britishness (cf. Chapman 2005, 130), which in turn has enabled critics to advance readings in which Bond can function as anything from a simple "old-fashioned British imperial hero" (Raymond Durgnat) to the "ultimate Orientalist" (Baron 136).[19] By contrast, we contend that Bond's nationality in both the novels and the films is sliding. The Bond character is more than a simple token for traditional Britishness,[20] he shares more and shifting affiliations. As far as national and ethnic constructions of the Bond persona in the novels are concerned, Vivian Halloran contends that Bond "is whiter than he is English": while his ethnicity is rarely questioned, his nationality, she argues, is just as hybrid as that of some of the villains (Halloran 159, 160f.).[21]

---

[19] Durgnat has described *Dr No* as nothing more than "Edwardiana in modern drag [...]. The British Raj, reduced to its Caribbean enclave, lords it benevolently over jovial and trusting West Indians and faithful coloured police-sergeants, the Uncle Toms of Dock Green" (Durgnat 151).

[20] Tony Bennett and Janet Woollacott have described him as a hero of the NATO alliance, imaginatively representing the West as a whole, not just Britain. Bond can also, for example, be both British and of another nationality (*You Only Live Twice*).

[21] Fleming often stresses the hybrid national status of Bond in his novels: in *You Only Live Twice* (1964), for example, Bond is described as the son of a Swiss mother and a Scottish father, who was a foreign representative for a British Arms manufacturer; with his early education being spent entirely abroad (cf. Halloran 160f.). Even his whiteness is in question in moments of "transraciality", when he reinterprets his physical features as being a sign of "the mixed blood of America" when he visits that country in *Live and Let Die*.

Such multiple national and transnational inscriptions become clearer if one moves away from 'character-readings' and considers instead, as Tony Bennett and Janet Woollacott have done, the visual signifiers, or composite myths, through which very different Bonds were most widely circulated (Bennett and Woollacott 34). In the 1960s, the Bond/Connery signifier is far from being a clear-cut 'gentleman John Bull': Connery was also cast as the first Bond precisely because he is not English, which in older British spy fiction served as a powerful metonymy for Britishness in general.[22] In its review of the film *Dr No*, *The Times* opined that "it is doubtful whether either his admirers or his detractors will recognize [Bond]" since Connery "exhibited an Irish-American look and sound, which somehow spoils the image" (qtd. in Chapman 1999b, 86). In fact, the nationality of Connery's Bond was widely described as Irish-American by audiences and critics both in America and in Britain.[23] Of the actors playing Bond up to the 1990s, only Roger Moore is English, both literally and in terms of his Bond/Moore screen persona – and his performances of Bond are the most ironic (Leach 97).[24] All this is not to say that the Bond/Connery and the Bond/Moore signifier cannot be reinscribed with national meanings by specific audiences, nor that Bond/Moore is not constructed to tap into mythologies of traditional Britishness. This 'Britishness' has always been, first, inflected by the demands of an international market, and, second, it is clearly distanced by layers of irony.

As Bennett and Woollacott have argued, Connery's Bond of the early to mid-1960s are not representatives of traditional myths of Englishness, they run counter to them, foregrounding themes of classlessness, sexual and political modernity, and professionalism.[25] This is achieved mainly through Bond's changed attitude towards his superior, M. Connery's Bond is increasingly distinguished from and constructed in opposition to the films' portrayal of a prewar fuddy-duddy establishment figure whose mythical Englishness now serves as a foil against which Bond can play out both his classlessness and the modern and professionalised values of a new meritocracy: "Bond belongs not to the breed but to a new élite – international rather than paro-

---

[22] Connery is Scottish with Welsh forefathers.
[23] Connery was subsequently cast in roles where he played Irish-Americans.
[24] The other actors portraying Bond until the 1990s are of Irish descent (Brosnan), have a Welsh background (Dalton) or are Australian (Lazenby).
[25] Cf. Bennett and Woollacott, who argue that Bond in the first part of the sixties functioned as "a condensed expression of a new style and image of Englishness [...] a mythic encapsulation of the then prominent ideological themes of classlessness and modernity, a key cultural marker of the claim that Britain [...] was in the process of being thoroughly modernized as a result of the implementation of a new meritocratic style of cultural and political leadership, middle class and professional rather than aristocratic and amateur" (34f.).

chially English in its orientation – committed to new values (professionalism) and lifestyles (martini)" (Bennett and Woollacott 34, 112).[26]

The matter of Bond's elusive rather than mythical Britishness is further complicated by the fact that since the mid-1960s, Bond films have established a self-referential system with its own intra-series memory and history: references to myths of Britishness in new films are understood more in relation to prior Bond films than to politics or history in any 'realist' sense, as intra-series-history has sublated more traditional history. This has consequences for the construction of nationality, since the self-referential Bond of the 1970s does not so much articulate any new images of nation and nationhood, he functions, according to Bennett and Woollacott, primarily "as a negative site in relation to which earlier conceptions of Englishness – including those represented by Bond in the earlier phase of his career – were parodied and debunked, punctured so as to release laughter, by means of carrying them to excess" (Bennett and Woollacott 38f.). Irony in excess plays a strategic role in the films; it is very obvious in the paraded Englishness of Moore/Bond, for example, which is excessive to the point of being a camp performance. Such ironic distancing, Bennett and Woollacott argue, allows for an appropriation of Bond by multinational markets, especially a US-American one:

> The comic strategy of the films also operated to recruit different [...] national audiences[;] the 'sending up' of some aspects of British post-imperialist ideologies combined with the buttressing of others was not only endorsed by British audiences but also allowed the Bond films to work in terms of other national reading formations, feeding in, for example, to American views of the British class system [...]. Bond can thus be conceived of as, if not an American agent, as an agent who is at the service of American interests. (Bennett and Woollacott 208f.)

One level on which the handover of empire does take place, therefore, is in the appropriation of Bond as "a trans-Atlantic hero" (Chapman 2005, 136-8). But Bond is not just a signifier ready for new national appropriations and inscriptions by different audiences, he is *a priori* constructed as a decentred subject that functionally moves through spaces in a sense that unsettles traditional concepts of nationhood.

---

[26] In their reading, Connery's Bond is distinctly liberal and his "tastes and lifestyle have a decidedly international and cosmopolitan flavour. In a word, Bond is not old-fashioned. M is, and it is in the relations between Bond and M that a space is opened up between, on the one hand, earlier fictional representations of the lifestyle and ethos of the traditional British ruling class and, on the other, the projection of a new set of élite values and styles" (Bennett and Woollacott 112).

The films habitually take the Bond character on journeys round the world (and beyond); he exemplifies above all a principle of almost constant mobility (cf. Leach 98). This mobility can be explained by claiming that the films allow for a vicarious tourist gaze. One could also argue that Bond's mobility establishes a new form of (cultural) imperialism: his journeys are either attempts to once more foreground and perhaps to reaffirm the traditions and values of a prewar British nation and a British Empire symbolised by Bond; or, Bond can also be seen as a mobile imperial marker travelling across parts of the globe in the attempt to test new, imaginative forms of empire, in which Britain can remain at the centre and all the world's her stage.

But we would argue that the mobility Bond exhibits is just as much a form of nomadism, and as a nomad, Bond has a subjectivity far less centred (say, on concepts of nationhood) than one would expect. It would be wrong to think of Bond's travels in terms of centre and periphery: Bond is already decentred; for the very centre of the old Empire, the office of M, is clearly not his. In fact, already in the novels, Bond's performances as a Brit are effortless only abroad, but he is at times even self-conscious about having to 'pass' as British in mainland Britain itself. When Bond roams about the globe, his functions and meanings are instead reconfigured through the specific locations he inhabits and the connections he makes. While Bond does travel to 'points' on a, more or less, 'customary path' (of established tourist destinations), these points are nothing but relays, reached only to be left behind – Bond's moves never stop. In *The Man with the Golden Gun* (1974), for example, he is constantly on the move as one clue leads him to the next: Beirut, then Macau, Hongkong and Bangkok are merely relays, reached only to be left behind again.

At the end of the films, Bond usually does not return 'home', but is frequently pictured in open, unlimited spaces such as the sea. At this moment in the narrative, M or other state officials inevitably try to reach and to 'contain' Bond again. Such containment (and with it, simple reinscriptions into traditional myths of nationhood) usually fails at the end of a picture (though it is often staged at the beginning of the next picture in the series, just before the state unleashes Bond again to fight its battles). We would argue that any diegetic act of reappropriation needs to fail because the way the Bond character is constructed, the State Apparatus can never quite contain a principle predicated on a different logic.[27] Instead, the film approximates such con-

---

[27] The relationship between M and Bond is thus structurally similar to Deleuze and Guattari's concept of State Apparatus and of War Machine; a War Machine that the State Apparatus can never quite contain because it is predicated on a different logic, but which it always tries to appropriate. Cf. Deleuze/Guattari, esp. 362, 380. "The life of the nomad is the inter-

tainment on an extra-diegetic level when it frames Bond's boat with titles that claim (in the face of actual practice, as we have seen) a national context of film production: "Pinewood Studios, London, England".

The handover of empire, therefore, needs to be deferred because as a restlessly mobile signifier, Bond refuses to be arrested. All this is not to say that the Bond franchise is not also heavily implicated in constructions of British national identities and mythologies. These, however, seem to be far more stable in the films' patterns of consumption than in the films themselves or in the character of Bond. Since 1975, Bond films on TV have become a regular feature during the holiday season in British households. ITV regularly transmits them on Christmas Day, and the audience expects them to be shown. This festive ritual constructs a sense of unity both in the family and among British families united in front of the television (Bennett and Woollacott 38).

But let us get back to the hapless Felix Leiter and his first film appearance in *Dr No*. It is interesting to note that there is no Felix Leiter in the novel *Dr No* – just as there is no Tom Sawyer in the graphic novel *The League of Extraordinary Gentlemen* by Alan Moore, the text on which the 2003 film of the same name is based. Inventing an American character enables both films to conjure up a handover of empire and to endlessly defer it. In *The League of Extraordinary Gentlemen*, there is a final intimation of immortality concerning Quatermain, the old hero of the Empire, who had died in the course of the film. Early on in the film, Quatermain had told the league's members: "[...] a witch doctor did bless me once. I had saved his village. He said Africa would never allow me to die". And indeed, the ending of *The League of Extraordinary Gentlemen* insinuates that Quatermain is not dead after all.

The last scene of the film shows Quatermain's burial in Africa. His spiritual son Tom Sawyer lays down his Winchester rifle on the grave of the spiritual father and leaves the burial ground as the last of the league's member. However, after the mourners have left, an African 'witch doctor' appears and starts conjuring up a fire and a thunderstorm. The fresh earth on Quatermain's grave positively vibrates with the energy of the thunderstorm, and the last shot of the film shows Sawyer's Winchester as it starts slipping from the mound. As an impersonation of the British Empire, Quatermain will return from the former colonies, which is to be expected of a film franchise that wants to keep its options open. But Quatermain's vibrating grave also opens up a rather grim ideological outlook. Imperialism itself is *undead*, an unfinished project haunting the collective unconscious which popular mass entertainment addresses. Imperialism will come back from the grave to claim more victims. The handover of Empire is once more deferred because the

---

mezzo", a well-known quote from Deleuze and Guattari (380), might just as well apply to Bond.

project of imperialism refuses to die – and cinemagoers the world over are invited to applaud, transnationally as it were.

Works Cited

Amis, Kingsley. *The James Bond Dossier*. London: Jonathan Cape, 1965.
Baron, Cynthia. "Doctor No: Bonding Britishness to Racial Sovereignty." *The James Bond Phenomenon: A Critical Reader*. Ed. Christoph Lindner. Manchester: MUP, 2003. 135-50.
Bennett, Tony and Janet Woollacott. *Bond and Beyond: The Political Career of a Popular Hero*. London: Macmillan, 1987.
Bergfelder, Tim. "The Nation Vanishes: European Co-Productions and Popular Genre Formulae in the 1950s and 1960s." *Cinema and Nation*. Eds M. Hjort and S. Mackenzie. London: Routledge, 2000.
Cannadine, David. "Ian Fleming and the Realities of Escapism." *In Churchill's Shadow: Confronting the Past in Modern Britain*. Oxford: OUP, 2003. 279-311. (orig. publ. as "James Bond and the Decline of England" *Encounter* 53.3 [1979])
—. "The Haunting Fear of National Decline." *In Churchill's Shadow: Confronting the Past in Modern Britain*. Harmondsworth: Penguin, 2002. 26-44.
Chapman, James. "Bond and Beyond: The James Bond Films and Genre." *Licence to Thrill: A Cultural History of the James Bond Films*. London: I. B. Tauris, 1999a. 19-68.
—. *Licence to Thrill: A Cultural History of the James Bond Films*. London: I. B. Tauris, 1999b.
—. "Bond and Britishness." *Ian Fleming and James Bond: The Cultural Politics of 007*. Eds Edward P. Comentale, Skip Willman and Steven Watt. Bloomington: Indiana UP, 2005. 129-43.
—. *Licence to Thrill: A Cultural History of the James Bond Films*. 2nd ed. London: I.B. Tauris, 2007.
Deleuze, Gilles and Félix Guattari. "1227: Treatise on Nomadology: The War Machine." *Capitalism and Schizophrenia*, Vol. II: *A Thousand Plateaus*. 1980. Trans. Brian Massumi. London: The Athlone Press. 1987, 351-423.
Durgnat, Raymond. *A Mirror for England: British Movies from Austerity to Affluence*. London: Faber & Faber, 1970.
Eco, Umberto and Oreste Del Buono, eds. *The Bond Affair*. London: Macdonald, 1966.

Haggard, Henry Rider. *King Solomon's Mines*. Ed. Dennis Butts. Oxford: OUP, 1989.

Halloran, Vivian. "Tropical Bond." *Ian Fleming and James Bond: The Cultural Politics of 007*. Eds Edward P. Comentale, Skip Willman and Steven Watt. Bloomington: Indiana UP, 2005. 158-77.

Kipling, Rudyard. *A Critical Edition of the Major Works*. Ed. and intro. Daniel Karlin. Oxford: OUP, 1999.

—. "The White Man's Burden." *Rudyard Kipling: A Critical Edition of the Major Works*. Ed. and intro. Daniel Karlin. Oxford: OUP, 1999. 479-80.

Leach, Jim. *British Film*. Cambridge: CUP, 2004. 94-9.

Low, Donald Anthony. *The Contraction of England*. Cambridge: CUP, 1985.

McFarlane, Brian. "Losing the Peace: Some British Films of Postwar Adjustment." *Screening the Past: Film and the Presentation of History*. Ed. Tony Barta. Westport, Con.: Praeger, 1998. 93-107.

Moore, Alan, Kevin O'Neill, Ben Dimagmaliw and Bill Oakley. *The League of Extraordinary Gentlemen*. Vol. I. No. 1-6 [La Jolla: America's Best Comics], 1999-2000.

Reynolds, David. *Britannia Overruled: British Policy and World Power in the Twentieth Century*. 2nd ed. Harlow: Longman, 2000.

Robbins, Keith. *The Eclipse of a Great Power: Modern Britain, 1875-1975*. 2nd ed. London: Longman, 1995.

Stoker, Bram. *Dracula*. Eds Nina Auerbach and David J. Skal. New York: Norton, 1997.

Street, Sarah. *British National Cinema*. London: Routledge, 1997.

—. "The 1960s: New Money, New Identities." *Transatlantic Crossings: British Feature Films in the USA*. London: Continuum, 2002. 169-92.

Sonja Fielitz

Fish and Chips with Marshmallows? Possibilities and Limitations of Trans-Cultural Intermediality

Against the background of the recent cultural turn in literary studies, this essay traces the role of intermediality for negotiating cultural identities on a global scale. It focuses on the field of film studies from a transatlantic perspective, since it lies in the nature of film to cross cultural borders, not only within and between nations but also across heterogeneous linguistic and social formations. In the field of film studies, one of the most salient incarnations of the global is to be found in Hollywood representing a forceful cinema industry that has put its competitors into the shade. Thus, it is a considerable challenge for producers in other cultural and national contexts to face up to Hollywood's international ubiquity and developing strategies, because the imperialism of an 'Americanisation' of film culture may devalue and influence national cultural identities, that is, in this case, British identity. Films discussed include William Shakespeare's *Macbeth, Much Ado About Nothing, Henry V, Romeo and Juliet*, Alan Bennett's drama *The Madness of King George III* (London, 1991), its film version *The Madness of King George* (released in America 1995) and the film version of Laurence Sterne's novel *Tristram Shandy* released as *A Cock and Bull Story* in 2006.

Introduction

In today's world, we are surrounded by newspapers, books, theatre, television, cinema, computer games, and the World Wide Web as a kind of intermedial library. In short: intermediality is our everyday life experience and, no doubt, deserves further critical investigation.

Theoretical Background: Definitions and Forms of Intermediality

Since the 1980s *intermediality* has become one of the most central ideas of scholarly debate, because postmodern critical discourse opened up new chances of interpretation in text as well as media studies. Derrida's reflections on the never-ending and permanently deferred line of signifiers, and deconstruction's abolishment of the focus on a separate notion of medium-inherent aesthetic qualities gave more weight to the potentiality of a text and a medium than to its defined form. Theory made us aware of the polyphonic chorus in the background of a text (in its very broad sense) that enabled its genesis and, at the same time, defined its implications. In literary criticism but also in performance studies this process prompted an attitude of transcendence in order to explore what lies beyond the boundaries of one defined meaning and form. From the 1990s on, performance studies took up the issue with fervour by paying particular attention to the dissolution of generic boundaries and styles in vogue with the attitudes of quotation and carnival transformations of art systems, and it is safe to say that the gradual shift of cognitive standards from (traditional) print culture to new modes of perception is still in progress. Originally separate media interact and merge, generic boundaries are blurred, and spatial blends and self-conscious reflexivity are the consequences.

Even if the concept of intermediality has been widely discussed since the 1980s, there is still a plethora of differing notions (Gross 335-66) of which I can only refer to the two most well known ones. Christopher Balme favours the notion of intermediality as the recreation of aesthetic conventions of one particular medium within a different medium in terms of quoting aesthetic strategies and importing techniques of a technological medium, such as film or video, into theatrical life performance (Balme 154). Werner Wolf's system of defining intermediality (Wolf 1999, 52) distinguishes between

1. Extracompositional intermediality and its two variants, i.e. transmediality and intermedial transposition.

a) Transmediality as a quality of cultural signification appears on the level of historical devices, that is, medially unspecific phenomena that occur in more than one medium, such as rhythm and thematic variation, or themes such as conflicts between generations. (This form was occasionally named extracompositional intermediality.) As is typical of this type in general, in all cases the intermedial quality is primarily located in the space between the two works, i.e. in the process of gestation, but not in the end product.

b) Intermedial transposition could be the transposition of a narrator into a film or a drama, or an operatic orchestra as fulfilling narratorial elements. The most common variant of intermedial transposition in contemporary culture applies to entire works, as for example in the transformation of novels and other pieces of art into films or the creation of an operatic version of a literary work. Intermedial transpositions characteristically result in relatively independent signifying units (in its extreme case, hardly any references to the original pretext are included in the end product).

2. Intracompositional intermediality (intermediality in a narrow sense) in which the existence of a reference to at least one other medium forms a constitutive part of the signification of an artefact. In this case, the involvement must be verifiable within the semiotic entity. Intracompositional intermediality can be subdivided into two variants: plurimediality and intermedial reference.

a) Plurimediality: This variant of intermediality applies to two or more media with their typical or conventional signifiers overtly present in a given work at least in one instance. It is an intermedial fusion, a medial hybrid and it is best exemplified in opera as a synthesis of drama and music, or ballet as a synthesis of dance, non-verbal dramatic elements and music.

b) Intermedial reference, on the other hand, does not give the impression of medial hybridity of the signifiers or of a heterogeneity of the semiotic systems used, but rather of a medial and semiotic homogeneity, since intermedial reference does not imply the incorporation of the signifiers in other media. This means that the involvement of another medium in intermedial reference takes place only indirectly. The medium referred to is only present as an idea. (In the field of intertextuality this is called system reference.)

Against this background, in recent scholarship the intracompositional field of image-text relations and the verbal rendering of visual works of art (generally termed *ekphrasis*) – be it in poetry, prose or drama – has proven an enduringly popular subject. In the field of drama and theatre, Freda Chapple and Chiel Kattenbelt, for instance, locate intermediality at a meeting point in-between the performers, the observers and the confluence of the media involved in a performance at a particular moment of time. Peter Boenisch (2006) and others see theatre as being challenged by the intermedial incorporation of digital technologies. A crucial element of digital media structures is hypermedia, in which each individual user creates his or her own navigation path and retrieves different versions of it by following the hyperlinks through a text.[1]

All these forms of intermediality, however, will not be in the focus of this essay. Since this publication is concerned with the practical side of intermediality, I will concentrate on the field of its extracompositional variants and intermedial transposition, in this case: film studies.

Intermedial Transposition: The Filming of Literary Texts

Within the field of film studies, I will follow up on Werner Wolf's statement in his article "Intermediality Revisited" (2002), namely that there have only been a few surveys focusing on the functions of intermediality "in contexts larger than that of individual works" (Wolf 2002, 16). Hence, in the recent wake of the cultural turn in literary studies, I will try to establish a larger cultural context and trace an aspect which appears to have been mostly neglected so far, that is, the role of intermediality for negotiating cultural identities on a global scale. As indicated in the title of this essay, I will be

---

[1] For instance, Herbert Fritsch's project *Hamlet-X* at the *Volksbühne Berlin*. Cf. Wiens 223-36.

particularly concerned with the filmic representation of British (represented by "fish and chips") and American ("marshmallows") cultural identities.[2]

Globalisation

No doubt, the international film scene is part of a configuration of flows and transfers of concepts on a global scale. Films cross cultural borders within and between nations and circulate across heterogeneous linguistic and social formations,[3] because more and more people across the globe are receiving the same messages from the same centres of communication. Besides music, food and fashion, media products such as films are also distributed globally – *Jurassic Park, Superman, Titanic* and *Star Trek* (films and TV-series), to name but a few, were from the beginning designed for a global market and became global box office hits.[4]

Hence, it is no longer feasible today to study a mass medium such as film solely from within the boundaries of national states. In addition, in the field of film studies, we find, in the sense of Edward Said, that a culture, a self, a national identity, is always produced in relation to its others, which in film industry is mainly Hollywood. For decades, Hollywood has been one of the manifestations of the global and, in the pure sense of the word, a global player, and other nations have always had to deal with its presence and its leadership in technology, capital investments and innovations.[5] Facing up to Hollywood's international ubiquity is a considerable challenge for producers in other cultural/national contexts, because the imperialism of a 'Holly-

---

[2] In this process I will neither trace the theatrical performance of the players of a text as adapted to suit the medium of the film (cf. Fielitz 1999), nor focus on the film narration, that is, the cinematic techniques of edit, cut, fade, wipe, soundtrack etc. (as this would require a case study) but focus on the film industry's cultural discourse.

[3] In times of satellite television reception, national boundaries are dissolving and national sovereignty cannot be retained. World events can be experienced simultaneously. Furthermore, in the global system various political, social, economical and cultural connections cross-cut borders between countries and decisively condition their fate. According to Welch (1977) the following factors are important in the development of globalisation: the increasingly global nature of capital and the rise of global markets, the increasingly global movement of people, the increasing importance of information technology in production, consumption and leisure, the increasing awareness of environmental issues that affect the whole planet, and a growing awareness that politics has stretched beyond the nation-state.

[4] In the strict sense of the word, 'global culture' is a contradiction in terms because cultures must be rooted in a sense of community, history and heritage, so that it would be impossible to speak of a 'global culture', since this would be universal and rootless.

[5] As recent studies such as *Global Hollywood* (Miller et al. 2001) and *Hollyworld: Space, Power and Fantasy in the American Economy* (Hozic 2001) indicate, the tendency has been to foster dominant screen images, practices and expectations that have dictated filmmaking in a variety of styles and environments.

woodisation' of film-culture may devalue and influence national cultural identities. Let us thus examine to what extent American media imperialism has shaped (British) national identity on the basis of a few examples.

Possibilities of Trans-Cultural Intermediality: The Globalisation of the British Bard

One of the best possibilities to trace intermedial transpositions in a global context, is, no doubt, William Shakespeare, because he is *the* British national poet and a British cultural icon. That academics were more than reluctant to allow an intermedial turn in Shakespeare studies for a long time was, at its time, shown by the following famous anecdote, that is, the reaction of an elderly distinguished textual scholar to Kosintsev's film version of *King Lear* at the first *Ohio Shakespeare Conference* of 1977. As soon as the chair of the session had advised the audience to keep their eyes on the entire frame to fully absorb Kosintsev's art rather than be distracted by the subtitles flashing along the bottom, and to forget the words, the elderly textual scholar rose to stammer in a voice choked with rage and incomprehension: "I must protest. This just won't do. I can't believe I've come all this way to a Shakespeare Conference to be told not to pay any attention to the words."

Fortunately, much has changed since these days. Since Jack Jorgens' now classic monograph on *Shakespeare on Film* (1977) at the latest, it has become common understanding that (not only Shakespeare's) plays were written for performance and that the script is not the work but, to use Jorgens' words, the 'score' for the work. Jorgens' analogy of the text as a musical score appears to be particularly appropriate since it implies an orchestral rendition that includes many strands in the dramatic texture. In his analogy Jorgens is summoning up an image of an orchestration of media and is also acknowledging that the text is just a starting point that will be explored through the rehearsal process, and completed in performance. Through his semiotic analysis Jorgens established how film adapts the performance skills associated with theatre: stage lighting, properties, set design, wardrobe, sound effects and acting. The most significant aspect of the move to a semiotic analysis of Shakespeare's films was, however, that it led to an interpretation which related to cultural rather than aesthetic values.

That globalisation was only a minor issue before the 1980s is aptly shown by Akira Kurosawa's Shakespeare films which were designed as meeting grounds for Western and Japanese classical modes. Local and global still met on an even terrain. In his *Throne of Blood* (1957), an adaptation of *Macbeth*, Kurosawa is clearly alert to cultural difference when he is highly ambivalent about how to represent a powerful woman (Lady Macbeth) and her role in the world. Some years later, in *Ran* (1985), his version of *King Lear*, the central character does not divide his lands among his daughters, but among his sons, since within the film's feudal Japanese setting daughters were not allowed to become heirs.[6] Here, Eastern hierarchy and loyal service are still in the forefront of trans-cultural intermediality.

A new stage in the globalisation of film culture began at the end of the 1980s when Kenneth Branagh infused the filming of Shakespeare with a marketeer's sense of popular culture. Branagh as actor/director led the way with *Henry V* (1989), *Othello* (1992), *Much Ado about Nothing* (1993) and *Hamlet* (1996). On the one hand, he continued a tradition drawn from the actor-manager of British Victorian theatre and established cinema by Laurence Olivier, since his films remain essentially theatre-based. No doubt, their strength lies in their actor-centred approach with their reverence for the text of the British Bard. What is particularly interesting from our point of view of (increasing) globalisation is that Branagh's *Henry V* (1989) still included an all-British cast. By the time of his *Much Ado about Nothing* (1993), however, things had changed, since Branagh had given in to Hollywood's dominance and subjected Shakespeare to American film imperialism. *Much Ado about Nothing* includes America's most popular black actor, the African-American Denzel Washington and America's most popular teen heart-throb Keanu Reeves. Two years later, in 1995, Hollywood's Laurence Fishburne played *Othello* (1995), and for his 1996 four-hour *Hamlet* Branagh casted Stratford-upon-Avon dignities such as John Gielgud (Priam), Judi Dench (Hecuba) in non-speaking appearances, while utilising Hollywood box-office stars such as Charlton Heston as the Player King, Jack Lemmon (Marcellus) and Robin Williams (Osric). Branagh's Americanisation of the British Bard was certainly pushed to a limit with his *Love's Labour's Lost* (2000), financially backed by Miramax, who had, among others, financed *Shakespeare in Love* (1999). This revival of the film musical ("There is no business like show business", for instance, replaces the Pageant of the Nine Worthies) cut no less than two thirds of the play (the film lasts only an astonishingly short 94 minutes) and flopped at the box office.

It was in this cultural discourse when we might assume that the Bard's name had come to be regarded in popular cultures as 'uncool', that the notably 'cool' Australian film director Baz Luhrmann put out a new *Romeo and Juliet* (1996). By deconstructing and reassembling Shakespeare's canonised play, the Australian director subverted the mono-vision of the British cine-

---

[6] The old lord (the Lear character) makes his eldest son Taro the lord of the first castle and head of the clan while the other two sons must content themselves with submission to Taro and with secondary and tertiary castles. The outspoken Saburo, the Cordelia figure, protests and is banished, along with a faithful retainer, Tango (representing Shakespeare's Kent).

matic discourse on Shakespeare by presenting a polyphonic, multi-cultural, self-reflective, multi-lingual, music and dance-driven version of this play. Luhrmann retells Shakespeare's story through a powerful combination of intermedial devices (there are references to other media-discourses such as theatre, film, the reading out of news, opera, television and pop music). Just as in narrativity, the referentiality and representational quality of fiction with its linear storytelling marked by clear causality, teleology and narrative closure as ways of creating narrative meaning, was called into question in this dramatic case.

In addition, Luhrmann reinforced the matter of globalisation from a linguistic point of view, when he moved the national British poet from the educated white UK to the immigrant Hispanic, African-American communities of the American city and took this as his starting point for distributing his product worldwide. His cast speaks Shakespeare's text in a variety of accents ranging over African-American, Hispanic, Italian, Rap etc. Luhrmann's *Romeo + Juliet* was Shakespeare, respectively British culture, in its most globalised form.[7] To mention but one example here: the self-reflexivity of performance across the media is immediately apparent in the opening section of *Romeo + Juliet*, a vibrant,[8] comic and immensely fast sequence that heralds the beginning and end of the play as the prologue, spoken initially on a television screen by a newsreader,[9] who reads the bare facts that will lead to the epilogue.[10]

---

[7] Further examples of globalisation in the 1990s are *Elizabeth* and *Shakespeare in Love*, cowritten by the American Marc Norman, the success of which lies with their international all-star cast. American stars Gwyneth Paltrow and Ben Affleck (as Ned Alleyn) work beside Australians, such as Oscar winner Geoffrey Rush and relative newcomer then Cate Blanchett, and the picture is completed by British 'quality' performers Judi Dench, Colin Firth, Richard Attenborough, and Joseph Fiennes. Nevertheless, it ends up at the shores of Virginia. *A Midsummer Night's Dream* (1999) casts Rupert Everett alongside Kevin Kline, Michelle Pfeiffer, and Sophie Marceau. In Franco Zeffirelli's *Hamlet* (1990), Mel Gibson's star persona was central since he brought well-established action-hero credentials from the *Lethal Weapon* franchise to the title role. Last but not least, *The Lion King* (1994) reworked *Hamlet* for a younger generation.

[8] From a further intermedial perspective, this opening of the film could also be interpreted as an overture by giving the audience the themes and stylistic structure of the piece. In fact dominating this 'overture' is the music of "O Verona" in which echoes of "O Fortuna" of *Carmina Burana* can be heard. In the tomb scene, a top shot of the dead lovers on their deathbed is accompanied by the *Liebestod* from Wagner's *Tristan and Isolde*.

[9] From an intermedial point of view it is particularly interesting that the story is framed by a television news report. The television slowly materialises from a dark screen until it takes over the frame. A black newsreader begins to tell us about the "two households both alike in dignity". The camera then turns away from the newsreader and we are drawn into the report itself. As the voiceover continues to tell us how civil war makes civil hands unclean, we are presented with a tabloid television montage of quickly edited images of chaos: some from a

British directors were, however, gradually opposing the American studios who allowed the Europeans to tell their stories mainly on their terms. This became obvious in the same year when Trevor Nunn's *Twelfth Night* (1996)[11] started a counter-movement. The film announcement asserts that "the film succeeds in part due to Nunn's decision to ignore the box office lure of Hollywood stars, and to cast all the parts with outstanding British actors[12] [such as Ben Kingsley, Helena Bonham Carter and Nigel Hawthorne] [...] who can actually speak Shakespeare's lines with proper cadence and clarity" (Boose and Burt 16).[13] That a further counter-movement back to national and away from global Shakespeare versions has taken place since then can be shown by a New Zealand *The Merchant of Venice* (2002) in Maori-language with subtitles in modern English.[14]

The Compromise: *The Madness of King George*, directed by Nicholas Hytner (1995)

Let us now turn from the British Bard to a distinctively British play. When the American film version of Alan Bennett's drama *The Madness of King George III* (first performed in London in 1991) was published under the title of *The Madness of King George* (released in America in 1995), there were rumours that the American promoters had insisted on the title change because they feared that the sequel-saturated Americans, not having seen the previous two Georges, would be confused. "This was a marketing decision", Bennett writes in the preface to the published version of the screenplay, "a survey having apparently shown that there were many moviegoers who came away from Kenneth Branagh's film of *Henry V* wishing they had seen its four predecessors" (Bennett xiv).

---

helicopter, some out of focus, some zooms and quick wipes. The end of the film reverses this process and the television newsreader fades to black when we are told that there "never was a story of more woe/than this of Juliet and her Romeo".

[10] This hybridisation of media was also employed by Michael Almereyda's *Hamlet* (2000) which closes with a television broadcast of the epilogue, and Michael Bogdanov's *Macbeth* (1998) which shows the title on a television set.

[11] It was backed by Fine Line Features, which generally finance films that do not cross the line from art house to mainstream immediately.

[12] In the same wake, Adrian Noble's cast or *A Midsummer Night's Dream* (1996) was a core of the same actors who played in the 1995 RSC production.

[13] Nunn had complained about the Hollywood executives and the pressures he was put under to charge his film in order to make it more saleable. He did not accept being told to provide novice audiences with more plot synopsis at the beginning of *Twelfth Night*.

[14] Director and producer Don C. Selwyn is a prominent player in New Zealand who apparently has a great interest in a 'national Shakespeare' again.

That in this case global transposition was at least a matter of compromises becomes first of all clear from what Bennett wrote in *The London Review* and elsewhere. The project started out as an accurate recreation of an episode in British political history and an exploration of the strange affinity between madness and power, but it reached the screen as a handsome piece of heritage cinema, full of English pageantry and stately homes.[15] Examples of heritage cinema of the 1980s in the field of the novel are the films of Henry James' *The Bostonians* (1984), E.M. Forster's *A Room with a View* (1985), *Maurice* (1987), Austen's *Sense and Sensibility*, or Ishiguro's *The Remains of the Day* and *A Passage to India*. Its success continued in the 1990s with films such as *Howard's End* (1992) and British television adaptations including *Brideshead Revisited* and the BBC's *Pride and Prejudice* (1995), to name only a few.

And indeed, as a diligent analysis of the text and film versions of Bennett's play show, the alterations were conditioned by the playwright's and the director's adjustments to the tastes of two different cultures. Bennett's play about a British King is meticulously respectful of historical data and incorporates many of the words actually spoken or written by its characters. In addition, it is to a large extent preoccupied with the political consequences of the King's indisposition (he suffered from porphyria, a rare metabolic disease, the symptoms of which were thought to include insanity at the time). The film version by Bennett and Nicholas Hytner, however, simplifies the political and constitutional issues featured in the British drama (for instance, the loss of the American colonies is characterised as a personal loss of the King's) and foregrounds the domestic melodramas of generational conflict and marital disruption (for instance, the film introduced Maria Fitzherbert, the secret wife of the Prince of Wales), thus alluding to popular family dramas or, much worse, soap operas.

---

[15] In the 1980s the so-called 'heritage cinema' emerged. Heritage films concentrate on the careful display of historically accurate dress and décor, celebrate rather than investigate (a theme park of) the past, use stars, use polished lighting and camera work, many changes of décor and extras and classical or classical-inspired music and are high-budget productions. In derogative terms these films were called the 'Laura Ashley school of filmmaking'. They usually display the middle class or aristocracy and use rather conventional filmic narrative style without distinct directorial voices. These films situate us firmly in the barricaded room of an English identity from which the outside world (e.g., the Italian, the working class) is viewed from above and without, not engaged with. They engage with the idea of crossing the border between cultures but in the knowledge that there is a safe haven to retreat to. Its success continued in the 1990s with films such as *Howard's End* (1992), *Elizabeth, Shakespeare in Love*, to name only a few. *Sense and Sensibility* was jointly created by Taiwanese director Ang Lee, British scriptwriter Emma Thompson and a British cast starring Thompson, Hugh Grant, and Kate Winslet. Later in the 1990s there were speculations whether we had reached a post-heritage phase with films such as *Orlando* (1992) and *The Piano*.

The structure of Bennett's British play rests upon the dichotomies of space and ideology that are described as Windsor, the King's place, and Westminster, the Parliament's place, between which the play moves back and forth.[16] In the film, however, this oscillation between Windsor and Westminster and their attendant implications is lost, when the film's opening sequences show a farmyard, a cricket ground, and a Lincolnshire field. In fact, the production crew appears so indifferent to the historical acumen of the (American) moviegoer that the film's opening scene contains a close-up of a door at Westminster, which actually is Eton College, with the clearly visible graffito '1862' cut into the wood.[17]

The film's most obvious invocation of an American film convention occurs, however, at the climactic political moment of the plot, that is, when the Regency Bill is about to be finally put to vote in Parliament. If the vote is taken, the Prince of Wales is sure to be declared Regent, and his father George III will be put away forever. In the play, news that the king has recovered his wits (and we will soon hear how this came about) is enough to stop the Prince of Wales' accession. The film, however, restages the classical cavalry rescue scene. Pitt cannot turn the tide with a few words in Parliament; the king himself must appear at Westminster, racing from Kew in a carriage to beat the clock, with the usual suspenseful technical cross-cutting between preparations for the vote and the progress of the king. Needless to say, the king does arrive in time, the MPs flood out of their chamber, Parliament hails George III as their monarch, the Prince of Wales faints at being foiled, and the film comes to a close. Order has been restored and moviegoers are invited to kick over their popcorn boxes and rush for the exit. What has been lost in the sophisticated (British) play's transfer to the global less sophisticated screen is its balance between personal and political narratives.[18]

---

[16] Such careful cross-cutting establishes both the centrality and fevered antagonisms of the political struggle at the time. In the play, George III (1738-1820), farmer George, who was very popular with the English people, is in many respects the embodiment of the state, and his own conflicted health of mind and body becomes emblematic of the nation's body.

[17] Further changes in the cast of characters between play and film also offer revealing glimpses into Bennett's and Hytner's strategies for their cultural orientation. When Edmund Burke disappears, and Richard Brinsley Sheridan is reduced to a spear carrier at Carton house, it becomes clear that the play's political content, with its complex relationship to the late Georgian literary sphere, is being diluted. Gone are the allusions to Goethe and Gibbon, as well as the witty exchange prompted by Burke asking Sheridan if he could ever abandon politics.

[18] Since Hollywood is big on humanity and sympathy, it was these changes and mostly Nigel Hawthorne's star performance in the title role that accounted for much of its transatlantic (still moderate) success: about 15 million dollars gross in the US compared to about 7 million dollars gross in GB is self-evident, and it may also be quite telling that the (American) Oscar in 1995 was awarded for Best Set Decoration, whereas no less than four British

Apart from its demanding cultural context, which appears to have been an obstacle for a global box-office hit, *The Madness of King George III* is also highly challenging from the point of view of intertextuality and intermediality: in Act Two, Bennett's stage directions explicitly compare the king and his servant Papendieck to Shakespeare's King Lear and the Fool (63-65). And it is indeed a reading performance of Shakespeare's play within Bennett's drama (a play within the play) that provides the turning point in the king's story, signalling his recovery.[19] Thus, this king has a much better ending than his counterpart in Shakespeare. What is more, by reducing Shakespeare's tragedy to a family quarrel with a happy ending, Bennett still includes another intermedial and intertextual reference here, that is, Nahum Tate's version of *King Lear* (1681), a reference, however, which most spectators will not notice. This also applies to George's "Pray, do not mock / I am a very foolish, fond old man. Fourscore and upward, / Not an hour more or less, and to deal plainly / I fear I am not in my perfect mind" (5.1.52-56, Folio text), which is, in fact, a quotation from Shakespeare's play.

Limitations of Trans-Cultural Intermediality: *The Cock and Bull Story*, dir. by Michael Winterbottom (2006)

That the possibilities and limitations of trans-cultural intermediality are not only a matter of dramatic but also of highly sophisticated narrative texts may be briefly exemplified by *A Cock and Bull Story* of 2005, which was released as a film in the US and in Australia as *Tristram Shandy: A Cock and Bull Story* in 2006. It is an attempt to adapt Laurence Sterne's essentially un-filmable novel *The Life and Opinions of Tristram Shandy, Gentleman* (1759). In this novel the narrator steps outside the narrative to address the reader, apologises for 'losing' chapters that later show up in their entirety, including an all-black page to mourn the passing of one character and a blank page for the reader to fill in his depiction of another figure. Amid the flashbacks and flash-forwards, Tristram never manages to get much further than the moment of his birth.

---

awards were granted to the film, among them The Alexander Korda Award for Best British Film in 1996. Trans-cultural intermediality appears to come to its limits where cultural and intermedial contexts become too complex.

[19] Bennett: "the Lear scene is the turning point [...]. The fact that [Doctor] Willis did actually read *King Lear* with George III, is actually a fact. If he'd read *Twelfth Night* or something like that, I would not have had the wit to change it to *King Lear*, so I'm glad he got it right. But it is a turning point. It is just like a pause in a symphony when a new theme comes in very sweetly somehow, it's just a very touching moment when suddenly it happens. It's quite a gentle turning-point, really, and it was wonderful to see that for the first time in rehearsal" (Introduction, xxi).

Filming a book that has such an idiosyncratic character would seem the very definition of folly on a director's part, but Michael Winterbottom, an intriguingly British director, takes the risk and succeeds in his project. His 94-minute version is a film about a film crew making a film of an unfilmable novel. The adult Tristram, as well as his father, are played by the British comic Steven Coogan. In a modern-day frame story that slowly takes over the film, Coogan does not play Tristram Shandy but Steve Coogan, an actor on the set of a film in progress entitled *Tristram Shandy*. Another British comic, Rob Brydon, plays Tristram's Uncle Toby, and in the modern-day scenes, Rob Brydon is the actor Rob Brydon. Steven Coogan and Rob Brydon thus play themselves as the egoistical lead and 'co- lead' actors in an adaptation of Sterne's novel, in which Coogan has his lead role in a film production brought into question half way through the film's chronology. The film may have a simple plot and numerous slapstick scenes (such as Coogan suspended upside down in a foam-rubber uterus), but has many layers of integrated narration making it highly complex. Hence, it is an exact rendering of the way of writing a book into the way of producing a film, since the graphemic level of the book has brilliantly been transferred to the cinematic level of the new medium here.[20]

All in all, *Cock and a Bull Story* embodies Sterne's (British) work perfectly from an intermedial point of view. The consequence, however, is that it is exactly this sophisticated nature of the film which hinders it from becoming a global box office hit.

Conclusion

Living in a globalised world, we cannot study a literary work from a monomedial perspective any longer. The speed and frequency of cultural transfers have given consumers throughout the world global 'tastes', accelerating the demand for cultural exchanges of all kinds. As I have shown, in the context of trans-national and trans-cultural film studies, the extreme cultural domination of film production by Hollywood has surely had a major influence on the idea of a national British film culture. As we have seen, actors and directors of British films became gradually aware that greater profits and prestige are to be found in a globalised film market (Branagh, Luhrmann). As it turned out, however, the possibility of such a cultural homogenisation is

---

[20] Most of the film is devoted to the 'frame' story about Coogan as the actor and the making of the film. The parts of the actual novel that are covered by the film are limited to Tristram's conception and birth, Uncle Toby's experiences at the Battle of Namur, Tristram's sudden and accidental circumcision at the age of three and the concluding scene of the novel: "L-d, said my mother, what is this story about? – A cock and a bull, said Yorick – And one of the best of its kind, I ever heard" (478).

double-faced, because it can be seen as part of the mechanisms that serve a sense of collective identity, but also as part of dis-establishing the same. Thus, in order to succeed in this process of hetero-identification on a global scale, various compromises have to be made in terms of target groups and their cultural expectations (Nunn, Bennett). The desire to use the medium of film in order to address specific matters of national cultural identity (*King George III*) appears to have reached its limitations in a globalised world, (a) when films require a high amount of cultural knowledge (Bennett) and (b) are highly complex (*A Cock and Bull Story*) with regard to their intermedial status.

Works Cited

Balme, Christopher. *Einführung in die Theaterwissenschaft*. Berlin: Erich Schmidt, 1999.
Bennett, Alan. *The Madness of King George* (Screenplay). London: Faber & Faber, 1995.
—. *The Madness of King George III*. London: Faber & Faber, 1995.
Boenisch, Peter M. "Aesthetic, Art to Aesthetic Act: Theatre, Media, Intermedial Performance." *Intermediality in Theatre and Performance*. Eds Freda Chattle and Chiel Kattenbelt. Amsterdam: Rodopi, 2006. 103-16.
Boenisch, Peter M. "coMEDIA electrONica: Performing Intermediality in Contemporary Theatre." *Theatre Research International* 28 (2006): 34-45.
Boose, Lynda E. and Richard Burt, eds. *Shakespeare, the Movie: Popularizing the Plays on Film, TV and Video*. London: Routledge, 1997.
Chattle, Freda and Chiel Kattenbelt, eds. *Intermediality in Theatre and Performance.* Amsterdam: Rodopi, 2006.
Fielitz, Sonja. *Drama: Text und Theater*. Berlin: Cornelsen, 1999.
Gross, Sabine. "Recent Research in Intermediality." *Monatshefte für deutschsprachige Literatur und Kultur* 93 (2001): 335-66.
Hozic, Aida. *Hollyworld: Space, Power and Fantasy in the American Economy*. London: Cornell UP, 2001.
Jorgens, Jack. *Shakespeare on Film*. Bloomington: Indiana UP, 1977.
Miller, Toby et al. *Global Hollywood*. London: British Film Institute Publishing, 2002.
Sterne, Laurence. *Tristram Shandy*. Intro. George Saintsbury. London: J.M. Dent & Sons Ltd., 1912, repr. 1956.
Welch, Jeffrey Egan. *Literature and Film: An Annotated Bibliography*. New York: Garland, 1977.

Wiens, Birgit. "Hamlet and the Virtual Stage: Herbert Fritsch's Project *Hamlet-X*." *Intermediality in Theatre and Performance.* Eds Freda Chattle and Chiel Kattenbelt. Amsterdam: Rodopi, 2006. 223-36.

Wolf, Werner. "Intermediality Revisited: Reflections of Word and Music Relations in the Context of a General Typology of Intermediality." *Word and Music Studies.* Ed. Suzanne M. Lodato. Amsterdam: Rodopi, 2002. 13-33.

—. "Musicalized Fiction and Intermediality: Theoretical Aspects of Word and Music Studies." *Word and Music Studies: Defining the Field.* Eds Walter Bernhart, Steven Paul Scher and Werner Wolf. Amsterdam: Rodopi, 1999. 37-58.

Susanne Gruss

Shakespeare in Bollywood?
Vishal Bhardwaj's *Omkara*

Othello has been portrayed by many of Hollywood's classic actors, including Orson Welles (1952), Laurence Olivier (1965), and, more recently, Laurence Fishburne (1995). In film adaptations, the play has thus already travelled far; in terms of literary criticism, *Othello* has also become a stock element of postcolonial criticisms of Shakespeare. Vishal Bhardwaj's *Omkara* (2006) adds a new twist to both trends in turning Shakespeare's play into a Bollywood film, including the typical features of the genre: song and dance-sequences. This article focuses on how this cross-cultural enterprise appropriates both *Othello* as 'master text' *and* the genre it uses, the Bollywood blockbuster, and scrutinises the commercial potential of the film's transnational visuals. Bhardwaj not only relocates *Othello* to India (and turns the race conflict into one of caste), he also carefully shapes and changes the Bollywood film: while *Omkara* could be interpreted as one of the family tragedies so popular with Indian audiences, the song and dance-scenes are more convincingly rooted in the plot than in typical examples of the genre and seem to accommodate the filmic tastes of a Western audience. *Omkara* is therefore read as a paradigmatic example of the fluidity of cultural borrowings and conventions in the early twenty-first century.

Adapting *Othello* – and Race

Othello has a long and complex screen history – "no Shakespeare play", Cartelli and Rowe point out in their recent *New Wave Shakespeare on Screen* (2007), "has been adapted to the screen as provocatively as *Othello* has in the last twenty years" (Cartelli and Rowe 120). By way of an introduction to the politics of adaptation that inevitably inform Vishal Bhardwaj's Bollywood *Othello*, I will therefore briefly touch on previous film versions of Shakespeare's play. While Orson Welles' *Othello* (1952) has been described as diminishing Othello's blackness through its black-and-white *film noir* approach, Laurence Olivier's *Othello* (1965) had to face severe criticism because of its "quite appalling projection of racist stereotypes" (Aebischer 62): his Othello is visibly othered by a thick layer of black make-up, an 'African' voice, rolling eyes, a West Indian accent, "a vulgar, open-mouthed, lip-smacking laugh, and an inclination to sensuality" (Aebischer 62f.).[1] It is of much more than anecdotal value that this Othello quite literally blackens

---

[1] Neil Taylor quotes from Olivier's *On Acting* (1986) to illustrate that Olivier's "own conception of 'being black' required him to 'be beautiful', to develop a deep sensuous voice ('dark violet – velvet stuff'), to speak with an accent and to walk 'like a soft black leopard'" (Taylor 269).

dead Desdemona when some of his make-up smudges her during his final monologue (cf. Aebischer 63). Although Oliver Parker's *Othello* (1995) was the first high-budget adaptation of the play with a black actor as the lead, the film has similarly been criticised as racist. Advertised by the director as an 'erotic thriller' (cf. Rosenthal 178), the film makes extensive use of Laurence Fishburne's corporeality; the moor is eroticised and exoticised through the use of jewellery and, more importantly, tattoos. The exploitative gaze on Othello's body, Deborah Cartmell points out, "reinforces a racial stereotype" (Cartmell 77). Several critics have identified Kenneth Branagh's Iago as the 'real hero' of this adaptation, the "wielder of the racist and misogynist gaze that has reduced Othello and Desdemona to their physicality and disabling 'otherness'" (Aebischer 69). The most recent Hollywood adaptation of *Othello* that I am aware of is Tim Blake Nelson's *'O'* (2001), an American high-school *Othello* that casts the moor as a basketball whizz kid, who, because of his sporting genius, is granted a scholarship at a white elite prep school in the US-American South. Even though it focuses on an analysis of teen violence, the film is similar to Parker's *Othello* in its depiction of a racialised sexuality; both *Othello* and *'O'* are therefore "most readily understood as reflections on the shifting and uneven processes of the formation of racial identities" (Thornton Burnett 68).

Othello has thus often been used to shed light on contemporary – and in these cases American – issues of race and violence. As the examples I have mentioned demonstrate, it is especially Othello's blackness[2] and what has often been identified as the latent (or blatant, depending on the critic's point of view) racism and misogyny of the play that make screen adaptations a challenge. As Shakespeare's plot "requires the gifted black protagonist to devolve once again to murder, [each production] locks these films into a storyline that suggests racial stereotypes are inevitably self-fulfilling. In different ways, each prompts the question: *can Othello be successfully updated?* and what would success mean if it could?" (Cartelli and Rowe 120) If *Othello* therefore "remains haunted by its own cultural history" (Cartelli and Rowe 123), what does it mean when the play is turned into an Indian film adhering to the principles of Bollywood? In this essay, I will delineate how Vishal Bhardwaj creates a unique cultural hybrid from Shakespeare's text. His *Omkara* (2006) convincingly integrates the bard's text into the conventions of Indian popular cinema, but at the same time also crucially alters these conventions through its revision of *Othello*; as I will show, *Omkara* appropriates both Shakespeare's play *and* the conventions of the Bollywood 'filmi' in order to create a contemporary *Othello* with a truly international

---

[2] See, for example, Hailey Rippey, who points out that *Othello* "embodies the simultaneous attraction to and repulsion from blackness as a sexual image" (Hailey Rippey 26).

appeal. Despite this potential, *Omkara* did not become an international blockbuster; I will illuminate in how far the film's generic hybridity can be seen as one of the reasons for its lack of success.

Shakespeare, Bollywood and the Global(ised) Marketplace

Shakespeare has been treated as an icon of high culture, a "cultural trophy" (Rothwell 168), for centuries. Especially in the context of the British Empire, the bard was also a token of Englishness that could be "used to legitimate Britain's imperial power" (Burt 2003b, 17). Turning *Othello* into a popular Hindi film as Vishal Bhardwaj has done in his recent *Omkara* (2006), entails – quite obviously – an appropriation of the play's Renaissance context and an integration of its politics into the cultural imaginary[3] and conventions of the Bollywood film. At the same time, the project might also be described as an attempt of postcolonial rewriting and therefore a possible revision of Shakespeare's position within a postcolonial Indian context. In the early twenty-first century, globalisation seems to enable "the indigenization and subversive appropriation of Shakespeare in postcolonial and developing nations" (Burt 2003a, 266). As British colonialism was characterised not only by the notion of a political, but also of "a corresponding literary and cultural hegemony" (H. Trivedi 11), Shakespeare's works and their association with colonial power politics might be perceived as inherently problematic for a Bollywood adaptation. Taught to Indian students as "a measure of England's general world-wide superiority" (H. Trivedi 14) and thus part of a discourse legitimising colonisation, the "complex fate of loving Shakespeare while living in India", as Harish Trivedi points out, "is a classic instance of the colonial double-bind" (H. Trivedi 25). Although Shakespeare's "tyrannical canonical dominance is not quite what it used to be in colonial times" (H. Trivedi 25), a Bollywood revision of the bard's notorious moor is nevertheless an ideological challenge – or so it seems.

As Poonam Trivedi notes, to "look for Shakespeare in the Indian cinema may evoke suspicions of bardolatry or even seem like a colonial throwback. Yet, a long look into the history of the Indian, and particularly the Hindi film reveals this co-relation as neither whimsical nor contrived" (P. Trivedi 2007, 148). Shakespeare can be described as a stable presence in Bollywood film since its beginnings, a presence that goes back to the Mumbai film industry's close links to traditional Paris theatre. Immensely successful from the nine-

---

[3] Cartelli and Rowe define the cultural imaginary that informs adaptation as "that prevailing set of fantasies, values, desires, and assumptions which effectively identifies a specific cultural moment and differentiates it from other cultural moments past or to come" (Cartelli and Rowe 25).

teenth century to the 1940s, Parsi theatre adapted many Shakespeare plays, thus producing an "anomalous situation in which a colonizing master text became, and remains to this day, the most translated, adapted, performed, and published Western author" (P. Trivedi 2005, 19).[4] As Rajiva Verma points out, however, the films based on Parsi theatre productions are not reverential adaptations of a master text – they are less "a matter of taking over a worldview or moral vision and more of one professional playwright borrowing plots and situations and other tricks of the trade from another" (Verma 272). Most early Indian films that adapt Shakespeare do not "assume prior knowledge of the original plays, and Shakespeare is present in them not as a cultural icon but as a resource to be exploited for characters and situations, often without acknowledgment. They thus point to a greater complexity in the relationship between metropolis and periphery than postcolonial theory would seem to allow" (Verma 270). Shakespeare's presence in popular Hindi film can be found in both direct adaptations, often influenced directly by Parsi theatre performances, and "in the use of several themes and motifs whose sources can be traced back to Shakespeare" (Verma 283). *Othello* was appropriated by Indian director Jayaraaj in 1997 – his *Kaliyattam* is an adaptation "in which a gifted but smallpox-scarred *theyyam* artist falls in love with a beautiful upper-caste girl" (Verma 285). Director Jayaraaj chose *Othello* as his source material because he perceived a similarity in what he dubs Othello's 'split personality' and the traditional art of *theyyam*,[5] and adapts "the key issue of racism in the play by transposing it on to the inequities of the caste system" (P. Trivedi 2007, 151). Although the film was received favourably and invited to several international festivals, it was of course not produced as a film appealing to a blockbuster audience – in contrast to *Omkara*, it is not a popular Hindi film meant to attract a huge, international audience.

Since Bollywood has developed into a 'buzz word' in Western Europe and the US over the last ten years (cf. Dwyer and Patel 217), most people are by now aware of the fact that Hindi popular films work according to a differ-

---

[4] Poonam Trivedi refers to *Dil Farosh* (1927), a silent film based on a stage adaptation of *The Merchant of Venice*, as the earliest Indian film adaptation of Shakespeare (cf. P. Trivedi 2007, 148), and notes that the advent of 'talkies' in India in the 1930s and '40s also coincided with several Shakespeare adaptations (cf. P. Trivedi 2007, 149). She points out that the "main contribution of these early Shakespeare films was to popularize the iconic poet and assimilate him into the mass consciousness often without the audiences' knowledge" (P. Trivedi 2007, 149).

[5] Jayaraaj argues that in *theyyam*, "when the artist dons the makeup, he is considered as god. [...] When he removes the makeup, he becomes a man once again. I saw in *theyyam* the best opportunity to express a split personality. I saw the same dichotomy in Othello's mind also" (in Warrier).

ent set of conventions than the films produced, for example, in Hollywood. 'Newcomers' to the Bollywood film are generally irritated by what they perceive as a strange mixture of genres – the prototypical Hindi 'filmi' cannot be conveniently labelled as tragedy, comedy or action film, but will probably contain all of these elements. Critics have identified a similarity to European melodrama in the clear delineation of good and evil, the extreme exteriorisation of excessive feelings and the escapist pleasure Hindi films offer. Although most critics agree on this generic similarity of popular Hindi film to melodrama, M.K. Raghavendra quite concisely points out that viewers have to keep in mind that Western melodrama "emerged through a specific historical impetus pertinent to Europe" (Raghavendra 25) and is therefore, of course, not identical with its Indian counterpart, which places "less emphasis upon individual motivation, subscribing to a more deterministic viewpoint" (Raghavendra 26). Intense emotions are most often shown in the songs, "where visuals and language are simultaneously foregrounded" (Dwyer and Patel 29). The famous song sequences can either be a diegetic element of the film (if the character is a singer, dancer or courtesan) or be included in a non-diegetic 'dream sequence', stereotypically a "lovers' fantasy that may take the form of a stage show" (Dwyer and Patel 37). Especially in the songs, but also in other scenes, popular Indian films do not follow the conventions that Hollywood has established as seemingly 'universal' and 'natural' for films – they depart "from continuity editing, naturalistic lighting, and realist mis-en-scene" (Ganti 141) and therefore often lack what Western audiences would call "a straightforward linear narrative" (Ganti 138). As Bollywood increasingly caters for the filmic appetites of non-residential Indians and their nostalgic longing for 'Mother India', the Mumbai film industry has produced many so-called 'family entertainers' since the late 1990s, films with plots driven by family conflicts and "love stories filled with songs, dances, elaborate cultural spectacles like weddings, set against the backdrop of extremely wealthy, extended, and frequently transnational, families" (Ganti 39). Often described as *masala*, a "potpourri of elements – music, romance, action, comedy, and drama" (139), it is both their inherent hybridity and the ensuing 'anti-naturalism' of Bollywood films that most people focus on to either explain Bollywood's attractions – or to ridicule them. The fact that the films are characterised by "meaningless digressions from the core narrative, maudlin melodrama, an embarrassingly juvenile conception of the comic as well as the romantic, and ahistoric, inconsistent sequencing" (Lal and Nandy xiv) has also made academics cringe from Bollywood as a 'serious' scholarly topic – a situation that has only changed over the last ten to fifteen years, which have seen the development of substantial academic analyses of the popular Indian film.[6]

Omkara and the Appropriation of Shakespeare

As Vishal Bhardwaj's renegotiation and appropriation of *Othello* and the play's meanings are embedded into the different production and reception context of the Mumbai film industry, his adaptation is dramatically different from the adaptations I have briefly discussed. With reference to Bollywood 'remakes' of Hollywood films, a practice that has led to the frequent perception of Hindi films as derivative of their Hollywood 'originals',[7] Tejaswini Ganti points out that the "three main elements of 'Indianization' are adding 'emotions', expanding the narrative, and inserting song" (Ganti 77). While one could argue that it is quite difficult to insert even more emotion into *Othello*, the other two elements are clearly discernible in *Omkara*.

The narrative itself is quite securely rooted in the setting of Uttar Pradesh, which not only accounts for the characters' accent, but also provides the messy setting of corrupt local politics.[8] Omkara works for a local politician known as 'Bhaisaab' and supports him in his ruthless campaign for a parliamentary seat, which entails the murdering of Bhaisaab's political opponents. Most of the action takes place in Omkara's home village, where he has taken his future bride Dolly while they are waiting for an auspicious date for their marriage. The seeds for Omkara's jealousy are sown when, in analogy to Shakespeare's play, Dolly's father warns him about his daughter's duplicity: "General [...] may you never forget the two-faced monster a woman can be!" (0:20:41). As in *Othello*, Dolly is as innocent and pure as can be. Langda, the film's Iago, is Omi's longtime friend and brother-in-law. In his sinister plots, Langda instrumentalises Raju, Dolly's former fiancé, and his wife Indu, and finally manages to make Omi believe that Dolly is having an affair with

---

[6] See, for example, R. Dwyer and D. Patel, *Cinema India: The Visual Culture of Hindi Film* (2002), V. Mishra, *Bollywood Cinema: Temples of Desire* (2002), T. Ganti, *Bollywood: A Guidebook to Popular Hindi Cinema* (2004), R. Kaur and A.J. Sinha, eds, *Bollyworld: Popular Indian Cinema Through a Transnational Lens* (2005), or V. Lal and A. Nandy, eds, *Fingerprinting Popular Culture: The Mythic and the Iconic in Indian Cinema* (2006).

[7] Susan Bassnett and Harish Trivedi highlight a similar problem for the more general topic of colonial translation: "The notion of the colony as a copy or translation of the great European Original inevitably involves a value judgement that ranks the translation in a lesser position in the literary hierarchy. The colony, by this definition, is therefore less than its colonizer, the original" (Bassnett and Trivedi 4).

[8] Bhardwaj points out that he "wanted a violent backdrop, and I think UP and Bihar are states of abject lawlessness. [...] These people have not been seen in our mainstream cinema – the characters of small towns, the little mafias, the street fights over girls – it's that crazy, Wild West kind of place." (Sen)

Kesu, his own rival. With the use of mobile phones (for example in the scene in which Omkara is eavesdropping on Kesu and his supposed 'date' with Dolly) and television, the setting is clearly marked as contemporary. Bhaisaab's election party is broadcast on TV, a technique that is reminiscent of the use of TV in other modern Shakespeare adaptations such as, most famously, Baz Luhrmann's *William Shakespeare's Romeo + Juliet* (1996), in which a news anchorwoman replaces the chorus, or Michael Almereyda's *Hamlet – The Denmark Corporation* (2000), which aptly replaces *Hamlet*'s metatextual discussions of theatre and stage conventions with a visual discussion of film and TV conventions.[9] Guns are generously employed in both the killings that take place during the film and in Omkara's suicide.

Although some of the British critics seem to have no more than a superficial knowledge of the conventions of Hindi film – one critic muses that Bollywood "is better known for producing lavish song-and-dance routines than the raging emotions of *Othello*" (Ramesh) – several critics argue that Bollywood seems to be the fitting context for another appropriation of *Othello*: nowhere, one of them writes, "are the themes of obsessive love, jealousy, betrayal and murder, more suited than amidst the excesses and emotional abandon of Indian cinema" (Joshi), while the *Guardian* critic points out that the adaptation is "appropriate, because Bollywood, with its liking for ingenuous fantasy and romance, has often seemed to me to resemble in style nothing so much as a late Shakespeare play" (Bradshaw). The problem of race (and racism), that all more recent adaptations of *Othello* struggled with, is cleverly circumnavigated: as in *Kaliyattam*, Omkara's 'difference' is not one of race but one of caste. Despite Dolly's quite metaphorical assertion that her lover's deficient social status does not diminish his humanity ("A crescent, though half, is still called a moon", 0:51:02), as the son of a slave girl, Omkara is a social outsider. In what might be seen as a remainder of the predominant discussion of race in *Othello*-films, the focus on skin colour persists: several people remark on Dolly's light skin in contrast to Omkara, and Omkara's sister Indu jokingly compares her to "a magic flute in the hands of the Dark Lord" (0:37:20). As readings of whiteness in a postcolonial context have shown, the "notion of whiteness as an explicit and implicit cultural ideal – of beauty, desirability, virtue, purity – lingers in the postcolonial world in surprising ways" (López 20). Dolly's whiteness is therefore not only a marker of her difference to Omkara, it is also an instance of criticism in the

---

[9] The 'to be or not to be'-soliloquy can serve as an evident example here: the set is a video shop, in which Hamlet prowls aimlessly, the shelves are decorated with signs apparently making fun of Hamlet (one of them says 'Go Home Happy') and a screen in the background shows *The Crow* (1994) – an action-saturated revenge tragedy that serves as an ironic commentary on Hamlet's procrastination.

film. In contrast to *Othello*, there is of course no cultural difference between Langda and Omkara; the question of hybridity or (unsuccessful) mimicry on Othello's side, which has become one of the predominant elements in postcolonial readings of the play, is therefore of no interest in Bhardwaj's film.

In accordance with the generic conventions, *Omkara*'s focus is in part shifted to family: in contrast to Shakespeare's play, Omkara is decidedly *not* an isolated outsider, but integrated into a social network. The film's equivalent of Shakespeare's Emilia, Indu, is also Omkara's sister, and the film adds a grandmother to complete his family. As already indicated, cunning Langda is married to Indu (with whom he has a young son), and is therefore also part of Omkara's family. Langda's frustration when his brother-in-law anoints Kesu as his lieutenant is therefore simultaneously more explicitly motivated than in the play and included into a context of family relations that is familiar to and popular with the Indian audience.[10] At the same time, his betrayal becomes even more perfidious, as he "betrays bonds of family as well as professional loyalty" (Rosenthal 190). Omkara himself is introduced as a dark and brooding hero who rarely smiles and who, as the chieftain of a group of criminals, is not averse to killing himself. The "constant political violence replaces the Turk's short-lived threat to Cyprus and enables the director to reflect the bloody world of contemporary politics in Uttar Pradesh by engineering a *Macbeth*-like cycle of attacks" (Rosenthal 188).

While some critics have pointed out the film's 'Western' aesthetics as reminiscent of the infamous 'spaghetti Western' à la Sergio Leone,[11] it is of course the Bollywood Western – with *Sholay* (1975) as the most famous example of the Indian 'curry Western' (if one wants to stick with culinary metaphors) – that has to be seen as the referential background. Going back to the genre of the *daku* (or outlaw, gangster) film in Indian cinema, *Sholay* does rely on Leone's *Once Upon a Time* (1968, cf. Raghavendra 38) and other Westerns,[12] but also "borrows liberally from other films" (Raghavendra 38) and therefore creates its own aesthetics. Bhardwaj thus embeds his updated *Othello* in a visual tradition that, curiously, refers to both Hollywood and Bollywood traditions and is therefore decipherable for both Eastern and Western audiences. Other scenes, one could argue, especially those of organ-

---

[10] Rosenthal notes that "Shakespeare's tragic love story is thus incorporated into a three-generation family tragedy of a kind very popular with Bollywood audiences" (Rosenthal 190).

[11] Rosenthal remarks that the "open-air shootouts and arid widescreen landscapes sometimes give *Omkara* a Western tang, and Saif Ali Khan's Langda has the tough, mischievous presence of Eli Wallach in *The Good, the Bad and the Ugly* (1996)" (Rosenthal 189).

[12] Raghavendra also mentions *The Magnificent Seven* (John Sturges, 1960), *The Good, the Bad, and the Ugly* (Sergio Leone, 1966) and *The Secrets of Santa Vittoria* (Stanley Kramer, 1969) (cf. Raghavendra 38).

ised crime and the killings, are reminiscent of classics like *The Godfather* (1972) or the *film noir*; again, however, the visual references are not that clear-cut – Indian popular film has a long-standing fascination with the world of organised crime and gangsters that *Omkara* alludes to, a world that Bhardwaj has already explored in his previous film, *Maqbool* (2003), an updated *Macbeth* set in the underworld of Mumbai. As Daniel Rosenthal points out, *Omkara* can even be interpreted in terms of "Uttar Pradesh folklore about a legendary band of brothers" (Rosenthal 189).

Omkara and the Appropriation of Bollywood

While Bhardwaj thus convincingly roots his *Othello* within the traditions of Bollywood cinema and finds convincing cultural equivalents for many elements from *Othello* – the symbolic handkerchief, to name another, is replaced by a precious cummerbund, a 'family heirloom' that Omkara gives to his prospective bride – the director at the same time "breaks the conventional mould of Bollywood into smithereens and does it with a panache that encompasses all departments of filmmaking" (Kazmi). *Omkara* is, as I will show, as much a unique appropriation of the paradigms of Bollywood film as it is of *Othello*.

One of the most strikingly obvious departures from Bollywood conventions in *Omkara* is certainly the inclusion of two sex scenes, one showing Langda and Indu in bed, one Omkara and Dolly, but the film departs quite radically from the 'rules' of popular Indian film in many more aspects. In contrast to the importance of celebrations in Hindi films, which also provide a social context in which protagonists can meet, *Omkara* is framed by two failed marriages. The position of the central wedding at the end of the film, when Omkara's and Dolly's relationship is already beyond repair, is thus another departure from Bollywood films. The wedding preparations in *Omkara* are overshadowed by bad omens, and prospective bride and groom are shown as unhappy and/or brooding. The wedding ceremony itself visually frames the couple as already divided, and Dolly's henna-fingerprints on the door of her new house can easily be associated with blood and her impending death. With a very subdued soundtrack, the scene figures as a stark contrast to the staging of the colourful, elaborate wedding scenes audiences expect from Bollywood flicks.

The authority of Indu (Emilia) is greatly increased in the film. As Omkara's sister, she does not merely provide the familial and social network that is so typical of many Bollywood products, her part is also one of female empowerment. Worried by the state of Dolly after her most serious argument with jealous Omkara, Indu tries to talk to Omkara about his marriage. 'Omi' confesses his jealousy ("Her father's voice keeps ringing in my ears all the time [...]", 0:32:15), and Indu quite sternly reminds her brother of the cultural status of women in Indian society: if the scriptures, she argues, sully women, how can men honour them? As women enter marriage with empty hands, they are dependent on their husbands' goodwill and trust; men, however, are too quick in their suspicions and judgements of their wives. If Omkara has any doubts, she admonishes him, he must not attend the marriage – the village community will take care of Dolly (cf. 0:33 ff.). With Indu's passionate statement, the film not only refers back to the misogynist heritage that has made *Othello* a problematic text for feminist readers, it also offers a critical glance at similar structures that can be found in contemporary India. Once again, the film's *modus operandi* therefore allows for both traditional 'Shakespearean' readings and readings that position *Omkara* more precisely in its Indian (and Bollywood) context. At the end of the film, it is Indu who turns into a figure of revenge when she finds out about her husband's machinations – she kills him with a single machete blow. The *Tragedy of Othello, the Moor of Venice* is therefore not simply remade into the *Tragedy of Omkara, Half-Caste*, in Bhardwaj's film, it becomes the tragedy of both Omkara and his sister Indu.

It is, however, with the songs that *Omkara* most clearly signals its hybrid status in its attempt to mediate between Hollywood and Bollywood conventions. Superficially, the film adheres to the 'rules' for songs in Bollywood films. There are seven songs that also serve to announce the film's status as a 'commercial' film: "Not having songs", Ganti points out, "communicates that a film is outside the mainstream of the Bombay film industry, possibly even an 'art film', and to most people in the industry this means death at the box office" (Ganti 84). Generally speaking, songs in popular Indian films are more often than not highly stylised – even if they are plot-affecting and diegetic, the song sequences are rarely mimetic or naturalistic. As Dasgupta argues, the spectator is therefore "in a position of constant awareness of the constructed and performed nature of the spectacle; you know that you are not seeing reality, and the way your complicity is elicited ensures that you know that the spectacle appeals to you by bringing your fantasies and desires directly into play" (Dasgupta 13).

Three love songs accompany the development (and decline) of Omkara's and Dolly's relationship. The first song, "Naina", is a non-diegetic song accompanying a flashback that accounts for the story of Omi and Dolly falling in love. A second love song, "O Saathi Re", fills the inevitable slot of the lovers' duet; triggered by Dolly's endearingly off-key version of "I Just Called to Say I Love You", the song differs considerably from the standard Bollywood mould. While the stereotypical love duet has the couple bursting "into song, mostly in picturesque locales such as gardens, meadows, and forests, far removed from the actual setting of the film, often with multiple costume changes, and sometimes with scores of dancers in the background" (Ganti 82f.), or might include a 'dream sequence' (cf. Dwyer and Patel 37), Omkara's and Dolly's song clearly demarcates the film's appropriation of Bollywood conventions. The non-diegetic song is used as voice-over; although the lyrics can of course be read as a comment on the flirtatious images of the couple in love, there is no choreography; the rural setting of Uttar Pradesh is far from exotic, and there are no changes of costume. Although the scene basically conforms to the convention of the love song, the 'rule' is at the same time changed, possibly to accommodate for the different viewing conventions and tastes of a Western audience. A last love song, "Jag Ja", is initially sung a cappella by Omkara to Dolly in the morning, and is then repeated as a non-diegetic voice-over by the end of the film, with a heartbroken Omi humming along to the lyrics, thinking about what he has lost before he kills himself.

"Omkara", the second song in the film, is meant to stage Omkara as a heroic figure. He helps an old woman at the well before a shoot-out, and when an agent of Singh, Bhaisaab's political opponent, tries to provoke him, he remains surprisingly calm: "Next time around," he coolly announces after the shoot-out, "bet on horses [...] not on tigers" (0:27:58). In an atmosphere strongly reminiscent of the Western, Omkara is staged as "the greatest warrior of them all [...] Omkara!" (0:28:00). The zoom on a washing Omkara fulfils stereotypical Bollywood stagings of the hero, while the fact that he is framed in between bodies also questions and problematises his heroic status. The two songs performed by 'Billo' (the Bianca-character in Bhardwaj's film), who is a dancer, are probably closest to what a Western audience would expect from a typical Bollywood film. "Beedi" is a bawdy duet between Billo and a drunken Kesu, "Namak Ishq" shows Billo entertaining Omkara's political opponent Indore Singh. Both scenes – and Billo's precarious moral status as a dancer – evoke a familiar Bollywood-feature, the courtesan (Ganti points out that "courtesans exist as characters in Hindi cinema, which has had a longstanding fascination with this institution", Ganti 14f.). In contrast to other films such as the quite recent *Devdas* remake (2002)[13] and its lavish staging of Madhurit Dixit's courtesan dances, Billo is, however, neither filmed in a sumptuous setting, nor is her choreography as elaborately staged as audiences might expect. The gritty realism of both bar-scenes is a decided move away from the 'anti-realism' of comparable scenes, the colours are subdued instead of luminous and saturated, neither scene is brightly lit and in both cases, the dancing sequences are clearly 'legitimated'

---

[13] I have chosen *Devdas* for comparison as it was also promoted both in India and in the West, and was meant to appeal to a similar audience as *Omkara*.

by the plot and not merely an occasion to showcase the dancing skills of the actress: the first scene is arranged by Langda – he has induced Kesu to drink and orchestrates the ensuing brawl that leads to Kesu's 'fall from grace'. In the second scene, Billo is not only used as a decoy for Omkara's political opponent while Omi and his men enter the club to take revenge for the failed assassination of Bhaisaab – Billo's playing around with the military cap and her seductive act with the gun is both a premonition of the ensuing shoot-out and a comment on the decrepit state of local politics in Uttar Pradesh.

Commercial Failure of Generic Hybridity?

With reference to what he dubs 'post-diasporic' cinema, Richard Burt points out that the "circulation of Shakespeare, Bollywood, and Hollywood does not translate, as some might expect, into hegemonic impositions, neo-colonialism, residual internalized colonialism, or subversive indigenizations" (Burt 2003a, 273). Poonam Trivedi celebrates the notion of a 'globalised bard' in Bhardwaj's *Maqbool*: "This kind of re-visioning that adds and expands the canonical text leads to the fourth and current stage in the engagement with, by now, a globalized bard, which is of a postcolonial confidence to 'play around' with and deconstruct Shakespeare for our own needs" (P. Trivedi 2007, 153); her assessment also holds true for *Omkara*. As my close reading of its adaptation of generic conventions has traced, *Omkara* seems to confirm both Burt's claim and Poonam Trivedi's more celebratory affirmation of recent Indian Shakespeare adaptations – the film is not overly interested in a postcolonial revision of *Othello*'s racial politics, as the evasion of the problem of race quite clearly states; it is also a self-confident appropriation that uses Shakespeare's text to explore specifically Indian genres and concerns. The film does, of course, 'indianise' Shakespeare's play through the use of culturally specific correspondents to Shakespeare's imagery and symbols. At the same time, *Omkara* is not a subversive critic of a colonial 'master-text', but quite consciously created as a hybrid product meant to please several dramatically different audiences: as Bhardwaj points out in an interview, he wanted to appeal to the Indian Bollywood audience and to "touch a cord with international audiences [...]. It was not for art or for literature" (Sen). In contrast to his earlier *Maqbool*, which had received good reviews but was perceived as an arthouse film (and thus not expected to do well at the box office), *Omkara* was advertised as a big Bollywood blockbuster – an intention that is clearly announced by the casting of popular Bollywood stars such as Ajay Devgan, Saif Ali Khan, and Kareena Kapoor in the lead roles.[14]

While some British critics mildly satirise the film's Bollywood conventions – "It's a bit rum when Iago breaks into a song-and-dance number, or when Desdemona's murder is followed by a trilling love song" (Matheou), writes *The Independent* –, British reviews were on the whole favourable, although almost none of the bigger newspapers devoted more than one or two paragraphs to the film. Similarly, Indian critics were in general favourable to the film, although one critic complains that the film "tends to get too realistic at times" (Adarsh) in its deviation from 'filmi' norms, while the critic for *The Tribune* indulges in a little wishful thinking: "It is then [at the end] that you wish Bhardwaj had cheated on Shakespeare a litte. The 'desi' version of *Othello* could well have ended with a 'baraat'", a marriage procession (Tandon). As these reviews indicate, *Omkara* was perceived as 'too Bollywood' by Western critics, while some Indian critics were irritated by its departure from 'filmi' conventions. Even though the film opened decently at the Indian box office, it did not develop into a big success; the Uttar Pradesh dialogue as well as the frequent swearing were used to explain the film's comparative failure.[15] The film did enter the UK top ten when it opened in 2006, but it cannot be called a hit in Europe, either. This seems to be part of a more general problem: although popular culture in both Europe and the US has incorporated Bollywood as a set of colourful conventions that are frequently quoted (cf. Baz Luhrmann's *Moulin Rouge*, 2001, Mira Nair's *Vanity Fair*, 2004, and other recent Hollywood films), and the visual culture of Hindi film has thus become quite visible internationally, nevertheless "Bollywood films themselves only rarely reach beyond South Asian diasporic audience" (Dwyer and Patel 217). Burt addresses this problem when he points out that, although "many thought that Bollywood, in the wake of *Lagaan*'s good notices, was poised to be in the West what Hong Kong cinema was in the 1990s, Bollywood basically bombed. *Lagaan* flopped, as did *Devdas*" (Burt 2003a, 276). Other Bollywood-adaptations of British classics, such as *Gur-*

---

[14] Several critics comment on the double appeal of *Omkara* as an *Othello* adaptation *and* a potential 'filmi' blockbuster. *Indiafm.com* notes that *Omkara* "is expected to prove a trailblazer, not only winning acclaim from those who appreciate realistic cinema, but also satisfying the needs of entertainment-seeking moviegoers" (Adarsh), and *bbc online* comments that *Omkara* "sees the play brought to life for the first time in a mainstream Hindi format" (Pandohar). In the *Guardian*, Randeep Ramesh quotes Anupama Chopra, a film critic for *India Today*, who compares *Omkara* to *Maqbool* and highlights that "*Omkara* is much more ambitious. It has big stars, it is a mainstream format. It is not arthouse" (Ramesh).

[15] The *Times of India* reports that especially families avoided *Omkara* due to the constant swearing, and that even in the North of India, where audiences are familiar with the Gujjar dialect, the film failed to be a blockbuster (N.N., *Times of India*).

inder Chadha's equally updated and bollywoodised Jane Austen, *Bride and Prejudice* (2004), have similarly failed the financial expectations. My explanation for this phenomeon is a rather bleak outlook – although the currency of Bollywood has risen in recent years, international audiences are not yet willing to accept films that incorporate and hybridise the double conventions of Hollywood and Bollywood. Despite the fact that "filmed Shakespeare is already multiracial and multinational in the West" (Burt 2003a 268), a globalised taste for a multi-generic Shakespeare with "a lot of masala", and a "vibrant, funny Othello" (Bhardwaj in Sen), has not yet developed.

Works Cited

Adarsh, Taran. "*Omkara.*" *indiafm.com*. 28 July 2006. 27 June 2008 <http://indiafm.com/movies/review/12773/index.html>.
Aebischer, Pascale. "Black Rams Tupping White Ewes: Race vs. Gender in the Final Scene of Six *Othellos.*" *Retrovisions: Reinventing the Past in Film and Fiction.* Eds Deborah Cartmell, I.Q. Hunter and Imelda Whelehan. London: Pluto, 2001. 59-73.
Bassnett, Susan and Harish Trivedi. "Introduction: Of Colonies, Cannibals and Vernaculars." *Post-Colonial Translation: Theory and Practice.* Eds Susan Bassnett and Harish Trivedi. London: Routledge, 1999. 1-18.
Bradshaw, Peter. "*Omkara.*" *The Guardian.* 28 July 2006. 27 June 2008 <http://arts.guardian.co.uk/filmandmusic/story/0,,1831260,00.html>.
Burt, Richard. "Shakespeare and Asia in Postdiasporic Cinemas. Spin-offs and Citations of the Plays from Bollywood to Hollywood." *Shakespeare the Movie II: Popularizing the Plays on Film, TV, Video, and DVD.* Eds Richard Burt and Lynda E. Boose. London: Routledge, 2003a. 265-303.
—. "Shakespeare, 'Glo-cali-zation,' Race, and the Small Screens of Post-Popular Culture." *Shakespeare the Movie II: Popularizing the Plays on Film, TV, Video, and DVD.* Eds Richard Burt and Lynda E. Boose. London: Routledge, 2003b. 14-36.
Cartelli, Thomas and Katherine Rowe. *New Wave Shakespeare on Screen.* Cambridge: Polity, 2007.
Cartmell, Deborah. *Interpreting Shakespeare on Screen.* Basingstoke: Macmillan, 2000.
Dasgupta, Probal. "Popular Cinema, India, and Fantasy." *Fingerprinting Popular Culture: The Mythic and the Iconic in Indian Cinema.* Eds Vinay Lal and Ashis Nandy. Oxford: OUP, 2006. 1-23.

Devdas. Dir. Sanjay Leela Bhansali. Perf. Shahrukh Khan, Aishwarya Rai and Madhuri Dixit. Mega Bollywood, 2002. DVD Eros International, 2002.

Dwyer, Rachel and Divia Patel. *Cinema India: The Visual Culture of Hindi Film.* London: Reaktion Books, 2002.

Ganti, Tejaswini. *Bollywood: A Guidebook to Popular Hindi Cinema.* New York: Routledge, 2004.

Hailey Rippey, Marguerite. "All Our *Othellos*: Black Monsters and White Masks on the American Screen." *Spectacular Shakespeare: Critical Theory and Popular Cinema.* Eds Courtney Lehmann and Lisa S. Starks. Cranbury, NJ: Associated UP, 2002. 25-46.

Hamlet. The Denmark Corporation. Dir. Michael Almereyda. Perf. Ethan Hawke, Julia Stiles and Sam Shepard. Prod. Double A Films. Miramax, 2000. DVD Kinowelt Home Entertainment, 2001.

Joshi, Poonam. "Omkara Review." *channel4.com.* 27 June 2008 <http://www.channel4.com/film/reviews/film.jsp?id=156817&page=1>.

Kaur, Raminder and Ajai J. Sinha, eds. *Bollyworld: Popular Indian Cinema Through a Transnational Lens.* New Delhi: Sage, 2005.

Kazmi, Nikhat. "*Omkara.*" *The Times of India.* 29 July 2006. 30 June 2008 <http://timesofindia.indiatimes.com/articleshow/1822973.cms>.

Lal, Vinay and Ashis Nandy. "Introduction: Popular Cinema and the Culture of Indian Politics." *Fingerprinting Popular Culture: The Mythic and the Iconic in Indian Cinema.* Eds Vinay Lal and Ashis Nandy. Oxford: OUP, 2006. xi-xxvii.

López, Alfred J. "Introduction: Whiteness After Empire." *Postcolonial Whiteness.* Ed. Alfred J. López. Albany, NY: State U of New York P, 2005. 1-30.

Matheou, Demetrios. "*Omkara.*" *The Independent.* 30 July 2006. 25 June 2008 <http://www.independent.co.uk/arts-entertainment/film-and-tv/film-reviews/omkara-nc-409924.html>.

Mishra, Vijay. *Bollywood Cinema: Temples of Desire.* New York: Routledge, 2002.

N.N. "Families Stay Away from *Omkara.*" *The Times of India.* 1 August 2006. 30 June 2008
<http://timesofindia.indiatimes.com/articleshow/1833494.cms>.

'*O'.* Dir. Tim Blake Nelson. Perf. Mekhi Phifer, Julia Stiles and Josh Hartnett. Chickie the Cop Productions, et al., 2001. DVD Concorde Home Entertainment, 2002.

Omkara. Dir. Vishal Bhardwaj. Perf. Ajay Devgan, Kareena Kapoor and Saif Ali Khan. Shemaroo Films/Big Screen Entertainment, 2006. DVD Eros International, 2006.

Othello. Dir. Oliver Parker. Perf. Laurence Fishburne, Irène Jacob and Kenneth Branagh. Dakota Films/Imminent Films, 1995. DVD Warner Home Video, 2007.

Othello. Dir. Stuart Burge. Perf. Laurence Olivier, Maggie Smith and Frank Finlay. Eagle Films/Warner Bros., 1965. DVD British Home Entertainment, 2003.

Pandohar, Jaspreet. "*Omkara* (2006)." *bbc online*, 22 July 2006. 27 June 2008 <http://www.bbc.co.uk/films/2006/07/31/omkara_2006_review.shtml>.

Raghavendra, M.K. "Structure and Form in Indian Popular Film Narrative." *Fingerprinting Popular Culture: The Mythic and the Iconic in Indian Cinema*. Eds Vinay Lal and Ashis Nandy. Oxford: OUP, 2006. 24-50.

Ramesh, Randeep. "A Matter of Caste as Bollywood Embraces the Bard." *The Guardian*. 29 July 2006. 9 June 2008 <http://www.guardian.co.uk/world/2006/jul/29/books.filmnews>.

Rosenthal, Daniel. *100 Shakespeare Films*. Forew. Julie Taymor. London: British Film Institute, 2007.

Rothwell, Kenneth S. *A History of Shakespeare on Screen: A Century of Film and Television*. Cambridge: CUP, 1999.

Sen, Raja. "Today Othello, Tomorrow Hamlet?" *rediff.com*. 27 July 2006. 16 July 2008 <http://www.rediff.com///movies/2006/jul/27vishal.htm>.

Tandon, Aditi. "Vishal Dares to Indigenize *Othello*." *The Tribune*. 28 July 2006. 01 July 2008 <http://www.tribuneindia.com/2006/20060729/cth1.htm#6>.

Taylor, Neil. "National and Racial Stereotypes in Shakespeare Films." *The Cambridge Companion to Shakespeare on Film*. Ed. Russell Jackson. Cambridge: CUP, 2000. 261-73.

Thornton Burnett, Mark. *Filming Shakespeare in the Global Marketplace*. Basingstoke: Palgrave Macmillan, 2007.

Trivedi, Harish. *Colonial Transactions: English Literature and India*. Manchester: MUP, 1993.

Trivedi, Poonam. Introduction. *India's Shakespeare: Translation, Interpretation, and Performance*. Eds Poonam Trivedi and Dennis Bartholomeusz. Newark: U of Delaware P, 2005. 13-43.

—. "'Filmi' Shakespeare." *Literature – Film Quarterly* 25.2 (2007): 148-58.

Verma, Rajiva. "Shakespeare in Hindi Cinema." *India's Shakespeare: Translation, Interpretation, and Performance*. Eds Poonam Trivedi and Dennis Bartholomeusz. Newark: U of Delaware P, 2005. 269-90.

Warrier, Shobha. "Meet Another Director in Love with Shakespeare." *rediff.com*. 1 August 2006. 16 July 2008 <http://specials.rediff.com/movies/2006/aug/01slid1.htm>.

Amira Nowaira

Text and Pretext: Reading Cultural and Ideological Paradigms in the Hollywood and Egyptian Movie Adaptations of Tolstoy's *Anna Karenina*

In this paper I will try to shed some light on the complex and often problematic relationship between 'original' text(s) and 'derivative' movie(s) as the new productions traverse national, cultural and temporal borders, acquiring new meanings and significations in the process. The paper will attempt to examine the cultural and ideological transformations of Tolstoy's *Anna Karenina,* published in serial installments from 1873 to 1877, as revealed by two movie adaptations of the novel: the Egyptian adaptation entitled *The River of Love* in 1960 and the Hollywood movie directed by Bernard Rose in 1997 entitled *Anna Karenina*. In so doing, I hope to uncover some of the underlying assumptions and hypotheses informing these two very disparate movies and separating them from Tolstoy's novel. *Anna Karenina* as an original source text thus becomes a mere pretext for the presentation of a very different set of ideological premises.

In this paper I will try to shed some light on the complex and often problematic relationship between 'original' text(s) and 'derivative' work(s) as they traverse national, cultural and temporal borders, acquiring new meanings and significations, exhibiting more ironies, and finally re-emerging in a totally new guise, transformed almost beyond recognition.[1] The paper will attempt to examine the cultural and ideological transformations of Tolstoy's nineteenth-century novel, *Anna Karenina,* as revealed by two movie adaptations: the Egyptian movie adaptation of the novel entitled *River of Love* in 1960 and the Hollywood movie directed by Bernard Rose in 1997 entitled *Anna Karenina*.[2]

In looking at these two disparate works, I'm hoping to uncover some of the underlying assumptions and hypotheses informing them as well as separating them from the original novel. *Anna Karenina* as a source text thus becomes a mere pretext, an excuse for promoting a set of ideological principles that are virtually, if not totally, absent in the original text. Seen from this perspective, the novel turns into a site of contestation where conflicting ideological and cultural assumptions battle for dominance.

---

[1] The vexed and often problematic relations between source text and movie adaptation as well as questions regarding the 'fidelity' of adaptations to their source inspiration have been explored in *In/Fidelity: Essays on Film Adaptation*, edited by David L Kranz and Nancy C. Mellerski.

[2] The number and variety of movie adaptations of Tolstoy's novel are simply staggering (cf. Makoveeva, 111).

Tolstoy's *Anna Karenina* was published in serial installments from 1873 to 1877. It depicts and addresses some of the salient problems of 19th-century Russia: an inflated aristocracy and an impoverished and huge urban and rural base, while giving voice to some of the teeming and conflicting ideologies, philosophies and controversies of the period. But it is the figure of Anna, rather than the ideas expressed through the novel, that has come to dominate the collective perception of Tolstoy's work. This is not only due to her privileged status as carrying the title of the book but, I think, more importantly because her story has come to powerfully tickle the collective romantic imagination of its readers, regardless of their geographical location or their cultural affiliations. Anna's story, however, is not the sole narrative dominating Tolstoy's novel. Equally important stands Levin. In fact, one can make a case that the presence of Levin is crucial to our understanding of the novel as a whole. He is the introverted, philosophising man, the aristocrat with a 'soul' who, perhaps more than anyone else in the novel, represents the restless and searching spirit of immortal Russia. Without the presence of Levin, the novel turns into the unfortunate love affair of a disaffected aristocratic woman whose feelings get the better of her in this highly stylised and rigid aristocratic system.

It would be interesting to see how the two movies selected deal with the double-bind created by Tolstoy, and to investigate the cultural assumptions and conceptions which inform and come into play in the new productions, concentrating on how the new messages are relayed and reinforced through visual representations. Seen from this angle, the visual becomes a tool which is manipulated for specific political ends. It becomes a signal whose power is immediate and should never be underestimated.

The Egyptian movie *Nahr El Hob*, or *River of Love*, was released in 1960. It was directed by Ezzel Din Zhul Faqqar, starring Faten Hamama, the doyenne of Egyptian cinema, and Omar Sharif before he achieved international stardom and acclaim in Hollywood. The movie was produced only eight years from the 1952 revolution, which not only overthrew the king and sent him packing, but also introduced vast ranging and – in so many instances – irrevocable changes to the social and economic structure of Egyptian society. The early 1960s are generally seen to represent the height of fervent nationalism endorsed and propagated by the socialist and revolutionary regime of Gamal Abdel Nasser. The movie also came at a point in time when Arab nationalism and unity were at their zenith, when the dream of political union between Egypt and Syria was still a reality.

In line with the nationalist pride in Egyptian heritage and history, and as a tribute particularly to the ancient Egyptian past, the movie opens on a view of the Nile and a narrative of Isis and Osiris, which seems like a far cry from

Tolstoy's conception. In the ancient Egyptian myth, the forces of evil come into headlong collision with those of good, with the evil Seth killing good Osiris. Thus, the faithful wife Isis embarks on a journey to collect the scattered pieces of his body. Through her devotion Osiris is restored to life. Because of his death and resurrection, Osiris has always been associated with the flooding and retreating of the Nile. But the movie presents a very different story.

Unlike the ancient myth, the Isis of the movie, the goddess of love, looks down on earth and finds it barren and fruitless because it lacks love. The goddess weeps for deprived earth and her tears create and replenish the River Nile. Thus, the movie takes its basic symbol, the Nile, and uses it to represent continuity, immortality and rebirth, a symbol that defies death and disintegration, making it clear that love, like the Nile, is the ultimate and indispensable source of life.

It is not hard to follow the reasoning and logic informing the opening sequence well before the events of the story unfold. The emphasis here falls unambiguously on the almost mythical value of love and its importance as a life force, and by inference of its unquestioned legitimacy. It is the *raison d'être* of life on earth and blessed are those who water the land with love. Even before the movie begins, we are getting a clear endorsement of the main character Nawal who represents Tolstoy's Anna and we are invited to see her love affair in a positive light. By donning the Egyptian robes of an Isis she becomes immortal Egypt, a woman who stands for life and regeneration.

The movie pays lip service to the original work by adhering to the general outline and the skeletal structure of the love triangle proposed by the Anna Karenina model, while totally ignoring the Levin strand. We have Nawal, the unhappy frustrated wife who is much younger than her more than off-putting husband. It is hardly surprising then that she should fall in love with the dashing and irresistible army officer Khaled whose very name in Arabic means 'immortal' to further complement the Osiris analogy.

The young officer is everything that Nawal's husband, Taher, is not. So while the would-be lover is presented as a man graced with tenderness and loving care, the husband, Taher, is shown to be an ogre, a monster in human clothing, for he is selfish, scheming and incapable of simple human sympathy.

The movie is set in Egypt in the late 1940s, the pre-1952 revolution era. Taher is made into an old pre-1952 revolution feudal lord. The fact that he carries the pre-Revolution title of *pasha*[3] and occupies a ministerial position in the cabinet to boot makes him inseparably linked to the political *ancien regime*. In him, the collusion of power and money is most apparent, and the emphasis on the mind to the disregard of everything else is made abundantly clear. The harshness of the features, the stiffness of the attitude, and the cunning twisted smile are all meant to stand in sharp contrast with the guileless innocence of Nawal (Anna) whose youth and inexperience put her at a serious disadvantage in her relationship with her husband. Equally clear is that both Nawal and the *pasha* belong to two different classes, two different worlds that can never meet. Nawal has been, in fact, virtually coerced to marry him for the sake of her brother and her marriage is seen in terms of a sacrifice on her part to save her brother from financial ruin. The sequence featuring the first meeting between Taher and Nawal, given as flashback, demonstrates the unbridgeable chasm separating these two characters.

Nawal, composed and peaceful, sits on a jetty on the Nile, with her fishing rod in the Nile. Taher appears at the distance towering ominously above her. Not knowing who she is, he starts scolding her for trespassing on his property because it is clear that the pier belongs to him. Unperturbed, Nawal mistakenly believes that the man is some kind of guard trying to harass her, and not the *pasha* himself, and treats him dismissively and scornfully. Quite noticeable is the way the angle of the shot magnifies Taher's already bulky stature in comparison with the youthful, fragile-looking Nawal. Although it is Nawal who is seen fishing, the real fisherman ironically enough is Taher who would eventually catch Nawal and smother her life. By marrying Taher, Nawal is implicitly bound to be a fish out of water.

Also notable is the answer Nawal gives to Taher when he reminds her that she is trespassing on his property. By vehemently retorting that "The Nile belongs to all Egyptians", she, in fact, voices the idea that the old feudal lords were usurpers and that Egypt's wealth, represented here by the Nile, should not be the private property of one class to the deprivation of all others.

The *pasha* as portrayed by the movie has no redeeming quality, and no saving grace. In fact, he is almost like a medieval symbol of vengeance and retribution, the embodiment of a political regime that is both corrupt and inhuman. The movie is not apologetic at all about demonising Taher and by implication the whole old order. The new regime is adamant about demolishing the old regime and exposing it as a sham, corrupt and altogether inhuman. Nawal is presented as frequently trying to reach out to him and to bridge the

---

[3] A couple of months after the 23 July 1952 revolution, the titles of Bey and Pasha (roughly equivalent to Sir and Lord) were abolished as a gesture indicating that a new era of equality had begun.

gap between them but, of course, to no avail. He does not relent and rejects her approach at reconciliation quite haughtily.

Far from condemning Nawal for indulging her feelings for Khaled, while still officially a married woman, the movie legitimises this relationship through recourse to the initial Isis-Osiris analogy. When Nawal and Khaled meet by chance at a fancy dress ball, she is referred to as Isis meeting her Osiris, almost through the machinations of fate, in order to replenish the earth.

If adultery is presented with some degree of ambivalence in Tolstoy's novel, it does not feature as a morally ambiguous element in the Egyptian movie. Instead, the love affair between Nawal (Egypt as a woman) and Khaled (the military regime) has to be seen as legitimate and inevitable. Unlike the original Vronski who survives Anna, Khaled dies heroically on the battlefield during the Arab-Israeli war of 1948. Driven to ultimate despair, Nawal finds herself cornered and hopeless, and ends up throwing herself in front of a train.

Even when Nawal physically dies at the end through the symbol of the ruthless and merciless machine (the train) which is the total opposite of the river, it is the river that will have the final say. The river never stops, the Nile will always flood, and Egypt will be regenerated through love. This is very different from Tolstoy's rather ambivalent moral attitude towards Anna. It has been pointed out that Tolstoy employs imagery of harlotry in the presentation of his unfortunate heroine. Ronald LeBlanc has suggested that one of the "subtle rhetorical strategies that Tolstoi pursues to communicate to us all the pathos of his heroine's tragic fall from grace involves surrounding Anna in this part of the novel with various images suggestive of harlotry" (LeBlanc).

No intimation of harlotry is made in the Egyptian movie. The triumphant note of the ending, reasserting the power of love to conquer even time itself is a marked divergence from the Tolstoy conception of Anna's descent into despair and finally death, her love misunderstood by a hostile society that leaves no room for the individual who strikes out on a different route.

Isis is Egypt, the source of life, growth and recreation. She is the immortal force sustaining Egypt. If she dies, her death is only one phase in the eternal cycle of life. The story of Anna Karenina was therefore used as part of the propaganda war waged against the old regime. The objective is clear. If people still have any nostalgia for a past world, this movie revises and reinvents the past in order to vindicate the revolution and its actions.

In many ways, Bernard Rose's movie *Anna Karenina* seems to me to be headed in the opposite direction. Produced in 1997, almost seven years following the collapse of the Soviet Union and after the disappearance not only of the haunting specter of the cold war but also of the obsessive fear of communism, the movie creates a lush and alluring picture of pre-Soviet Russia. Visually, the movie is simply stunning: the ballroom interiors, the opulent style of living, the green landscapes as well as the period costumes. No less stunning is the music drawn from works by Tchaikovsky, Rachmaninoff, and Prokofiev. The splendor and sheer magnificence of the surroundings are recreated, with long sequences taking place in or around them. In the ball sequence, for example, where Anna and Vronski meet for the first time, we are overwhelmed by the sheer magnificence of the setting and the breathtaking beauty of the music no less than the beauty of the personages involved in this drama.

It is actually from the ball scene that the drama of Anna's narrative begins. In contrast with Kitty's superb, upbeat entry into the ball hall, Anna's departure from it is presented in terms of a descent into a dark abyss, foreshadowing the events yet to unfold. The abyss is used in the movie as a dominant and haunting image. Although both Anna and Kitty, who later becomes Levin's wife, inhabit the same opulent space, their fates are markedly different and their lives move in opposite directions. While Anna's fate is seen to follow a path of destruction ending in her death under the wheels of the train, the Levin strand follows a markedly different path. Levin's predicament at the beginning of the movie is fraught with pain and suffering but ends with reconciliation and harmony. The opening sequence of the movie places emphasis on his psychological/philosophical dilemmas, beginning as it does with the harrowing nightmare of wolves in pursuit of Levin representing the lack of purpose that haunted him at the beginning of the novel.

An interpretation of this nightmare along Freudian lines would not be too misguided. The movie pits Levin's plight against that of Anna. While she descends into despair and suicide, Levin regains his sense of purpose and the will to live. As Gillian Slovo points out, "While Tolstoy uses society's casting-out of Anna to tell us about the nature of aristocratic society, it is Levin who is his conduit to the wider world he so brilliantly evokes" (Slovo).

It is clear that the last impressions we have at the end of the movie are not those of Anna's despair, but of a reinvented Levin who is finally reconciled to his world. The beauty of the world presented in the movie is finally justified and endorsed.[4]

---

[4] The centrality of Levin in the novel has been commented on by Gillian Slovo who says: "What a contrast this feckless Vronsky is to that other main character – the tortured Levin. And here came my second adult realisation. The novel I had chosen to remember was the ill-fated love story between Anna and Vronsky; what I was reading now had a much more complex structure. I had forgotten or ignored that through the centrality of the book also runs the coming to terms with life, faith and death, of the Tolstoy-like Levin. Here, in many

The movie recreates a fantasy world that is imaginatively set in contrast to the dreary drabness of the communist world of twentieth-century Russia, as it largely came to be projected and perceived in the west. Conspicuously absent in the movie, however, are the Russian working classes and their voices, except for a fleeting moment, where a poor elderly man appears on the screen, sitting aimlessly and looking vacantly in front of him. The single image is designed to pay lip service to the realities of Russian life in the nineteenth century. This apart, the movie is entirely designed to stun and overwhelm by opulent magnificence and social grace. Focusing its interest exclusively on the aesthetically pleasing surroundings, it reinvents pre-Soviet Russia as a visually magnificent world to be appreciated and envied, an object of desire to be dreamed about.

It is clear that both movies depend to a great extent on visuality to communicate their messages. For the nascent Egyptian regime in the 1950s, the graphic representation of the new order as a young and lovely woman who desperately needs love stands in sharp contrast with the totally decadent regime that should to all intents and purposes be eradicated. Bernard Rose's work also uses visual glamour in recreating a pre-Soviet world that epitomises iconic grace and refinement, a world to be envied and emulated, and hopefully to be made to rise again from the ashes of almost a century of communist drabness.

Works Cited:

Anna Karenina. Dir. Bernard Rose. Perf. Sophie Marceau, Sean Bean and Alfred Molina. Icon/Warner, 1997.

Kranz, David L. and Nancy C. Mellerski, eds. *In/Fidelity: Essays on Film Adaptation*. Newcastle: Cambridge Scholars Publishing, 2008.

LeBlanc, Ronald. "Levin Visits Anna: The Iconology of Harlotry." *Tolstoy Studies Journal* 3 (1990): 1-20.

Makoveeva, Irina. "Cinematic Adaptations of *Anna Karenina*." *Studies in Slavic Cultures* 2 (2001): 111-34.

Nahr El Hob (*River of Love*). Dir. Ezzel Din Zhul Faqqar. Perf. Faten Hamama and Omar Sharif. 1960.

---

ways, lies the real love story: not between Anna and Vronsky, as I had thought, but between Levin and Kitty. Theirs is a much more traditional, and successful romance: the oddball Levin fighting his own incapacity to embrace life, so that he might ask the humiliated, but eventually all-knowing Kitty, to marry him" (Slovo).

Slovo, Gillian. "Love in a Cold Climate." *Guardian* 20 March 2004. 6 October 2008
<http://www.guardian.co.uk/books/2004/mar/20/featuresreviews.guardianreview30>.

Noha Hamdy

Revisiting Transmediality:
9/11 Between Spectacle and Narrative

In this paper I argue that textual production in post- 9/11 visual and literary culture is an open transformational topology where American national subjectivity is caught up in a web of endless configurations and constitutes an intertextual function of psycho-social overdetermination. The paper examines the various narrative templates of "Falling Man", a pixilated photograph from the (tele)visual and journalese archives of 9/11, which, for a few years, was trapped in an 'iconic impermissibility'. In 2003, however, the resurrection of Falling Man as a potential template in the trans-semiotisation of suppressed signification reenacts a psychic investment in the desire to repeat and adapt particular acts of narrative and visual consumption of 9/11, which were suppressed in the immediate aftermath. Tom Junod's transcoding of the static photograph into a quasi-national(ist) narrative in the Esquire issue of September 2003 features as a pseudo-detective investigation of 9/11 iconography. This resensibilisation of perception prompts a further visual appropriation of the freighted symbol in a 9/11 documentary film, also entitled *Falling Man*, which was directed by Canadian film-maker Henry Singer and released in 2006. DeLillo's revisiting of this 'daunting spectacle' in his latest *Falling Man* (2007) constitutes a further intertext in a galaxy of post-9/11 trans-modalities of American subjectivity. The paper focuses on the various adaptations (literary and visual) of Falling Man as trans-semiotisation processes, which, though modelled through cultural myth and containment, subscribe to a post-structuralist ethic of topological pliability.

Howling Spaces, Folding Topologies

In DeLillo's novella *Players* (1977) the Twin Towers didn't seem like "permanent structures [...]. They remained concepts, no less transient in all their bulk than some routine distortion of light" (DeLillo, *Players* 26). In what appears to be an almost prophetic analogy that visually anticipates the two giant laser shafts of light that annually commemorate, or metonymically simulate where the twin towers once stood, DeLillo's prophecy has enacted, decades ahead of time, the substitution of the modernist skyscraping craze for a postmodernist fascination with virtual metonymies. The impressionistic cover photograph of *Underworld,* published two decades later in 1997, which shows the Twin Towers dissolving into fog as a bird tilts towards them, outstretching its wings against the skyscraping march of parallel lines, amazingly overlaps with media representations of 9/11; the fog in the background triggers visual associations with the mushroom clouds of smoke and fireballs that were emanating from the buildings upon the impact; the bird flying towards the towers in a diagonal manoeuvre recalls the replay scenes of a Boeing aeroplane crashing into the South Tower. The visual parallels seem to suggest that DeLillo's evanescent towers, though improbably, were a potential semantic template for the 9/11 terrorist plot. Interestingly, this impressionistic evanescence lapses further into a crisis of signification, when DeLillo writes his "In the Ruins of the Future", groping for analogies and similes and yet failing to represent a visually stunning singularity:

> The event itself has no purchase on the mercies of analogy or simile. We have to take the shock and horror as it is [...]. The writer [...] begins in the towers, trying to imagine the moment, desperately [...]. People falling from the towers hand in hand [...] hands and spirits joining, human beauty in the crush of meshed steel. In its desertion of every basis for comparison, the event asserts its singularity. There is something empty in the sky. The writer tries to give memory, tenderness and meaning to all that howling space. (DeLillo 2001, 39)

And I would like to start with the 'all that howling space' trope and graft the metaphor onto narrative topologies of 9/11. To start with, DeLillo's 'howling space' obviously extends beyond the ontology of Ground Zero and well into a 'semiotic' black hole in which language, too, falls short of generating the analogies, similes, tropes and metaphors that would adequately describe it. It is in and through this signifying opacity that writers, artists and documentary film-makers continue to grope for a narrative, visual and cultural framing of 9/11. Hirsch describes it as the challenge "to look at an undescribable event, to make it manageable, frame it [...] make it small enough to fit into our living rooms or even our pockets" (Hirsch). Randy Kandel remarks:

> The diverse narratives of the immediate events, the planes hitting the buildings, the buildings burning, the people crossing bridges covered with ash, resonate with an effort to document the surreal, and to emotionally assimilate the unthinkable. (Chermak 187)

Alfred Hornung speaks of an opaque juncture where "virtual textuality meets the concrete reality, [as] the verbal displacement of signifiers on the page makes way for the physical disfigurements of humans and their habitat" (Hornung 385). In Ian McEwan's novel *Saturday* (2005) Henry is caught "watching death on a large scale, but seeing no one die [...] and into this emptiness, the obliging imagination set free" (McEwan 16). What particularly intrigues me here is how this opacity enacts the challenge of *presenting the unpresentable in presentation* (cf. Lyotard, "Answer to the Question: What is the Postmodern?") in terms of a narrative topology that has a migratory, transmedial potential. Hence my own metaphoric extension of DeLillo's: *Howling Spaces, Folding Topologies*.

Cultural analysts concur that the way in which 9/11 has been mediated in photographic archives and televisual documentation is entangled in a web of other visual intertexts, a fact which further complicates emergent interpretations and discursive framings of the attacks. The live footage of the WTC is said to have evoked visual parallels to simulacral scenarios from Hollywood movie disasters, a sense of what Miles Orwell calls the 'destructive sublime' (Orwell 2006). Orwell claims that the images of the planes that capture the moment of penetration recall Harold Edgerton's early strobe photographs of bullets penetrating apples and light bulbs. Ulrich Baer speaks of a "hijacking of our imagination" (Baer 7), and Baudrillard notes that "the spectacle of terrorism forces the terrorism of the spectacle upon us" (Baudrillard 2002, 30).

In this paper I propose to look at the trans-mediatisation of 9/11 as a redistributive function of semiotic synergies within and across textual topologies by examining the various narrative configurations of *Falling Man* in light of several theories: Kristeva's geno-/phenotext model, Deleuze's notion of *le pli* or the fold, Derrida's theory of the archive and finally Freud's concept of trauma. I wish to concoct out of them a model for a textual production in post-9/11 visual and literary culture that is an open transformational topology, where American subjectivity constitutes an intertextual function of psycho-social overdetermination.

This I propose to do through an examination of "Falling Man", a pixilated photograph from the (tele)visual and journalese archives of 9/11 which appeared on the cover page of the *Morning Dew* on September 12th 2001, and which showed a man jumping or falling from the North Tower, suspended in a moment of artistic composure and a stunningly perfect verticality to the steel bars in the background. The image was not the only one that captured victims succumbing to the laws of gravity; in fact, it was singled out as a moment embodying the 'destructive sublime' (cf. Orwell 2006) in a series of captures showing the utter chaos during the falling act.

Despite the ubiquity of traumatological images that were broadcast upon the impact, the iconic image has become in no time a notorious instance of photographic voyeurism and exploitation and has been refuted in a puritanical gesture of self-censorship. A few years later, however, the resurrection of Falling Man as a potential template in the trans-semiotisation of suppressed signification reenacts a psychic investment in the desire to repeat and adapt particular acts of narrative and visual consumption of 9/11, which have been suppressed in the immediate aftermath. Tom Junod's transcoding of the static photograph into a national narrative in the *Esquire* issue of September 2003 features as a pseudo-detective investigation of 9/11 iconography, a probing into the narrative and visual strategies used by the media to elevate specific meanings of the attacks and to suppress others. This resensibilisation of perception prompts a further visual appropriation of the freighted symbol in a 9/11 documentary film entitled *Falling Man*, which was made by film-maker

Henry Singer and released in 2006. DeLillo's revisiting of this daunting spectacle in his latest *Falling Man* (2007) constitutes a further intertext in a galaxy of post 9/11 trans-modalities of American subjectivity. Jonathan Safran Foer's *Extremely Loud & Incredibly Close* (2005), an example of immersive fiction and visual interactivity, closes with a flip-book collection of *Falling Man* images, rotated at 180 degrees, so that ultimately *Falling Man* appears to be flying upwards instead of hurtling to the ground.

I am particularly interested in the narrativity of Falling Man and its lateral trans-semiotisation in and across different textual topologies. By lateral trans-semiotisation I mean media adaptations of Falling Man as a series of substitutive, metonymic significations, to use Kristeva's words, as "a metonymical concatenation of deviations from the norm signifying a progressive creation of metaphors" (Kristeva 1980, 40), or to use Baudrillard's more eloquent multimediatic metaphor "the play of infinitesimal signifiers" (Baudrillard 1976, 92). Accordingly, I wish to show how the narratives spun around the ontogenetic image of "Falling Man" in the three texts dissolve into an infinite semiosis, a negativité.

Kristeva's conceptualisation of intertextuality as the passage of one sign system into another (Kristeva 1984) finds resonance in transmediality as a function of sign transference and transcoding across literary and visual interfaces.

> This process comes about through a combination of displacement and condensation, but this does not account for its total operation. It also involves an altering of the thetic [from the Greek *thetos*, 'placed'] *position* – the destruction of the old position and the formation of a new one [...]. The term *inter-textuality* denotes this transposition of one (or several) sign system(s) into another; but since this term has often been understood in the banal sense of 'study of sources', we prefer the term *transposition* because it specifies that the passage from one signifying system to another demands a new articulation of the thetic – of enunciative and denotative positionality. If one grants that every signifying practice is a field of transpositions of various signifying systems (an intertextuality), one then understands that its 'place' of enunciation and its denoted 'object' are never single, complete, and identical to themselves, but always plural, shattered, capable of being tabulated. In this way polysemy can also be seen as the result of a semiotic polyvalence – an adherence to different sign systems. (Kristeva 1984, 59f.)

Such redistributive function of semiotic synergies constitutes a dynamic model of signification, a space open to varied articulations in which new modes of structuring words, images and narratives, new ways of positioning bodies in time and space evolve. More so, Kristeva's imbrication of a literary structure in a social ensemble to create a topology of texts which are assimilated into the general text of culture offers an explanatory frame for the intersection of textual arrangements with semiotic practices. Though Kristevan 'intertextuality', having been conceived within the rigid and scientistic enclaves of poststructuralism, may indeed be dated in comparison to recent studies in transmediality, it does, in my view, offer a useful analytical toolbox for the trans-mediatisation of 9/11 news broadcasting material across different visual and literary channels. The 'ideologeme' here, a productivity, would be that intertextual function, where the 9/11 (news) text is continually rearranged across the different topologies and intersects with semiotic practices which serve to mobilise national mythologies and foreground the primacy of American cultural myth.

The archetypal pheno/genotext binary as a model of disruptive signifying productivity, for example, may find a correlate in (trans)mediality as a frame of research that draws on and explores modes of narrative circulation, appropriation, transposition, and archiving. As François Jacob argues in *The Logic of Life: A History of Heredity* (1982), it could serve as a general model for theorising the creation of possible worlds and the modelling of unfinalisable processes of transformation through infinite combinations of symbols that may be actualised variously. The genetic model involves a function of mutations and infinite recombinations. So, where the genotype represents a pool of infinite genes (the applicational model), the phenotype is the observable manifestation of a particular genotypal assemblage (actualised model). Kristeva's increasing focus on subjectivity as an unstable effect of psycho-social processes of transformation, what she calls, 'sujet-en-process' or 'subject-on-trial' is modelled on her notion of the genotext as an unfinalisable field of signifying energy. I propose to use this poststructuralist-psychoanalytic model of the genotext in my analysis of the psycho-social intertexts which tend to overdetermine representations of post-9/11 American subjectivity. By genotext I mean the continuous deferral of denotative meaning and the oversymbolicity which tend to characterise the various 9/11 narrative configurations.

Equally interesting in this regard is Deleuze's notion of 'Le Pli' or 'The Fold' (cf. G. Deleuze 1992), which he elaborates within the context of a rhizomic topology as a pliable space with movements and permutations that have no fixed points or suggestive identities. I am interested in Deleuze's notion of 'le pli' as a space which is no longer detached from the event but where the folding process becomes the event itself. In more concrete terms, the 9/11 story as 'two planes crashing into the Twin Towers' is not the real event but how it folds and unfolds in narrative and visual representations, the fold being the 'Event'.

Derrida's theory of the archive offers another example of a topology of textual permutations, and could be grafted on the Kristevan notion of the interaction between textual arrangements and semiotic practices in 9/11 narratives. In his *Archive Fever: A Freudian Impression* (1996), Derrida defines the archive as an institution that is governed by a generic tension between two contradictory impulses: conservation and suppression. While the archive hosts, stores and preserves data in its subscription to a historicising impulse, it simultaneously guards against the event it processes in a movement that is directed towards massive replication and infinite expansion, one that we could connect to Kristeva's genotext in its unfinalisable semiosis and Deleuze's pliable topology. The archive is precisely that intertextual site (a negativity) that generates the gap through which the desire to disseminate and store particular forms of knowledge, yet also to suppress others, emerges. In this regard, it would be interesting to mention German system theorist Niklas Luhmann who speaks of a "communication that avoids communication" (Luhmann 11), in which an event is ritualised, but where this last itself is not directly represented; rather it is its ritualising which is foregrounded. This would open up the debate of how far the staging of 9/11 in, by and through the media was a ritualisation which precisely evaded communication and rather mobilised that (intertextual) intersection between ritual and otherwise dormant cultural/national mythologies.

Speaking of gaps and structuring absences, trauma theory has been advanced as a template through which to understand how alternate significations of 9/11 have been suppressed by the 'archive' in favour of specific recurrent frames which resonated with cultural ideals. In particular, in *Beyond the Pleasure Principle* (1919) Freud's concept of trauma seems to accord with the orthodox view of many 9/11 cultural analysts who try to map the ways in which trauma becomes the central axis of storytelling. The biology-theatre-consciousness triad traces the transition from biology to theatre in the constitution of post-trauma consciousness, the first storyline being that of a wounding set in the register of biology, the second that of a performance set in the register of theatre, which, together, collapse into the sphere of the psychological.

Media theorists agree that September 11 has been narrativised by the media into a primary recognisable discourse marked by the emergence of dominant hegemonic agendas of patriotism but what often remains undisclosed is that this puzzling unanimity is structured around fluid interactions and multiple thresholds. In the following, I will show how 9/11 trans-semiotisation processes are largely determined by an ethic of topological pliability, especially in the televisual documentary adaptation *The Falling Man*.

Tom Junod's transcoding of the Falling Man photograph into a lengthy article points to the narrative potentialities inherent in the art and practice of photography; the reading of the photograph is an instance of how 9/11 iconography can be used to mobilise national mythologies, holding out the promise of a purgatory healing and transcendence. Singer's documentary film *The Falling Man* is largely based on Junod's article, with its focus on polarised reactions to 9/11 iconography, the identity of the Falling Man as well as its appropriation of Junod as an author-detective-therapist into the filmic material; a fact which shows that 9/11 trans-mediatisation is modeled through containment and cultural myth.

Both the article and the documentary are structured around a self-reflexive questioning of the ethics of representation in the immediate aftermath of 9/11; they attempt a remodelling of the archive by reclaiming the picture of the Falling Man into the canon of historical registry. The realisation that the initial narratives of 9/11 have been organised around the central axis of heroic rescue operations is coupled with a desire to explore alternate visual significations of 9/11, which have been suppressed in the immediate aftermath of the attacks; while the images of rescue workers and firefighters were among the most frequently disseminated, those of people jumping from the towers were trapped in an iconic impermissibility.

The emergent narratives in the article and the documentary have no inherent news value of the original event. Instead, they dissolve into an infinite semiosis, exploit the unfinalisable energy which is latent in the psycho-social genotexts and convert them into a phenotext, a primary recognisable structure, which through its folding processes and signifying energies, becomes the real event. In Junod's piece this signifying energy is actualised through a particular discursive framing of the Falling Man who appears to be a free-floating signifier in a series of metonymic substitutions; the narrative is clearly threaded with the ultra-nationalistic discourse of war. Falling Man is transformed from victim into hero-soldier who has fought in a war and thus emerges as a martyr. In a gesture of heroisation, even the soldier-analogy undergoes a further metonymic digression when Falling Man is described as falling with the precision of a "missile, a spear bent on attaining its own end". Junod's narrative slides further into the deep mythographic reserves of the American cultural imaginary as Falling Man appears to be flying, an image which evokes a parallel to the superman myth and Jonathan Safran Foer's flip-book collection. Such loops and digressions are an actualised instance of Deleuze's fluid topology, where the folding of 9/11 in and through these textual permutations constitutes a healing of a wounded corporeality.

> One of the most famous photographs in human history became an unmarked grave, and the man buried inside its frame – the Falling Man – became the Unknown Soldier in a war whose end we have not yet seen [...]. In the picture, he departs from this earth like an arrow [...] he appears to have, in his last instants of life, embraced [his] fate. If he were not falling, he might be very well flying. He appears relaxed, hurtling through the

air. He appears comfortable in the grip of unimaginable motion [...]. [The Falling Man] is perfectly vertical, and so is in accord with the lines of the buildings behind him. He splits them, bisects them [...]. [He] is the essential element in the creation of a new flag, a banner composed entirely of steel bars shining in the sun [...]. There is something almost rebellious in the man's posture, as though once faced with the inevitability of death, he decided to get on with it, as though he were a missile, a spear, bent on attaining its own end. (Junod 2003)

Singer's adaptation of the story to filmic material further complicates Junod's emergent narrative of *Falling Man* and its discursive framing. The challenge of reframing *Falling Man* as static photograph and a national narrative within a motion picture is largely determined, and quite beneficially so, by the medium specificity of film; the loose prepositional filmic syntax allows for the appropriation of multiple discourse and visual fragments from the archive of American history into the smooth operational surface of news reportage. Thinking of the intrinsic semiotic configuration of film, the scenic syntax not only allows for a succession of images and narratives around the *Falling Man* topos, but also offers the possibility of introducing a principle of transformation, a folding within that succession.

This is sublimated however, at the beginning, as the documentary comes as a recognisable interpretative package, a media frame that validates information as well as discursive engagements with the event. In its subscription to the historicising impulse, it seeks to place 9/11 within an authentic historic frame by providing factual information about the history of the towers in a scene showing the Manhattan Skyline. Furthermore, the opening scene of the film raises the standard of the historical record in its replaying of the WTC footage, a reenactment which accords with Freud's dialogic transition from wounded biology as primordial text to recovering theatre as meta-text. The ubiquity of trauma and its perpetual presentness is visually impinged on the consciousness of the viewer through a recurrent staging of traumatological images which show the chaos and the destruction upon the impact, for example, the scenes where people are shown jumping from the upper floor windows of the WTC in utter desperation or waving with their shirts for help. Some of these shots are in black and white, which underscores the historical record, while others are freeze-frames inserted into the motion picture. The possibility of oscillating between the topology of static photography and that of a motion picture accords the documentary a historically authentic frame, in this way sublimating the genotextual psycho-social aberrations which surround and overdetermine the Falling Man topos.

This loop-structure unfolds in a myriad of totemic images: symbols, icons, and statues which are reborn from the imaginary tomb of Falling Man as the unknown soldier, like a phoenix rising from its ashes. One of the most intriguing images which is played in the documentary at rather frequent intervals is that of the Crucifix, especially when the camera moves away from the Twin Tower scenes to individual stories, families mourning the loss of close ones, crosses hung on the walls at home. The vertical posture of Christ on the cross evokes a parallel to the steel bars of the towers (which are immediately played afterwards), a visual association which anchors the Falling Man within the topos of religious mythology and ritualises its replaying as a means to transcendence and spiritual recovery. It is quite evident that the documentary makes use of an editing device known as 'associational juxtaposition', which allows the qualities of an object or person in one image to be transferred to, or more precisely, to flow into those of an object or a person in a subsequent scene. This myriad of images creates a new intertextual, rhizomic topology out of the intersection of the Falling Man topos with the latent mythographic reserves of American cultural heritage. Speaking of mainstream news and ways in which 9/11 was documented visually, Michelle Brown, Leia Fuzesi, Kara Kitch, and Crystal Spivey in their article "Internet News Representations of September 11: Archival Impulse in the Age of Information" (cf. Chermak) explain the therapeutic machinations of 9/11 news representation:

> mainstream news representations of 9/11 attempt to create a particular historical order out of the chaos of September 11. The multiple accounts (visual, audio, textual) that mix personal and national tragedies and reactions serve to preserve the memory of September 11 as the single most shocking and tragic day in American history, but one that Americans rapidly overcome through the deep mythographic reserves of cultural heritage and a unified impulse toward war. (Chermak 9)

Furthermore, in its appropriation of the Ground Zero picture showing two firefighters hosting the flag on top of the WTC debris, the documentary evokes a direct historical parallel to the Iwo Jima photograph of 1945.[1] As Hariman and Lucaites concur, the Iwo Jima becomes a "discourse fragment [that] artistically [coordinates] available structures of identification within a performative space open to varied and continual articulation" (Hariman and Lucaites 387).[2]

---

[1] The Iwo Jima photograph, possibly the most reproduced photograph of all time, is a historic one taken on February 23, 1945 by Joe Rosenthal. It depicts five United States Marines and a U.S. Navy corpsman raising the flag of the United States atop Mount Suribachi during the Battle of Iwo Jima in World War II. Lucaites and Hariman concur that "the Iwo Jima flag-raising demonstrates how iconic photographs have strong qualities of strong performance, a series of transcriptions that carry deep resources for public identification, a rhetorical richness, open emotionality" (Hariman 127).

[2] In their *No Caption Needed* (2007) both Hariman and Lucaites engage in a profound reflection on the role which iconic journalistic photographs play in democratic liberal societies,

The filmic syntax unwinds into pictures from the Vietnam War, the bombing of Hiroshima, the Holocaust concentration camps of WWII and mass genocide. These images are wrested from the archives of world history and re-functionalised as parallels to the Falling Man in terms of an exposed or wounded corporeality.

The closure of the documentary discloses a quasi-mythic narrative structure, and represents a function of etherialisation, as the image of the Falling Man dissolves into a myriad of chants, hymns, birds flying or rather floating in the sky. The camera angle, looking buttom-top, suggests, a kinesis which is then arrested in the 'eternal' symbolism of the Statue of Liberty; the closure discloses a structure which Michiko Kakutani has described as a "therapeutic arc [...] from shock [...] toward [...] resolve" in a *from fall to redemption* kind of pattern (Michiko Kakutani 2).

DeLillo's *Falling Man* is the last adaptation of Falling Man in a series of photograph trans-/decodings. This time the fictional archive is sprung on a web of ambivalent topological surfaces which oscillate between a compliance with and a resistance to the 'society of the spectacle'. On the one hand, DeLillo's staging of 9/11 is overdetermined by visual representations devised by the mass media to induce ambivalent feelings of corporeal involvement and surreal fantasmagoria on the part of the viewer.

> It was something that belonged to another landscape inserted, a conjuring that resembled for the briefest second some half-seen image only half-believed in the seeing. (*Falling Man* 103)

> Every time she saw a videotape of the planes she moved a finger toward the power button on the remote. Then she kept on watching. The second plane coming out of that ice blue sky, this was the footage that entered the body [...] first one plane, and then the other, the one that was nearly cartoon human [...]. (134)

I tried to track down the visual equivalent to this description in the documentary to catalogue some of the parallels in terms of a narrative transmediatics. Indeed, the documentary is threaded by these typical replay scenes of the footage where the planes are seen hitting and crashing into the towers, which evoke a sense of fantasmagoria. DeLillo's characters, too, seem to be governed by this compulsion to replay the footage, which shows that they have internalised the media's traumatising of 9/11.

On the other hand, and quite paradoxically, the DeLillo version of Falling Man seems to veer away from conventionalised topologies of motion picture and manifests instead a resistance to photographic decoding. First, falling is

---

more precisely, how these are used, transformed and appropriated continually to converge to different ideological totems.

refunctionalised as a systemic pathology of a post-9/11 subjectivity, a howling space in which traumatised individuals are trying to recover from the 9/11 drama, yet are constantly caught in a different gravitational field of drifts: religious trances, amnesia, depression and self-estrangement. Characters seem to be caught in drift-like spells, their motion arrested, like puppets in a spectacle. Keith keeps remembering "the timeless drift of the long spiral down" (137), as he descends the stairs of the WTC upon the impact. "Estranged from his wife, he finds himself drifting into spells of reflection" (66). A group of Alzheimer patients are shown trying to record their personal stories yet keep "receding into tinted mist" (142). "Rosellen, [one of Lianne's Alzheimer patients] could not remember where she lived [...] the breathless moment when things fall away, streets, names [...] every fixed grid of memory" (156). Instead of communicating with her patients, Lianne finds herself "fading into time, dropping back into some funnelled stretch of recent past" (127). Acts of terrorism are described as embroiled in a pattern of "falling and dying" (77).

This time, in a DeLillesque twist, and according with the puppet drifts above, Falling Man is an incognito performance artist appearing in a business suit and haunting Manhattan with his performance, as he is seen jumping from different elevations in New York using a safety harness.

> He brought it back of course, those stark moments in the burning towers when people fell or were forced to jump [...]. There were people shouting at him, outraged at the spectacle, the puppetry of human desperation [...] the single falling figure that trails a collective dread. (33)

DeLillo stages the act as a cryptic, arty performance which almost verges on a mystic and coded rituality. It may be interesting to go back to Luhmann's idea of rituals as "communication that avoids communication". In fact, DeLillo's world is a space of non-communication where individuals recoil into themselves as they are daunted by the rituality of spectacle. In the middle of it, Lianna seeks an "exchange of glances" but finds it virtually impossible to expand a field of communication beyond that. In contrast to Junod's and Singer's proposal of decoding Falling Man into cultural myth, DeLillo's *Falling Man* unfixes the meaning that the media have accorded to the photograph. That sprawling filmic syntax is frozen here into a meditation on mediation. DeLillo, the choreographer of slow motion, wrests the image of Falling Man from the infosphere of brisk, free-floating signifiers and anchors it in a process of introspection. He discloses an aesthetic of suspension as the falling act is modulated to one of dangling, with Falling Man hanging in mid-air. What makes DeLillo's version problematic, though, is that this aesthetic of arrested motion accords with the original photograph in its stillness, and is again refunctionalised as a stretched time in which the partitions between self and other dissolve. After all, much like the photographic prototype, the performance demands our bodily engagement with the spectacle and seems to self-replicate in an auto-referent circularity: "She thought the bare space he stared into must be his own, not some grim vision of others falling" (167). and yet, in the middle of all this, when DeLillo's descriptions of *Falling Man* seem to be inflected by those of Junod and the ritual of mediated representations, DeLillo attempts to capture the original falling motion in its original signification as it unwinds from the memory of Keith, a 9/11 survivor, a twist that unfixes the aesthetics of the photographic prototype.

> Things began to fall, one thing and then another [...]. Then something went past the window [...]. He could not stop seeing it, twenty feet away, an instant of something sideways, going past the window, white shirt, hand up, falling before he saw it. (242)

Lianne, similarly, intrigued by the spectacle of the performance artist, embarks on a journey in search of an original signifier.

> She thought it could be the name of a trump card in a tarot deck, Falling Man, a name in gothic type, the figure twisting down in a stormy night sky [...]. [She] knew which photograph the account referred to. It hit her hard when she first saw it, the day after in the newspaper. The man headlong, the towers behind him. The mass of the towers filled the frame of the picture. The man falling, the towers contiguous [...]. The enormous soaring lines, the vertical column stripes. The man with blood on his shirt, she thought, or burn marks, and the effect of columns behind him, the composition, she thought, darker stripes for the nearer tower, the north, lighter for the other, and the mass, the immensity of it, and the man set almost precisely between the rows of darker and lighter stripes. Headlong, free fall, she thought, and this picture burned a hole in her mind and heart, dear God, he was a falling angel and his beauty was horrific. She clicked forward and there was the picture. She looked away into the keyboard. It is the ideal falling motion of a body. (221f.)

Lianne's (hypertext) search for an original signifier winds into an abyss of non-signification as the multiple meanings of Falling Man accumulate, and the line between the real Falling Man and that of the performance artist becomes blurred. This oscillation between Falling Man as original motion, photographic voyeurism, performance art, and a chronicle of the age of terror reflects DeLillo's view of the unfinalisable signifying energy of the Falling Man topos and shows how the different media such as photography, televisual documentation and (hypertext) narrative indulge further in the ritualisation of spectacle. DeLillo's dangling characters subscribe to the archival impulse of preserving the memory of 9/11, as it is constructed in and through a self-replicating ritual of representation which avoids communication of facts, truths and as Lianne feels, "an exchange of glances".

To conclude, all of the three texts, Junod's article, the documentary film and DeLillo's novel deploy an ethic of topological pliability in their semiotisation of 9/11 and in particular the topos of Falling Man. The challenge is to try and measure that degree of pliability across these different surfaces and to link it to a post-9/11 subjectivity. What is self-evident, however, is that the topology of film has a generic potential for pliability as it rearranges and subordinates narrative structures to a sprawling, depthless visual intertextuality. This explains, at least partly, why documentary films with their topological pliability and visual oversymbolicity were among the most popular archives/theatres in the healing of the 9/11 trauma.

My aim has been to flesh out a semiological model for a narrative transmediatics, and to establish a correlation between topological surfaces and psycho-social processes in the trans-semiotisation of 9/11 visual material, and I hope I have managed to do so, at least tentatively. I would like to conclude with DeLillo's photographic closure in *Falling Man*, one that transposes us back into that howling space where falling man dwindles into waving arms, a metonymic capture, a simile which vanishes in the desperation of the camera to frame falling motion in yet human terms.

> That's where everything was, all around him, falling away, street signs, people, things he could not name. Then he saw a shirt come down out of the sky. He walked and saw it fall, arms waving like nothing in this life. (246)

Works Cited

Baer, Ulrich. *110 Stories: New York Writes after September 11*. New York: NYUP, 2002.
Baudrillard, Jean. *Echange Symbolique et la Mort*. Paris: Gallimard, 1976.
—. *The Spirit of Terrorism and Requiem for the Twin Towers*. Trans. Chris Turner. New York: Verso, 2002.
Chermak, Stephen, Frankie Bailey and Michelle Brown, eds. *Media Representations of September 11*. USA: Praeger, 2003.
Däwes, Birgit. "On Contested Ground (Zero): Literature and the Transnational Challenge of Remembering 9/11." *Journal of American Studies* 52.5 (2007): 517-44.
Deleuze, Gilles. *The Fold: Leibniz and the Baroque*. Minnesota: MUP, 1992.
DeLillo, Don. *Players*. New York: Ballentine Books, 1987.
—.*Underworld*. New York: Scribner, 1997.
—. "In the Ruins of the Future: Reflections on Terror, Loss and Time in the Shadow of September." *Harper's Magazine* (Dec. 2001): 33-40.

—. *Falling Man*. New York: Scribner International, 2007.
Derrida, Jacques. *Archive Fever: A Freudian Impression*. Trans. Eric Prenowitz. Chicago: CUP, 1996.
Foer, Jonathan Safran. *Extremely Loud & Incredibly Close*. London: Penguin, 2005.
Freud, Sigmund. *Beyond the Pleasure Principle*. Trans. C.M. Hubback. New York: Digireads, 2008.
Hariman, Robert and John Lucaites. *No Caption Needed: Iconic Photographs, Public Culture and Liberal Democracy*. Chicago: CUP, 2007.
Hirsch, Marianna. "The Day Time Stopped." *The Chronicle of Higher Education Online*. 25 Jan. 2002. 6 Feb. 2006
<http://chronicle.com/free/v48/i20/20b01101.htm>.
Hornung, Alfred. "'Flying Planes Can be Dangerous': Ground Zero Literature." *Science, Technology and the Humanities in Recent American Fiction*. Eds Peter Freese and Charles B. Harris. *Arbeiten zur Amerikanistik 36*. Essen: Die Blaue Eule, 2004. 383-403.
Hutcheon, Linda. *A Theory of Adaptation*. New York: Routledge, 2006.
Jacob, François. *The Logic of Life: A History of Heredity*. Princeton: PUP, 1993.
Junod, Tom. "The Falling Man." *Esquire,* 2003. 15 January 2008
<http://www.esquire.com/features/ESQ0903-SEP_FALLINGMAN>.
Kakutani, Michiko. "The Information Age Processes a Tragedy: Books and More Books Analyse, Exorcise and Merchandise the Events of Sept. 11." *New York Times*. (28 August 2002): B1.
Kandel, Randy Frances. "Narrative Reconstruction at Ground Zero." *Media Representations of September 11th*. Eds Stephen Chermak, Frankie Y. Bailey and Michelle Brown. Westport, Conn: Praeger, 2003. 187-200.
Kristeva, Julia. "The Bounded Text." *Desire in Language: A Semiotic Approach to Literature and Art*. Ed. Leon Roudiez. Trans. Alice Jardine, Thomas Gora and Leon Roudiez. New York: Columbia, 1980. 36-59.
—. *Revolution in Poetic Language*. Trans. Margaret Waller. New York: Columbia UP, 1984.
Leys, Ruth. *"Trauma": A Genealogy*. Chicago: CUP, 2000.
Luhmann, Niklas. "Kommunikationsvermeidungskommunikation." *Die Gesellschaft der Gesellschaft*. Frankfurt: Suhrkamp, 1997.
Lyotard, J.F. "Answer to the Question: What is the Postmodern?" *Literary Theories: A Reader & Guide*. Ed. Julian Wolfreys. Edinburgh: EUP, 1999. 371-80.
McEwan, Ian. *Saturday*. London: Vintage, 2005.

Orwell, Miles. "After 9/11: Photography, the Destructive Sublime, and the Postmodern Archive." *Michigan Quarterly Review* (Spring 2006): 239-256.

Santrac, Alexander S. *The Deconstruction of Baudrillard: The Unexpected Reversibility of Discourse*. New York: The Edwin Mellen Press, 2005.

Singer, Henry. "9/11 The Falling Man." 16 March 2006. Online Video Clip. *YouTube*. 22 December 2007 <http://www.youtube.com/watch?v=BXnA9FjvLSU>.

Wolfram R. Keller

"Long Live the New Flesh"?
David Cronenberg's *Videodrome* and the Limits of Ovidian Metamorphosis[*]

In his *Ovid's Poetics of Illusion*, Philip Hardie observes that Ovid's texts speak in interesting ways to current poetological concerns, given that "something like the presence of a postmodernist critic lurks already in Ovid's "ancient texts" (29). While scholars frequently (if tacitly) allude to the presence of Ovidian themes – abandonment, transformation, and exile – in postcolonial literature, a sustained engagement with this 'structural Ovidianism' in narrative texts and film is hitherto lacking. While Canadian writers, such as Margaret Atwood and Carol Shields, utilise Ovid's counter-imperial poetics in order to articulate an alternative to the Virgilian literary endeavour of empire-making (e.g. Ziolkowski), the translation of Canadian Ovidianism into David Cronenberg's cinematographic aesthetic of metamorphosis points up limits to the transformation of ancient 'postcolonial' paradigms. Although Cronenberg's films are distinctively Canadian (Lasierra), the liberating force of Ovidian transformation for the construction of counter- and trans-national communities is thwarted by the problematic ontological status of emergent forms of social organisation and of what Max, in *Videodrome*, hails as the 'New Flesh'. Thus, Cronenberg's films become an insightful reflection on the possibilities and limitations of positing alternative models of nationhood as well as showcasing the risks of parodying Virgilian imperial discourses.

The Roman poet Ovid was not very popular in the mid-twentieth century; the first two postwar decades were rather an *aetas Virgiliana*, since Virgil, especially in Europe, enjoyed a wide readership. This began to change in the 1960s, and during the 1970s and 1980s Ovid was fully rehabilitated (Ziolkowski 153). Artists and scholars alike were particularly interested in Ovid's *Metamorphoses*, a renewal of interest coinciding with the popular reception of postmodern philosophy. In the words of Theodore Ziolkowski: "The eighties saw the rise and revival of two forces that pervaded much of the intellectual life of the decade: postmodernism and metamorphosis" (167). Moreover, "The belief in a constantly shifting world no longer governed by rationality, logocentrism, and oppressive master narratives and in which myth was open to ceaseless reinterpretation cleared the way for a new appreciation of metamorphosis" (Ziolkowski 168). Classicist Philip Hardie likewise ob-

---

[*] The following poetological and cinematological musings on Cronenberg's *Videodrome* stem from many a discussion with Jocelyn Keller, who first made me realise that there was something Ovidian about it. I would further like to thank Renate Brosch and Mary Orr for their helpful comments and their feedback on the occasion of the *Semiotic Encounters* Conference in Freudenstadt.

serves that Ovid's texts speak in interesting ways to current poetological concerns, given that "something like the presence of a postmodernist critic" lurks already in Ovid's "ancient texts" (29). It is perhaps no accident, then, that "two landmark studies of postmodern aesthetics and fiction take their titles from Ovid: Ihab Hassan's *The Dismemberment of Orpheus* and Linda Hutcheon's *Narcissistic Narrative*" (Terry 15).

Ovid is not only *the* poet of change, but also the poet of exile and abandonment, which makes Ovid particularly relevant to postcolonial concerns, as Christine Walde has recently argued in a different context: "Ovid ist einer der Autoren, der auch von kulturellen Grenzgängern rezipiert wird, etwa in der *post-colonial literature*, vielleicht auch deshalb, weil die *Metamorphosen* eine gewisse (trügerische) Affinität zu fernöstlichen Wiedergeburtslehren zeigen" (323).[1] I believe that within this postcolonial context, however, it is not so much the direct allusions to the works of Ovid or Ovid himself that matter. Ziolkowski, Hardie, Walde, and many other scholars have diligently assembled and discussed a plethora of intertextual references or immediate adaptations of Ovidian tales or works in which Ovid himself features centrally, most importantly, David Malouf's *An Imaginary World* (1978), Christoph Ransmayer's *Die letzte Welt* (1988), David Wishart's *Ovid* (1995) and Jane Alison's *The Love-Artist*. Beyond these direct literary allusions, though, there is a *structural* Ovidianism, a large-scale reception of Ovidian structures, sometimes embedded within a recourse to the Ovidian canon that is not characterised by any immediate references to the Roman poet. Thus, Ulrich Schmitzer argues – in a chapter aptly titled 'Instead of a Reception History' – that reference is often made to Ovid without explicit or implicit acknowledgement, sometimes perhaps even unwittingly: "Das ist nicht das Ende der poetischen Wirksamkeit Ovids, vielmehr ein erneuter Beweis dafür, in welchen Wandlungen sich die Verwandlungsgeschichten dem Leser präsentieren können: *ille referre aliter saepe solebat idem* (*ars* 1,128)" (210-16, quotation 216).[2] While postcolonialists have, of course, discussed classic (Ovidian) *topoi* like abandonment, exile, and metamorphosis frequently – albeit often independently – a sustained engagement with what I referred to as 'structural Ovidianism' in narrative texts and films is still lacking, or more adequately: almost lacking.

---

[1] "Ovid is one of those writers, who is read by those transgressing cultural borderlines, for example, in postcolonial literatures, perhaps because his works demonstrate an affinity to far-Eastern theories of rebirth" (my translation).

[2] "This is not the end of Ovid's poetical influence, but rather new evidence for the metamorphoses in which the stories of metamorphosis can be presented to the audience: *ille referre aliter saepe solebat idem* (*Ars amatoria* 1.128)" (my translation).

Discussing works that directly allude to Ovid or feature him as a central character, Ziolkowski does draw attention to a common denominator in the works of "commonwealth writers" like David Malouf, Derek Mahon, C. H. Sisson, Seamus Heaney, and Anne Carson, all of whom, he contends, "transcend the narrow political reading of Ovid-in-exile to see in him, by means of poetic vision, an existential model for contemporary humanity" (Ziolkowski 130). While this is certainly true of the texts analysed by Ziolkowski, I am not convinced that the political reflection upon exile is irrelevant. The only other study I am aware of that engages with the question of Ovidianism in the New Literatures in English – in this case Canadian literature – suggests that humanist and aesthetic concerns in the reception of Ovid do not override but rather amplify the political dimension of postcolonial Ovidianism.

In his investigation into parody in U.S.-American and Canadian literatures, Canadian author and critic David Williams observes that Canadians "like to fancy their own history as a separation from America, from its history and habits. But lacking any genuine myth of origin, we have had to live in the shadow of one of the most original cultures in the world". This situation is analogous to that of the ancient Romans, who lived "in the shadow of a truly original literature". It is Virgil who finally "found his originality only through the deeply serious art of parody". Accordingly, Virgil becomes "the world's first modernist poet, manipulating a continuous parallel between the age of Homer and his own age to invert the whole ethos of the *Iliad* and the *Odyssey*". Virgil's epic was quickly superseded by the *Metamorphoses*, however, which is "akin to the world's first postmodern poem", a poem tremendously sceptical of the gods and representative of Ovid's suspicion of "Augustan majesty and morality" that are ridiculed and parodied. Williams concludes that "the epic of endless change, like the 'Rules of Love', turns into an elaborate, cheerfully degraded game, a deliberate vulgarization of the more lofty Augustan ideals" (Williams 1994, 8f.). In this context, it is important to keep in mind that the *Metamorphoses* are ultimately the parody of a parody.[3] In the absence of an historical analogue to the U.S. War of Independence, "Canadian writing, like the vernacular literatures of Europe which Bakhtin describes, had to learn how to repel 'the foreign-born word' through the 'dialogized operation' of parody," placing Canadian writers in a predicament resembling that of the ancient Romans and their attempts to overcome their status of merely imitating Greek literature (Williams 1994, 10). Insofar as Canadian "independence" ultimately depends on the "ability to write 'bilingually', to parody both the languages of gender and culture which threaten to colonize us", Williams ultimately aligns Canadian writers with an Ovidian

---

[3] For David Williams' and Carol Shields' Ovidianism, see Keller 2006, 77-92; Keller 2008, 200-15.

poetics that parodies the seriousness of Virgilian epic. Whether or not it is ultimately possible to transcend the logocentrism of an 'empire without end' by means of an Ovidian poetological or cinematological model is an important question. And it is precisely this question, I believe, that informs David Cronenberg's 1983 horror film *Videodrome*.[4]

Videodrome, a film that is often seen as a watershed movie in David Cronenberg's oeuvre, has entered the pantheon of *Canada's Best Features* (Walz) and has also been immensely popular beyond Canada, irrespective of the partially scathing critique of many Canadian parliamentarians who were outraged by the explicit depiction of sex and violence which was funded by the government and, ultimately, by Canadian taxpayers – a critique that is possibly less related to the actual depiction of sex and violence than the uncomfortable questions *Videodrome* raises about the paradoxical question of what it means to be Canadian – as opposed to being a United States citizen. While this indicates the important Canadian dimension of *Videodrome*,[5] at least as regards the reception of the film, criticism locates its popularity mainly in Cronenberg's proto-Baudrillardian postmodernism. Most scholars, William Beard summarises, "emphasize the film's paranoid dimension of social manipulation and mind control, which connects individual anxieties about identity engulfment and transformation through media images with political analysis that asks questions about who wields media power and to what ends" (125). The film's "political and social implications," he argues,

> are also much more serious: deep and widespread, offering a kind of postmodern paranoid model of manipulation of helpless private individuals by predatory corporate forces under conditions of universal technological penetration and colonization. At the same time, the protagonist whose psyche and body become the uncontrollable landscape of transgressive sexuality, boundaryless transformation and abjection, and murderous violence becomes also in the end the foundational example of Cronenberg's many suicidal melancholiacs. (124)

Rather than illustrating recent permutations within postmodern, postcolonial, or post-whatever theory, Cronenberg's oeuvre, Beard claims, bespeaks a certain "nostalgia for the old unified subject" (128).[6] While I agree with

---

[4] That is, Cronenberg's Ovidianism is intensely political. As Suzie Sau-Fong Young observes, the "business" in and of Cronenberg's films "always means the business of oppression and the politics of hegemony. The politics of *Videodrome*, in a word, is the politics of everyday life, with all of its madness uncensored" (151).

[5] For the role of Canada for Cronenberg, cf Lasierra.

[6] Beard argues that "Cronenberg is not at all convinced that unified subjectivity is a false and undesirable construct, and he is not at all sanguine about what state will follow its loss" (126). Beard also qualifies his earlier statement: "Nostalgia", to be sure, is not at all the right word to describe the horror and despair dramatised in the protagonist of every film from

Beard concerning Cronenberg's critique of an all-too optimistic, postmodern view of subjectivity, I want to add that *Videodrome* tests (one is tempted to say: tests experientially) two competing narratives of transnationalism as well as two competing versions of parody. And Cronenberg's *Videodrome* thus offers two very different evaluations of Ovidian (read: postmodern) metamorphosis as a cinematological, narratological model.

First of all, it is important to note that metamorphosis, as the main theme of the film, occurs within a structurally Ovidian context insofar as the film replicates *en miniature* the Ovidian canon, that is, the movement from the art of love (Ovid's *Amores*, *Ars amatoria*, and *Remedia amoris*) to abandonment (*Heroides*), and thence to metamorphosis (*Metamorphoses*) and exile (esp. *Tristia*, *Epistulae ex Ponto*). At the beginning of Cronenberg's "horror" film,[7] viewers are introduced to Max Renn, who is the president of the Toronto-based television station Civic-TV, the mission of which is to provide sex and crime for the Canadian public. During a talk show, in which Max stoutly defends his mission against accusations of promoting violence, he becomes attracted to Nicki Brand, the hostess of a radio show, who has strong reservations about Civic-TV's mixture of sex and crime. She is also attracted to Max, though, and subsequently seduces him, introducing him to sadomasochism, her sexual preference. This somewhat perverted *Ars amatoria* soon gives way to abandonment and metamorphosis, as Nicki leaves behind an increasingly feminised Max: she intends to travel to the United States, to audition for 'Videodrome', a torture program run out of Pittsburgh to which she was, ironically, first introduced by Max. The emphasis on deviant, violent sexuality may, at a first glance, appear crude and 'un-Ovidian', but it is far from unusual in contemporary and near-contemporary reworkings of Ovid. The (recent) reception of Ovid's works indicates that those myths dealing with water, dreams, sexuality, deviance, ill-advised passions or showcasing a particular realism in the depiction of violence are particularly favoured, whereby the multifaceted and intertextually-complex Ovidian sto-

---

Videodrome to *M. Butterfly*, in response to the dreadful leaching-away of stable personal identity. The fact that these identities were not so stable to start with, or that they were beset with serious and fundamental problems, or even that their sense of self was not rooted in any kind of existential truth, is ultimately irrelevant, since their last state is always much, much worse than their first" (128).

[7] While Cronenberg's films are usually classified as horror films, "they challenge rather than constitute much that is conventional in the genre. In the horror scene, what is terrifying is death and dying; in Cronenberg's (ob)scene, what is terrifying is life and living" (Young 151).

ries are often reduced to – and become paradigms of – crises of identity or pathologies (Walde 30).[8] The latter is particularly true of Cronenberg's film.

After Nicki abandons Max, the latter finds solace in "Videodrome", which, it transpires, transmits a signal that induces brain tumours in the viewers. The brain tumours, in turn, prompt hallucinations. The tumour growing in Max's brain intensifies his sadomasochistic tendencies, and Max's reality begins to take interesting new shapes. It is through the induced hallucinations that Max stays in contact with Nicki, who now "appears" on Max's television screen on the "Videodrome"-set. In this emerging, Pyramus-and-Thisbe-like love-story,[9] the television screen literally becomes the hole in the wall separating the lovers. In fact, the television set transforms into Nicki, the screen becoming her mouth that protrudes into Max's livingroom and which he then kisses. By means of the screen, the lovers are united for a brief moment. On the downside, however, Max is increasingly unable to distinguish between reality and hallucination, and he begins to metamorphose into a cyborg after inserting a gun into a vagina-like opening in his abdomen, which he later removes through the same opening, the gun and his hand having merged into a gun-hand-hybrid. In what follows, the audience learns with Max that the owners of 'Videodrome', apparently a company called Spectacular Optical, take advantage of Max's hallucinations by programming him to kill his partners at Civic-TV and using his station to disseminate the tumour-inducing Videodrome-signal across Toronto (and, presumably, the rest of Canada). Moreover, they want him to kill Bianca O'Blivion, the daughter of the co-inventor of 'Videodrome', Professor Brian O'Blivion, who had reservations about his partners' "marketing schemes". Bianca O'Blivion, though, manages to reprogram Max, who now turns on the people in charge

---

[8] "Die Mythen, die mit Wasser und Traum, Sexualität, Devianz, schicksalhaften Leidenschaften zu tun haben oder einen sezierenden Realismus in der Darstellung von Gewalt zeigen, bekommen den Vorzug. In einer Reduktion der Komplexität, die bei Ovid durch die intertextuelle Dimension und die Vielzahl der in wechselndem Rhythmus erzählten Geschichten entsteht, werden in der allerneuesten Rezeption die mythologischen Figuren zu Paradigmata für Identitätskrisen oder gar Pathologien."

[9] This analogy is instructive in the context of the feminist reception of the film insofar as the two lovers represent seemingly different worldviews: in the television show, where the two meet for the first time, Max represents the industry of sex and violence that deals primarily in external images while Nicki represents the moralist antidote, counselling people in emotional, internalised distress. The love story of Pyramus and Thisbe ends with a suicide. Pyramus, misinterpreting the bloody veil of Thisbe, decides to kill himself. Once Thisbe realises that Pyramus is dead, she follows her lover into death (*Met.* 4.148-63). In line with the emasculation and feminisation of Max in *Videodrome*, it is Nicki who is first killed – or chooses death by auditioning for the show and wanting to be on it (as it emerges in Max's hallucinations) – Max follows later, leaving the viewer to decide whether (and what kind of) transformation will take place.

of 'Videodrome'. She also presents him with *the* central slogan of the film, namely, "Death to Videodrome. Long Live the New Flesh". At the end of the movie, after having killed his partners and two representatives of the 'Videodrome' program, Max has become a persecuted killer who sees only one redemption from this grave error. He takes refuge – that is to say, he exiles himself – in an abandoned vessel anchored in the Toronto harbour, in a ship that is fittingly marked with the word "Condemned". Nicki, present yet again on a television screen, prepares him for the final metamorphosis into exilic selfhood. The television screen shows him a scene of himself aboard the empty vessel – which in terms of colour coding and background resembles the aesthetic of 'Videodrome' – lifting his hand-turned-gun to his head, shooting himself. Once more declaring "Long Live the New Flesh", Max shoots himself in the same fashion. The screen goes blank.

Significantly, Max's Ovidian metamorphosis and his general progression through the Ovidian *cursus* occurs within a very Canadian context. As Young contends, "*Videodrome* is arguably the most 'Canadian' of Cronenberg's films", a claim based on several convincing reasons: first, the characters of Professor Brian O'Blivion and Max Renn are modelled on public Canadian personalities, namely, on Marshall McLuhan, Professor of Communications Theory at the University of Toronto,[10] and Moses Znaimer, founder of Toronto's City TV, which broadcast erotic films in the 1970s, respectively; second, the film is primarily about television without which the 'imagined community' of Canada would not be possible; and third,

> the film's central concern is the border transgressions of technology and ideas into Canada from the South, and the subsequent breakdown of boundaries and previous ways of seeing and being. It is a theme familiar to all Canadians, whether or not we accept the "Canadian Content Regulations" as a solution, and it is only a slight step away from what Northrop Frye has famously called the "garrison mentality" – an acute awareness of an indifferent but always encroaching Other. (Young 149)

Ultimately, Young asserts that *Videodrome* is not so much about the policing of borders; the film "is not a fascist film" that speaks out against the "the infiltration of 'undesirable elements'". Moreover, *Videodrome* "does not advocate a protectionist response to perverse 'purity' or to insulate against change. On the contrary: *Videodrome* is Canada's *Bacchae*, and just like Pentheus, the king of Thebes in Euripides' play, Max in Cronenberg's film is both destroyed and released after he gives in to what he really wants and that which he had first sneered at – femaleness" (149f.). On Young's view, then, *Videodrome* rather represents a testimony to the liberating powers of change-

---

[10] Cronenberg was a student at the University of Toronto at the time and most likely knew McLuhan.

ability and of the transgression of gender identities. In my opinion, Max's Ovidian metamorphosis on account of a television signal, (allegedly) transmitted from South of the Canadian border, has a very different dimension and does not offer an exclusively positive assessment of the liberating possibilities of Ovidian metamorphosis in the Canadian context. I believe that the different perspectives offered within the film (and by the film) suggest that one individual's changeability and liberation inevitably rests upon another person's bondage. The film thus showcases that the seemingly liberatory force of Ovidian parody is ultimately just a different form of Virgilian parody, which it replicates with the ideological agenda inverted.

Videodrome is mediated chiefly from Max's perspective – and given his hallucinations, he becomes a very unreliable first-person narrator. Trying to make sense of *Videodrome* – and of what is happening to him – Max first seeks out Professor Brian O'Blivion, who is modelled on "media prophet" Marshall McLuhan and who,[11] in the film, is reduced to a collection of videotapes (itself a kind of video*drome*) maintained by his daughter Bianca. The latter enjoys sending video messages, which are the product of her multimedial bricolage, to the media and other interested parties, like Max.[12] In the first video message for Max, O'Blivion expounds the ideological agenda that seems to inform *Videodrome*. He explains:

> The battle for the mind of North America will be fought in the realm of the video arena, the videodrome. The television screen is the retina of the mind's eye. Therefore the television screen is part of the physical structure of the brain. Therefore whatever appears on the television screen emerges as raw experience for those who watch it. Therefore television is reality, and reality is less than television.

As one would expect from a television man, Max's curiosity is roused by the tape, and he wants to consult Brian O'Blivion to learn more about his mission. Instead of encountering the man himself, Max learns more about his 'Videodrome' problem from Bianca O'Blivion, who tells Max that O'Blivion is one of the fathers of 'Videodrome', which he hailed as "the next stage in the evolution of man as a technological animal. When he realized what his

---

[11] As Beard has it, "Brian O'Blivion is clearly a 'radical' pastiche of McLuhan as a 'media prophet'" (124).

[12] Bianca is not only in charge of the videotape recordings that literally *are* her father, but she is also in charge of the quasi-religious institution of Cathode Ray Mission, "a Salvation Army-like soup kitchen where derelicts are parked in front of televisions to 'help patch them back into the world's mixing board'. Such sentiments could hardly be more in tune with the Baudrillardian sense that virtuality has supplanted history and simulacra the real" (Beard 131). Given Brian O'Blivion's idea as to the significance and importance of television, the intended beneficial mission of Cathode Ray represents the other side of the *Videodrome*-coin.

partners were going to use it for, he tried to take it away from them. And they killed him – quietly". Evidently, O'Blivion's ideas about an all-encompassing metamorphosis of contemporary culture and society is at odds with the fascist-sounding mandate of Spectacular Optical. O'Blivion is very optimistic about the possibility of the transformative potential of 'Videodrome', about Ovidian metamorphosis, as Max learns from one of the tapes:

> I believe that the growth in my head – this head, this one, right here – I think that it is not really a tumor, not an uncontrolled, undirected little bubbling part of flesh, but that it is in fact a new organ, a new part of the brain. I think that massive doses of the "Videodrome"-signal will ultimately create a new outgrowth of the human brain, which will produce and control hallucinations to the point that it will change human reality. After all, there is nothing real outside our perception of reality, is there?

After being thus introduced to O'Blivion's confidence in the "Videodrome"-project, Max's metamorphosis into a cyborg begins, but the transformation itself appears to contradict O'Blivion's belief in benevolent metamorphosis. It is a gun that Max introduces into his abdomen, which fittingly represents his recently acquired taste for a more violent way of exploring his sexual identity. Brian O'Blivion's optimism vis-à-vis the change of human reality through television finds an analogue in Marshall McLuhan's hopefulness concerning the role of television and electronic media in general. McLuhan had hoped that

> electronic media will undo the visual hegemony of print, enabling the recovery of vocal, auditory, and mimetic values repressed by print and, thereby, reversing the bias of visual culture with its fixed points of view and promoting "the acceptance of multiple facets and planes in a single experience" [...]. So McLuhan concludes that electronic technology reverses the movement from centre to margin since "electric speech creates centers everywhere. Margins cease to exist on this planet". (Williams 2003, 233, citing McLuhan 1966, 247, 92)

McLuhan's vision of television represents an egalitarian, transnational society, encapsulated in his observation that "certainly the electro-magnetic discoveries have recreated the simultaneous 'field' in all human affairs so that the human family now exists under the conditions of a 'global village'" (McLuhan 1962, 31). For O'Blivion, the 'Videodrome' signal offers a transformation of the world from the bottom up – a liberation of the individual and individual desires from the shackles of the nation and the nation-state, and, to some extent, a liberation also from collective norms.

The transnational community Max partakes in via 'Videodrome' is a creation of Spectacular Optical, however, a corporation that suspiciously specialises in "inexpensive glasses for the Third World and missile-guidance systems for NATO". As Max further learns upon his first introduction to the makers of 'Videodrome', notably in a message that is itself mediated through a television screen, "[w]e also make *Videodrome*, Max. And as I am sure you know, when it's ready for the marketplace, things will never quite be the same again. It can be a giant hallucination machine – and much, much more. But it's not ready, those were test transmissions that you picked up". At this point in the film, it seems as if 'Videodrome' is merely a new entertainment system that needs fixing (and whose ideological underpinnings might require some adjustment). In fact, Barry Convex, one of the partners of Spectacular Optical, kindly and helpfully offers to check on Max's hallucinations to find out why the latter is not yet in "intense psychiatric care", as are all the others who had hitherto been exposed to the signal. A little later, it emerges that Max's right-hand man Harlan had exposed Max to the signal intentionally in order for Max to clear the way for the exposure of a certain segment of society to the tumour-inducing signal.[13] The transnational signal is thus already, one is tempted to say "always already", a home-grown permutation, enlisted in an ultra-nationalist enterprise that unites only to separate, to purify the nation. In Harlan's words,

> North America's getting soft, *patron* – and the rest of the world is getting, very very tough. We're entering savage new times, and we're going to have to be pure and direct and strong if we're going to survive them. Now you, and this [...] *cesspool* you call television station, and your people who [...] *wallow around in it*, and your viewers, who [...] *watch you do it* – you're rotting us away from the inside. We intend to stop that rot.[14]

After this explanation, Convex sticks a videotape into Max's abdomen, which minutes later "gives birth" to the fleshgun, which Beard describes as the male offspring of Max's "vagina" – a child fathered either by Convex's tape or the gun which Max inserted into his abdomen earlier (Beard 147). Max uses the fleshgun to kill first his partners and later, after being reprogrammed by Bianca O'Blivion, Harlan and Convex. The entertainment system and hallucination machine 'Videodrome' has become appropriated by

---

[13] Harlan's name is possibly an oblique allusion to the company now called Harlan-Sprague, which is one of the leading suppliers of laboratory animals.

[14] Harlan, who has not been exposed to the 'Videodrome' signal, provides possibly one of the few neutral perspectives throughout the film. Harlan's perspective, though, is severely curtailed since he has never seen 'Videodrome', and the film nowhere suggests that he has any foundation for his claims about the actual viewers of Civic-TV's programming. Ironically, Convex *is* rotting away from the inside – after Max shoots him with his fleshgun, tumours that apparently outlive their host's death are sprouting everywhere, tearing Convex from the inside out.

a pseudo-fascist enterprise, whose ultimate goal appears to be the purification of the Canadian nation, keeping the transmitted content exclusively Canadian, purging it of foreign influences – after all Max's world is very globalised: at the beginning of the film, he negotiates with representatives of a Japanese company that offers him *Samurai Dreams* for Civic-TV, he is then offered pornographic material set in ancient Rome, and meets his friend Martha in a Turkish bar in the background of which a belly-dancer is performing; Max's world is rather multicultural. Although the objectives of Spectacular Optical seem to be pseudo-fascist at this point, the motives of Spectacular Optical ultimately remain opaque.[15]

With O'Blivion's benign vision of technological progress and Spectacular Optical's mandate to purify Canada, the film offers Max two mutually exclusive perspectives on his own metamorphosis. For the audience, these perspectives are multiplied and become increasingly confusing as the film approaches its end, which pivotally raises the question as to the ontological status of the "New Flesh". After taking refuge on the condemned vessel, Nicki appears again on a TV screen – this time as a kind of spiritual counsellor.[16] She informs Max that "[she] learned that death is not the end. [She] can help [him]". She also tells him that *Videodrome* still exists: "It's very big, very complex. You've hurt them, but you haven't destroyed them. To do that, you have to go on to the next phase". Max (together with the audience) wants to find out what that next phase is, to which Nicki answers: "Your body has already done a lot of changing. But that's only the beginning. The beginning of the New Flesh. You have to go all the way now. Total transformation. Do you think you're ready?" Max is more than willing to go along with her suggestion, even as it entails his death: "To become the New Flesh, you first have to kill the Old Flesh. Don't be afraid. Don't be afraid to let your body die. Just come to me, come to Nicki". First seeing his suicide on the TV, Max puts his fleshgun to his head and kills himself, after saying "Long Live the

---

[15] For Beard, the film throws into relief "Max's private quagmire of desire and guilt. The relentless movement of the film is *inward*. Spectacular Optical's project and motives become more and more opaque, and are finally irrelevant; at the end Max is alone with his gun, his personal organic television set, and his image of Nicki, while Spectacular Optical has evaporated" (Beard 133). Nicki, at the very end of *Videodrome*, tells Max, however, that 'Videodrome' is still around, even more powerful and more complex. From an audience's perspective, that is, Spectacular Optical and "Videodrome" become anything but "irrelevant".

[16] Besides the metamorphosis of Max into the New Flesh, the female characters also metamorphose: Bianca first manipulates and then cares for Max; Nicki is transformed from a temptress and manipulator into "Max's private voice of wisdom, consolation, and reassurance" (Beard 149).

New Flesh", but significantly *without* prefacing the phrase with "Death to Videodrome".

The ending of the film complicates the plot of an already very complex movie, but it is tempting to see in Max's final transformation the rebirth of Max's female identity. Discussing the ending, Young observes that "after he has killed these 'fathers'" – that is, Harlan and Convex – Max heads "literally into the sea of rebirth", entering "a condemned vessel (a no longer useful body)". The suicide, on her view, is not an act of despair; rather, Max "is re-creating himself" (Young 159). The ontological status of the New Flesh, however, remains opaque: "What is this promise of the new flesh that carries him out of the world? A life-after-death, on TV? It is possible, but unlikely: the screen is at last black/blank when we hear the gun's report. The answer seems to lie elsewhere – in seeing and hearing while in the flesh, while alive, by being alive to life's irreducible pain. And this is a step beyond simulacrum, beyond Baudrillard" (Young 169). Obviously, it is undesirable to reduce the meaning of a complex film to one and only one reading. The complementary Ovidian reading that I would like to offer is one that is at once optimistic about the possibilities of metamorphosis while simultaneously pointing out the problematic epistemological underpinnings of metamorphosis itself. What an Ovidian reading of the film suggests, I think, is a separation between poetological and cinematological metamorphoses, a poetics of parody parodied cinematologically.

Poetologically, Max's choice of location – the condemned vessel (or vessel for the condemned) – is telling. Setting off, unfurling the sails, as it were, on a maritime journey is a classical poetological metaphor, one that is characteristic particularly of Ovid, as he has to traverse a turbulent ocean in order to reach the imperial hinterland; he survives, ultimately because he keeps writing and continues his literary activities. While Max is also condemned and about to embark on a journey, the viewer does not get a glimpse of ongoing creative activity of any kind – the blank screen might signify the kind of empty page the audience might use to reconsider Max's transgressions against a Canadian nationhood, to be more precise, a kind of print-nationhood in which postmodern self-explorations of one's repressed violence cannot (and should not) result in the kind of reality that Max deigns appropriate. Cinematologically, Max's choice of location is equally telling. With the prominence of Nicki's TV-image and the doubling of Max's suicide, first on TV, then in the film's reality, the audience continues to watch both 'Videodrome', the program within the movie, and *Videodrome*, Cronenberg's film. In fact, Cronenberg has often been taken to task for satisfying the very voyeurism that his films repudiate or attempt to repudiate (cf. Kotte 154). In *Videodrome*, though, this doubling appears to be quite deliberate insofar as audiences are watching a Canadian-made film that is transmitted and distributed across the world, including, of course, the United States of America – and Pittsburgh. The reversal of this movement on the meta-filmic level, then, exhibits the quintessential similarity of a transnational film industry, regardless of the origin of the signal. More problematically, it also showcases the problems inherent in the kind of electronic transnationalism advocated by scholars like Marshall McLuhan.

The metamorphosis of the Old Flesh into the New Flesh indeed promises the kind of postmodern liberation of the subject represented by Brian O'Blivion – and like O'Blivion, Max is asked to let the old body die; earlier, Bianca O'Blivion informed Max that her father was not afraid to do just that. To let the Old Flesh die, however, is to be oblivious to the fact that this metamorphosis cannot but result in the kind of selfhood represented by O'Blivion: a collection of videotapes at the disposal of whoever wants to play them, for whatever purposes. Like Ovid, then, who wished to immortalise himself through his books – that is, he desired to be transformed into the medium in which he worked – Max Renn metamorphoses into the medium that is the message, into a phantasmorganic world of simulacra, into metamorphosis itself. Here, Max Renn, the television producer, whose aggressive entrepreneurial nature had much in common with that of Spectacular Optical's corporate thugs, correlates with David Cronenberg, the filmmaker.[17] Max thus ultimately dramatises the perennial quandary of the Canadian, Ovidian parodist in the quest of a New Flesh. Whatever one takes *Videodrome*'s New Flesh to be, whether it embodies a print-nationalist self or a cyber-transnational self, its ontological status, along with its possibly liberating potential, cannot be realised in Croneberg's Ovidian film – neither poetologically nor cinematologically.

Works Cited

Beard, William. *The Artist as Monster: The Cinema of David Cronenberg*. Toronto: U of Toronto P, 2001.
Hardie, Philip. *Ovid's Poetics of Illusion*. Cambridge: CUP, 2002.

---

[17] In passing, Beard refers to Max as a "confident, aggressive, entrepreneurial hero" (134). Towards the end of his chapter on *Videodrome*, Beard further emphasises the analogies between Max Renn, who runs Civic-TV against public censorship, and David Cronenberg, who likewise had his battles with censors (162f.). Moreover, throughout *Videodrome*, "artistic creation and sexual sadism are very close to each other; and knowing yourself, having the artist's courage of truth in self-knowledge, is knowing yourself to be a sadist. When you 'go all the way through' your primal, instinctive inspiration, this dreadful scene is what you discover, and it is what converts the transgressor, the creator, into a melancholic" (Beard 164).

Keller, Wolfram R. "Ovid Sailing the Prairies: Abandonment and the Creative Process in Carol Shields's *Various Miracles*." *Reading(s) from a Distance: European Perspectives on Canadian Women's Writing*. Eds Charlotte Sturgess and Martin Kuester. Augsburg: Wißner, 2008. 200-15.

—. "'Trying to Glimpse the Man Behind the Mask of the Monster': David Williams's Mythological Construction of Regional Counter-Nationhood in *Eye of the Father*." *Zeitschrift für Kanada-Studien* 48 (2006): 77-92.

Kotte, Claudia. "Das anglokanadische Kino von 1960 bis heute." *Kanadischer Film: Geschichte, Themen, Tendenzen*. Eds Markus Heide and Claudia Kotte. Konstanz: UVK, 2006. 141-88.

Lasierra, Mertxe. "Cronenberg: A Modern Canadian Myth." *Screening Canadians: Cross-Cultural Perspectives on Canadian Film*. Eds Wolfram R. Keller and Gene Walz. Marburg: Universitätsbibliothek, 2008. 135-59.

McLuhan, Marshall. *The Gutenberg Galaxy: The Making of Typographic Man*. Toronto: U of Toronto P, 1962.

—. *Understanding Media: The Extensions of Man*. 2nd ed. Toronto: Signet, 1966.

Schmitzer, Ulrich. *Ovid*. Hildesheim: Olms, 2001.

Terry, Philip. Introduction. *Ovid Metamorphosed*. Ed. Philip Terry. London: Chatto & Windus, 2000. 1-18.

Videodrome. Dir. David Cronenberg. Perf. James Woods, Sonja Smits and Deborah Harry. Universal, 1983.

Walde, Christine. "Auferstehungen – Literarische Ovidrezeption an der Wende vom 20. zum 21. Jahrhundert." *Ovid: Werk – Kultur – Wirkung*. Eds Markus Janka, Ulrich Schmitzer and Helmut Seng. Darmstadt: Wissenschaftliche Buchgesellschaft, 2007. 317-48.

Walz, Eugene P., ed. *Canada's Best Features: Critical Essays on 15 Canadian Films*. Amsterdam: Rodopi, 2002.

Williams, David. *Imagined Nations: Reflections on Media in Canadian Fiction*. Montreal: McGill-Queen's UP, 2003.

—. "'Where is the Voice Coming from'? 'Bilingual' Parody in the Canadian Novel." *Canadian Literature: Perspectives*. Ed. Jameela Bagum. Madras: Macmillan, 1994. 1-20.

Young, Suzie Sau-Fong, "'Forget Baudrillard': The Horrors of 'Pleasure' and the Pleasures of 'Horror' in David Cronenberg's *Videodrome*." *Canada's Best Features: Critical Essays on 15 Canadian Films*. Ed. Eugene P. Walz. Amsterdam: Rodopi, 2002. 147-72.

Ziolkowski, Theodore. *Ovid and the Moderns*. Ithaca: Cornell UP, 2005.